"THE PYGMIES WERE
OUR COMPASS"

Recent Titles in
Social History of Africa Series
Series Editors: Allen Isaacman and Jean Allman

"THE PYGMIES WERE OUR COMPASS"

BANTU AND BATWA IN THE HISTORY OF WEST CENTRAL AFRICA, EARLY TIMES TO c. 1900 C.E.

Kairn A. Klieman

Social History of Africa
Allen Isaacman and Jean Allman, Series Editors

HEINEMANN
Portsmouth, NH

Heinemann
A division of Reed Elsevier Inc.
361 Hanover Street
Portsmouth, NH 03801-3912
www.heinemann.com

Offices and agents throughout the world

ISBN 0-325-07104-7 (cloth)
ISBN 0-325-07105-5 (paper)
ISSN 1099-8098

Library of Congress Cataloging-in-Publication Data

Klieman, Kairn A., 1962–

"The Pygmies were our compass": Bantu and Batwa in the history of west central Africa, early times to c. 1900 C.E. / Kairn A. Klieman.
    p.   cm—(Social history of Africa, ISSN 1099-8098)
   Includes bibliographical references and index.
   ISBN 0-325-07104-7 (alk. paper)—ISBN 0-325-07105-5 (pbk. : alk. paper)
   1. Batwa (African people)—History. 2. Banta-speaking peoples—Africa, Central—History. 3. Historical linguistics—Africa, Central. I. Title III. Series.
DT650.B372K55 2003
967'.0049639461—dc21   2003044984

British Library Cataloguing in Publication Data is available

Printed in the United States of America on acid-free paper
07 06 05 04 03 SB 1 2 3 4 5 6 7 8 9

To my parents and siblings,
who have supported me through thick and thin.

CONTENTS

LIST OF MAPS, FIGURES, AND TABLES

MAPS

FIGURE

TABLES

ACKNOWLEDGMENTS

Given the financial, logistic, institutional, intellectual, and emotional support it took me to complete this book, I consider it nothing less than a group project. I began work on the project in 1992; as a result, there are a myriad of individuals I would like to thank. In doing so, however, I am bound to forget a few. To those individuals omitted from these pages, please accept my apologies in advance.

I would like to thank the institutions that provided the material support to carry out this work. Preliminary archival research in Belgium (1992–93) was made possible through the auspices of the Belgian-American Educational Foundation. A Fulbright-Hays Department of Education grant allowed me to travel and research in Congo and Gabon for one year (1993–94), and support from the Social Science Research Council allowed me to stay on for another six months (1994). In 1998 I returned to Belgium to gather linguistic and archeological data for revisions of the manuscript. This research was made possible through a Research Initiation Grant from the University of Houston, as well as a grant from the African American Studies Program at the same institution. Finally, the Department of History at the University of Houston has played an ongoing role in supporting the completion of this book. I especially thank the former chairperson Tom O'Brien for arranging course releases, and current chairperson Joe Pratt for providing funds for maps.

In Belgium I benefited greatly from the guidance and kindness of Professor Pierre de Maret, who provided me a place to study, work, and socialize in the Prehistory Section of the Africa Museum at Tervuren. A very special note of gratitude must go to Professors Yvonne Bastin and Claire Gregoire of the Linguistic Section, Tervuren, who have welcomed me back time after time. The resources, data, advice, and hospitality they provided were essential to the completion of this work. I am also greatly indebted to Els Corneilson, Olivier Gosselain, Philippe Lavachery, Christophe Mbida, Alain Assoko-Ndong, Aimé Manima-Moubouha, Pascale Piron, Geneviève Thiry, and Annaliese Bulkens. I continue to benefit from both the knowledge and friendship that each one of these individuals was kind enough to share. Great thanks also to Hélène Pagezy and daughter, who so kindly hosted me in Aix-en-Provence.

During my stay in the Congo Republic, I was graciously welcomed and aided in research by the following individuals: M. Leopold Mpika "et famille," M. Mikolo Jean Roger "et famille," Professor Jean Boyi, M. Ango Simon, Anneliese Simmons, and Dan Irvine. I would also like to thank the staff and researchers associated with the Societé International de Linguistique (SIL) who allowed me to use their library and other facilities. Among such researchers were John and Elizabeth Philips, who were especially helpful during my long stay in Ouesso. Thanks also to Mike Fay and Richard Ruggiero for allowing me to carry out research at Bon Coin in the Nouabali-Ndoki National Park. In Gabon, research was greatly facilitated by Bernard Clist, Pierre Ondo and his wife Jean-Marie, Alexis Massala and his wife Nicette, Patrick Mougiama-Daouda, Alyssa LaGamma, and my special Peace Corps "family": Meg Thorley, Angela Heartfield, and Brad Arsenault.

In preparing the manuscript for publication, a number of accomplished scholars have played a great part. Three among these deserve special mention: David L. Schoenbrun, Gregory Maddox, and Axel Köhler. I have been amazed and humbled by their commitment to this project over the very long haul, and I appreciate the hard questions they continuously asked. I especially thank Axel for his patience and support in my times of stress, both in Congo and at home. Also indispensable were the comments of Jim Denbow, Edwin Wilmsen, Gerda Rossel, Jerome Lewis, Ibrahima Tchiaw, Philippe Lavachery, Jaime Monson, Sheryl McCurdy, and Jan Shetler, all of whom read various sections of the book. Although all of these scholars do not agree with all of my conclusions, their thoughtful and incisive comments forced me to go deeper in my attempts to articulate historical hypotheses and theories alike. Jean Hay provided crucial advice at a critical moment in the writing of the manuscript; I thank her for her expert and ongoing mentorship. I would also like to thank Eugenia Hebert, Joseph Miller, and Wyatt MacGaffey, all of whom read the book in its latest stages of production. I am indebted to them for highlighting both the strengths and weaknesses of the work; their comments helped me to produce a much more polished book. Of course, all of the mistakes are mine.

A most heartfelt debt of gratitude must be sent to Christopher Ehret, who has unwaveringly supported this project from inception to end. First as an academic advisor, and then as colleague and friend, he has been consistently willing to share his expertise on both African history and historical linguistics. I only hope that I can someday repay the intellectual debt I owe him— perhaps by being as supportive to my students as he has been to me.

Three very special research assistants aided me over the past two years. First among these was Daniel Brown, who did a great deal of research on the Idea of the Pygmy and helped develop a bibliographic database. I thank him for his patience and commitment to the project, especially after he ceased to be an official student and had more interesting things to do. Myra Williams also played an integral role by editing and formatting chapters as they came "off the press." Her careful and meticulous work has been essential to the timely completion of this work; she is not only an expert editor, but a person of infinite patience and grace. Last but not least is my own stepson Elias Kamal. Although only 14 years old (and motivated by a desire to buy a PlayStation 2), his skills in computers, English, and French proved invaluable in preparing the footnotes and bibliography.

Of course, not a word could have been written if dozens of individuals in Congo and Gabon had not been willing to share with me knowledge about their languages and lives. For their kindness, patience, and willingness to sit down and talk with me time after time, I thank the following individuals: M. Mutelu Auguste, M. Zidzala Margarite, M. Gaul Jonas, M. Nguadi Francis, Mme. Motaboka Elise, M. Romain Agolli Numbau, Mme. Koussooumbou Martial, M. Yenzo Marcel, Chef Mbandza Pascal, Mme. Mbandza Margarite, M. Balouma David, M. Moiwa Michel, M. Djah Simon, Mme. Logete Martine, M. Wawa Alphonse, M. Bwaka Mopina, M. Ndundu Michel, M. Bokube Emile, M. Mosidere Ely, M. Ikuni Sylvain, M. Bagondzo Patrice, M. Bokoba Andre, M. Tendza Alphonse, M. Diboka Jacques, M. Manyali Raphael, M. Zamongo Jean Bernard, M. Mwanza Serge, M. Samuel Ngano, Mme. Soumba Veronique, Mme. Ibuta Madeleine, M. Moundemou Denis, Mme. Andzangi Jaqueline, Mme. Bosane-Dzute Philomene, M. Ngondulu Raphael, Mme. Lydie Essobe, M. Kumu Eugene, M. Moyipele Philipe, M. Mangonda Jean, M. Mingongue Julien, Mme. Mossouma Florentine, M. Mbuka Pierre, M. Masande Pascale, M. Nzengui Yves, M. Kouimbe Francois, M. Muanga Yves, M. Moghongho Ferdinand, Mme. Muhabu Caroline, Chef Ngona Gabriel, M. Ngoyignaka Maurice, Mme. Matana Susanne, Mme. Mohama Perine, Chef Leyonza Etienne, Mme. Bimbamba Charlene, Mme. Muhondo Christine, Mme. Mikolo Jaqueline, M. Mwele Francois, M. Panga Pierre, Mme. Ndula Evaline, M. Tsamba Thomas, M. Mahoungou Daniel, M. Mampassi Pierre, M. Iwungu Simon, M. Madungu Antoine, Mme. Mougetou Josianne, M. Mambundu Yves, Mme. Mwisi Elie, Chef Mbina Maganga, M. Moungungui Serge, Chef Kumba Matsinga, M. Mbumba Jean Claude, M. Ntsatsi Alphonse, and M. Ndembi Antoine.

James Young, current chair of the Department of Geography and Planning at Appalachian State University, created the earliest versions of many of the maps that appear in this book. I thank him for his contributions, as well as his willingness to allow his work to serve as a base for further mapmaking by others. The final versions of maps (both old and new), were created by members of the Cartography and Geographic Information Science Center at the University of Wisconsin, Milwaukee. Ms. Donna Genzmer Schenström, Director, deserves special mention; her patience and professionalism made working with the center a joy. Special thanks to Don Cole, photographer at the Fowler Museum at UCLA, for the beautiful cover photo on the paperback edition.

Finally, I could not have completed this work without the ongoing support of family and friends. I thank my parents for never questioning their daughter's fascination with Africa, encouraging me to pursue my passion from age 22 on. For supporting me emotionally when I was dead tired of writing and revising, I thank my very dear friends: Kendahl Radcliffe, Gail Kennedy, Barbara Wallace, Christine Ahmed-Zaidi, and Jo Ellen Hunter. In Houston I owe a great debt to the teachers and students at Guru Ram Das Ashram; through the benefits of yoga and constant encouragement, I was able to bring balance to both writing and life. Most important of all has been my husband Yasin K. Jabir. Throughout the entirety of our relationship he has had to "share" me with this book. I thank him for his patience and constant loving support, and look forward to starting the next "chapter" of our lives.

INTRODUCTION

This book presents a history of a very large and important region of Africa, a history that for the first time brings Batwa (Pygmy) actors onto the stage. It focuses on the western regions of the equatorial rainforest (Congo Republic, Gabon), chronicling interactions between agriculturalists and forest specialists for a period of more than two thousand years. In a region of the globe where written evidence for periods beyond the past two hundred years is very rare, the reconstruction of such a long-term history might seem an unattainable goal. It is made possible, however, through a multidisciplinary approach. By using evidence from linguistics, archeology, oral traditions, and ethnography, this work seeks to reconstruct the changing nature of relations between Bantu and Batwa during the watershed periods of central African history: early Bantu settlement in the rainforest, the introduction of metallurgy and bananas, the rise of long-distance trade and centralized polities, and finally, the era of Atlantic trade.

My motivation to take on such a large project was originally rooted in a discomfort with the way that modern-day Batwa societies are treated in historical works. This did not arise from a sense of protective fascination with hunter-gatherers or a desire to defend indigenous peoples' rights. Instead, it originated in my amazement at the way nineteenth-century ideas about race, progress, and social evolution continue to go unquestioned when it comes to the Batwa. In general surveys of African history, Batwa tend to be mentioned only once, in the first chapter where discussions of early humans appear. Modern-day subsistence strategies are taken as a model for those that existed in the Late Stone Age past, and the reader is left with the idea that there are societies in Africa that have remained unchanged through time. In cases where Batwa societies are mentioned in later eras, they tend to be portrayed as perpetual clients to more powerful agriculturalist neighbors, a notion that has its roots in social evolutionary discourse and observations of forest specialists over the past 150 years. Perhaps most perplexing is the fact that no historian has ever attempted to reconstruct the history of the Batwa. Although a number of anthropologists have written regional surveys that include these populations, these surveys tend to focus on the last couple of centuries and do not employ the full array of methodologies that historians of pre-colonial Africa are trained to use.

The reasons for the historical neglect of Batwa peoples are multiple and complex. One must first consider the nature of Western epistemologies, which relegate the study of hunting and gathering societies to the anthropologist's domain. In the case of the Batwa, however, there are even more influential factors at work. Most important is the central role that legendary Pygmies have played in Westerners' attempts to explain the origins and nature of humanity. I refer to this phenomenon as the "Pygmy Paradigm," and chronicle its history in chapter 1. These ideas can be traced as far back as Aristotle's *scala naturae* and the Medieval Great Chain of Being, for mythical Pygmies are situated between apes and humans in both. Associations between semi-human status and the idea of the Pygmy influenced Western thinking well into the modern era, providing a conceptual model for the development of the Missing Link paradigm, evolutionary theory, and scientific racism.

It was these latter ideologies that prevailed when Europeans first came into contact with short-statured forest dwellers of Central Africa (1850s–1890s). Assuming that they had "discovered" the Pygmies of the Ancients, Europeans rapidly unloaded centuries of ideas about a mythical people onto the Batwa. Following nineteenth-century notions of progress and race, the Batwa were relegated to the bottom of the social evolutionary scale and their short-statured bodies became the objects of endless scientific investigation. These strains of thought continued into the twentieth century, although the assumed primordiality of the Pygmies was often cast in an approbatory light. This phenomenon reached its apogee with Colin Turnbull's *The Forest People,* which presented a romanticized vision of the Mbuti peoples' lifestyle (Ituri Forest, Democratic Republic of Congo) largely in an effort to critique the West.[1] Although his work led thousands of Westerners to question their assumptions about race, progress, and human relations, it did little to challenge evolutionary tenets of the Pygmy Paradigm. Thus, in the modern-day context, the Batwa continue to be seen as a people whose biology and lifestyle can help us to decode the human genome, understand human adaptation, and reconstruct the deep hunting and gathering history of all human beings.

It is important to recognize that although the evolutionist approach might provide certain data to help us understand early human societies, it leads scholars to neglect the actual history of the Batwa. Until recently there has been very little interest in understanding the lives that Batwa peoples' ancestors lived over the past few thousand years, how they participated in and were affected by regional or global historical events, or whether their subsistence strategies and interactions with agriculturalists might have changed over time. Indeed, evolutionary theory has become so closely associated with Batwa history that it seems impossible to imagine a different approach.

This is, as I see it, the key reason historians have been so hands-off when it comes to the Batwa. On one hand it is exceedingly difficult to break free from and/or propose an alternative to evolutionist models (both biological and social); on the other, it is awkward and disconcerting to confront the vestiges of nineteenth-century thinking that continue to influence us today. I make this argument from my own experience, for I have often felt uncomfortable informing fellow historians that I work on the history of central African Pygmies. Without a full explanation of my motives, they generally assume I am a "tree hugger" (i.e., environmental activist) or someone who embraces the racial paradigms academicians now so heartily disdain. Furthermore, I have intellectually battled my own reliance on evolutionist models for more than nine years of work on this book. It was only in the latter stages of its writing—after having assessed the plethora of Batwa-related myth, tradition, and ethnographic data through the lens of Igor Kopytoff's "frontier thesis"—that I was able to conceive of an alternative approach. I refer to this as the "first-comer" paradigm, a model that focuses on the contributions that Batwa societies have made to the social, political, and religious systems of central Africa in their role as expert intercessors to the supernatural world.

THE BATWA OF CENTRAL AFRICA: TRUE AUTOCHTHONS OR AN "ETHNOGRAPHIC FICTION"?

One of the central questions surrounding modern-day Batwa societies is whether they are in fact the biological descendants of Late Stone Age peoples who lived in central Africa before agriculturalists arrived. Although this is commonly assumed to be the case, there is actually no archaeological or biological evidence to directly link the two. This issue is made further enigmatic by the fact that not one Batwa community of central Africa speaks its own language. Instead, they all speak languages or dialects of the Bantu, Adamawa-Ubangian, and Central Sudanic families, that is, the languages that immigrant agriculturalists carried into the equatorial regions as they settled from the north. Working from the assumption that the Batwa are direct descendants of Late Stone Age populations, Africanist scholars have long been perplexed as to how, when, and why Batwa communities adopted these immigrant languages and lost their own.

Although this work suggests historical hypotheses as to how the latter kind of development might have occurred, the data employed do not cover a deep enough time period to discern the ultimate origins of the Batwa. For example, although I have dated between 500 B.C.E. and 1000 C.E. the existence of a speech community linguistically ancestral to modern-day Batwa communities of northern Congo, the language this community spoke was decidedly Bantu. Furthermore, this was an era long after Bantu speakers had arrived and when Late Stone Age technologies had been replaced by the use of Neolithic tools (polished stone axes) and iron. Reconstructed lexicon from this ancestral language does, however, suggest the emergence of an increasingly forest-oriented lifestyle during this time.

This evidence supports previous scholars' suggestions that the Batwa lifestyle might have been a Neolithic adaptation, that is, engendered by the shift in economies as a fully agricultural lifestyle began to prevail.[2] As chapter 4 shows, I argue that it developed as one of many regional forms of economic specialization, through which the ancestors of modern-day Batwa communities gradually took up the task of supplying forest products for expanding systems of trade. This hypothesis explains my use of the term "forest specialist" instead of "hunter-gatherer" for periods after the introduction of bananas and iron. It rests on the notion that the subsistence strategies and economic practices of these communities would have differed greatly from those of simple hunter-gatherers, who did not focus their economic efforts on participating in regional systems of trade.

The lack of evidence to link Late Stone Age autochthons with modern-day Batwa communities should not be taken lightly. Without it, we cannot simply dismiss out of hand revisionist theories such as that recently proposed by Blench, who argues that the Pygmies are an "ethnographic fiction" and simply the descendants of Bantu or Adamawa-Ubangi speakers who took up forest dwelling at some point in the past.[3] Such a scenario seems plausible for at least some of the Batwa, considering that genetic studies carried out among forest specialists and agriculturalists of southern Cameroon show the two communities to be genetically indistinguishable.[4] Furthermore, some biologists are now asserting that the adaptive process that produced the smaller stature of many Batwa communities could have taken place over the last few thousand years.[5]

Viewed from this perspective, there are a number of scenarios one could put forth regarding the origins of the modern-day Batwa. Whether they are the descendants of Late Stone Age populations (whether short in stature or tall), one cannot assume their ways of life remained unchanged through time. On the other hand, the data attesting a linguistic "distancing" might be read as supportive of Blench's theory, but only if we accept that the biological adaptations to produce smaller stature took place in the last twenty-five hundred years. A third possibility is that the linguistic distancing occurred between members of a single speech communities that, although comprised of autochthons and immigrants, had intermingled to such a degree that languages, cultures, technologies, and genes had come to be shared. This latter scenario is the one I find most plausible in interpreting the archeological, linguistic, oral, and ethnographic evidence. Given the ambiguity of data regarding the actual origins of the Batwa, I feel it is necessary to explain my preference for this model at the outset.

A central premise of this book is that social distinctions between immigrants and autochthons have been of vital importance ever since Bantu speakers first settled the western equatorial rainforest. Such distinctions were undoubtedly made during the era of original settlement (c. 4000–2000 B.C.E.), for archaeological evidence attests the presence of autochthonous hunting and gathering populations during this time.[6] Chapter 5 argues that this social category remained relevant well into the Early Iron Age (c. 500–1000 A.D.) and that it was during this era that Bantu agriculturalists developed a new political charter designed to recast relations with first-comer populations, whose political and ritual power was being usurped by the rise of Bantu territorial chiefs. Remnants of this ancient charter can be discerned from the great many shared motifs found in central African myths, rituals, and cosmologies that involve the Batwa. Documented over the past five hundred years, these ideologies clearly reflect the continued importance of first-comer Batwa populations (both mythical and real) as legitimizing agents in the politico-religious systems of the Atlantic Age.

The Bantu view of Batwa peoples as religious experts is found widely across central Africa, attesting that social distinctions between the two groups are at least partially rooted in ideological constructs that date very far back in time. But the enduring nature of the first-comer social category—and especially the profound influence it has had on the development of central African politico-religious institutions—makes it clear that an actual population of outsider autochthons has never ceased to exist within the rainforest itself. The earliest of these autochthons, however, need not have been identical to modern Batwa peoples in physical, cultural, or economic ways. Indeed, this is the reason I have chosen to use the term "Batwa" as a generic reference to first-comers of both modern and historical times.[7] As Thilo Schadeberg has shown, the term was invented in the equatorial rainforest and originally made no reference to physical characteristics or a lower social status.[8] Its primary connotations can be discerned from attestations found across the Bantu-speaking world, for in the majority of contexts, it refers simply to non-Bantu-speaking autochthons, usually (but not always) ones that lead a nonagriculturalist lifestyle.[9]

Thus, although I do not go so far as to assert that modern-day Batwa communities are genetically unchanged descendants of Late Stone Age populations, I do argue that they, as well as their linguistic ancestors of the last millennium B.C.E., have been cast in the same first-comer role as the autochthonous peoples that early Bantu immigrants met. By focusing on the social rather than biological aspects of Batwa identity, we are able to establish a sense of historical continuity across the eras—especially regarding the manner in which Bantu societies interacted with peoples they deemed "original owners of the land."

STRUCTURE AND CENTRAL ARGUMENTS OF THE BOOK

Writing a history of Bantu and Batwa interactions is a complex and multi-faceted task. It requires far more than the reconstruction of Batwa history and its insertion into established narratives of the central African past. Historians must also disentangle the complex web of myth and reality that is presented as Batwa history, distinguishing elements of ethnographic fiction from data that might encode actual historical fact.

Furthermore, it is essential to recognize that the tendency to meld myth with reality is not limited to the Euro-American sphere: this book illustrates that Bantu agriculturalists have carried out similar processes over (at least) the last millennium, thereby creating their own unique vision of "the primordial Batwa." It is therefore essential that the historian articulate differences between the two primordialist paradigms, identifying their origins, transformations, and the historical moments in which they began to intersect.

To this end, the book begins with a chapter examining Western myths about both Pygmies and the Bantu expansion. Chapter 1 begins with an intellectual history of the Pygmy Paradigm, illustrating how its tenets have impacted Western notions about evolution, race, and the central African past. Drawing from references to legendary Pygmies from the Greco-Roman, Medieval, and Early Modern past, I argue that the Idea of the Pygmy has consistently been used as a similarity-creating device to mediate emergent knowledge about human origins, nature, and diversity. A second section examines more modern myths about Bantu agriculturalists and historical settlement south of the equator. This discussion focuses on the ways that Post-World War II antiracialist paradigms—especially that of the Neolithic Revolution—limited our understanding of the Bantu and Batwa past. Because chapter 1 focuses heavily on Euro-American culture and ideas, it must be seen as a further introduction to the book. I have chosen to let it stand alone, however, because the ideas it seeks to challenge are so hard to dislodge. Chapter 1 encourages readers to question the assumptions they might already hold. As a result, they are better able to assess central African historical data on its own terms.

Chapters 2 through 6 comprise the heart of the book. Two distinct modes of historical argumentation are followed in these chapters, depending on the type of data employed. Chapters 2 and 4 work from archeological and historical linguistic evidence, relying on what readers will recognize as a classically historical approach. Dating through radiocarbon and glottochronological techniques allow for the constructing of a chronology and a historical narrative that traces economic and linguistic transformations during the era of early Bantu expansion (chapter 2) and after the introduction of bananas and iron (chapter 4). Chapters 3 and 5 focus on these same eras, respectively, but use oral and ethnographic data to construct historical hypotheses about the changing nature of social relations between Bantu and Batwa. They rely on a much more heuristic mode of argumentation, for they seek to illustrate the fruitfulness of employing a particular interpretive framework, the first-comer paradigm, for reconstructing long-term histories of the Bantu and Batwa.

This dual approach is mandated by the very different nature of the sources used. The classical historical mode presupposes that archeological and linguistic methods provide historical data reflective of lifeways and beliefs that existed in ancient times. The oral and ethnographic materials, however, cannot be approached in the same way: all were collected over the past four hundred years and are essentially etiological in nature. Accordingly, one cannot assume that they are literal remembrances of the distant past. However, by attempting to reconstruct the history of these myths, that is, by identifying common elements, theorizing as to how, when, and why they were created, and tracing their change over time, the historian can begin to discern a certain type of historical "truth"—namely, a history of transformations in relations between Bantu and Batwa.

By juxtaposing rather than integrating the two historical approaches, the integrity of both types of sources are retained. At the same time, readers are encouraged to assess the reliability of such sources on their own. The structure of the book, however, asks readers to consider the possibility that the economic transformations documented in chapters 2 and 4 underlaid, generated, or gave shape to the nature and transformations of social relations proposed in chapters 3, 5, and 6. In this way, the two approaches intersect, providing a more complete history of relations between Bantu and Batwa.

Although many studies have focused on the Bantu expansion, the history presented in chapter 2 is unique in a number of ways. First, it focuses on the northwestern regions of the equatorial rainforest, an area that has not received detailed attention in earlier works. Second, by drawing from recent linguistic and archeological evidence, it argues for an earlier arrival of Bantu speakers than has previous been acknowledged—ranging from as early as the fifth millennium B.C. along the coast to the fourth millennium B.C. in the interior. By combining evidence from these sources, chapter 2 illustrates that Bantu immigrants underwent periods of six hundred to sixteen hundred years (depending on location) when they obtained the majority of their food from hunting, gathering, and fishing, carrying out lifestyles very similar to those of the autochthons they met. Accordingly, chapter 2 proposes that it was during these early periods that Bantu and Batwa interactions were most intimate, allowing for the transferal of languages, cultures, technologies, and genes.

Chapter 3 presents historical hypotheses about the politico-religious nature of Bantu and Batwa interactions during these earliest times. Working from a modified version of Kopytoff's frontier thesis and ethnographic data from the southern Central African Republic, it proposes that early Bantu immigrants eagerly sought to establish alliances with Batwa communities to meet their own religious needs. I refer to this dynamic as the first-comer model, and argue that it arose from ancient Niger-Congo beliefs the Bantu brought with them. Key among these is the belief that the spirits of first-comers controlled the fertility and fecundity of both people and land. As a result, Bantu lineage heads submitted to the religious authority of Batwa communities to gain access to ritual knowledge that could be used to influence the spirits of the land. An understanding of this phenomenon helps to explain why Bantu genesis accounts, origin stories, and migration myths consistently cast ancient Batwa societies as teachers, "civilizers," or guides. It is from one such account I have derived the title for this book: during the 1960s a Punu man (Gabon) reported to Hubert Deschamps that his ancestors survived in the rainforest only because the Pygmies served as a compass, guiding the Punu to "good lands."[10]

Chapter 4 focuses on the dramatic socioeconomic transformations that occurred during the Late Stone-to-Metal and Early Iron Ages, when Bantu societies adopted banana cultivation and the production of iron. As a result, their lives became more sedentary, regional economic specializations developed, and long-distance trade began to thrive. Chapter 4 argues that these transformations impacted Batwa communities in important ways as well. Linguistic evidence illustrates that the ancestors of certain Batwa groups began to lessen their contacts with Bantu agriculturalists at this time, and began to develop their own unique economic specialization as procurers of forest products for entry into regional systems of trade. In the centuries that followed, simple hunter-gatherers were increasingly integrated into both agriculturalist and forest-specialist communities, while socioeconomic distinctions between forest specialists and agriculturalists became complete. This history explains why no Batwa societies have ever been observed using stone tools, subsisting exclusively on rainforest resources, or speaking indigenous languages unique to them alone. They are not the descendants of Late Stone Age hunter-gatherers, but rather, forest specialists, peoples that had undergone long periods of intimate interaction with agriculturalist communities before striking out on their own.

Chapter 5 returns to oral and ethnographic evidence, expanding upon the first-comer model and documenting its working in the politico-religious systems of numerous west-central African societies. Through comparative analysis of genesis myths and origin stories, this chapter argues for the existence of an ancient cosmological belief focused on the image of the primordial Batwa. Because the mythical first-comers are in most societies associated with territorial spirits, it is argued that Bantu agriculturalists conceptually fused their image of ancestral Batwa spirits with those associated with the land. This led to the development of distinctly central African notions of leadership and its ultimate origins, for the transformative powers associated with leadership are considered to be passed from territorial/ancestral spirits to the Batwa, and from the Batwa to Bantu politico-religious heads. A second section of chapter 5 documents how this ideology came to be spread so widely across the central

African world. Drawing from Vansina's reconstruction of Bantu political history, it argues that myths, rituals, and traditions regarding the primordial Batwa were part of a broader set of institutions designed to legitimize the power of territorial chiefs, and that they were found widely across central and parts of southern Africa by the last half of the first millennium C.E. Because of this, Bantu territorial chiefs became known as the new owners of the land, and the Batwa were relegated to essentially symbolic roles in the politico-religious systems of the more centralized societies in west-central Africa.

Chapter 6 deals with the period between 1000 and 1900 C.E. This was an era of great transformations in west-central Africa, encompassing the rise of centralized kingdoms in the southwest (1000–1400 C.E.) and the socioeconomic upheavals of the Atlantic Age (c. 1500–1900 C.E.). After a brief overview of these historical events, chapter 6 presents broad outlines of Batwa history in three distinct regions: the northern Congo Republic, central Gabon, and the southwestern regions of Congo Republic and Gabon. A central theme of this chapter is that there is no one history of Batwa peoples during the Atlantic Age; one must take into account overarching political, economic, and social systems to understand how different communities fared. In the more forested regions (northern Congo/Central Gabon), where centralized polities did not come to exist, Batwa societies retained social and economic autonomy as forest specialists until very late in the Atlantic Age. In the southwestern regions, however, Batwa communities began to suffer political and economic subordination with the rise of centralized states. This dynamic intensified as Atlantic economies began to penetrate the region, causing both primary producers and traditional authorities to loose standing in the socioeconomic systems that came to prevail.

By the late nineteenth century, the violence and upheavals associated with the Atlantic slave trade came to affect Batwa and Bantu relations throughout the rainforest region. Accordingly, chapter 6 argues that it was during this later period that Bantu practices of extreme social and economic discrimination toward the Batwa came to be widespread. Such dynamics were exacerbated during the era of colonial rule, when Bantu societies used violence and intimidation to force the Batwa to collect forest products demanded by the colonial regime. At the same time, Bantu communities began to adopt social-evolutionist notions from the West, using them to justify their exploitation of the Batwa. The result was that Batwa communities came to occupy a distinct position as a marginalized underclass, with, until recently, very little opportunity for participating in regional markets beyond the local sphere.

SOURCES, METHODS, AND THEORETICAL APPROACHES

My work on this project began with an 18-month period of fieldwork in the Congo Republic and Gabon. The goal of this research was to gather linguistic

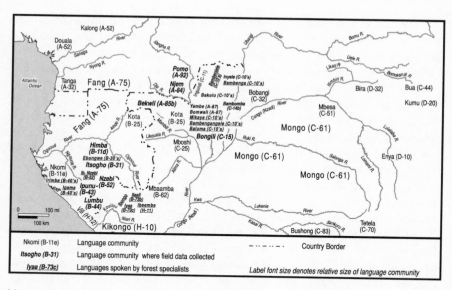

Map 1. Speech Communities Included in Lexicostatistical Classification

data from Batwa communities and the agriculturalists they currently interact with. All told, language data were collected from 14 different Batwa communities and 32 of their neighboring agriculturalists and/or fishing neighbors. Although a number of these communities speak languages of the Ubangian branch of the Adamawa-Ubangian language family, those data are not treated at length here. Instead, this work deals with Bantu languages as spoken by both forest-specialist and agriculturalist societies, focusing primarily on communities located in the regions of northern Congo Republic, central Gabon, and the southwestern regions of both Congo Republic and Gabon. Map 1 in this section illustrates the locations and names of these various speech communities; they are indicated by italic font, with forest-specialist languages also underlined.

The collection of oral histories was not an initial goal of this work; although I developed a systematic way of eliciting lexical data, I did not work from a specific set of questions regarding peoples' perceptions of the near or distant past. In the course of linguistic investigations, however, such information often came up. The interviews were generally conducted with individuals whom the chief or headmen of a village considered the most capable of completing the task; in many instances, these were very astute elders (if not the chief himself) who inevitably had much to say about the past. These types of sources are used sporadically in chapter 6 of the book; where they appear, they are noted with the location and the date when the information was passed on. It also happened that historical memories—and sometimes even esoteric vocabulary items—were "corrected" by an audience of community members who had gathered to observe the interview process at work. This phenomenon was most common among Batwa communities, whose social relations tend to be less hierarchical in nature. Where such correcting did occur, whether among agriculturalist or forest-specialist societies, it was clear that a group consensus was being created or retained. Because of this, research carried out in only one specific region reflects the historical or linguistic "memories" of at least a segment of a larger group, despite the fact that the members of such speech communities were sometimes located across wider expanses of land.

In nearly all of the speech communities, I collected words for the same approximately five hundred meanings. Although these were divided into different semantic fields,[11] most wordlists were developed with the more tangible elements of the Batwa cultures and economies in mind. In retrospect, I realize that it would have been effective to focus more heavily on religious and cosmologically related vocabularies of Bantu and Batwa societies alike. This should be the goal of future fieldwork, so that more thorough lexical evidence can be presented to substantiate and/or challenge hypotheses regarding the first-comer model and the paradigm of the primordial Batwa. Along these same lines, the myths, rituals, and oral traditions that I have drawn from to uncover this ancient paradigm were mostly collected by previous ethnographers and historians and not by me. Although such sources refer to Batwa populations (both mythical and real), the majority were gathered among agriculturalist societies. A future and fruitful direction of research will be to compare how Batwa societies view these cultural and historical representations, or how their own myths differ from those the Bantu tell. It is likely that such research would allow for a somewhat less Bantu-centric perception of the central African past.

Although methods of comparative historical linguistics have been used to reconstruct African history for more than four decades, there remains a degree of uncertainty among general audiences as to how exactly the process works. In recent years, a number of historians and linguists have produced explanations of how such methods are or should be employed.[12] For the reader seeking a more nuanced understanding, I recommend a thorough reading of these sources. Following I present only a thumbnail sketch of the sources, methods, and theoretical approaches I have applied in this work.[13] This brief introduction makes readers aware of the relevant controversies surrounding not only modes of dating historical and comparative linguistic evidence, but also the issues that arise when attempting to correlate linguistic results with the chronologies and cultural sequences established through archaeological research.

Historical Linguistics and the Reconstruction of Human History

Historians who use linguistic methods to reconstruct the human past work from a very fundamental assumption: that human languages provide vital information about the people who speak them, and that by reconstructing the history and vocabularies of ancient languages, we can begin to understand various facets of ancient peoples' lives.

To understand how language data can be used to reconstruct history, one must first recognize that words are historical artifacts in and of themselves. Although spoken in the present by modern-day communities, words do not simply appear out of the blue. Each and every word has its own particular history (i.e., etymology), and these histories can help us to understand the lifeways of peoples who spoke them in the past.

There are three possible origins for most of the words we speak. They can be inherited from our linguistic forebears, communities that spoke languages ancestral to ours in the distant past; they can be internal innovations, words that were invented to describe new social, economic, or technological phenomena that occurred in a specific historical time and place; or they can be loanwords, terms that were borrowed from outsiders who spoke different languages—but with whom contact was made nonetheless.

Each of these alternatives provides important information about the past. The identification of inherited words, for example, helps the historian to discern the ancient technologies, cultural practices, or beliefs that served as the foundation of the ancestral speech community under study. The identification of internal innovations, on the other hand, allows the historian to discover which historical events most impacted a society, in both tangible and cognitive ways. Finally, the identification of loanwords provides important information about the nature and direction of cross-cultural contacts. Such contacts often served as a generative force for historical transformations as well; they therefore provide the scholar with another important avenue for identifying historical events and their impact.

To determine whether words are inherited, innovated, or borrowed, historian linguists must move beyond the analysis of a single language to assess commonalities between related languages. The first task in this type of analysis is to develop a genetic classification of languages based on comparative analysis of their inherited traits. Such classifications can be based on any component of language (i.e., phonology, morphology, syntax, etc.). The most common preliminary approach is to begin with the identification of cognates.[14]

The identification of cognates, however, is not always a simple task. This is because as members of ancient speech communities begin to distance themselves socially or geographically from each other, new patterns of pronunciation appear. For example, the old Bantu root word *-pìcí, "bone," is pronounced as *epese, gyes, or ndjyehe* among various speech communities of northern Congo[15]; to the untrained eye, the common origin of these terms would be very difficult to detect. Likewise, there are cases in which words might have very similar meanings and forms, yet be derived from entirely different ancestral words. The historian-linguist must therefore spend a great deal of time determining the phonological changes that produced these variant forms; this process is referred to as the "establishment of regular sound change rules" for each language under study.[16] Once these sound change rules are determined, one can begin to reconstruct ancient vocabularies.

The genetic classification of languages is produced through the use of lexicostatistics or the "counting" of cognates, which determines the relationship of single languages and subgroupings of languages to one another. Lexicostatistical methods apply to a limited set of terms, most often a one-hundred-word list of core vocabulary terms that have been determined by linguists to be most resistant to replacement over time.[17] This approach allows for a cognation rate (i.e., percentage of cognation) to be established for each pairing of compared languages, or, alternatively, a core cognation range for groups of languages compared. Languages and/or groups of languages that hold higher percentages of cognation with each other are considered to have separated from an intermediate mother language in more recent times. Likewise, those that hold lower rates of cognation to each other diverged from an ancestral mother language that was spoken further in the past.

The results of lexicostatistical analysis are most commonly illustrated by a "dendogram" (tree diagram) of languages divergence, a two-dimensional rendering of the sequential stages by which new languages came to be formed. The dendogram for this study's classification is presented in chapter 2 (Figure 2.1). It illustrates the manner in which the original proto-Bantu language of southern Cameroon diverged over a 5,000-plus-year period, giving rise eventually to all the modern-day Bantu languages and dialects and, most germane, to the 49 languages that serve as the database for this study (see bottom of Fig. 2.1). The names and historically recent locations of these 49 speech communities are indicated on Map 1. As indicated earlier, I collected linguistic data in the field for those speech communities whose names are indicated by italicized font.[18]

The historical significance of such classifications can be further enhanced by transposing the results to geographical space. This provides hypotheses as to the regions where ancestral speech communities most likely lived. To identify such locations, one works from the "fewest moves principle." This is a postulate based on Occam's razor, which states that (1) the simplest, most parsimonious theory is preferable, and (2) an explanation of unknown phenomena should first be attempted in terms of what is already known. Thus, one works backward from the present-day locations of daughter languages, deducing and plotting the most probable location of each preceding proto-group according to the location of its subgroups.[19]

A final task for the historian-linguist is to provide broad estimates of the periods in which proto-speech communities came to be formed. This is achieved through the use of glottochronology, a dating technique that works from the same percentages of cognation used to determine genetic relatedness between languages. Based on the empirical observation that vocabulary changes and/or replacements have occurred at about the same rates in what is by now a great number of datable language studies around the world, the glottochronological method holds that two languages, after about one thousand years of divergence from their mother language, will normally still retain in common about 75 percent of the 100 core vocabulary items.

Thus, if two languages hold 86 percent cognation they can be estimated to have diverged from the ancestral proto-language roughly five hundred years prior; likewise, a range of cognation centering around a median of 41 percent indicates that the divergence took place roughly three thousand years ago. By applying this formula to cognation figures associated with each of the divergences documented by the classification, the historian-linguist can provide a chronology based on very rough estimations of calendrical dates.[20]

It must be acknowledged that a certain amount of controversy has emerged regarding the viability of glottochronology as a dating tool.[21] These debates center around linguists' arguments that vocabulary is not always replaced or changed at a regular rate, and that languages diverge over a long period of time rather than at a specific date. However, as Christopher Ehret has pointed out, this opinion derives from a misunderstanding of the phenomenon glottochronology actually describes. It "identifies, however imperfectly, a real phenomenon with strong analogues in the natural world, namely, the *patterned accumulation of individually random change among quanta of like properties.*"[22] Thus, it should be recognized that "individual lexical changes in basic vocabulary take place randomly—unless particular and usually overtly identifiable historical influences intervene—but the over-all rate of accumulation of such random changes over long time periods tends to form normal distributions."[23] As a consequence, historian-linguists do not assert that divergences occur at a given point in time. They present their chronologies in terms of time spans, not specific dates. The broadest of such time spans in the present work covers a period of roughly one thousand years, whereas the most limited refer to periods of roughly three hundred years.

Although reconstructed vocabularies, lexical innovations, and the identification of loanwords play a key role in revealing the local histories provided in this book, it is the classification of Bantu and Batwa languages that provides the historical framework upon which this work is built. By chronicling the formation of new speech communities within the rainforest over the past five thousand years, a new understanding of the spread of Bantu languages within the equatorial region emerges.[24] As chapter 2 illustrates, this history should not be envisioned as the result of human migration alone. In several cases, new speech communities emerged in situ, that is, among peoples who had inhabited a specific region for hundreds of years. Thus, it should be recognized that economic, social, and cultural factors drive language divergence as often as migration does.

Correlative Approaches for Linguistic and Archeological Data

As with most works based on methods of comparative historical linguistics, this book presents numerous illustrations of instances in which the chronologies and geographical distribution of archeological artifacts seem to correspond with evidence for the emergence of new Bantu speech communities. It must be recognized, however, that there is no way to determine beyond all doubt which languages that the manufacturers of a certain pottery tradition spoke. Likewise, one cannot assume that specific styles of pottery were always produced by members of the same language or ethnic group, because trade and contact can account for the transfer of decorative techniques or pottery itself. To deal with this issue, historian-linguists prefer to work from the notion of "parallelism"—the identification of commonalities in time and space between the diffusion of specific speech communities and archeological traditions.

This requires the laying out, side by side, of chronologies and data derived independently from each field, and then highlighting the points at which their respective conclusions intersect. This approach has proven fruitful for the eastern regions of the Bantu-speaking world, where archeological and linguistic data are considerably more advanced. In those regions, and west-central Africa as well, the constant recurrence of parallels between linguistic and archeological data suggests that similarities are not simply the result of chance. However, readers should be made aware that associations between archeological and linguistic data can never be proven, only inferred. It is this type of logic that informs the comparative analysis of linguistic and archeological results presented in chapters 2, 4, and 6.

It must also be recognized that neither historical linguistics nor archeological dating techniques (radiocarbon 14) provide finely calibrated chronologies. Accordingly, parallels are identified by the overlapping of time ranges in this book, rather than exact correlations between years or centuries reckoned in calendrical dates. Furthermore, because of fluctuations in atmospheric levels of carbon 14, only very imprecise chronologies can be provided by radiocarbon dating for certain periods of time. This is especially the case for the last millennium B.C.E., a crucial period for the history reconstructed in this book. As de Maret has noted, even when calibrated, "dates between 2520 and 2400 B.P. (570–450 B.C.E.) cannot be resolved to better than anywhere in the 780–420 B.C.E. range, and dates between 2260 and 2160 (310–210 B.C.E.) spread in a 380–200 B.C.E. interval."[25] Again, I deal with this issue by highlighting overlapping ranges of dates, rather than asserting parallels in terms of specific years.[26]

Finally, this book does not work from the standard archeological classificatory schema, for I have elected to replace the Neolithic with de Maret and

Lavachery's notion of the "Stone to Metal Age."[27] This classificatory category is more suitable for this study, for it was developed through analysis of specifically central African archeological data. In adopting this model, however, I have retained an important assumption associated with central African versions of the Neolithic paradigm: that it was Bantu-speaking populations who introduced ceramics and polished stone tools into the western regions of the rainforest. Although I do not attribute each and every site containing such artifacts to Bantu agriculturalists, I do suggest that autochthonous populations gained access to polished stone tools and ceramics through trading contacts that linked them, either directly or indirectly, with Bantu communities living within a relatively local geographical sphere.

Theoretical Approaches

Theories and models developed by a number of scholars have deeply influenced historical reconstruction presented in this book. First and foremost is Igor Kopytoff's model of the frontier process; it provided an initial insight into the commonalities that Bantu/Batwa relations hold with other first-comer and late-comer societies of the Niger-Congo world. Likewise, in his discussion of the term Batwa as chief among the Fipa of Tanzania, Thilo Schadeberg laid out the argument that agriculturalist communities held ancient autochthons in esteem because they relied on them to gain access to the spirits of the land.[28] This observation stuck with me for many years, eventually to form the central premise of the first-comer paradigm. Luc de Heusch's most recent work, *Le Roi de Kongo et les monstres sacrés,*[29] served as a model of how one can use oral and ethnographic data to reconstruct the history of religious and political ideologies over time. His insight into the Kongolese "mythology of the body" provided me with an understanding of how human dwarfs came to serve as symbolic equivalents for the primordial Batwa, and I have drawn heavily from his interpretations of ethnographic and oral evidence regarding peoples of the Kongolese cultural sphere.

Perhaps most influential was the article "Wealth in People as Wealth in Knowledge: Accumulations and Composition in Equatorial Africa" by Jane Guyer and Samuel M. Eno Belinga [30] Their compelling explanation of the role that knowledge has played as a political force in equatorial Africa allowed me to view Bantu and Batwa interactions in an entirely new light. By following their suggestion to move beyond the "lineage mode of production" and "wealth-in-people" models, I was able to see that it was the quest for knowledge—esoteric, supernatural types of knowledge—that kept Bantu leaders tied to Batwa communities for centuries on end.

Finally, as with all works focused on the equatorial regions of Africa, this book owes a great debt to the scholarly corpus of Professor Jan Vansina. Especially important have been his more recent works, which have argued against the notion of a Neolithic Revolution and technological superiority on the part of early Bantu settlers.[31] The topic and methodologies employed here address, among other things, what Vansina has called the "fatal flaw" of anthropological work on the Pygmies—the tendency to focus on Batwa societies exclusively and neglect the societies with whom they are linked.[32] To use his words, "Rather than stress discontinuities between foraging communities and their successors, historians should now look more closely at the continuities between them."[33]

NOTES

1. Colin Turnbull, *The Forest People* (New York: Simon and Schuster, 1961).

2. James Denbow, "Congo to Kalahari: Data and Hypotheses about the Political Economy of the Western Stream of the Early Iron Age," *The African Archaeological Review* 8 (1990): 139–76; R. C. Bailey et al., "Hunting and Gathering in Tropical Rainforest. Is it Possible?" *American Anthropologist* 91, no. 1 (1989): 59–82. Bailey et al.'s central thesis, that there are not enough food sources in the rainforest to sustain human life, has been disproved. The authors did suggest, however, that the lifestyle observed today might have arisen as agriculture developed.

3. Roger Blench, "Are the African Pygmies an Ethnographic Fiction?" in *Challenging Elusiveness: Central African Hunter-Gatherers in a Multidisciplinary Perspective,* ed. Karen Biesbrouck, Stephan Elders, and Gerda Rossel (Leiden: CNWS, 1999), 41–60.

4. L. Luca Cavalli-Sforza, Paolo Menozzi, and Alberto Piazza, *The History and Geography of Human Genes,* (Princeton: Princeton University Press, 1994), 178.

5. For references to these sources, see note 83, chap. 1.

6. Bernard Clist, "Traces des très anciennes occupations humaines de la forêt tropicale au Gabon," in *Challenging Elusiveness: Central African Hunter-Gatherers in a Multidisciplinary Perspective,* ed. Karen Biesbrouck, Stefan Elders, and Gerda Rossel (Leiden: CNWS, 1999), 62–75.

7. Although ethnonyms derived from *-twa* are used widely in reference to autochthonous peoples in the central Congo basin and to the southeast, this term is not commonly used in the more western regions of Congo Republic and Gabon. More common in Gabon is "Babongo" or variants thereof; both agriculturalists and forest specialists assert that this ethnonym originated in agriculturalist communities. In northern Congo, a number of ethnonyms are used. These are discussed in chapters 2–5.

8. This is in contradistinction to Vansina, who has reconstructed "twa" to the proto-Bantu stage (*-tóa*) and assigned it the meaning "serf." See *Paths in the Rainforest: Towards a History of Political Tradition in Equatorial Africa* (Madison, Wisconsin: University of Wisconsin Press, 1990), 279.

9. Thilo Schadeberg, "Batwa: The Bantu Name for the Invisible People," in *Challenging Elusiveness,* 27. It should also be mentioned that I am not adamantly opposed to the use of the term "Pygmy," because in some instances it is embraced by Batwa peoples themselves. However, in most central African contexts, it holds a negative connotation. It is for this reason, as well as its non-African origin, that I prefer not to employ it regularly in this work.

10. The original citation is derived from migration accounts collected at Mouila, Ndende, and Tchibanga. Deschamps writes, "guidés par les Pygmées (Babongo) qui 'fai-

saient la boussole' vers 'les bons pays,' ils ont suivi les savanes de la Ngounié." H. Deschamps, *Traditions orales et archives au Gabon: Contribution à l'ethnohistoire* (Paris: Éditions Berger-Levrault, 1962): 25.

11. Word lists comprised terms related to these themes: core vocabulary word lists, residence, hunting, gathering, agriculture, fishing, metals, clothing, cooking, rituals, and social relations. They were compiled through analysis of ethnographic studies on the Batwa lifestyle in southern Central African Republic and northern Congo, especially the numerous works of Serge Bahuchet (see Bibliography) and that of Lucien Demesse (1978).

12. The most comprehensive is that of Derek Nurse, "The Contributions of Linguistics to the Study of History in Africa," *Journal of African History* 38 (1997): 362; see also Christopher Ehret, "Language Change and the Material Correlates of Language and Ethnic Shift," *Antiquity* 62 (1988) and "Bantu Expansion: Re-Envisioning a Central Problem of Early African History," *The International Journal of African Historical Studies,* 34, no. 1 (2001): 5–41; David Lee Schoenbrun, *A Green Place, A Good Place: Agrarian Change, Gender, and Social Identity in the Great Lakes Region to the Fifteenth Century* (Portsmouth, New Hampshire: Heinemann, 1998), introduction and chap. 1; and Vansina, *Paths,* 9–16 and "New Linguistic Evidence and the 'Bantu Expansion,'" *Journal of African History,* 36, no. 2 (1995): 5–58.

13. Chapters 2 and 4 offer rather detailed presentations of both linguistic and archaeological data to document the nature of Bantu settlement patterns within the rainforest, largely because these results have not been published anywhere else. For information concerning the more technical aspects of how such hypotheses were arrived at (e.g., the establishment of regular sound change rules, techniques used in determining core cognation ranges) see K. Klieman, "Hunters and Farmers of the Western Equatorial Rainforest, Economy, and Society, 3000 B.C. to A.D. 1880" (Ph. D. diss., University of California, Los Angeles, 1997) and K. Klieman, "Comments in Response to Christopher Ehret, 'Bantu Expansion: Re-Envisioning a Central Problem of Early African History,'" 28–32.

14. Cognates are terms that share similar forms and meanings, and which can be proven to be derived from a common ancestral source.

15. These words appear in the Mikaya (C-10s), Bekwil (A-85b), and Njem (A-84) languages, respectively. Also, readers should note that this specific presentation—a term written in phonological script, preceded by an asterisk and followed by a definition—refers to a reconstructed word; it comprises a form and a meaning that has been determined through comparative analysis of cognates within a given branch of a language family or across the Bantu-speaking world.

16. Regular sound change rules for languages collected in the field can be seen in Klieman, "Hunters and Farmers," 310–53.

17. Core vocabularies are therefore considered the most stable set of words to use in determining genetic relationships between the various descendants of a common ancestral language. Morris Swadesh, "Towards Greater Accuracy in Lexicostatistical Dating," *International Journal of American Linguistics* 21 (1955): 121–37.

18. Lexical data (i.e., 100-word lists) for the languages I did not study in the field were kindly provided by the directors of the Linguistic Section of the Africa Museum in Tervuren, Belgium. These latter languages were chosen to serve as representatives for each of the branches and subbranches of the Bantu language family spoken within the equatorial region today. Also, to facilitate cross-referencing of Guthrie's materials, each mention of a language is followed by a capital letter (e.g., A, B, C, H) as well as a number (e.g., A-80, C-10). They refer to Guthrie's geographical indexing of the Bantu languages, in which the letters identify a broad zone of languages and the numbers identify subzones and individ-

ual languages. It should be pointed out that Guthrie's scheme is not genetic, and he often includes, even in the same numbered subzone, languages that belong to entirely different subgroups of Bantu.

19. This technique has been carried out for the classification presented in this study; the resultant maps are presented in chapters 2 and 5. It is also important to note that only the most probable core areas of ancient speech communities can be identified through these mapping techniques; it is possible that the extension of a given speech community could have been larger than the areas identified on such geographical maps, and it could have been differently configured.

20. Sheila Embleton, *Statistics in Historical Linguistics* (Bochum: Brockmeyer, 1986); C. Ehret, "Testing the Expectations of Glottochronology against the Correlations of Language and Archaeology in Africa," in *Time Depth in Historical Linguistics,* vol. 2, ed. Colin Renfrew, April McMahon, and Larry Trask (Cambridge: McDonald Institute for Archaeological Research, 2000), 373–99.

21. For arguments supporting the validity of glottochronology as a dating method, see M. Swadesh, "Towards Greater Accuracy"; R. Antilla, *Historical and Comparative Linguistics* (Amsterdam: John Benhamins, 1989), 396–98; Vansina, *Paths,* 16; and Ehret, "Language Change." For arguments against its validity, see Theodora Bynan, *Historical Linguistics* (Cambridge: Cambridge University Press, 1977), 266–72; Henrick Birnbaum, *Linguistic Reconstruction: Its Potential and Limitations in New Perspective* (Washington, 1978), 17; and a number of much older articles such as D. L. Olmstead, "Three Tests of Glottochronological Theory," *American Anthropologist* 59 (1957): 839–42, K. Bergsland and H. Vogt, "On the Validity of Glottochronology," *Current Anthropology* 3, no. 2 (1962): 115–52, K. V. Teeter, "Lexicostatistics and Genetic Relationships," *Language* 39, no. 4 (1963): 638–48.

22. Ehret, "Testing the Expectations," 373.

23. Ibid.

24. Although other classifications of the Bantu languages have been carried out, many using a number of the languages included here, none have focused exclusively on rainforest languages, nor have they systematically incorporated data from the various Batwa communities that inhabit the region. See, for example, Y. Bastin, A. Coupez, and B. De Halleux, "Classification Lexicostatistique des Langues Bantoues (214 relevés)," *Bulletin des Séances: Académie Royale des Sciences d'Outre Mer,* 27:2 (1983), 174–199; Y. Bastin, A. Coupez, and M. Mann, *Continuity and Divergence in the Bantu Languages: Perspectives from a Lexicostatistic Study* (Tervuren: MRAC, 1999); B. Heine, H. Hoff, and R. Vossen, "Neuere Ergebnisse zur Territorialgeschichte der Bantu," in *Zur Sprachgeschichte und Ethnohistorie in Africa,* ed. F. Möhlig Rottland and B. Heine (Berlin: Reimer, 1977); and Vansina, *Paths,* 49–55. Vansina's interpretation is based on Bastin et. al.'s 1981 classification. Although Vansina's *Paths* presents a history of the equatorial region as a whole, it does not focus heavily on the history of speech communities located in modern-day Congo Republic and Gabon. A detailed comparative analysis of this classification and those presented in Vansina and Heine, Hoff, and Vossen can be found in Klieman, "Hunters and Farmers," 49–61.

25. P. de Maret and G. Thiry, "How Old Is the Iron Age in Central Africa?" in *The Culture and Technology of African Iron Production,* ed. Peter R. Schmidt (Gainesville: University Press of Florida, 1996), 31. I have altered the authors' usage of "B.C." to "B.C.E." in this quote for purposes of consistency.

26. Although this work presents calibrated dates wherever possible, archeologist reports and article do not always provide them. I thus follow archeologists' orthographies

for indicating these differences: calibrated dates are indicated by uppercase punctuated abbreviations such as B.C.E. ("before the common era") and C.E. ("common era"), whereas those that are not calibrated are indicated by lowercase unpunctuated abbreviations (e.g., bp [before present], bce).

27. P. de Maret, "Pits, Pots, and the Far West Streams," in *The Growth of Farming Communities in Africa from the Equator Southwards,* ed. J. E. G. Sutton (*Azania* special vol. 29–30, London/Nairobi: British Institute of Eastern Africa, 1994/95): 320; P. Lavachery, "De la pierre au metal: Archéologie des dépots Holocènes de l'abri de Shum Laka (Cameroon)" (Ph.D. thesis, Université Libre de Bruxelles, 1997–98), 367.

28. Schadeberg, "Batwa," 30–31.

29. L. de Hersh, *Le Roi de Kongo et les monstres sacrés* (Paris: Éditions Gallimard, 2000).

30. J. Guyer and S. M. E. Belinga, "Wealth in People as Wealth in Knowledge: Accumulation and Composition in Equatorial Africa," *Journal of African History* 36 (1995): 91–120.

31. Vansina, "New Linguistic Evidence," 173–95; Vansina, "Historians, Are Archaeologists Your Siblings?" *History in Africa* 22 (1995): 369–408; Vansina, "A Slow Revolution: Farming in Subequatorial Africa," in Sutton, *Growth of Farming Communities,* 15–26.

32. Vansina, *Paths,* 29.

33. Vansina "Historians," 394.

1

(RE)CONSTRUCTING HISTORIES: CENTRAL AFRICAN SOCIETIES AND THE BURDEN OF MYTH

> Objectivity must be operationally defined as fair treatment of data, not absences of preferences. Moreover, one needs to understand and acknowledge inevitable preferences in order to know their influence, so that fair treatment of data and arguments can be attained!
> Stephen J. Gould, *The Mismeasure of Man* (1996), 36.

As Jan Vansina has so aptly pointed out, the equatorial rainforests of central Africa have long remained terra incognita to historians of Africa and the world at large. In his classic *Paths in the Rainforest,* he attributes this phenomenon to Western visions of the rainforest itself—an environment utterly foreign and menacing to those Europeans who sought in the nineteenth century to conquer its inhabitants and wealth. Portrayed as a hostile, primeval environment, a green hell where humans could do nothing more than survive, the forest came to take on anthropomorphic attributes in the minds of Westerners. As such, it was used to explain not only the tragedies induced by the European presence in the region, but the perceived lack of civilization among central African peoples as well.

Steeped in notions of social Darwinism, Westerners of the late nineteenth century located central African forest societies at the bottom of a presumed scale of evolution. Batwa peoples were deemed remnants of the earliest age of humankind, groups of isolated hunter-gatherers who had simply become lost in time. Their Bantu neighbors, considered somewhat more advanced thanks to their knowledge of agriculture and ironworking, were nonetheless seen as peoples only just beginning the long march toward civilization. This view was based on European conceptions of African political systems, which were often noncentralized and kin based, a type of political organization that was largely incomprehensible to the Western mind. Vansina asserts that the end result of such thinking was a legacy of scholarly dismissal, one based on the notion that "environment determines history," and the "unlucky" peoples of central Africa "have no history because they have never changed."[1]

Although environmental determinism and social Darwinism most assuredly played a large role in the nineteenth-century conceptualizations of central African people as primordial remnants, these beliefs do not fully explain the lack of historical interest in this region that prevailed throughout the larger part of the twentieth century. For example, the practice of classifying humans into hierarchically arranged racial categories was discarded after the atrocities of World War II. Why then, do the Batwa remain essentially a "people without history," still regarded as the perennial objects of anthropological and biological studies geared toward understanding the origins and behavior of early humankind? Furthermore, beneficent visions of the tropical rainforest environment have prevailed among Westerners since the 1970s. How then can we explain the fact that attempts at reconstructing the history of the Bantu expansion focused so heavily on the eastern, nonforested regions of the continent? Although scholars of Africa generally attribute this phenomenon to a simple lack of data, such reasoning is tautological; it provides very little information as to why such a vast lacuna in historical documentation endured until the publication of Vansina's *Paths*.

This chapter argues that our lack of information regarding central African forest societies can be attributed to a whole series of myths, not simply those that arose with nineteenth-century ideologies. These pertain to both Batwa and Bantu peoples, and have become so naturalized in discourses of central African history that they often go unrecognized. As such, I consider them "unconscious mental habits,"[2] ideas that influenced the collection, interpretation, and synthesis of data obtained in the central African context. In the case of the Batwa, these myths are exceedingly ancient and related to the Idea of the Pygmy, a Western construct that has been posed as a foil to European societies since the Greco-Roman age. Myths about the Bantu, on the other hand, are of a much more recent origin. I argue that they developed during the "Bantuist" era of African studies (1960s and 1970s), when Africanist scholars strove to distance themselves from the racist elements of the nineteenth-century diffusionist thinking. Because these myths have been prevalent for a much shorter period of time, their analysis is a less complex story to tell.

By presenting this analysis as an introduction to my own historical work, I do not mean to suggest that these myths are hopelessly misguided and should all be rejected outright. Indeed, as Matt Cartmill has suggested, it is important to realize that all myths are not simply false stories, and that "good myths often embody big truths."[3] I do suggest, however, that we begin to test some of them, or at least recognize the influence they have had on our perception of central African history. Following Gould's logic, it is hoped that an initial exposure to the "inevitable preferences" that guide our thinking will clear the way for readers to assess the linguistic and archaeological evidence on its own merit, and begin to contemplate alternative visions of the Bantu and Batwa past.

THE PYGMY PARADIGM

The Idea of the Pygmy is an entirely Western construct, one that was applied to peoples of central Africa relatively late in the history of the idea. By the nineteenth century, the term "Pygmy" had come to signify a very complex and multilayered aggregate of meanings, all of which were unpacked onto newly discovered forest specialists of central Africa. I refer to this aggregate as the Pygmy Paradigm because its primary use has been to generate and test theories about human origins and evolution. The widespread acceptance of this paradigm in the subsequent century has obscured the fact that many of its precepts were originally propositions, and most remain to be proven through scientific and/or historical analysis.

This discussion seeks not only to illustrate the ancient origins of the association between Pygmies and evolution, but also to explain why this association is so difficult to discard. I will argue that the Idea of the Pygmy has been one of the most enduring root metaphors of Western culture, mediating successive shifts in Western thinking about human origins, human nature, physical variation, and cultural difference.[4] The power of the idea lay in its role as a commonplace referent to the non-Western or nonhuman "other," one that was readily and freely evoked by both the masses and intellectuals alike. This phenomenon can be attributed to the location of legendary Pygmies between apes and humans in both Aristotle's *scala naturae* and the Medieval Great Chain of Being, and the resultant vision of the Pygmy as an exceedingly humanlike yet primordial being. As is illustrated following, Westerner intellectuals from nearly every era of history have relied on the Idea of the Pygmy to seek answers to the most fundamental of human queries—*who am I, and from whence did I come?*

Finally, although a history of Western ideas about Pygmies would seem to have little to do with the realities of the central African past, this discussion serves an important purpose by illustrating to readers exactly how root metaphors work. By adjusting and expanding their meanings to fit major transformations in social, political, and intellectual thought, some are able to remain vital and viable for centuries on end. An understanding of this phenomenon will better allow readers to follow the arguments presented in chapters 3, 5, and 6, where I build a case that Bantu speakers of west-central

Africa developed their own unique root metaphor centered on the image of the primordial Batwa.

The Origin of an Idea: Dwarfs and Pygmies in the Ancient World

Although it is generally accepted that the Idea of the Pygmy was a Greek invention, I argue that we must go much further back in time to understand the intellectual context in which it emerged and the complex of ideas that came to be attached to it. A key set of associated ideas traces back to Ancient Egyptian conceptions of abnormally short-statured peoples, individuals commonly referred to as dwarfs. For Egyptians, dwarfism was a condition imbued with mystical and very positive connotations, largely because of the association of dwarfs with the creator god and the process of childbirth itself. These notions were encoded in the worship of the dwarf gods Ptah and Bes, whose cults spread widely in the Mediterranean during the first millennium B.C.E. Because of this development, the notions became commonplace among the general populace and intellectuals alike, providing a fertile context for the creation and reception of Greek legends about miniature, human-like beings living on the borders of the known world. As we will see, these two themes—one linking the Pygmies to creation and the other tending toward a positive evaluation of their differentness—have remained two of the most enduring premises of the Pygmy Paradigm, influencing Westerners' perceptions of people they deem Pygmy ever since.

Iconographic studies of artifacts, paintings, and papyri make it clear the Egyptians recognized several forms of pathological dwarfism. The majority of representations refer to disproportionate types of dwarfism, medically described as *achondroplasia* and *hypochondroplasia*. Both of these conditions result in very distinct facial and bodily characteristics such as small facial bones, depressed nasal bridge, severely shortened limbs, normal-sized trunk, pronounced pelvic tilt, bowed legs, and in the case of achondroplasia alone, large cranium. A New Kingdom magic spell confirms that dwarfs were revered specifically because of these deformities, for it states, "O you dwarf of heaven! You whose face is big, whose back is long, and whose legs are short."[5]

Images of dwarfs are present in nearly every era of Egyptian history, but are especially prominent in the Old and New Kingdoms. The earliest known representations are two ivory figurines found along the Middle Nile at the predynastic sites of Naqada and Ballas (c. 3000 B.C.E.).[6] In the Pyramid Texts, King Pepy I himself is personified as a dwarf, performing a sacred dance in front of the throne of the sun god, Re.[7] From the Middle Period on, dwarfs were increasingly represented as attendants to royal personages. One notable example of this tendency is found at El-Amarna, where Mwt-bnrt, the sister of Queen Nefertiti and wife of King Ahkenaton, is accompanied by two dwarfs named "the sun" and "forever."[8] In the tomb of a wealthy man of the thirtieth dynasty, a sarcophagus of a dwarf named pwenhtf was found. His nude figure was engraved on the lid, and the accompanying texts indicate that "he wanted to dance on some religious occasions related to the burials of the bulls Hp-Wsir and Wsir Mr-wr."[9]

Two key motifs, as is evident in these examples, surrounded Egyptian representations of dwarfs—an association with the sun and a role in the performance of ritual dances at burials. Magical texts from the late and Greco-Roman periods explain these associations, for they indicate that dwarfs were used as symbols for the creator/sun god, Re. In certain passages, Re is referred to as "that dwarf of the sky,"[10] and "that great dwarf who goes around the two lands (i.e. the nether world) at twilight."[11] Others show a direct parallelism with Re (e.g., "The sacred child who is in the house of Re, the holy dwarf who is in the cave"),[12] or use the dwarf as a symbol of his original creation ("A lotus emerged in which there was a beautiful child who illuminates the earth with its rays, a blossom in which there was a dwarf whom Shou loved to see").[13]

Dassen has argued that the association between Re and dwarfs derives from what was considered the ambiguous physical appearance of the latter. Seen as an embodiment of both youth and old age, dwarfs were considered reminiscent of Re's rebirth each morning (with the rise of the sun) and his passage to the netherworld (i.e., death) each night.[14] With the unification of Upper and Lower Egypt, Re eventually came to be intermingled with the fertility god Osiris. The two were considered counterparts in life and death, representatives of day and night, as well as the east and the west.[15]

Beliefs about the divine attributes of dwarfs came to be embodied in the worship of two Egyptian dwarf gods, Ptah and Bes. First recognized in the Middle Kingdom era, their cults came to enjoy great popularity in the late Egyptian and Greco-Roman periods. Ptah was originally a creator god of the Memphitic religion, as well as the patron deity of craftsmen. In Memphis he came to rival and eventually overpower Re as the most senior of creator gods, for he was considered to have generated all of the Heliopolis pantheon by thinking and speaking the cosmos into existence.[16] From the New Kingdom on, he is portrayed in protective amulets as a dwarf, identified by a flat-topped head that was often adorned with a scarab.[17] Ptah's association with Re is made apparent in a hymn to Ptah of the twenty-second dynasty: "the child who is born everyday, the radiant who causes the gods to live, the glowing who shines in his horizon, who causes the two lands to unite with his brilliance, lord of the light, the light of the day, the lion of his night."[18]

The final lines from the "Hymn to Ptah" (i.e., the lion of his night) provide an allusion to Bes, the second dwarf god worshipped by Egyptians. He was considered the counterpart of Ptah, representing the evening aspect of the creator god (i.e., Osiris). Depicted as an achondroplastic dwarf with leonine features (mane, ears, and tail) and a menacing demeanor (grimacing face, protruding tongue), Bes was revered for his ability to ward off disease, dangerous animals, evil spirits, and invading armies. As a reflection of his links to the creator god, he was also considered the guardian deity of women in childbirth and the protector of women's sexuality and fecundity.[19] Like Ptah, his image became widespread through the use of protective amulets, some of which have been found in locations as far away as Britain and Syria.[20] These were made from inexpensive local stones, attesting his appeal among the masses.[21] The worship of Bes eventually spread to the Greeks, where he took on a strongly erotic guise and was associated with the Dionysian cult. In Egypt, Bes was worshipped well into the early Christian era; some Coptic texts indicate that he was placed alongside Jesus as a benevolent spirit, and his amulets have been found in numerous Coptic sepulchers.[22]

Given the popularity of the cults of Ptah and Bes, it is not surprising to see that the earliest Greek manifestations of the Idea of the Pygmy recall numerous aspects of Egyptian religious beliefs. A direct association is found in the earliest depictions of dwarfs of the Archaic and Classical eras, where figures resembling Ptah and Bes appear on votive terra-cottas and vase painting. Although nearly all of the Greco-Roman artistic renderings illustrate dwarfism of the achondroplastic sort, later scholars have divided the depictions into two types—those of dwarfs, and those of Pygmies. This distinction arises from correlations with contemporaneous literary references that begin to make mention of miniature peoples living in faraway lands. The earliest is in Homer's *Iliad* (ninth–eighth centuries B.C.E.), where the term "Pygmy" first appears as a reference to peoples only one cubit *(pygmæ)* tall, and who annually fight off the advances of migrating cranes. Accordingly, depictions of dwarfs battling cranes are considered representations of Homer's legendary figures, a distinction clearly made by the Greeks and Romans themselves.[23]

Numerous later references to Pygmies appear in Greek travelers' accounts, a genre of writing that fancifully mixed fact and fiction.[24] The most detailed comes from Ctesias of Cnide, a Greek physician who worked in the Persian royal court.[25] Among the peoples he purportedly encountered was a population of "small black men" who lived in the center of India. Ctesias described these men as less than two cubits tall, flat-nosed, and ugly. They were also reported to have penises that reached their ankles and hair so long that it served as bodily covering.[26] Despite their rather frightening physical appearance, Ctesias considered these men to be extremely just, stating that they lived by the same laws and spoke the same language as other Indians.[27] Herodotus (485–425 B.C.E.) described the Pygmies as well, stating that they were troglodytes (cave dwellers) of Africa (Aethiopia) who ate serpents and lizards and spoke a language that sounded like the screeching of bats. He described Pygmies, "for those who have never seen them," as resembling a statue of the Greek dwarf god Hephaistos, with bent and deformed legs.[28] In the *History of Animals,* Aristotle (384–282 B.C.E.) argued that the Pygmies of Homer's tale were no fable. Working from Herodotus's studies of bird migrations, he posited that they were located in the "lakes of Upper Egypt"—because cranes migrated to that region each winter.[29]

Seen in light of earlier Egyptian beliefs about dwarfs, many elements of these stories appear to conflate actual travelers' accounts and ideas derived from the cults of Ptah and Bes. For example, Ctesias's description of small-statured Indians with snub noses, large phalli, hairy bodies, and ugly faces clearly recalls the image of the leonine dwarf-god Bes. Herodotus's description of Pygmies as cave dwellers recalls the ancient text associating dwarfs with Re's attribute to the child Horus ("The sacred child who is in the house of *Re,* the holy dwarf who is in the cave"), and Herodotus's mention of their diet of snakes and reptiles may reflect a memory of the same, because Ptah in his Horus aspect was renowned for his ability to vanquish such animals along the Nile. The generally favorable depiction of Pygmies may also be seen as a continuation of the Egyptians positive evaluation of dwarfs' "otherness." Indeed, the traits attributed to them—the possession of speech, laws, and a sense of justice—are the very criteria by which Greeks judged and measured the potential humanity of alien peoples.

The Idea of the Pygmy as a link between animals and humans was foreshadowed in Aristotle's theory of human gestation, which posited that the embryo becomes a fetus through a series of stages, first taking on a fungus-like form, and followed by that of an unshaped animal, an ape, a Pygmy, and finally, a fully-formed human. Aristotle's theory of human gestation is especially significant because it presents his vision of the *scala naturae*—essentially a nascent version of the Great Chain of Being. Formalized nearly four centuries later by Plotinius, the Great Chain of Being was used by Westerners from the Medieval to Modern ages as a metaphor for a perceived hierarchy in the nature, function, and organization of the universe. Aristotle's contribution was his view that nature should be seen as a continuum—a series of classes whose properties shaded off into those of the next. Although he did not propose a hierarchy for the continuum, he did see it as a linear series of classes, and in his work ordered beings according to their degree of development at birth. Thus was added the principle of linear gradation and the idea of arranging animals in a single-graded *scala naturae.*

Although it is likely that Aristotle was actually referring to pathological forms of dwarfism in his theory of human gestation, later scholars and translators did not especially concern themselves with this issue. The Idea of the Pygmy came to be intimately associated in subsequent ages in the West with theories of human origins and natural science, a characteristic of the Pygmy Paradigm that continues to prevail today.

The Pygmy in Medieval Theology and Thought

With the rise of Christianity, the Great Chain of Being came to be conceptualized in religious terms, and the objects of creation were ranked according to their resemblance to God. Under this thinking, the Great Chain of Being came to be seen as a series of linked stages: from God, to Angel, to Man, to Animal, to Plant, and to Dust. In such a schema, important questions were raised about the status of legendary peoples such as the Pygmies. As Friedman has noted, a new more philosophical line of reasoning was applied; did these "abnormal" creatures have a soul? Had they descended from Adam? In what ways did their strange appearance link them to God, and, most important, how was the Christian to deal with them?[30] This shift in thinking was partly induced by the occupational concerns of clergymen, for priests were required to determine the humanity of anomalous births before going forth with baptism. A long series of debates were carried out in the church, allowing scholars to define the nature of humanity in distinctly Western ways. Two distinct strains of thought developed regarding the nature and origins of anomalous peoples.

The first was *inclusionist*. Following Plato's idea of plenitude, proponents of the inclusionist view saw the monstrous races as an indication of God's creative capacity. This view came to be associated with the universalist notions of Christianity, most strongly extolled by St. Augustine in *City of God*. Arguing that bodily form is not indicative of human or nonhuman status, he proposed instead that the possession of reason and descent from Adam should be the determinative criteria for inclusion in the human race.[31] The Medieval scholars came to term such beings *monstrum* (from the Latin *monstra*, "portent") and considered them the showing forth of divine will.[32] Such is the etymological origin of the "monstrous races," an appellation originally associated with positive connotations.

This view, as well as the ancient approbation of Pygmies, helps to explain their frequent appearance in Medieval Christian texts and art. A thirteenth-century example presents the Pygmy as a miniature European male, cradled in the hand of a three-faced Giant and accompanied by a Sciopod.[33] The tympanum of an eleventh-century cathedral in Vezelay, France, presents carved images of Pygmies as well. In this context they are clearly designated as an "alien other" by their location across a symbolic body of water. As Friedman has pointed out, pilgrims and crusaders were encouraged to view them as examples of God's wonder, and as possible converts to the religion.[34]

Although the Church promoted a universalist version of Christianity, an *exclusionist* vision of the monstrous races was developing as well. This approach was associated with the rise of rhetoric and focused on the questions that St. Augustine neglected to address—exactly *how* and *why* these beings came to be so abnormal.[35] Scholars of this persuasion worked from the Ancients' notion that extremes of bodily form and geographical location could be considered a mark of vice. Like the Ancients, they considered differences in the appearance of men to be caused by climatic variation. However, in the Medieval era these differences were additionally considered to be reflective of a spiritual state; God had relegated the monstrous races to the ends of the earth as punishment, and out of concern for the rest of mankind. It is in this genre of text that we see the first mention of ideas that are used to justify African slavery in later periods: the curse of Cain, Ham, and the idea that certain peoples had suffered a biblical fall from grace.[36]

Given the location of Pygmies between apes and humans on the Great Chain of Being, Medieval thinkers of both persuasions considered them to be the most human of the monstrous races. As such, they figured prominently in Scholastics' debates about the true nature of humanity. For example, Albertus Magnus (1193–1280) used the Idea of the Pygmy to argue that the true measure of humanity was the possession of *Ars*—the ability to formulate syllogisms and to argue from universals. Taking a decidedly exclusionist line, Albert states:

> The pygmy is the most perfect of animals. Among all the others, he makes most use of memory and most understands by audible signs. On this account he imitates reason even though he truly lacks it . . . accordingly, he perceives nothing of the quiddities of things, nor can he comprehend and use the figures of logical argumentation.[37]

It is important to remember that at this point in history, Albert is referring to an entirely legendary race. His ideas regarding the Pygmies' lifestyles and customs were drawn from a common cultural metaphor, one that had been developing among Europeans for over a thousand years. The level of assumption about these legendary beings, especially as pertains to their human characteristics and mental capacities, leads one to believe that the Idea of the Pygmy was widespread among intellectuals of the thirteenth century.[38] With Albert's work, however, an entirely new element is added to this paradigm; the Pygmy becomes a symbol of the subhuman, and the seeds of a much more injurious idea about the non-Western "other" are sown.

Although thirteenth-century European ideas about Pygmies cannot be considered a discourse on race per se, they clearly contributed to the incipient stages of such. They serve to substantiate Foucault's contention that the development of modern racism was formed not through a break with the past, but rather, through a "discursive bricolage whereby an older discourse of race is 'recovered,' 'modified,' 'encased,' and 'encrusted' in new forms."[39] As we will see, Westerners would once again turn to the Idea of the Pygmy during the age of slavery and science, when the Pygmy Paradigm contributed to Western notions of race and evolution in much more overt ways.

The Pygmy in the Age of Exploration, Science, and Slavery

With the opening of global trade routes in the fourteenth century, considerable numbers of Westerners began to travel the globe. Although they fully expected to meet members of the monstrous races, they were faced with a much more daunting reality—the incredible diversity of humankind. Although the church continued to call for a universalist approach, numerous new exclusionist theories developed as well. Most famous among these was Paracelsus's proposal (1520) that the aborigines of the New World were descended from a "second" Adam, the same that had generated "nymphs, griffins, salamanders and sirens . . . all beings without souls."[40]

Although Paracelsus's theory was considered highly heretical, it illustrates the manner in which increased knowledge of the world led many to question biblical revelation as an authoritarian source. A preponderance of new data on animals, plants, peoples, and places flooded Europe, challenging ancient notions about both the origins of humans and their place in the natural world. Empirical approaches came to be valued over the ancient disciplines of theology and moral philosophy, and the age of modern science was born. Although still working within the scheme of the Great Chain of Being, scholars of this intellectual revolution strove to replace ancient beliefs in miracles and the marvelous by using science to reveal the majesty of God's creation. In such a context, belief in the monstrous races declined. They represented that which the new empiricists sought to discard: a fanciful, superstitious, unobservable form of knowledge. Perhaps because of its appeal as a commonplace icon for the alien "other," the Idea of the Pygmy seems to have survived this era, for it is represented in very distant locations (the New World, northern Europe, the North Pole) on some of the earliest maps of the globe.[41]

Friedman has argued that the decline of the monstrous races took place in two stages: "First, the monstrous men of antiquity were reduced to a single figure, the Hairy Wild Man, and second, the figure became conflated with the aboriginal peoples found in the New World."[42] Although this is clearly the case in terms of European perceptions of New World inhabitants, it neglects to evaluate the African side of this transformation. As we will discover, the Hairy Wild Man was incorporated into the Pygmy Paradigm through an association with anthropoid apes, leading to the notion of the "missing link" and its enduring association with Africa.

References to both hairy wild men and hairy wild women are found in ancient texts, the earliest of which appear in the legends of Alexander. They were usually portrayed as human in bodily form, yet covered entirely with hair and oftentimes exhibiting abnormalities such as six fingers or hands.[43] St. Augustine associated them with the wandering (undesirable) life of the hunter. In early Christian exclusionist thought they were usually considered inhabitants of the desert and associated with sin through the perceived physical aberration of blackness. This interpretation was carried into the Medieval era, when they came to be considered enslaved by nature and their own libidinous desires. By the late twelfth century, however, ancient ideas about nature had been reintroduced, and the Hairy Wild Man became fodder in debates about the value of life in the "polis."[44] Those disenchanted with Medieval lifestyles saw nature as the ultimate escape, and tended to portray the Hairy Wild Man as entirely beneficent in nature, a protector of wildlife and teacher of wisdom to peasants. Those who saw in nature nothing but an endless and horrible struggle for survival continued to view the Hairy Wild Man as sinful and evil, a symbol of the dangers faced if one abandoned civilization.

It is easy to imagine how the Hairy Wild Man came to be combined with the Idea of the Pygmy. Both were considered to be semi-human, of a libidinous nature, and oftentimes associated with the inner regions of Africa. But what really clenched this association was the European "discovery" of Old World apes. Although monkeys had been known to Europeans since the time of the Greeks, increased travel in the tropics exposed Europeans to the closest relatives of our own genus homo—chimpanzees, gorillas, and the orangutan of southeast Asia.

The first live specimen of such an ape arrived in London in 1698. It was given to the renowned naturalist Edward Tyson, who quickly set about dissecting it, seeking specifically to identify what place it occupied on the Great Chain of Being.[45] He eventually published his results in a monograph entitled *Orang-outang sive Homo Sylvestrus, or the Anatomy of a Pygmie compared with that of a Monkey, and Ape, and a Man; to which is added A Philological Essay Concerning the Pygmies, the Cynocephali, the Satyrs and the Sphinges of the Ancients, wherein it will appear that they were all either Apes or Monkeys; and not Men, as formerly pretended* (1699). In it he argued that the legendary Pygmies had never existed at all, that ancient references to them were simply a mixing of legend and mistaken identity, and that travelers had mistaken apes for the Pygmies when viewed from afar. At the same time, however, he argued that the orangutan/wildman/Pygmy (i.e., chimpanzee) should be considered as a possible missing link on the Great Chain of Being, one that tied humans to other creatures physically, if not intellectually.[46] Tyson's theories rapidly became the accepted explanation of the age: not only did they provide an exceptionally neat repudiation of ancient mythologies, but they also reinforced faith in the Great Chain of Being as a tool for interpreting the patterns and organization of nature. The idea of the legendary Pygmy was seemingly dead, and the term "Pygmy" came to be used exclusively in the construction of biological nomenclature as it referred to apes.[47]

Although Tyson's argument presented a sensible, scientific explanation of a legend that had long perplexed Western thinkers, it also reflected an important epistemological leap—one that was necessary to the development of the human and biological sciences. As Marks has noted, the relationship of humans to the natural world was a philosophical question of long standing, but with the work of Tyson it became an empirical one as well.[48] Equally important was the method Tyson employed to make this leap, for he applied the premises of the Pygmy Paradigm to mediate emergent knowledge about an unknown area of fact—the study of anthropoid apes. As such, it stands as one of the earliest examples of the use of metaphor in modern science.[49]

Long ignored as an integral element of scientific research, the role of the metaphor has only recently begun to be analyzed and articulated by scholars. Kuhn has argued that the similarity-creating process engendered by the use of metaphors is similar to that of the scientific model—both are used to generate new hypotheses, programs of research, and, eventually, data. Such processes have traditionally been downplayed, however, in an attempt to portray science as an objective, universal form of knowledge. Stepan argues that this "dichotomization" has led many to dismiss obviously metaphorical approaches as "pre-scientific" or "pseudo-scientific," allowing "the metaphorical nature of much modern science to go unrecognized."[50]

This appears to be the case for Tyson's study. Discussed in terms of its con- tributions to seventeenth-century notions of the missing link and The Great Chain of Being, the elements of his argument that pertain to the Idea of the Pygmy are treated in a very cursory, almost anecdotal manner. It therefore goes unrecognized that, although Tyson replaced the legendary Pygmy with a more "scientized" symbol (the missing link), the major premises or categories of the Pygmy Paradigm remained intact. These premises eventually came to be naturalized in the human and biological sciences, helping to establish a set of rules and constraints that would guide evolutionary research for centuries to come. As such, the newly developed missing link paradigm served to struc- ture the experience and understanding of human variation and origins— essentially creating objects of difference at the same time.[51]

In the seventeenth- and eighteenth-century context, such objects of differ- ence were created through the application of the missing link paradigm to anthropoid apes and southern African pastoralists. Although both were per- ceived of as missing links on the Great Chain of Being, European experience conditioned which aspects of the Pygmy/Hairy Wild Man paradigm would be applied to each. Anthropoid apes, posing little threat to European interests abroad, came to be associated with the more approbatory aspects of the Pygmy/Hairy Wild Man paradigms. Such is the source of what Harraway has described as "Simian Orientalism," a specifically Western discourse in which "the monkeys and apes have a privileged relationship to nature and culture," occupying "the border zones between those potent mythic poles."[52]

On the other hand, southern African pastoralists such as the Khoi and the San (referred to as "Hottentots" and "Bushmen" by the Europeans at that time), were portrayed as brutes, savages, and degenerates,—populations infe- rior in physical, mental, moral, and spiritual ways. This was largely due to European ambitions in southern Africa, which led to more than two hundred years of genocidal wars over access to resources and land. Although such imagery drew heavily from ancient ideas about the Hairy Wild Man,[53] it relied on the same criteria that had been used to deny human status to the leg-

endary Pygmies, that is, a lack of reason. Take for example, the writings of
Soame Jenyns, published in 1790:

> Animal life rises from this low beginning in the shellfish, through innumer-
> able species of insects, fishes, birds, and beasts, to the confines of reason
> where in the dog, the monkey and the chimpanzee it unites so closely with
> the lowest degree of that quality in man, that they cannot easily be distin-
> guished from each other. From this lowest degree in the brutal Hottentot,
> reason, with the assistance of learning and science, advances, through the
> various stages of human understanding, which rise above each other, till in
> a Bacon or a Newton it attains the summit.[54]

Although it was eventually decided that Khoi and San peoples were in fact
human, they continued to represent the lowest limits of humanity in the
majority of Western minds. Like the legendary Pygmy, they were posed as a
foil to European society; in this era, however, they were used to create
increasingly ethnocentric explanations of what the highest echelons of
humanity (i.e., northern Europeans) were *not*.

In the context of an expanding and exclusively African global slave trade,
the ideas of the brutal savage and the missing link were eventually extended
to include all Africans. In the eighteenth and nineteenth centuries, this discourse appropriated the exclusionist aspect of the combined Pygmy/Hairy
Wild Man paradigm, yet used newly developed scientific methods of observation, measurement, and classification to support its claims. Some of these
were based on attempts to establish physiognomical links between Africans
and apes (Camper's infamous facial angles). Others, such as the "science" of
phrenology (measuring the exterior dimensions of the skull), worked from
Albert's original notion that rationality was the ultimate determinate of
human status. Debates about the place of man in nature were often conducted
in terms of the differences between Africans and apes, and the foundations for
the emergence of "racial science" in the nineteenth century were set in place.

Modern Manifestations of the Pygmy Paradigm

Appalled at the use of The Great Chain of Being as a classificatory device
to render Africans and other non-Europeans less than human, many leading
scientists of the eighteenth century rejected the paradigm as unscientific and
absurd. However, subsequent discoveries in the fields of anatomy, geology,
and paleontology reinforced what appeared to be the naturalness of gradation
between distinct species.[55] The notion of a graded human hierarchy was thus
reinforced, and emerged in the nineteenth century with the notion of biological race at its core. Race came to be seen as an indelible, inherited essence,
one that determined intelligence, culture, even national character. Nineteenth-

century scholars from all fields of the human and biological sciences strove to develop theories and methods that would aid in the classification of all humanity along racial lines.

In this new context, the Pygmy Paradigm resurfaced in racialistic form. The event that provoked this development was the discovery of short-statured forest specialists in the equatorial region of central Africa. Although the earliest encounter took place between the French-American traveler Paul Du Chaillu and certain Babongo peoples of Gabon,[56] a more enduring and influential link between central Africans and the legendary Pygmies was drawn by Georges Schweinfurth.

After traveling through Sudan in search of the source of the Nile, Schweinfurth arrived in the Ituri forest of northeastern Congo in the early 1870s. There he encountered several Aka individuals, all of whom were caught up in the warfare and strife that ravaged this region at the time. Both their military prowess and geographical location led Schweinfurth to associate the Aka with the Pygmies of the Ancients—in this case, particularly Aristotle's accounts, which had located the Pygmies in the "upper lakes of the Nile."[57]

Schweinfurth's hypothesis led Western scholars to once again pore over the plethora of Ancient and Medieval references to Pygmies and dwarfs. Key to the scientific validation of his theory were the late-nineteenth- and early-twentieth-century discoveries in Egypt and the Nile, for the numerous illustrations and references to dwarfs were interpreted as literal references to central African peoples. Drawing on their own experience of the African slave trade, Western scholars hypothesized that such populations were captured by Egyptians and sent to the courts of the great pharaohs.[58] Depictions of Bes in his warlike stance were interpreted as bellicose Pygmies, as were the images of Ptah in his childhood aspect vanquishing crocodiles along the Nile. In some instances data appear to have been created as a part of this legitimization process; noteworthy is a still frequently cited reference to Marietta's discovery of the word "Akka" below an illustration of a dwarf in a fifth-century tomb. Scholars immediately assumed this inscription linked Egyptian Pygmies to the Aka forest specialists that today inhabit the Ituri Forest (northeastern Democratic Republic of Congo). As Bahuchet has noted however, the actual references to this inscription have never been found in Marietta's work, and the precise determination of the term would be extremely difficult given the fact that the Ancient Egyptian orthography consisted of consonants only.[59]

Although Batwa peoples continued to be associated with the missing link paradigm well into the twentieth century,[60] the approbatory premise of this association was influential from the start. It came to be expressed in visions of the Batwa as primitive in the original sense of the word, an example of an infantile race that illustrated the earliest stages of humankind. This notion was promoted by the anthropologists Hamy and de Quatrefages, the two leading scholars on Pygmies at the end of the nineteenth century.[61] Working from the same traits attributed to Pygmies and hairy wild men (i.e., short stature, nudity, dark skin, "hairiness," and a hunting lifestyle), they argued that short-statured peoples from Africa, the Philippines, Malaysia, and India were the remnants of an original Pygmy race, the first humans to inhabit the globe. This theory incorporated diffusionist notions that emerged in the late nineteenth century, for the Pygmies were considered to have enjoyed a great prosperity until the arrival of more advanced migrating races.[62] Rather amazingly, de Quatrefages's notion of a "global Pygmy race" was widely accepted until the 1960s, when Boyd used blood group studies to illustrate that the Pygmies of the various regions more closely resembled their neighbors than they did each other.[63]

The approbatory premise appears in other contexts as well. It can be seen in the efforts of missionaries to substantiate the universality of monogamy and monotheism through ethnographies of Batwa religious beliefs,[64] as well as in the tendency of colonizers to apply more tempered forms of state control over Batwa populations. In the post-World War II era, however, the Idea of the Pygmy reached a rather exalted status, one comparable to that of ancient times. This new level of approbation was linked to the rise of the Man the Hunter evolutionary narrative, and its use of both San and Batwa peoples as analogical sources for understanding the origins of early humankind.

Appalled by the atrocities of World War II, scientists of the 1950s and 1960s strove to abolish the notion of graded human hierarchies. In an effort to prove the unity and equality of all human beings, they developed a new paradigm—one that focused on notions of a "universal mankind." Contrary to the racial model, this paradigm gathered all human populations into a single category (The Family of Man), and strove to make sharp distinctions between animals and human beings.[65] Both the origins of humanity and physical diversity were explained through adaptation, that is, processes of natural selection that initially differentiated humans from animals, and later, allowed for development of physical variation. Under this rubric, reliance on notions of biological race could be discarded, and human evolution came to be talked about exclusively in terms of behavior, environment, and adaptation.

It was in this context that the "hunting hypothesis" emerged—it posited that hunting and its selection pressures had differentiated human beings from their ape-like ancestors.[66] This theory was rapidly embraced for both political and scientific reasons; it not only argued for a common evolutionary history for all humans, but also reinvigorated faith in Darwin's theory of natural selection by providing the first (seemingly) substantive evidence of its function in human evolution.[67] By the 1960s, it dominated nearly all fields of the human and biological sciences; as Foley has argued, evolutionary research virtually *became* a search for the origins of the hunting lifestyle during this time.[68]

Key to the development and diffusion of this paradigm was the work of the physical anthropologist Sherwood Washburn and his school of "new physical anthropology." Seeking to reconstruct the very origins of humankind, he encouraged his students to draw data from the fields of primatology, physical anthropology, social anthropology, and archaeology. Underlying this cross-disciplinary approach was an assumption that the study of primate and hunter-gatherer behavior would provide a rich analogical source for the generation of new hypotheses, especially those concerning the all-important shift to hunting. Such thinking served as the intellectual springboard for Washburn's students Lee and Devore, who established the Harvard Bushman (San) Project (1963–74), to study San peoples in what was considered their original domain—the Kalahari.

Even if unconsciously, the inaugurators of this scientific approach drew heavily on the premises of the Pygmy Paradigm. Washburn and his students turned to commonplace conceptualizations of the primitive in attempts to explain the origins and nature of humankind. Because the goal of this work was to eliminate racism from the evolutionist model, the more positive premises of the Pygmy Paradigm came to the fore. The San and other hunter-gatherers of Africa came to be viewed as noble, knowledgeable, and altogether rational beings, a beneficent and harmless people whose very culture and customs could be used as didactic tools for the West.

This approach also informed the work of Colin Turnbull, who provided the West with its most complete accounts of Batwa lifestyles through his works on the Mbuti peoples of the Ituri Forest (Democratic Republic of Congo), *The Forest People* (1961) and *Wayward Servants* (1965). As Hewlett has noted, these works were so influential that most people, including anthropologists, continue to view Mbuti and Pygmy culture as synonymous.[69] The importance of Turnbull's work is also seen in the fact that Marshall Sahlins used his data to develop his theory of hunting and gathering as the "original affluent lifestyle," an idea "which has laid the foundations for the anthropological study of modern hunter-gatherers."[70] As the years have progressed, however, scholars have begun to acknowledge the ways that Turnbull's vision of the Mbuti as "Noble Savages" impacted his interpretation of data.

For example, the anthropologist Pascal Boyer has noted the manner in which Turnbull strove to portray the Mbuti (in *Wayward Servants*) as a people without strong beliefs in witchcraft or specialized rituals and beliefs, despite the fact that his text is replete with examples of Mbuti mysticism and ritual practice. Boyer sees in these a theme of connivance that informs nearly all work on the Batwa—a sense of complicity that is established between the author and the Batwa subject, and presumed to be understood by the Western reader as well.[71] Identifying what he considers an exaggerated attempt to portray the Pygmy as sensible, rational, and entirely practical beings, he argues that this theme of connivance is introduced as a means of rendering Pygmies closer to Western sensibilities, thus positioning the Bantu as the more exotic, irrational "other."[72] Unaware of the approbatory premises inherent to the

Pygmy Paradigm, Boyer attributes this phenomenon to the frustrations all anthropologists face when confronted with such intellectual traps as magic and witchcraft.

Produced in an age of Western anxieties about warfare, ecological devastation, and social strife, works such as Turnbull's borrowed directly from ancient notions of the Pygmy/Hairy Wild Man as remnants of a lost Golden Age, recalling an era when humans lived in harmony with community, economy, and nature. Although such depictions were put forth with honorable intentions (i.e., the elimination of racism from the evolutionary model), it must be recognized that these views essentially rendered the San and Batwa peoples without history. This was due not only to exaggerated romanticism, but also to the analogical method itself. As Stepan has noted, an important function of the metaphor in science is its "ability to neglect or even suppress information about human experience of the world that does not fit the similarity implied by the metaphor." Because of this, "metaphors often involve the scientist in a selection of those aspects of reality that are compatible with the metaphor."[73]

It was recognition of this fact that led Wilmsen to produce his groundbreaking work *Land Filled with Flies* (1989), in which he argued that members of the Bushman project consistently overlooked data to indicate that the San were *not* primordial hunter-gatherers. Using archaeological and ethnographic evidence to support his case, he argued that the appearance of San as foragers was "a function of their relegation to an underclass" that took place through historical processes of the last millennium.[74] Although the very vitriolic debates Wilmsen's work produced are generally considered evidence of the Western desire to cling to neo-evolutionary theory, they additionally illustrate the enduring power of the Pygmy Paradigm, whose premises predate and were, in fact, essential components in the development of the evolutionary model. Here we see an example of what occurs when the role of metaphor goes unrecognized in science. Scholars begin to "mistake the model for the thing modeled,"[75] and African hunter-gatherers are deemed primordial rather than recognized for the role that they played in producing Western definitions of primordiality itself.

As the perennial objects of biological and anthropological research, Batwa societies have played an important role in this process. Their association with primordiality has most recently been manifested in human population genetics, a field of scientific inquiry originally intended to dismantle the Euro-American racial worldview. This goal was never achieved, however, for as Mukhopadhyay and Moses have noted, "old racial groupings were creatively integrated into the modern paradigm through the invention of new typologies such as micro, geo, and local races."[76] Such were the origins of the "Forest Negro" type, a genetic classification for central African Batwa that is commonly posed as an original or representative African population.[77] As was the case in the nineteenth century, this category remains based primarily on morphological and cultural characteristics alone.[78] Thus, the evolutionary premise remains—the small body size of the Batwa continues to be explained as a process of natural selection that took place over many millennia in the rainforest environment, and the Batwa (especially the Mbuti) are portrayed as the earliest branch of the human genetic tree.[79]

Recognizing the notion of a Pygmy race as a social construction, a number of scholars have begun to challenge the primordial premise as it appears in genetic studies. For example, Froment has noted that the results of genetic trees (designed to represent the ancient divergences between human populations) largely depend on the methods used to construct them. As an example of very suspect results, he cites the work of Vigilant et al. who proposed a date of 119,000 B.C.E. for the divergence between Pygmies of the East and the West, a period that predates the emergence of modern humans.[80] Keita and Kittles have further argued that "the use of genetic systems not responsible for morphology in order to study groups that are defined by morphophenotype is theoretically unsound, especially when divergence times are the subject."[81] And as was mentioned in the introduction, a general shift in thinking is reflected in biologists' estimates of how long it might have taken to develop the small body stature that some Batwa people exhibit. Although earlier works often spoke in terms of tens of thousands of years, more recent accounts suggest a period of as few as three to four thousand years.[82]

Although of more recent origin than the approbatory and primordial premises, the racial premise of the Pygmy Paradigm has had an equally great impact on the collection of data among central African societies. Grounded in notions of ancient, discrete, and non-overlapping racial communities, Westerners often work from the notion that pure Pygmy and pure Bantu populations once occupied the central African terrain. This assumption has held such sway that a whole host of historical possibilities has been precluded. For example, it is only rarely acknowledged that the categories of Pygmy and Bantu might be no more than social constructions of identity, and that these categories may not have existed in the deep past. The belief in distinct original races has also led geneticists to classify Batwa into two population types—Pygmy and Pygmoid—the latter being people socially defined as Batwa, but whose bodies and economic lifestyles do not conform to the ideal type.[83] Such individuals or communities are considered to be the result of admixture, that is, sexual unions between Pygmy and Bantu that took place in the distant past. Although this hypothesis appears to be supported by genetic data that indicate certain Batwa populations are genetically indistinguishable from their Bantu neighbors, it could also be interpreted as evidence that they derive from a single original population.[84]

Because racial categories have been intrinsically linked to economic practices, a tendency to dichotomize subsistence practices has prevailed in interpretations of both ethnographic and archaeological evidence from central Africa. Furthermore, only the "purest" of Batwa peoples were considered suitable objects of biological and anthropological studies. Knowledge of Batwa lifestyles during the twentieth century was thus derived from a few select communities—those of the Ituri (Bambuti, Efe, and Tua), southern Cameroon (the Baka), and the Central African Republic (the Aka). The result is that comparative data that might challenge, alter, or confirm the notion of the Batwa as primordial hunter-gatherers have often been ignored, and the racial premise has been in turn reinforced.

Finally, the notion of a discrete Pygmy race has often led to the assumption that various and far-flung Batwa communities should exhibit a degree of cultural, biological, and/or genetic homogeneity. Comparative studies of the twentieth century thus tended to focus on similarities rather than on differences. This notion has been recently refuted by genetic evidence, however; studies by Chen et al. have indicated that for some loci, Batwa communities are as different from each other as they are from populations located on the other side of the globe.[85] Such data should encourage scholars to contemplate alternative explanations for the similarities they do observe, perhaps by integrating Batwa peoples into larger analyses of regional histories and economies, as this study tries to do. In this manner, difference may be used as an analytical tool in itself, and a more complete understanding of the Batwa past might be achieved.

As is evident, modern manifestations of the Pygmy Paradigm remain linked to the premises of primordiality, approbation, evolution, and race. Although scholars have made valiant efforts to eliminate the racist elements of the nineteenth-century version, they inadvertently replaced one paradigm (social evolutionism) with another (the "noble savage"). As such, the racial premise remains implicitly understood, providing the foundations for the evolutionary premise as well. As a virtual poster child of natural selection theory, the modern-day Idea of the Pygmy plays much the same role it did in the past—mediating emergent knowledge about the origins and nature of human beings. It is for this reason that both the primordial and racial premises remain so difficult to reject; to do so would require greatly recasting current understandings of human cultural evolution as well.

Such is the source of the phenomenon highlighted at the beginning of this chapter—that Batwa people figure significantly in scientific, but not historical, research. Uncritically accepting Batwa as primordial in origin, historians assume that the only data to attest the Batwa past are the bones, stones, and fossilized fauna of the Paleolithic ages. Even language data have been discounted as source material for historical reconstruction; because Batwa peoples speak Bantu, Ubangian, or Central Sudanic languages, it is commonly assumed that they lost their original languages, and thus, historical linguistic methods could be of no avail. The primordial premise has held such sway that scholars failed to recognize that the Batwa speak *their own* forms of these languages, perfectly fine sources for use in historical reconstruction.

This book will work from such data, chronicling a history that reaches back to the fourth millennium B.C.E. Because the Pygmy Paradigm presumes a far more ancient, primordial Batwa presence, the data from the era 3000 B.C.E. to 1900 C.E. cannot directly refute or confirm the premises of the paradigm. Rather, it serves to relocate Batwa peoples in historical time, providing evidence of their social and economic contacts with Bantu peoples over the past few millennia. As is the case for all human societies, the Batwa *do* have a history, whether descendants of ancient populations or not. Because reconstructing this history also relies on an understanding of common conceptualizations of the Bantu past, we turn to that topic for the last part of this chapter.

THE "PROBLEM" OF THE BANTU EXPANSION

This section seeks to present and assess the impact of myths about the historic dispersal of Bantu languages across the southern half of the African continent. It must be acknowledged from the start that these are not myths of the legendary sort, but rather, commonly accepted ideas and narratives that have guided generations of scholars in their pursuit to recover the history of the establishment of Bantu-speaking communities across such vast regions. The first of these myths were developed during the nineteenth century and were greatly influenced by Darwinist and diffusionist thinking. As was the case with the Idea of the Pygmy, scholars of the post-World War II era valiantly strove to eliminate the racist elements of this nineteenth-century paradigm, yet failed to assess the central tenets of the diffusionist paradigm itself. As a result, its premises were integrated into the notion of the Neolithic Revolution, a universalist paradigm intended to rehabilitate the African past. The impact of both of these paradigms—one exclusionist and one universalist—is assessed here, especially as they pertain to our understanding of the central African past.

Bantu languages are today spoken across a vast expanse of the African continent, covering more than one-third of its surface area. Comprising more than 450 closely related languages and dialects, their distribution approximates the shape of an irregular trapezoid, with one corner located in the northwestern regions of Cameroon, another in northwestern Namibia, still another on the Kenya coast, and the fourth on the southeastern edge of the continent. Although the full extension of the Bantu language family was unknown until the last century, European travelers in Africa remarked upon the great similarity between these languages from early on. In 1515, the navigator Andrea Corsali noted that "from the Cape of Good Hope to the Red Sea, the inhabitants speak the same language," and travelers in the more interior regions of the continent documented the commonalities between languages during the eighteenth and nineteenth centuries.[86]

Although the first dictionaries, grammars, and classifications of the Bantu languages were produced by Christian missionaries, the real pioneer of the field of comparative Bantu languages was the German philologist Wilhelm Bleek (1827–75). Based on his observation of common linguistic features among south African languages (including the use of the root *-ntu,* "person"), Bleek coined the term "Bantu" (people) as a referent to the wider language family. Influenced heavily by the diffusionist paradigm,[87] he proposed that all of the Bantu languages derived from a single ancestral source (proto-Bantu), and that the history of the Bantu could be discerned by tracing their patterns of migration across geography and time. Although later works by linguists such as Carl Meinhoff and Harry Johnston confirmed the genetic relationships between Bantu languages, these linguists did not provide any information as to exactly how and why the Bantu languages came to be spoken across the southern half of the continent. Such is the crux of the "Bantu problem," a historical enigma that subsequent generations of Africanists have tried to solve through the prominent epistemologies of their time.

Unfortunately, nineteenth-century theories of cultural diffusion were steeped in notions of racial hierarchies, social evolution, and the struggle between races to survive. Viewing language as a prime expression of racial or national identity, the earliest scholars of the Bantu expansion sought to combine methods of comparative philology and ethnology in an attempt to construct the histories of African "races" and "tribes." An example of the assumptions that underlie such work can be seen in the words of Bleek, who claimed that comparative philology could provide knowledge of

> the descent and mixture of different nations inhabiting South Africa, their consanguinity with and influence upon each other, their gradual breaking up into several tribes, or the confluence of different tribes into one powerful nation. We shall be able to learn by these means, whence and by what races South African was originally peopled, how they came into contact with each other, whether they peacefully commingled, or whether the stronger drove the weaker race victoriously before them.[88]

In this construction, the Bantu expansion came to be portrayed in primarily militaristic and racial terms—as a series of conquering migrations by the "superior" and "virile" Bantu "race" who subjugated hunter-gatherers previously occupying the land. Although such theories clearly mirrored European visions of their colonial experience in Africa, the linguistic classification of African peoples additionally aided Europeans in making sense of a world they were trying to control. The effects of such work could be highly negative; as Dubow has noted, linguistic classifications played an integral role in the creation of the various racial and tribal categories upon which apartheid and its system of Bantustans (i.e., "homelands") were eventually built.

   Given this history, it is easy to understand how the "problem" of the Bantu expansion has come to signify much more than a historic dispersion of languages across the landscape of subequatorial Africa: its central tenets and questions were framed by the discourse of social Darwinism, and it relied heavily on the notion of biological race. It is therefore not surprising that the issue of the Bantu expansion was placed center stage in the revisionist era of the 1950s and 1960s, when the field of African history first emerged. Working from the aforementioned paradigm of a "universal humankind," scholars of this era sought to neutralize racial narratives by integrating the Bantu into what they considered a universal theme of global history—the Neolithic Revolution. Although the notion of the Neolithic had been around since the mid-nineteenth century (associated primarily with the appearance of the "new lithics," i.e., polished stone tools), in the post-World War II era, it came to be seen in a primarily socioeconomic sense. As such, it was viewed as an integral stage of human evolution in which subsistence practices underwent fundamental and irreversible alteration—shifting from hunting and gathering economies to more sedentary kinds of production such as animal raising, cultivation, and the manufacture of ceramics.[89]

   The integration of Africans into this global chronology was based on increasing amounts of archaeological evidence emerging from eastern and southern Africa during the 1970s. Most indicated that the earliest appearance of sedentism was in fact accompanied by ceramics, polished stone tools, the domestication of animals, and in the more southern regions, the smelting of iron. Because the ceramics seemed to show a basic unity in shape and decoration, it was widely accepted that they represented the arrival of Bantu-speaking peoples, and that they brought with them the full package of the Neolithic lifestyle. Thus, the racial conquest narrative was dropped, and the Bantu migration came to be seen in terms of population expansion, one of the benefits assumed to have accompanied the shift to an agricultural lifestyle.

   At the same time, these archaeological discoveries were being made, more refined classifications of the African, and particularly Bantu languages, emerged. Key among these were Greenberg's *The Languages of Africa* (1963), which posited that the original area of Bantu dispersion should be located where the greatest diversity of languages was found, that is, the northwestern regions of Cameroon. Malcolm Guthrie's four-volume *Comparative Bantu* (1967–71) appeared at this time as well. Although he argued incorrectly for an alternative Bantu "homeland" in southeastern Congo-Zaire,[90] his work was groundbreaking in that it included a compendium of more than 2,300 reconstructed "common" Bantu root words. Many of these substantiated the notion that the Bantu had begun their migration with Neolithic subsistence and technological practices, providing direct correlation with emerging archaeological data from the east. Guthrie was also the first to suggest that the Bantu language community divided into a western and eastern branch early on, although this was based on evidence of word retention rather than analysis of genetic relations. Finally, numerous scholars employed the methods of glottochronology to date the time depth of the Bantu language family; the eventual accumulation of data coalesced around an estimate of roughly five thousand years. By the 1980s and 1990s, it was generally accepted that the Bantu expansion began from southern or western Cameroon near the beginning of the third millennium B.C.E.

These great advances in the fields of African linguistics and archaeology contributed to what is commonly termed the Bantuist era of African history (1960s–1980s). This period saw an unprecedented amount of cross-disciplinary research and debate as historians, linguists, and archaeologists brought their data to bear on the problem of the Bantu expansion. Commenced during the era of nationalist struggles, these efforts were heavily influenced by a desire to rehabilitate and valorize the African past. The notion of the Neolithic Revolution served this purpose well, for it not only integrated Africans onto the stage of global history, but it also substantiated the parity of their intellectual and technological skills far back into the past. As was the case with the "new physical anthropology," this must be seen as an admirable goal. At the same time, however, the new paradigm served in many ways to limit our knowledge of the central African past.

The most obvious problem for central Africa was a lack of archaeological and linguistic data. It was not until the 1980s that systematic archaeological excavations were undertaken, and these were primarily carried out along the peripheries of the rainforest region.[91] As such, early Bantuist research had a decidedly "east-centric" focus, and the western regions—where the Bantu expansion actually began—were largely neglected. Nineteenth-century notions of "impenetrable forest" seem to have prevailed, for the forest was generally portrayed as a region to be avoided, overcome, or rapidly traversed in early Bantu expansion narratives.

The heavy focus on migration as the key event in Bantu history also had a number of deleterious effects. First, and as Vansina has pointed out, the desire to identify migration routes often encouraged archaeologists to carry out excavations for the sole purpose of identifying a Neolithic presence (i.e., ceramics, bones of domestic stock, etc.).[92] Once such evidence was found, the excavation was considered complete, and later settlement histories often went neglected. In many cases, these methods produced what was essentially only survey data, resulting in incomplete archaeological records for many areas of the continent. Linguistics studies were affected in a similar way; the desire to reconstruct migration routes on a continental scale led to classifications carried out on the broadest of scales. As such, only very sweeping narratives of the Bantu expansion were provided, and classifications at the intermediate level were largely ignored. The end result was a lack of information about the development of Bantu societies *after* they settled, as well as the nature of their interactions with neighbors over time.

Another problem arose from the fact that, although the Bantuists succeeded in eliminating the racist elements of the diffusionist paradigm, its main premises often remained intact. Archeologists continued to rely on migration as the source of all cultural and technological innovation, largely neglecting the alternatives of in situ development or the spread of new technologies or culture traits on their own. This thinking heavily impacted nonspecialists' conceptualization of language spread as well; given the thesis of Vansina's 1995 article "New Linguistic Evidence and the Bantu 'Expansion,'" it appears that many scholars continued to consider geographical movement as the only possible explanation for new language formation well into the 1990s.

A number of additional problems arose from the epistemologies that inform archaeology itself. As Vansina has noted, the discipline relies heavily on notions of cultural and technological evolution. Archaeologists long classified their findings into one of a series of "progressive" technological stages (i.e., the Late Stone Age, Neolithic, Early Iron Age, etc.), each considered to be an advancement over the last.[93] In the context of the Bantu expansion, this requirement often led archaeologists to make sharp dichotomies between the Late Stone Age and the Neolithic, where they did not clearly exist. This has been a significant problem for central Africa, because soil acidity causes a rapid decomposition of organic materials and evidence for ancient subsistence practices is extremely rare. Having little to go on other than the theory of the Neolithic Revolution, many archaeologists assumed the presence of the full farming complex at sites where only polished stone tools and/or ceramics were found. This practice has not only skewed our understanding of the earliest stages of Bantu settlement and expansion, but has also obfuscated evidence that may in fact have been related to Late-Stone-Age hunter-gatherers rather than Bantu settlers.

The notion of a progressive technological advancement often led to an assumption that introduction of a new technology (e.g., polished stone tools or iron) would rapidly render all previous technologies obsolete. Again, the archaeological record attests that this is not the case for central Africa. Current data from Gabon suggest that the Neolithic overlapped with both the Late Stone Age and Early Iron Age for periods of at least four hundred years at each end. This phenomenon is somewhat perplexing to archaeologists; to solve the problem, they generally call for an increase in excavations.[94] Rarely, however, is it acknowledged that central Africa might simply have a unique history of its own, one that does not fit into the preconceived classificatory categories at all. Finally, and as numerous scholars have previously pointed out,[95] the cross-disciplinary approach that prevailed in the Bantuist era often resulted in scholars allowing results from one field to influence interpretations in another. This has especially been the case in the forested regions of central Africa, where archaeologists often disregarded radiocarbon dates for the Neolithic that did not fit with the linguistically derived date of c. 3000 B.C.E. for the commencement of the Bantu expansion.

These examples make clear that although the Bantuist agenda produced great advances in the fields of archaeology and linguistics, the interpretation of resultant data has in many ways been limited by the theories and epistemologies that prevailed at that time. Sensing that the "problem" of the Bantu expansion had devolved into somewhat of an intellectual cul-de-sac, archaeologists began to turn to new models of analysis in the 1980s. As Vansina has noted, this "new archaeology" was consciously designed to counter neo-evolutionary thought, for it strove to "go beyond a narrow interpretation of artifacts to elaborate hypotheses about the organization of the societies which apparently created them."[96] As a result of this shift in thinking, the notion of a Bantu expansion came to be seen as outmoded, and oftentimes came under attack. For example, the editors of the 1993 volume *The Archeology of Africa: Food, Metals, Towns* appear to have associated any mention of a Bantu expansion, dispersal, or diffusion with the racialized nineteenth-century conquest narrative. Accordingly, they rejected the very *notion* of the Bantu expansion, relegating it to the category of "discredited racial ideas."[97] For many nonspecialists, Vansina's 1995 article "New Language Evidence and the Bantu 'Expansion'" appeared to do the same. In it he argued for the rejection of the diffusionist notion of a "single continuous migration" and called for the use of an alternative model ("wave theory") to uncover a history of "gradual diffusion in successive spreads."[98]

The result of these revisionist approaches has been a great deal of confusion among generalists as to whether the Bantu expansion ever occurred! This problem arises from the fact that scholars who reject the entire idea of the Bantu expansion have failed to discriminate between the historical reality of a Bantu language spread and the impact that Western theories and epistemologies have had on the interpretation of related data. As such, they have simply thrown the proverbial baby out with the bathwater and decided to work from an entirely different set of questions. Although fruitful in terms of developing new theories and paradigms, this approach precludes the possibility of further advances in the study of the Bantu expansion, and consequently, the reconstruction of early settlement histories. Vansina's critique, which does not reject the idea of the Bantu expansion, asks scholars to consider their data according to an alternative paradigm, one that is in fact not entirely new. It parallels the approach of the "new archaeologists," for it encourages us to reconstruct histories at the more local level, and insists that we recognize the role of contingency in each region and set of linguistic data we treat.

This approach has already commenced among archaeologists working in the northwestern region of the Bantu-speaking world; indeed, it is their data that has infused new energy into the problem of the Bantu expansion, allowing for the modification and refinement of earlier Bantuist hypotheses and beliefs. For example, the accumulation of exceptionally early dates for the appearance of ceramics and polished stone tools in Gabon has led archaeologists to consider that Neolithic technologies may have been introduced in two distinct phases—one beginning in the third millennium B.C.E. and the other near the end of the last millennium.[99] These data implicitly challenge the notion of a single continuous migration, as well as the firm dating of c. 3000 B.C.E. for the commencement of the Bantu migration.

De Maret and Phillipe Lavachery's conceptualization of the "Stone to Metal Age" has also provided an alternative model, allowing scholars to avoid the socioeconomic assumptions that have come to be associated with the Neolithic. Defined as a "stage without metals but advanced technical traits, such as ceramics and polished stone, and sometimes possible indications of food-production,"[100] this classificatory category allows us to envision introduction of new technologies as a process of transition rather than a rupture with the past. It was likely a familiarity with such data that led Vansina to argue that the Neolithic was not introduced as a complete package, and as such, was not revolutionary at all. Both of these alternative conceptualizations have played a large role in the writing of this book, for they inform the interpretation of archaeological data presented in chapters 2 and 4.

Having laid out the myriad of ways that our unquestioned assumptions, "inevitable preferences," and "unconscious mental habits" can affect historical interpretations regarding Batwa and Bantu societies alike, we are now ready to look at the data itself. We begin by chronicling the early history of Bantu settlement within the equatorial rainforest, the topic of chapter 2.

NOTES

1. J. Vansina, *Paths in the Rainforest: Towards a History of Political Tradition in Equatorial Africa* (Madison, Wisconsin: University of Wisconsin Press, 1990), 3.

2. I borrow this turn of words from Arthur O. Lovejoy, *The Great Chain of Being* (Cambridge: Harvard University Press, 1953), 7; this work greatly influenced and guided my analysis of the Idea of the Pygmy.

3. Matt Cartmill, *A View to a Death in the Morning: Hunting and Nature through History* (Cambridge: Harvard University Press, 1993), 27, 226.

4. My use and definition of the root metaphor is derived from the work of Stephen C. Pepper, *World Hypotheses: A Study in Evidence* (Berkeley: University of California Press, 1942), 84–114. Like all metaphors, a root metaphor serves as a similarity-creating device that mediates structural correspondences between two concepts—one well-known and the other less so. The root metaphor is unique, however, in its ability to expand and adjust its constituent categories over time, allowing for the incorporation of data from all fields of human knowledge.

5. V. Dassen, "Dwarfism in Egypt and Classical Antiquity: Iconography and Medical History," *Medical History* 24, no. 2 (1988): 258.

6. These figurines can be seen in G. Steindorff, *Catalogue of the Egyptian Sculpture in the Walters Art Gallery* (Baltimore: The Trustees, 1946), 19, pl. 1.3; W. S. Smith, *The Art and Architecture of Ancient Egypt* (Harmondsworth: Pelican History of Art, 1981), 29–30, fig. 7; E. A. W. Budge, *A Guide to the Egyptian Collections in the British Museum* (London: The Trustees, 1909), 24, 26, fig. 8. All cited in Dassen, "Dwarfism in Egypt," 260.

7. Ola El-Aguizy, "Dwarfs and Pygmies in Ancient Egypt," *Annales du Service des Antiquites de l'Egypte (Le Caire)* 71 (1987): 54.

8. Warren R. Dawson, "Pygmies and Dwarfs in Ancient Egypt," *Journal of Egyptian Archeology* 24, no. 2 (1938): 188.

9. El-Aguizy, "Dwarfs and Pygmies," 56.

10. H. O. Lange, *Der Magische Papyrus Harris,* 8th ed. (Copenhagen, Høst & Søn: 1927), 9–10; cited in El-Aguizy, "Dwarfs and Pygmies," 56.

11. Scott, *Bulletin of the Metropolitan Museum of Art* 9 (1951): 210–221, line 223; cited in El-Aguizy, "Dwarfs and Pygmies," 56.

12. F. Ll. Griffith and Herbert Thompson, *The Demotic Magical Papyrus of London and Leiden* (Milan: Instituto editoriale Cisalpino, 1976), 2:6–7; cited in El-Aguizy, "Dwarfs and Pygmies," 56.

13. Edfou, 10, 289; cited in El-Aguizy, "Dwarfs and Pygmies," 57.

14. Dassen, "Dwarfism in Egypt," 263. It is also possible that an association between dwarfs and birth/creation was based on the observation that both newborn infants and dwarfs possess disproportionately large heads. This association is seen in sub-Saharan Africa, where human dwarfs came to be viewed as symbolic equivalents of the primordial Batwa in the Kongolese cultural sphere, and mythical dwarf first-comers are portrayed or described as having overly large heads (among the Kuba, Chewa, Nyanja, Tonga, and Venda). See chapter 5 for more details.

15. El-Aguizy argues that it was likely the association with Re/Osiris that explains the presence of dwarfs at the funeral rites of prominent Egyptians. Dwarfs were considered to embody one of the various manifestations of the creator god, and the dwarf dances could have been directed to Re (whose horizon the deceased desired to reach) or Osiris, the judge of the dead. The ritual importance of dwarfs at funerals is attested throughout the Egyptian era, with the earliest reference being that of King Pepy I in the Pyramid texts and the latest in the Ptolemaic era. See El-Aguizy, "Dwarfs and Pygmies," 59.

16. Michael Jordon, *Encyclopedia of Gods* (London: Kyle Cathie Limited, 1992), 249.

17. Dassen, "Dwarfism in Egypt," 263. A symbolic element linking Ptah to creation, the scarab was considered by Egyptians to represent the morning aspect of the sun god.

18. Wolf, *Zeitschrift der Deutschen Morgenlandischen Gesellschaft* 64 (1929): 18, 31; cited in El-Aguizy, "Dwarfs and Pygmies," 58.

19. Primarily considered a household god, very few sanctuaries were dedicated to Bes, although two rather impressive ones were built in the late first millennium B.C.E. at Saqqara and Abydos. Instead, Bes's image was found on furniture, toilette accessories, and the walls of birth houses. His role in childbirth is most apparent in an incantation from the Magical Papyri at Leiden called "The Spell of the Dwarf"; it instructs that the spell should be repeated four times "over a dwarf of clay placed on the vertex of the woman who is giving birth." See Dawson, "Pygmies and Dwarfs," 188.

20. A. Delatte and Ph. Derchain, *Les Intailles Magiques Gréco-Égyptiennes* (Paris: Bibliotheque Nationale, 1964), 18.

21. Ibid.

22. Dimitri Meeks, *Genies, Anges, Demons en Egypt,* 8th ed., 1971; (Paris: Editions Seuil, 1987), 54.

23. Another set of images that should not so readily be associated with Pygmies—of either the legendary or the central African kind—are those depicting dwarfs in Nilotic environments, generally found in mosaics and wall paintings. These are clearly disproportionate dwarfs, depicted with dark-colored skin, short limbs, and overlarge phalluses. As H. Whitehouse has demonstrated, many of these Nilotic images were associated with the

cult of Ptah; the dwarfs are often depicted wearing sidelocks and holding sticks that recall the snakes strangled by the child Horus (H. Whitehouse, "In Praedis Iuliae Felicis," *Papers of the British School at Rome* 45 (1977): 52–68; cited in Dassen, "Dwarfism in Egypt," 275). The overlarge phallus can be associated with Bes as well, who in Greek imagery came to take on a satyr-like relation to women. Dassen cites a case of a pelike in Oxford ("Dwarfism in Egypt," 272) in which a veiled woman dances with a dwarf and a winged phallus flies toward the woman, symbolizing the sexual energy of the dwarf.

24. For example, Pygmies are mentioned alongside such populations as the Cynocephali, dog-headed men who communicated through barking; the Astomi (apple smellers), hairy, mouthless men who live by smell alone; and the Bragmanni (Indian Brahmins), naked wise men who spend their time in caves. For more on these "monstrous" races, see John B. Friedman, *The Monstrous Races in Medieval Art and Thought* (Cambridge: Harvard University Press, 1981).

25. It is not actually clear whether Ctesias traveled to India; the stories he recounts appear to be based on tall tales about India that he heard from merchants in Persia. Nonetheless, Ctesias's work had a great influence on his contemporaries and later travel writers, for the exaggerated and entertaining manner in which he described various Indian peoples, both legendary and real, set a precedent for the creation of fantastic travelers tales. Friedman, *Monstrous Races*, 5.

26. Edward Tyson, *Orang-outang sive Homo Sylvestrus, or the Anatomy of a Pygmie compared with that of a Monkey, and Ape, and a Man* (London: Dawsons of Pall Mall, 1699), 23.

27. Although it is not certain that Ctesias used the word "Pygmy" to describe these peoples, later translators have, and the description has thus come to be considered an early reference to Pygmies in ancient literature. S. Bahuchet, "L'Invention des Pygmées," *Cahiers d'Études Africaines* 129, 33-1 (1993): 154, footnote 5.

28. Ibid., footnote 6.

29. Bahuchet makes this point in "L'Invention," 154, footnote 6. He cites Aristotle, *Histoire des Animaux,* 3 vols., ed. and trans. P. Louis (Paris: Les Belles Lettres, 1964–1969).

30. Friedman, *Monstrous Races,* 2.

31. Ibid., 92.

32. Ibid., 109.

33. Westminster Abbey Library MS 22, fol. 1v., thirteenth century. The Sciopod, or "Shadow Foot," was considered to be from India. As Friedman notes, they "spent their days lying on their backs protecting their heads from the sun with a single great foot." This particular image can be seen in Friedman, *Monstrous Races,* 113.

34. For more details, see Friedman's interpretation of this tympanum in *Monstrous Races,* 77–86.

35. Ibid., 89, 92.

36. See Friedman, *Monstrous Races,* chap. 5 ("Cains Kin") for a thorough analysis of such theories in the Medieval era.

37. Hermann Stadler, ed., "Albertus Magnus de Animalibus," in *Beiträg zur Geschichte der Philosophie des Mittelalters,* 16 vols. (Münster: Aschendorff, 1920), 1328, cited in Friedman, *Monstrous Races,* 256, footnote 40.

38. This is attested by the work of another Scholastic, Peter of Croc (or Auvergne) who is recognized for a series of six *quodlibeta*—a form of discursive argument presented in public in the great learning centers of the Medieval period. In 1301, he posed the quodlibeta "Whether Pygmies be Men," the underlying premise of which was whether two things that agree in form also agree in nature. For a detailed discussion of Peter's logic and conclusions, see Friedman, *Monstrous Races,* 192–196.

39. A. L. Stoler, *Race and the Education of Desire: Foucault's History of Sexuality and the Colonial Order of Things* (Durham, North Carolina: Duke University Press, 1995), 61. Cited in Eugenia Shanklin, "The Profession of the Color Blind: Sociocultural Anthropology and Racism in the 21st Century," *American Anthropologist* 100: no. 3 (1999): 675.

40. Nancy Stepan, *The Idea of Race in Science: Great Britain 1800–1860* (London: MacMillan, 1982), 29.

41. The 1375 *Atlas de Catalan* represents Pygmies as inhabitants of the New World, the 1448 *Mappemonde* locates them in northern Europe, and the 1539 Mercator Map illustrates Pygmies as inhabitants of the North Pole. Information cited in Bahuchet, "L'Invention," 160.

42. Friedman, *Monstrous Races,* 197.

43. Ibid., 15–16.

44. Haydn White, "The Forms of Wildness: Archaeology of an Idea," in *The Wildman Within: An Image in Western Thought from the Renaissance to Romanticism,* ed. E. Dudley and M. E. Novak (Pittsburgh: University of Pittsburgh Press, 1972), 28.

45. Tyson worked from previous knowledge about monkeys, as well as a superficial description and illustration of an anthropoid ape that had been provided in 1641 by the Dutch naturalist Nicolaas Tulp. Although Tulp indicated that he had seen the animal in Angola, he applied the Bornean term for a similar species to describe it, that is, orangutan, or "man of the forest." See Jonathon Marks, *Human Biodiversity: Genes, Race, and History* (New York, Aldine de Gruyter, 1995), 3–6 for a more detailed explanation.

46. Ibid., 5.

47. In 1758, the English naturalist Edwards described the Malaysian orangutan as "man of the woods, satyr, or pygmee," and in 1760, Christophe Hoppius provided the biological name *Simia pygmaeus* for the same species (both cited in Bahuchet, "L'Invention," 161). Other scholars attempted to explain the origins of ancient legends in light of this evidence. For example, Buffon states in his *History of Natural Birds* (1787) that the legendary Pygmies were nothing more than monkeys, which unskilled observers with a taste for the fantastic simply took for men. The Abby Antoine Banier proposed in his *Explication Historique des Fables* (1711) that Homer had simply "miniaturized" unknown races as a form of exaggeration, as many poets of the era were wont to do (both cited in Bahuchet, "L'Invention," 162).

48. Marks, *Human Biodiversity,* 8.

49. Tyson's analogical use of the Idea of the Pygmy provides a classic example of root-metaphor extension, a process whereby "a world theory beginning promisingly with a root metaphor fresh from vital common sense grows for a while, meets obstacles in fact, is incapable of overcoming these obstacles, desperately juggles its categories, forgets the facts in the juggling of the categories, till these presently become so empty that some men can cast half of them overboard, devoutly believe the other half, substitute concepts for the facts, and deem it unnecessary to look back upon forgotten facts" (Pepper, *World Hypotheses,* 94–95).

50. N. Stepan, "Race and Gender: The Role of Analogy in Science," in *Anatomy of Racism,* ed. David Theo Goldberg (Minneapolis: University of Minnesota Press, 1990), 38–57.

51. This understanding of the ways that metaphor can create objects of difference is taken from Stepan, "Race and Gender," 41–42.

52. D. Harraway, *Primate Visions: Gender, Race, and Nature in the World of Modern Science* (New York: Rutledge, 1989), 10–13. Although Harraway attributes this tendency to the human-like characteristics of anthropoid apes, the way Westerners conceptualize such simi-

larities is clearly derived from the Pygmy/Hairy Wild Man paradigm. For example, "apes and monkeys have been subjected to sustained culturally-specific interrogations of what it means to be 'almost human,'" the very role that the legendary Pygmy played in Ancient and Medieval times. Apes are also (like the legendary Hairy Wild Man/Pygmy) associated with the overtly sexual and lewd, and, in the modern context, considered to live in primordial (often Edenic) environments and social configurations. Finally, like the Pygmy (both legendary and central African), apes have played a privileged role in a vast array of academic disciplines, always eliciting a "keen interest among the general populace."

53. A fact made evident in the origins of the term "Bushman" itself; Lehman has argued that the original *Bosmanneken* was simply the Dutch version of the Malayan word *"Orang-Outang"* (i.e., "man of the forest"). Mathias G. Guenther, "From Brutal Savage to Harmless People: Notes on the Changing Western Image of the Bushman," *Paideuma* 26 (1980): 127.

54. Soame Jenys, "On the Chain of Universal Being," in *The Works of Soame Jenys, Esq.,* ed. C. N. Cole (London: T. Cadell, 1790), 179–185; cited in Lovejoy, *The Great Chain of Being,* 197.

55. Stepan, *Race in Science,* 12–13.

56. As Bahuchet has noted, it was not Du Chaillu himself, but his translator Malte-Brun who first associated these populations with the legendary Pygmies (P. Du Chaillu, "Le pays d'Ashango," *Annales des Voyages* 2 [2001]: 256–290). Du Chaillu took up this notion and highlighted it in his later work *The Country of the Dwarfs* (1872; New York: Negro Universities Press, 1969). Both cited in Bahuchet, "L'Invention," 153–181.

57. Schweinfurth wrote, "Trois ou quatre siècles avant l'ére chrétienne, les Grecs connaissaient l'existence d'un peuple remarquable par sa taille réduite, habitant la région des sources du Nil. Ce fait peut nous autoriser, peut-être, a designer du nom de 'pygmée,' non pas des hommes litteralement hauts d'un empan, mais dans le sens d'Aristote, les races naines d'Afrique équatoriale." G. Schweinfurth, *Au cœur de l'Afrique* (Paris: Hachette, 1875), 105; cited in Bahuchet, "L'Invention," 163.

58. This refers to the oft-cited inscription from the tomb of Harkhuf at Aswan, a minister for King Pepy II of the Sixth Dynasty. During his service, he made four trips to the southern regions of Nubia, and on his last he wrote to King Pepy (at the time only eight years old!) that he had secured a *dng*—commonly translated as "Pygmy." King Pepy's reply to this letter was inscribed on the walls of Harkouf's tomb; it illustrates his great excitement in the procurement of a *dng* who will perform "dances of the gods" for the King himself, and asks Harkouf to take all necessary measures to avoid a possible escape. It is argued that this *dng* was a central African Pygmy, based on its similarity to the Amharic word *denk,* "dwarf," and the fact that the term *nmi* appears more commonly as a referent to dwarfs in Egyptian writing. However, Amharic had not come into existence at that time, and there is no evidence to indicate that it meant anything other than dwarf in the proto-Afroasiatic. Furthermore, El-Aguizy has noted that the Egyptians used several words as referents to varieties of dwarfism; *nmi* for achondroplastic, *iwhi* for those exhibiting characteristics of pituitary dwarfism, and *iw* for those with a hunchback. Given the fact that the southern lands were considered to be the domains of the gods, and that female dancers from Nubia were especially prized in the royal courts, it is possible that King Pepy II was simply referring to a dwarf of Nubian origin, borrowing a term common to that region. See El-Aguizy, "Dwarfs and Pygmies," 53–54.

59. Bahuchet, "L'Invention," 166.

60. The most blatant example of the use of the Batwa in the missing link paradigm is the case of Ota Benga, a Pygmy from the Kasai region of Congo-Zaire who was brought to

the United States by the missionary/entrepreneur Samuel P. Warner. Originally displayed with a group of his compatriots in the 1904 St. Louis World's Fair, Ota Benga was put on individual display in the primate section of the Bronx Zoo in 1906. Although a prominent group of local African Americans finally negotiated his removal, his presence at the zoo provided great fodder for the general populace's fascination/revulsion with the idea of the missing link and African primitivity in general. See Phillips Verner Bradford and Harvey Blume, *Ota Benga, The Pygmy in the Zoo* (New York: Delta, 1992) for the full details of this disturbing episode in the history of social evolutionary thinking.

61. E.-T. Hamy, "Essai de coordination des matériaux récemment recueillis sur l'ethnologie des négrilles ou pygmées de l'Afrique équatoriale," *Bulletin de la Société d'Anthropologie de Paris* 2 (1879): 79–101; A. de Quatrefages, "Les Pygmées d'Homère, d'Aristote, de Pline, d'après les découvertes modernes," *Journal des Savants* (1881): 94–107; id., *Les Pygmées* (Paris: Baillère, 1887).

62. Originally developed by the German cultural historical school, diffusionist theory worked from the assumption that similarities and innovations among cultures could be explained by identifying the geographical/cultural origin, or *kulturkreis,* of various peoples and tracing the history of their migrations through time. The approach, however, was heavily infused with notions of race and social Darwinism. As such, it inevitably focused on the histories of "superior" and "inferior" races. See Saul Dubow, *Scientific Racism in Modern South Africa* (Cambridge: Cambridge University Press, 1995), 75–76, for a more detailed explanation.

63. W. C. Boyd, "Four Achievements of the Genetical Method in Physical Anthropology," *American Anthropologist* 65 (1963): 335–338.

64. Made most famous in the works of Father Wilhelm Schmidt, who produced an 800-page work entitled *Der Ursprung der Gottesidee* ("The Origin of the Idea of God"), in which he posited that the notion of monotheism had originated among the "Pygmies." As Bahuchet has noted ("L'Invention," 171), Schmidt's students were the "pioneers of Pygmology": Monseigneurs Le Roy and Briault, as well as the Fathers Tastevin, Schebesta, Gusinde, and Trilles.

65. Cartmill, *A View to a Death,* 200.

66. Ibid., 14.

67. As Cartmill explains, Darwinian theory was largely rejected by scientists of the early twentieth century, especially the theory of natural selection. Biologists influenced by the rise of population genetics tended to see it as "a more or less random process driven by chance mutation," or others saw it as the result of mysterious internal forces that were unrelated to the environment. By the 1930s, a Darwinian counterrevolution had taken place, and by the end of World War II, neo-Darwinism had become the cornerstone of biology (*A View to a Death,* 198–199.)

68. Robert Foley, "Hominids, Humans, and Hunter-Gatherers: An Evolutionary Perspective," in *Hunters and Gatherers 1: History, Evolution, and Social Change,* ed. T. Ingold, D. Riches, and J. Woodburn (Oxford: Berg Publishers, 1988), 207.

69. Barry Hewlett, "Cultural Diversity among African Pygmies," in *Cultural Diversity among Twentieth-Century Foragers: An African Perspective,* ed. Susan Kent (Cambridge: Cambridge University Press, 1996), 215.

70. N. Bird-David, "Beyond 'the Original Affluent Society.' A Culturalist Reformulation," *Current Anthropology* 33, no. 1 (1992): 25.

71. P. Boyer, "Pourquoi les Pygmées n'ont pas de Culture?" *Gradhiva* 7 (Winter 1989–90): 4.

72. Ibid., 8.

73. Stepan, "Race and Gender," 49.

74. E. Wilmsen, *Land Filled with Flies: A Political Economy of the Kalahari* (Chicago: University of Chicago Press, 1989), 3.

75. Colin M. Turbayne, *The Myth of the Metaphor* (Columbia: University of South Carolina Press, 1970), 24. Cited in Stepan, "Race and Gender," 38.

76. Carol C. Mukhopadhyay and Yolanda T. Moses, "Reestablishing 'Race' in Anthropological Discourse," *American Anthropologist* 99, no. 3 (1997): 519. For examples of how such categories were created and used, see William C. Boyd, *Genetics and the Races of Man: An Introduction to Modern Physical Anthropology* (Boston: Little, Brown, 1950); Stanley Garn, *Human Races,* 2d ed. (Springfield, Illinois: Charles C. Thomas, 1965); and Carlton Coon, *The Origins of Races* (New York: Alfred A. Knopf, 1962).

77. See, for example, A. Bowcock, "High Resolution of Human Evolutionary Trees with Polymorphic Microsatellites," *Nature* 368 (1994): 455–57 and L. L. Cavalli-Sforza, P. Menozzi, and A. Piazza, eds., *The History and Geography of Human Genes* (Princeton, New Jersey: Princeton University Press, 1994), cited in Rick Kittles and S. O. Y. Keita, "Interpreting African Genetic Diversity," *African Archaeological Review* 16, no. 2 (1999): 88.

78. Cavalli-Sforza, Menozzi, and Piazza acknowledge this point, for they point out the difficulty in distinguishing Pygmy populations from their neighbors based on genetic sampling alone. As they state, "Physical characteristics (e.g., stature) and Pygmy customs are usually the major criteria employed for the Pygmy classification." See *History and Geography,* 178.

79. Although certain Batwa populations have been sampled and their genetic profiles do show them to differ from more distant African populations, adequate sampling has not been carried out among the agriculturalist populations that currently live as their neighbors (ibid.). The genetic data therefore remain somewhat ambiguous, for it is unclear whether these specific communities are similar or distinct from their immediate farming neighbors. As was noted previously, these distinctions do not prevail between Batwa and farming populations of southern Cameroon (where sampling has been conducted on both groups) and only slight variations in genetic make-up are noted for those of Central African Republic. For a detailed discussion of the problems surrounding Cavalli-Sforza, Menozzi, and Piazza's genetic classification of Pygmy communities, see Alain Froment, "Le peuplement de l'Afrique Centrale: Contribution de l'anthropobiologie," in *Paléo-anthropologie en Afrique centrale: Un bilan de l'archaeologie au Cameroon,* ed. M. Delneuf, J.-M. Essomba, and A. Froment (Paris: Editions Harmattan, 1998), 13–90. For a broader discussion of the fit between genetic, archeological, and ethnographic data, see Scott MacEachern, "Genes, Tribes, and African History," *Current Anthropology* 41, no. 3 (2000).

80. Froment, "Le peuplement," 45.

81. S. O. Y. Keita and R. Kittles, "The Persistence of Racial Thinking and the Myth of Racial Divergence," *American Anthropologist* 99, no. 3 (1997): 537.

82. For example, L. L. Cavalli-Sforza cites a period of 10,000–20,000 years for the separation between "Khoisan, Mbuti (*Batwa of the Ituri Forest*) and "Bantu" in *African Pygmies* (London: Academic Press, 1986), 414. More recent works, however, argue for a much shorter time. Among these are studies designed to test the theory that a failure to produce the insulin growth factor I (IGF-I) after puberty is an inherited genetic trait, and that this is the cause of short stature among certain Batwa. Studies by Dulloo et. al. ("Dissociation of Systemic GH-IGF-I Axis from a Genetic Basis for Short Stature in African Pygmies, *European Journal of Clinical Medicine* 50 [1996]: 371–380) have indicated that the lack of

IGF-I is not genetic, and that the short stature of the Batwa "must thus be attributed to contingent environmental effects. This is what would be expected if the pygmies have adapted to the forest relatively recently." (This quote and concise explanation is drawn directly from R. Blench, "Are the African Pygmies an Ethnographic Fiction?" in *Challenging Elusiveness: Central African Hunter-Gatherers in a Multidisciplinary Perspective,* ed. Karen Biesbrouck, Stefan Elders, and Gerda Rossel [Leiden: CNWS, 2001], 45). Also, R. C. Bailey et al. ("Hunting and Gathering in the Tropical Rainforest: Is it Possible?" *American Anthropologist* 91, no. 1 [1989]: 59–82) have suggested that the ancestors of modern-day Batwa peoples may have developed small body size over the last 3,000 years, as a result of being driven into the forest by the arrival of the Bantu. For a discussion of the issue of Bailey's work and the issue of Batwa peoples short stature in general, see Jared M. Diamond, "Why Are Pygmies Small?" *Nature* 354 (1991): 111–12. Finally, Froment proposes a period of roughly 2,000 years or more ("Le peuplement," 45.)

83. See E. J. Wijsman, "Estimation of Genetic Admixture in Pygmies," in *African Pygmies,* ed. L. L. Cavalli-Sforza (London: Academic Press, 1986), 349–356, as well as Cavalli-Sforza, Menozzi, and Piazza, *History and Geography,* 177–80 for explanations and discussions of these categories.

84. As was stated in the introduction, this idea has recently been put forth by Blench, "Ethnographic Fiction?," 41–60. He hypothesizes that Batwa communities might be a "sub-caste of the Adamawa-Ubangian and Bantu speaking peoples which evolved to seasonally exploit the tropical rainforest."

85. Chen et al., "Analysis of mtDNA Variation in African Populations Reveals the Most Ancient of All Human Continent Specific Haplogroups," *American Journal of Human Genetics* 57 (1995): 133–49. A shift in thinking away from the homogeneity premise has also been made apparent in Susan Kent's edited volume *Cultural Diversity among Twentieth Century Foragers: An African Perspective* (Cambridge: Cambridge University Press, 1996).

86. See, for example, the discussion of the works of Heinrich Lichtenstein (1808), the "orientalist" William Marsden (1816), and the missionary Dr. Phillip (1824) in C. M. Doke, "The Growth of Comparative Bantu Philology," in *Contributions to the History of Bantu Linguistics,* ed. C. M. Doke and D. T. Cole (Johannesburg: Witwatersrand University Press, 1961), 55–57. Cited in Dubow, *Scientific Racism,* 77.

87. For a fine analysis of the impact of diffusionist theory on early philology, see Dubow, *Scientific Racism,* 74–82.

88. W. H. I. Bleek, *A Comparative Grammar of South African Languages. Part 1: Phonology* (London: Trübner, 1862), 7. Cited in Dubow, *Scientific Racism,* 79.

89. Although the concept of the Neolithic had been used in Europe since the mid-nineteenth century, it was generally conceived of as a period of technological innovation, that is, the period during which macrolithic polished stone tools were introduced. The newer vision developed after the publication of V. G. Childe's *Man Makes Himself* (London: Watts, 1956), in which he envisioned the shift to agriculture as analogous to the life-changing effects of the Industrial Revolution. For more explanation, see Shaw et al., *The Archaeology of Africa: Food, Metals, Towns* (London: Routledge, 1993), 3–8.

90. Malcolm Guthrie, "Some Developments in the Prehistory of Bantu Languages," *Journal of African History* 3 (1962): 273–282.

91. For example, De Maret's work at Shum Laka in the Grasslands region of Cameroon, Clist's multiple excavations along the Gabonese coast, and De Maret's earlier excavations in the region of Bas-Zaire.

92. J. Vansina, "A Slow Revolution: Farming in Subequatorial Africa," in *The Growth of Farming Communities in Africa from the Equator Southwards,* ed. J. E. G. Sutton (*Azania* special vol. 29–30; London/Nairobi: British Institute of Eastern Africa, (1994/95): 16.

93. See J. Vansina, "Historians, Are Archaeologists Your Siblings?" *History in Africa* 22 (1995): 370–77 for a full discussion of "multilineal neo-evolutionism" and its impact in archaeology.

94. M. K. H. Eggert, for example, regarding the central African archaeological record, states "the contemporaneity and partial areal coexistence of 'neolithic' and iron technology communities suggested by radiocarbon denies any straightforward explanation." ("Central Africa and the Archaeology of the Equatorial Rainforest; Reflections on Some Major Topics," in *The Archaeology of Africa,* ed. T. Shaw et al. [New York: Routledge, 1993], 304).

95. See Vansina, "A Slow Revolution" and "Historians"; P. de Maret, "Pits, Pots, and the Far West Streams," in Sutton, *Growth of Farming Communities,* 318–23; and Eggert, "Central Africa" for brief mention of this problem.

96. Vansina, "Historians," 374.

97. Shaw et al., *The Archaeology of Africa,* 11.

98. Although his suggestions are well-founded, the assumption that most historians viewed the migration as a single continuous event was not, because other specialists in the field of have been working with notions of a gradual diffusion since the 1970s. See, for example, B. Heine, "Zur genetische Gliederung der Bantu-Sprachen," *Afrika und Übersee* 56 (1973): 164–185 and C. Ehret, "Linguistic Inferences about Early Bantu History," in *The Archaeological and Linguistic Reconstruction of African History,* ed. C. Ehret and M. Posnansky (Berkeley, Los Angeles: University of California Press, 1982).

99. An alternative hypothesis regarding these phases is provided in chapter 2, where we discuss the nature of early Bantu/Batwa interactions.

100. de Maret, "Pits, Pots, and the Far-West Streams," 320.

2

Bantu Expansion in the Western Equatorial Rainforest, c. 4000–1500 B.C.E.

This chapter sets the stage for a history of Bantu and Batwa interactions by laying out a broad history of Bantu settlement in the western regions of the equatorial rainforest. Building on a linguistic classification of exclusively rainforest Bantu languages, the chapter proposes the first detailed account of how Bantu languages and societies came to be established in these regions. The first part of this chapter describes the geography and vegetational history of this region. The second section presents linguistic evidence for the progressive divergence of the early Bantu settlers into new speech communities, as well as for the adoption of Bantu languages by Batwa societies in the northern Congo Republic and southwestern Congo/Gabon. The third section of the chapter charts the parallels between this evidence and the archaeological record from Cameroon and Gabon.

Based on linguistic data and accumulating evidence for the exceptionally early appearance of ceramics and polished stone tools, this chapter argues that Bantu-speaking populations were present in the western equatorial rainforest earlier than scholars generally presume. Working from Vansina's theory of a "slow revolution" of farming in subequatorial Africa, I show that the archaeological record of central Africa attests both an "initial" and "formative" phase of agricultural development.[1] These data are used to explore the nature of economic and technological exchanges between Bantu and Batwa during the initial phases of settlement and farming, whereas chapter 3 uses oral, ethnographic, and linguistic data to develop hypotheses regarding social, political, and religious interactions that took place during this period.

GEOGRAPHICAL CONTEXTS

The Land

This study focuses primarily on the western regions of equatorial Africa, an area defined by the latitudes of 5° north and south of the equator and 9°–19° east of Greenwich meridian (see Map 2.1). These coordinates encompass the geographical limits of modern-day Gabon, Republic of Congo, and the southern regions of Cameroon. Climatically speaking, the most striking characteristic of this region is its high rate of annual rainfall, averaging 1,600–2,200 mm per year for most of the forested regions, 1,500 mm for savannas and forest/savanna mosaic regions, and reaching as much as 2,800–3,000 mm per year at locations along the northern coast.[2] Temperatures are consistently warm (23°C –27°C), rarely fluctuating by more than two to three degrees from that range within a given year. Located in the intertropical convergence zone, rains arrive from both the Atlantic and Indian Oceans, producing an annual cycle of two seasons, one dry (June, July, August) and one rainy (September to May). This pluvial cycle can vary, however, according to location. For example, some regions of the northern Congo Republic experience no dry season at all,[3] and in central Gabon the rainy season is punctuated by a dry period of short duration (mid-December to January).

Another striking characteristic of this region is its low relief. Located on the western flanks of the shallow Congo depression (250–480 m above sea level), it comprises low-lying plains, hills, and plateaus; where mountains do exist, they rarely exceed 1,000 m in height. The western regions are characterized by a series of coastal plains and hills (0–100 m) that are covered by both savanna and forest environments. Two parallel plains of the same latitude, the Nyanga and Ngounié River valleys, are located in the southwest. They are separated by the Ikoundou massif (500–1,000 m) and flanked by the forested massifs Mayombe (200–500 m) and du Chaillu (500–1,000 m). Farther north a forested plateau extends across southern Cameroon, central and Western Gabon, and into the western portions of Congo.

The high rates of precipitation feed great networks of rivers. Most important is the immense Congo River, extending around the Congo basin along a length of 4,374 km. Second in volume in the world only to the Amazon, it is fed by a vast number of tributaries, among them the Ubangi, Sangha, Likouala-aux-Herbes, and Kwa Rivers. In central Gabon the Ogooué River extends along a length of 1,200 km; it finds its source in the Bateke plateau in the southwest. The Okano, Ivindo, and Offoué Rivers feed into it from the north, and near the coast it is met by the Ngounié River. To the far southwest are the Nyanga and Kouilou-Niari Rivers, both flowing westward toward the Atlantic Ocean.

The tropical climate, low relief, and extensive drainage systems all contribute to the unique nature of central African soils. Because the region is

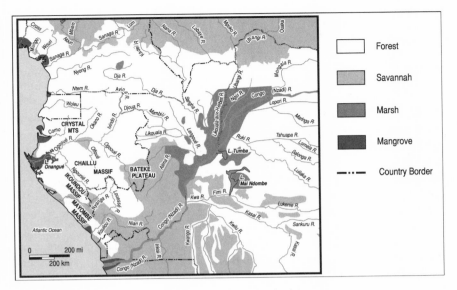

Map 2.1. The Physical Geography of West-Central Africa

located within the intertropical zone, its soils were not removed by the glacial or aeolian processes of erosion that occurred in more temperate or arid regions of the world. As a result, central Africa contains some of the thickest, most ancient, and least fertile soils found on the globe.[4] Its topsoils are primarily of two types: ferralitic (iron-rich and generally infertile) or hydromorph (waterlogged and slightly more fertile). Hydromorph soils are found in the central Congo basin, as well as the alluvial valleys and estuaries of rivers such as the Ogooué and Congo.[5] Ferallitic soils predominate in the rest of the region, comprising the horizon layer of nearly all dryland forests. Although these soils are chemically very iron rich, veins of iron are rare to the region.

The Forests, Past and Present

It is important to recognize from the start that the rainforests of central Africa are not primordial in origin, but have undergone periods of vast geographical expansion and retreat conditioned by climatic shifts of a global nature. In central Africa, paleoclimatologists have found evidence of at least four distinct climatic shifts since the onset of the Würm glaciation in Europe (c. 100,000 B.P.) These are the Maluekian (70,000–40,000 B.P.), the Ndjilian (40,000–35,000 B.P.), the Leopoldian (35,000–12,000 B.P.), and the Kibangian (12,000–5000 B.P.). The Maluekian and Leopoldian were periods of significantly lower rainfall and cooler temperatures than today; these conditions led to the retreat of rainforests and extension of grassland savannas in the equatorial region. The Leopoldian era was the most severe; during this period water levels at the coast dropped 120 m and tropical rainforests retreated to distinct refuges found only along rivers and in the most humid massifs.[6] Palynological analysis has indicated that the majority of these refuges were located in western equatorial Africa, especially in higher altitude regions such as Mount Cameroon, the Monts Cristal, and the du Chaillu, Ikoundou, and Mayombe massifs.[7] By 12,000 B.P. the Kibangian humid period commenced, allowing the re-expansion of forests. The distribution of forests in Africa as a whole at that time was even wider than today, and in the western equatorial regions rainforest was as at least as widespread as it is now, covering a region of more than 204 million hectares in area. Since 5000 B.P., however, a drying trend has been underway. Combined with the impact of human action upon the rainforest, it has led to a receding of forests, especially along the northern and southern fringes.

In the modern context the rainforests of Cameroon, Congo, and Gabon are especially renowned for their seemingly undisturbed nature and for their richness of biological diversity. Covering more than 300,000 km^2, their species diversity is immense. Cameroon is considered to support the richest flora in continental Africa, Gabon is reputed to harbor more than 8,000 plant species (22 percent endemic), and the western regions of northern Congo are described as one of the most species-rich areas of the entire Congo basin.[8] Scientists explain this phenomenon by the refuge status of these regions during the Leopoldian era, as well as their low human population density of today. In eastern Gabon, one hectare of land can contain as many as one hundred different tree species, each interlaced by such an abundance of woody and herbaceous lianas and/or epiphytes that sunlight barely reaches the forest floor.[9] This proliferation of plant matter—the "supreme luxuriance" of the central African rainforest,—has led some biologists to describe it as "the apex of creation."[10]

Rain, temperature, relief and soil quality, and sunlight all determine which species grow at given locations. Because the soils of central Africa used to be considered universally nutrient poor, botanists long attributed the lush rainforest foliage to the development of a rapid and highly efficient system of nutrient cycling through the litter layer of the forest floor. This hypothesis helps explain the unusual concentration of most rainforest tree roots within 30 cm of the surface level of the soil. Recent research has considerably complicated this hypothesis, however, for it indicates that forest soils are highly variable in nutrient content. Not all minerals are concentrated in the aboveground biomass, and additional sources of nutrients, such as aerosols, play a significant role in the nourishing of forest foliage as well.[11] Such research has only begun to elucidate the incredibly intricate workings of the central African rainforest ecological systems, a research problem that remains full of enigmas to this day.[12]

Research from Gabon has led biologists to revise myths about rainforests that have developed over the years. For example, detailed studies of forest composition have indicated that the portrayal of central African rainforests as storied (composed of two or three discrete and superimposed strata) is amiss. Instead, they are more aptly described as "complex juxtapositions of biovolumes" whose height and shape are characterized by their unique intermingling of tree and liana species.[13] It is the overlapping of these biovolumes that accounts for the closed nature of central African rainforests, and that produces the mass of foliage generally described as the forest canopy. Although taller (emergent) trees are contained in each biovolume, and smaller fruit trees, seedlings, and herbs (underbrush) do compete for light under the canopy, none of these categories are statistically demonstrated to exist across extended areas of land. The result is thus a "mosaic of forest patches," each containing a unique combination of trees that can best be classified as immature, mature, and decaying.[14]

The notion of a forest mosaic extends across the western equatorial region as well, for there are numerous types of rainforests found under the vast expanse of green. Dry land forests are the densest and cover the largest area. They are classified into two primary categories: "dense humid seasonal evergreen" and "dense humid semi-deciduous" forests. Seasonal evergreen forests are found across the central regions of Gabon and into western Cameroon.[15] Although they appear to remain green all year, they actually contain emergent tree species that shed their leaves during the short dry season (though not simultaneously). Semi-deciduous forests are slightly drier; they contain both emergent and canopy species that shed leaves in the dry season, with emergent trees being especially drought resistant. These drier forests are located along the northern edges of the region under study—in the westernmost reaches of northern Congo and southern Cameroon/Central African Republic. A third type of dry-land forest, described by some as "in transition from evergreen to semi-deciduous" or "mixed deciduous forest" exists as well.[16] It is found in the north along the borderlands of Gabon, Equatorial Guinea, and Cameroon and into eastern Gabon, as well as in the southern Mayombe, Ikoundou, and du Chaillu massifs.

Wetland forests comprise two types: permanently inundated swamp forests and seasonally inundated marsh forests. The largest remaining expanse of wetland forests in Africa is found along the floodplains of the Congo River. These forests cover an area of more than 8,000 km^2 and culminate in the west in an extensive complex of floodlands and swamp forests around the confluence of the Congo, Ubangi, and Sangha Rivers.[17] Adjacent to these rivers, and extending westward into the central and northern regions of the Congo Republic, are vast expanses of marsh forests. Although flooded during the rainy season, many contain adjacent patches of higher land that have made human habitation possible the year round. Smaller patches of freshwater swamp forest surrounded by mixed deciduous forests are found in the north-eastern regions of Gabon, as well as mangrove swamp forest in saltwater-inundated areas along the coasts of Cameroon and Gabon.

To the southwest is yet another distinct type of environment, the savanna/forest mosaics of the Ngounié, Nyanga, and Kouilou-Niari valleys. Although these regions are covered primarily by savanna-woodland formations (tall trees and perennial grasses), the rainforests penetrate deep into the plains, appearing as remnant forests or gallery forests along riverbanks. Because inhabitants of these regions gain access to a wide variety of plant and animal products, it is often assumed that savanna/forest mosaics were preferred environments for central African agriculturalists. Thus, it is believed that human clearing of the land (after the introduction of agriculture) may have created the savannas of paleoclimatic origin. This was probably the case along the southern fringes of the rainforest, as well as in the intercalary savannas of the middle Ogooué River.

Human action in the rainforest can be detected away from savanna regions as well. The abundance of *Lophira alata* and *Aukoumea* trees in the seasonal evergreen forests of western Gabon, as Vansina has pointed out, indicates prior clearing and historical occupation of the land.[18] Along the middle Ogooué, archaeologists have found evidence of burnt taproots 30 cm below the soil surface. These taproots are considered to be evidence of slash-and-burn agriculture carried out during the Early Iron Age (500 B.C.E.–500 C.E.) Together these different types of data indicate that truly virgin rainforests do not exist. As Grainger has stated, "Even in western equatorial Africa, where great expanses of closed forests still exist and appear untouched by human hands, closer examination often reveals evidence of disturbance long ago."[19]

Indeed, archaeological data indicate that humans have been living in the forested area of central Africa for millennia on end. The earliest evidence for human habitation of the rainforests is found in geological strata for the Ndjilian humid phase (40,000–35,000 B.P.), when the forest refuges of Gabon were first formed. Roughly hewn stone tools of the "Sangoan" Middle Stone Age tradition are associated with this era and are found in nearly every province of Gabon, along the Kouilou-Niari and Sangha Rivers in Congo, and in the southern regions of Cameroon.[20] Most of the sites are located on the summits of hills (in both lower and higher altitudes) near running water. Because the inhabitants of these sites made tools from raw materials procurable within 30 km of the sites, archaeologists have concluded that these Middle Stone Age peoples did not participate in medium- or long-distance exchange networks.

The lifestyles of central Africans appear to have changed dramatically with the recolonization of the forest during the humid Kibangian era (from 12,000 B.P.).

During this period, the forest reached an extension similar to that of today, and people began to produce smaller, less heavy, microlithic tools. Archaeologists assign these tools to the Late Stone Age Tshitolian tradition found across most of central Africa during this period. The newly evidenced presence of the bow and arrow attests important technological innovations, as does the production of small bifacial tools from flakes of stone.[21] The quantity of tools increased dramatically at this time, and in the Gabon estuary, raw materials were procured from as far away as 90 km. These findings lead archaeologists to hypothesize that Late Stone Age peoples of the rainforest participated in medium-distance trade networks and perhaps even traveled by canoe.[22]

Although it is commonly assumed that modern Batwa peoples descend from populations who produced these Late Stone Age tools, there is as yet no archaeological evidence to confirm this link. The most powerful evidence to affirm such connections is found in oral and ethnographic data from this region of Africa. Because these data provide a great deal of information about early Bantu and Batwa relations, they are treated separately in chapter 3. Before presenting such data, however, we must provide a vision of the geographical and economic contexts in which the two societies met. We turn to this task now, focusing on a reconstruction of early Bantu subsistence and settlement patterns within the western equatorial rainforest.

BANTU EXPANSION IN THE WESTERN EQUATORIAL RAIN FOREST

Proto-Bantu Subsistence Strategies and Technologies

Until recently, the lack of archaeological research in equatorial Africa has led to a reliance on comparative historical linguistics to reconstruct a history of the earliest Bantu-speaking communities. This has been done through reconstruction of proto-Bantu lexicon, which can provide insight into the subsistence strategies, technological skills, social systems, and religious beliefs that Bantu-speaking peoples may have carried with them as they moved into the equatorial region. Because a knowledge of subsistence strategies and technologies aids in understanding both archaeological and linguistic evidence for Bantu settlement, a preliminary overview of the information provided by these lexical reconstructions is provided here.[23]

Reconstructed vocabularies indicate that Bantu settlers moved outward from western Cameroon with a knowledge of agriculture centered on the cultivation of root crops. Among the plants they cultivated were yams (of many varieties), gourds (edible and bottle types), the castor bean, black-eyed peas, and the *Voandzeia* groundnut. They used stone axes and digging sticks to prepare and plant fields. Oil and raphia palms were important to the early Bantu as well, although they may often have managed these trees in their natural state rather than cultivated them outright. Because palm trees, yams, and gourds require a high-rainfall environment and sunlight to thrive, it is generally assumed that the earliest Bantu lived in regions that included woodland savanna and forests alike. At present the only environment-related terms reconstructible to proto-Bantu are "forest," "wild area," and "grassy area in forest."[24] Such data lead us to believe that proto-Bantu speakers conceived of their world as a primarily forested one, but that they made use of interspersed woodland-savanna niches. In the earliest stages of Bantu settlement, these niches would have existed as a result of natural conditions—locations with somewhat lesser rainfall or sandier soils that did not well support forest. Upon settlement, however, the Bantu communities may have extended these areas by the use of polished stone axes and controlled fires. Proto-Bantu peoples raised three types of domesticated animals: dogs, goats, and guinea fowl. All are animals able to survive in the forest environment.

Agriculture was by no means the only subsistence strategy that proto-Bantu speakers practiced. The verb "to hunt or chase," is reconstructible to proto-Bantu, as well as words for snares, bows and arrows, and spears. Proto-Bantu peoples applied well-developed fishing techniques, as attested by their terms for "to fish with a hook," "fishhook," and "to fish with a basket." Although these activities could be carried out from the shore, the presence of terms for "canoe," "to paddle," and "row" attest that proto-Bantu speakers traveled and fished along riverine routes as well. Although gathered foodstuffs such as caterpillars, mushrooms, and roots undoubtedly played a large role in proto-Bantu speakers' diets, the only terms scholars have so far reconstructed relating to such subsistence strategies are "bee," "honey," and (naturally) "beehive."

Both linguistic and archaeological data confirm that proto-Bantu communities manufactured pottery. Reconstructed vocabulary indicates not only the process and products of ceramic manufacture ("to make pot," "pot," and "water [?]pot"), but its eventual deterioration as well ("potsherd"). There is also linguistic evidence to attest the art of basketry ("to plait") as well as the numerous types of artifacts produced through such skills ("basket," "large tall basket," "wicker hamper," and "palm mat").

Although the linguistic data indicate that Bantu speakers were able to practice agricultural lifestyles within the rainforest, it should not be assumed that these subsistence strategies always prevailed, nor that they allowed the Bantu a great deal of cultural or economic superiority over their foraging or fishing neighbors. As Vansina has noted, the "fully mature farming way of life" developed only after a period of agricultural experimentation at each new location, and the earliest Bantu immigrants may have depended on agriculture for as little as 20 percent of their food intake.[25] Social and environmental factors also played a role in deciding which elements of the Bantu subsistence and technological package would come to the fore, because early villages were neither socially nor economically self-sustaining. The nature of the resources at hand, as well as the need to establish and maintain alliances and exchange relationships with communities that already occupied the land, surely influenced economic and subsistence choices among early Bantu settlers. All of these factors undoubtedly lent an air of historical and geographical contingency to the settlement experience, a phenomenon that is often overlooked in presentations of linguistic and archaeological evidence related to the Bantu expansion.

The Bantu Expansion: Preliminary Overview and Periodization

The history of Bantu expansion into the western equatorial rainforest falls into four periods or phases, each defined by a differing trend of settlement that prevailed during that era. These patterns can be read historically as successive periods of societal divergence among the early Bantu speech communities. The detailed arguments and evidence for this linguistic history are presented elsewhere, namely, in the author's doctoral dissertation.[26] Here we will adopt the historical subclassification of "narrow" Bantu that was arrived at in that work, and show how we build a history of societies from it.

The Bantu group proper, or "narrow"-Bantu as it is sometimes called, forms one branch of the Bantoid (or "wide"-Bantu) division of Africa's Niger-Congo language family. The other branchings of the Bantoid division consist of languages spoken today in south-central Cameroon and neighboring parts of eastern Nigeria—languages such as Tiv, Jukun, and Ekoi in Nigeria and the Mambila and its relatives in the Cameroon grasslands region. The early ancestral forms of all of these languages—including the particular ancestral language of the whole modern-day vastly spread Bantu grouping of languages, which we call proto-Bantu—came to be spoken across these Nigerian and Cameroonian areas in the periods between about 5000 and 3000 B.C.E. Proto-Bantu itself was originally the language of a set of communities residing at the south of the region, most probably somewhere in the rainforest fringes of southern Cameroon.

The first phase of the Bantu expansion into parts of the equatorial rainforest began sometime before 3000 B.C.E. Preliminary glottochronological estimates suggest a time between 4500 and 4000 B.C.E.[27] It was during this era that the proto-Bantu society was formed, most likely through a southward movement away from its nearest Grassland Bantoid neighbors (see Map 2.2). Continued southward extensions of the proto-Bantu communities led to the formation of two distinct daughter societies, possibly as early as c. 4000 B.C.E. One of these eventually came to occupy the coastal region of Gabon. Because of its lasting establishment near and at the coast, we call it the proto-Coastlands community. The modern-day linguistic heirs of the proto-Coastlands people are the Myene, Mpongwe, Orungu, Nkumi, Galwa, and Adjumba, who cluster in limited coastal areas of Gabon today. The second daughter speech community of the proto-Bantu took shape in the forested

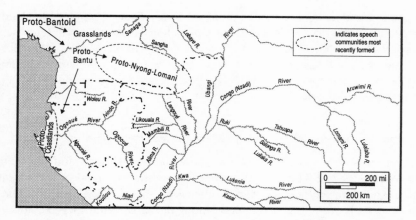

Map 2.2. Initial Divergence out of Northwestern Cameroon, c. 4000–2700 B.C.E.

regions of southern Cameroon. All the rest of the Bantu languages, today spoken across most of the southern half of Africa, descend from this second community. Because the eventual divergence of this group led to the formation of language groups all across the rainforest—from the Nyong River Cameroon to the Lomami River in eastern Democratic Republic of Congo—this ancient speech community is referred to as the proto-Nyong-Lomami.

The second phase of Bantu expansion lasted from roughly 3000 B.C.E. to 1500 B.C.E. This is the period when the cultural and linguistic heirs of the proto-Nyong-Lomami embarked on a succession of geographical extensions across and into different parts of the equatorial rainforest. The classification used for this study documents three distinct (but chronologically overlapping) clusters of language divergences for this period of history in the regions of southeastern Cameroon, the lower Sangha River, and the middle reaches of the Congo River. The linguistic descendants of these various speech communities appear to have traveled extensively along the major rivers of the central African region, for they eventually came to settle both the interior and far eastern reaches of the rainforest. It is this period of Bantu expansion that is treated in this chapter.

After 1500 B.C.E. a third phase of Bantu settlement began. I refer to this as the "filling in" era, because the majority of new speech communities were formed through movement into areas already circumscribed by the earlier Bantu settlement. This process intensified between 500 B.C.E. and 1000 C.E., characterized by an ongoing divergence of the existing Bantu societies into new local communities within and at the peripheries of previous regions of settlement. As we see in chapter 4, this era of linguistic and social divergence was conditioned by the adoption of ironworking technologies and banana cultivation, as well as the development of economic specialization at the local level.

The fourth period began c. 1000 C.E. and continued to the close of the nine-teenth century. Expansion across large areas of land or along rivers had ceased by this time, and the majority of Bantu-speaking communities were present in the regions they inhabit today. I refer to this as the period of "set-tling in," because new speech communities were formed very locally and only in the earliest stages of the era. This history is the subject of chapter 6, where we deal with the period from c. 1000 to 1900 C.E.

Bantu Settlement in the Interior Forest Regions, c. 2700–1500 B.C.E.

To understand how this or any similar history unfolded, the historian who uses linguistic evidence must first establish what we call a linguistic stratigra-phy. A dendogram or family tree of language relationships is a convenient and illuminating model for understanding such a stratigraphy. It presents, in schematic form, a history of the successive divergences of the proto-Bantu language community, documenting the development and genetic relation-ships of modern-day Bantu languages at the same time. The family tree of language relationships for this study is presented in Figure 2.1. It presents the linguistic stratigraphy we draw from in this and later chapters of this book.

In this chapter, we discuss only those linguistic strata that pertain to the eras before 1500 B.C.E. The earliest stratum after the divergence of proto-

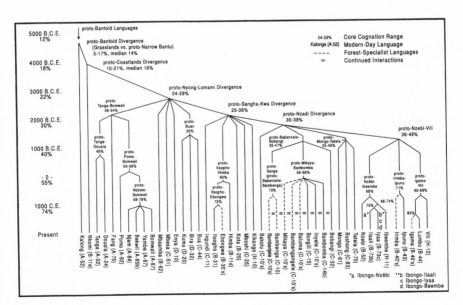

Figure 2.1. Successive Divergences of the Proto-Bantu Speech Community

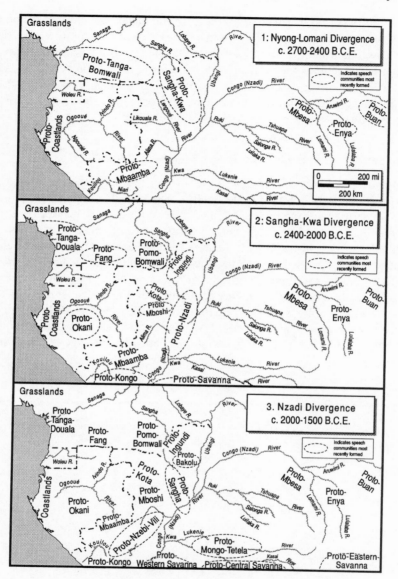

Map 2.3. The Formation of New Speech Communities, c. 2700–1500 B.C.E.

Bantoid is represented by the proto-Bantu language community (second node, upper left). As was noted earlier, this community diverged to form the proto-Coastlands and proto-Nyong-Lomami branches. Because we are primarily interested in the history of the interior regions, only one of the descendants of proto-Coastlands was included in this study (proto-Nkomi) and no further information about the divergence of this group is provided for later eras. It is likely, however, that a number of sister societies of proto-Coastlands languages were formerly spoken in northern Gabon as well. Their prior existence is impossible to document, however, because the spread of Fang speakers into the region since 1500 removed and/or absorbed peoples who would have belonged to these communities.

The second branch of proto-Bantu, the proto-Nyong-Lomami, provides a far more complicated stratigraphy. At the close of the proto-Nyong-Lomami period, six separate branchings of the Nyong-Lomami speech community took place (see Map 2.3, "Nyong-Lomami Divergence"). In the modern-day context, most of the descendant branches of the proto-Nyong-Lomami occupy great expanses of the equatorial rainforest. Descendant languages of the proto-Tanga-Bomwali branch (represented here by the languages of Tanga, Douala, Fang, Pomo, Njem, Bekwil, Yambe, and Bomwali) are spoken across the southern reaches of Cameroon, the northern regions of Gabon, and into the far northwestern regions of the Congo Republic. The Mbaamba language is today spoken in the southeastern regions of Gabon, in what appears to be relict distribution with the closely related Mbete language. It is likely that these languages were formerly spoken in regions farther north, because the simultaneous arrival of Fang speakers and guns during the nineteenth century set off a chain reaction of southward migrations among peoples of this region (see chapter 6). Also formed through the divergence of proto-Nyong-Lomami was the proto-Sangha-Kwa speech community. Speakers of this language most likely lived along the Sangha River and around its confluence with the Congo; it is referred to as the "proto-Sangha-Kwa," however, because the linguistic descendants of the community eventually settled into regions around the confluence of the Congo and Kwa Rivers. The proto-Sangha-Kwa speech community was ancestral to the C, B, and H groups of Bantu languages (currently spoken in Gabon, Congo Republic, and the Democratic Republic).

Finally, three linguistic descendants of the proto-Nyong-Lomami are today located in the far eastern regions of the Congo basin. Mbesa and Enya are spoken along the Congo River south of its confluence with the Aruwimi, and the Buan languages (Kumu, Bira, Bua) are spoken farther to the northeast along the upper Aruwimi River and between the Aruwimi and the Bomokandi and Uele Rivers. Thus, all but the primary descendant branches of proto-Nyong-Lomami initially spread across an expanse of land that stretches across the northern equatorial rainforest.

Glottochronological estimates place the Nyong-Lomami divergence between c. 2700–2400 B.C.E.[28] We can thus envision Bantu-speaking communities settled across a vast expanse of the equatorial rainforest by the early and middle third millennium B.C.E. During this period, as in those that followed, such communities were most likely not isolated pockets of Bantu-speaking peoples, because only in rare instances would individuals establish settlements so far away from family and friends that communication was rendered impossible. Furthermore, and as Vansina has previously noted—the Bantu did not move into a region that was uninhabited.[29] The archaeological record clearly indicates that the rainforest already contained peoples who hunted, gathered, fished, and traded to meet their subsistence needs.[30] It is quite possible that Bantu speakers sought specifically to settle among or in between such communities, especially in the earliest stages of expansion. Such a scenario would not only account for the settlement across such vast expanses of the equatorial rainforest (which was only sparsely settled at that time[31]), but could also explain the presence of potsherds in a number of Late Stone Age sites across the region. This issue is followed up in the section on archaeological parallels. Such details are important for the moment, however, so that readers might divest themselves of any diffusionist notions provoked by this rather sweeping account of Bantu expansion and settlement.

The next major cluster of divergences took place among one of the Nyong-Lomami branches, the proto-Sangha-Kwa. The proto-Sangha-Kwa language, as we have seen, was most probably spoken in the regions west of and around the confluence of the Sangha and the Congo Rivers, in the northern panhandle region of the modern-day Congo Republic. Again, river routes of expansion may have been very important to this history. Glottochronologically, this divergence is estimated to have begun between c. 2400 and 2000 B.C.E., indicating that its earliest stages overlapped with the later stages of the Nyong-Lomami expansion.[32]

According to this classification, at least six, and probably seven, new language communities evolved out of the Sangha-Kwa society: four through geographical movements south out of the confluence regions of the Sangha and Congo Rivers, and two through in situ processes of language differentiation (see Map 2.3, "Sangha-Kwa Divergence").

The proto-Okani community formed the farthest west offshoot of the proto-Sangha-Kwa expansions.[33] The modern-day Okani-speaking peoples (i.e., the Tsogho, Himba, Pove, Okande, Gevia, and Pindji) reside along the middle Ogooué and in the forested regions to the immediate south. Because the arrival of the Fang so changed the ethnic distribution of northern central Gabon, we cannot rule out that Okani languages were spoken formerly by people living farther north in central and northeastern Gabon as well. It is perhaps this history that is reflected in modern-day Okani-speaking peoples origin stories, which claim that their ancestors arrived on the middle Ogooué through migration from areas just to the north of there, along the Ivindo River.[34]

Languages ancestral to the modern-day Kota (C-25) and Mboshi (B-25) of central Congo diverged out of the proto-Sangha-Kwa society as well. The locations of their modern-day descendants allow us to place the proto-Kota and proto-Mboshi communities in regions centered around the upper reaches of the

Mambili and Likouala Rivers, respectively. The southernmost offshoot of the proto-Sangha-Kwa was the proto-Kongo community. Although the Kongo group's various members play only peripheral roles in this study, the latter-day distributions of these peoples along the Congo River show that the proto-Kongo moved downstream from the Sangha-Congo confluence region.

One of the two Sangha-Kwa communities that remained in the older proto-Sangha-Kwa lands spoke a language distantly ancestral to modern-day Ingundi; the other spoke what we call the proto-Nzadi language. The ancestors of the Ingundi evolved in the northernmost part of the Sangha-Kwa territory, whereas the proto-Nzadi language, spoken by peoples in the middle reaches of the Congo River, began to undergo its own divergence into four daughter languages. The emergence of these daughter languages of proto-Nzadi thus constitutes the third major cluster of divergences to take place in these regions central to the early expansion of Bantu populations. Glottochronologically, this divergence is dated to the period between 2000 and 1500 B.C.E.

Two of the new language communities formed from the Nzadi divergence were located in the Congo panhandle: they are termed in this study the proto-Bakolu and the proto-Sangha (see Map. 2.3, "Nzadi Divergence"). The proto-Sangha language was ancestral to nearly all the modern Bantu agriculturalist languages spoken in the panhandle today, such as Bongili, Inyele, Bambomba, and Bobangi, as well as those spoken by Batwa forest-specialist communities (e.g., Bambenjele, Bambenga, Aka, Mikaya, Bambengangale, and Baluma). The territories of this set of communities appear to have remained centered on and around the Sangha River, whereas proto-Bakolu may have emerged as a distinct language through an eastward movement of people away from this central location.[35]

Toward the south, two other new societies also emerged out of the proto-Nzadi cluster of communities, the proto-Mongo-Tetela and the proto-Nzebi-Vili. From the locations of their descendant languages, the simplest explanation is that these new communities emerged from a successive spread of settlement to the east and west of the Congo River, respectively. The proto-Mongo-Tetela speech community may have emerged along and east of the Congo, to the north of the Kwa River's confluence with the Congo. In later times the descendants of the proto-Mongo-Tetela spread eastward up the Lukenié and perhaps Sankuru Rivers. The proto-Nzebi-Vili society probably emerged among communities that moved into the southern regions of modern-day Congo Republic, spreading along an east-west axis that traversed the Louessé, Niari, and eventually the Kouilou Rivers. As we see with the continuation of this history in chapter 4, the westward spread of proto-Nzebi-Vili speakers was greatly aided by the introduction of bananas and iron.

Although this classification does not specifically deal with Bantu languages spoken in the more southern and southeastern regions of the continent, it is

likely that these languages developed from another southern offshoot of the
Sangha-Kwa divergence. They derive, in other words, from a probable seventh
branch of proto-Sangha-Kwa. This can be deduced from previous scholars'
classifications, which have identified a subgroup of the Bantu languages ancestral to all of the languages spoken outside of the equatorial rainforest. Referred
to as the "Zambezi,"[36] "Kongo-branch,"[37] or "Savanna Bantu"[38] in various
studies, this group holds cognation percentages with other Bantu languages that
parallel those of the Sangha-Kwa (high 20s to low 30s). Ehret has proposed that
speakers of this "Savanna-Bantu" language first emerged among those Bantu
communities who settled near the Kwa-Congo confluence region and subsequently spread east along the savanna/forest ecotone. This farthest eastern offshoot eventually gave rise to the proto-Mashariki (proto-Eastern Bantu) speech
community.[39] Because this history, as well as that concerning the later formation of Mashariki Bantu language communities in eastern and southern Africa,
is only peripheral to this study, we will not deal with it in detail here.

To sum up, the information presented earlier represents the first two phases
of Bantu expansion into the western equatorial rainforest. After the initial
two-way split of proto-Bantu in the fifth millennium B.C.E., proto-Coastlands-
speaking peoples settled the coastal region of Gabon, and the proto-Nyong-
Lomami group began to develop in the more southern forested regions of
Cameroon. Thereafter followed a succession of periods of rapid settlement in
various northern and western parts of the equatorial rainforest. This was the
result of three successive clusters of language divergences. They took place
among language communities located first in the southern/southeastern
Cameroon (the proto-Nyong-Lomami), then in the Congo panhandle (the
proto-Sangha-Kwa), and finally around the middle reaches of the Congo
River (the proto-Nzadi).

Because the cognation ranges of these three divergence periods overlap at
their high and low ends, we can envision the commencement of the proto-
Sangha-Kwa and proto-Nzadi divergences to have taken place even as distinct
languages were still being formed among the descendant communities of the
previous divergence. In other words, each divergence can be seen as the formation of a new dialect chain, one that was created within the older, still evolv-
ing, dialect chain of the immediately preceding era.[40] Although the speakers of
many of these new dialects settled in regions adjacent to areas that had been
occupied by Bantu speakers for centuries on end, others progressively moved
out of these central regions on riverine routes, carrying the incipient language
with them. As contacts with the ancestral speech community lessened, new
languages were developed, and as members of the new language community
again spread out, the chaining process was begun once again.

Thus, from the proto-Nyong Lomami period through proto-Sangha-Kwa
era, and then the proto-Nzadi stage, what we see taking place was a succession of periods of expanding settlements, each overlapping with the one that

came before it, filling in a succession of adjacent areas with Bantu-speaking societies. The proto-Sangha, proto-Mongo-Tetela, and proto-Nzebi-Vili expansions continued these processes; they are documented in chapter 4. Thus, by the middle of the second millennium B.C.E., Bantu-speaking communities were established widely across the equatorial rainforest, although their distribution probably tended to concentrate in areas on and around the Sangha, Congo, and Ogooué Rivers and their numerous tributaries (Mambili, Likouala, Kwa, Aruwimi, Lomami). Having presented a vision of Bantu expansion based on linguistic evidence alone, we now turn to an analysis of the archaeological record to see where possible parallels can be drawn.

ARCHAEOLOGICAL PARALLELS

Classificatory Schema

Archaeological data for west-central Africa, although rather spotty and uneven in coverage, nonetheless allows us to draw a number of important parallels with the linguistic hypotheses presented earlier. In the earliest stages of the Bantu expansion, these parallels are based upon temporal and geographic correspondences between the appearance of ceramics and linguistically derived hypotheses for the location of early Bantu-speaking communities.[41] Such correspondences arise through analysis of Late Stone Age sites that contain ceramics, as well as a distinction between the early and late phases of the Stone to Metal Age (formerly referred to as the early Neolithic and Neolithic).[42] Thus, this work employs a four-part classificatory paradigm to assess the rainforest archaeological record of the last six millennia B.C.E. The categories of the paradigm are the Ceramic Late Stone Age, the Early Stone to Metal Age, the Late Stone to Metal Age, and the Early Iron Age. A description of each is provided in Table 2.1.

Because these classificatory categories are derived from the realities of the central African (rather than global) archaeological record, they do not rely on the notion of a Neolithic Revolution to explain the early Bantu past. Instead, they allow us to build up a history of gradual change in the midst of cultural continuity, especially as related to subsistence and technological practices. When viewed from this perspective, archaeological data from west-central Africa go a long way toward substantiating Vansina's notion that the development of the full farming complex took place through a "slow revolution" in the equatorial context.[43] As seen in the following chapters, an acknowledgment of this reality is crucial to an understanding of the Bantu and Batwa past.

The Ceramic Late Stone Age

Beginning in the far northwest, Ceramic Late Stone Age assemblages have been uncovered in the lower assemblage of the Shum Laka rock shelter in the

Table 2.1 Classificatory Schema for Archaeological Data

_____

<u>The Ceramic Late Stone Age</u> (Ceramic LSA) -
 Characterized by the predominance of microlithic industries (small flaked
 stone tools), but which contain a few shards of ceramics and/or
 macrolithic polished stone tools (i.e., hoes or axes).

<u>The Early Stone to Metal Age</u> (Early SMA) -
 Characterized primarily by an early appearance of ceramics outside the
 LSA context and a limited distribution of the ceramics in question.
 Sometimes accompanied by macrolithic polished stone axes and hoes, or
 one or two elements of the full agricultural complex described below.

<u>The Late Stone to Metal Age</u> (Late SMA) -
 Characterized by a full fluorescence of the agricultural lifestyle: village
 settlements, deposit pits, large quantities of ceramics at one site and/or the
 identification of similar ceramics in numerous, geographically distant
 sites, the remains of palm nuts, cola nuts, and/or the fruit of *Canarium
 schweinfurthii*, mortars and pestles, and in rare cases, domesticated plants
 and animals. Also at some sites, the initial appearance of iron.

<u>The Early Iron Age</u> (EIA)
 Characterized by the widespread production and use of iron, as well as the
 full complex of the agricultural lifestyle (see above).

_____

Grassfields region of Cameroon. In recent excavations carried out by Philippe
Lavachery, four potsherds, a few polished stone fragments (3 percent of the
entire lithic industry), and the remains of the fruit of *Canarium schweinfurthii*
were found in a Late Stone Age context dated to between 6160 and 4200
B.C.E. [44] A polished stone tool was also discovered in a Late Stone Age context
at the nearby Abeke rock shelter (11 km north); this tool was dated to between
4750 and 4000 B.C.E.[45] These data can be compared with Ceramic Late Stone
Age assemblages found farther to the west in Nigeria. The earliest of these
assemblages are at Iwo Eleru (southeastern Nigeria), which saw the appearance of bifacial polished stone tools c. 6000–5690 B.C.E., and Dutsen Kongba
(Jos plateau, Nigeria), which attests the presence of microlithic tools with
pottery (24 shards) c. 6050–5400 B.C.E.[46] The pottery at this site was decorated in a fashion similar to that found at Shum Laka. From these data,
Lavachery has posited that pottery, macrolithic tools, and the polishing of
stone axes and hoes was widespread in the Gulf of Guinea (Ghana, Nigeria,
Cameroon) from the sixth millennium B.C.E.[47]
    These data provide a striking parallel with the history of Bantu expansion
provided earlier, which indicated that the proto-Bantu speech community
began to be formed sometime before 4000 B.C.E. through southward move-

ment away from the proto-Bantoid speech community in the Grasslands region of Cameroon. Although we cannot know which language the earliest producers or procurers of ceramics and polished stone tools spoke, we can posit that peoples of the Grassfields region were using pottery and polished stone axes/hoes for nearly a millennium before the proto-Bantu moved south. It is possible that the acquisition of pottery allowed for demographic growth (stewed foods provide higher nutrition), and that polished stone axes/hoes aided some communities in clearing settlements as they moved into the forest. Indeed, words for both of these technologies exist in proto-Bantu, attesting their use in the earliest stages of the Bantu expansion.

A net increase pottery and macrolithic tools uncovered at Shum Laka for periods roughly fifteen hundred years later may reflect an augmentation of production at the site, and as such, a growing demand by local populations for the products that were produced there. In levels dated to c. 2500–2000 B.C.E., the percentage of bifacial macrolithic tool increased to 39 percent, and 443 shards of pottery were found as well.[48] The entirety of these data has led archaeologists to conclude that Shum Laka was used as an intermittent hunting station where animals were butchered and smoked. Because there is no direct evidence of sedentism or agriculture at Shum Laka, we cannot unequivocally assert that agriculturalist populations used the shelter. Given the long history of human occupation at the site (32,000–7000 B.C.E.), it is possible that Late Stone Age hunter-gatherers continued to use the shelter and simply integrated the new technologies into their preexisting toolkit. This scenario would explain the small quantities of ceramics and polished stone tools in the earliest assemblages, as well as the continued use of polished stone tools until the later dates of the second phase of occupation.

Another important set of Ceramic Late Stone Age data has been found 600 km south in the Gabon Estuary. At the Sablières site near Libreville, small quantities of potsherds were found amid Late Stone Age tool assemblages and dated to the eras of 5441–5282 B.C.E., 4940–4722 B.C.E., and 3757–3541 B.C.E.[49] Because these discoveries were made in what is essentially a sand-dune formation, a number of archaeologists have rejected these exceedingly early dates, citing probable soil disturbances.[50] However, Bernard Clist (one of the excavators at the site) has argued for their acceptance on the basis of data from the sites of Nzogobeyok 1 and 2, located to the north of Sablières. Excavations at Nzogobeyok 1 uncovered small quantities of potsherds in association with flaked microlithic tools. Nzogobeyok 2, dated to between 5259 and 5000 B.C.E., contained a fragment of a polished stone ax and pieces of basalt and dolerite, raw materials not found in the region.[51] The nearest source of basalt is 26 km across the Estuary at Pointe Denis, and dolerite is found nearly 90 km to the northwest.[52] Given this evidence, Clist asserts that both Sablières and Nzogobeyok were occupied by Late Stone Age peoples who participated in regional trade networks that carried raw materials and ceramics from the fourth millennium B.C.E.[53] The basalt may have been obtained through contacts with peoples living south of Point Ngombe on the other side of the estuary. There, Clist excavated two village sites along the banks of the River Denis (Rivière Denis 1 and 2). Flat-bottomed ceramics decorated in a similar fashion to those uncovered at Nzogobeyok were uncovered, as well as flaked stone tools and more fragments of basalt. The sites are dated to the third millennium B.C.E.[54]

Farther south along the Gabonese coast are the Late Stone Age sites of Tchengué A and B, located to the south of Port Gentil on the peninsula of Cape Lopez.[55] Tchengué B contained 19 potsherds, all decorated in a style that resembles that of the later Stone to Metal Age Okala tradition that appears near Libreville.[56] These sherds were found in association with marine shells and a lithic industry that was primarily microlithic, but which contained one polished stone adze made of dolerite as well. The nearest sites of this material are located 350 km to the southwest near Pointe Kunda in the Mayumba, or 230 km to the northwest near the Ngoulaé/Song in the Estuary province. From this fact, the lead excavators (Peyrot and Oslisly) have postulated that the inhabitants of the Tchengué sites may have traveled long distances to settle the regions of Cape Lopez, and that they were involved in direct or indirect exchange relationships with their neighbors.[57] Because there are no dates available for this site, the excavators postulate that it was settled sometime between 4800 and 2200 bp (2850 b.c.e. to 250 b.c.e., uncalibrated), the range of dates associated with similar Ceramic Late Stone Age assemblages along the Gabonese coast.[58]

The early appearance of ceramics along the Gabonese coast provides important parallels with the linguistically derived hypothesis for the spread of Bantu language speakers. If we work from the evidence of ceramic-using village settlements alone, the archaeological evidence from the River Denis (the fourth millennium B.C.E.) corresponds to the linguistic hypotheses for the development of a proto-Bantu speech community from as early as c. 4000 B.C.E. The earlier appearances of ceramics at Sabliéres and Nzogobeyok (sixth to fourth millennium B.C.E.) might be explained in a number of ways. Because we know that ceramics were present in the Grasslands region from the sixth millennium B.C.E. on, the data from Sabliéres and Nzogobeyok might attest exchange relations with proto-Bantoid-speaking peoples who inhabited the coastal regions of Cameroon and northern Gabon. It may also attest the presence of an avant-garde of Bantu settlers, peoples whose numbers were so small that they were eventually integrated into the later-developed proto-Coastlands linguistic communities.

A final set of archaeological data for the ceramic Late Stone Age has been found along the lower reaches of the Kouilou River on the Congolese littoral.[59] The earliest appearance of pottery was uncovered at the site of Tchissanga West, where four crushed yet nearly complete pots were found in association with a large quantity of microlithic pieces (45.7 per square meter).[60] Radiocarbon dates for this assemblage ranged from the tenth to the sixth century B.C.E. (580 ± 60 B.C.E., 575 ± 85 B.C.E., 500 ± 70 B.C., and 930 ± 90 B.C.E.), although Denbow (the lead archaeologist) considers the earliest to be suspect because of the unfavorable conditions in which the sample was taken.[61]

In another series of excavations located 125–140 m to the east (Tchissanga East), ceramics were discovered as well. Although stylistically distinct, they appeared to be evolved from the Tchissanga West tradition. This pottery was also found in association with Late Stone Age lithics, although of a quantity substantially decreased (only 13.5 per square meter), and iron fragments and slag were uncovered in the upper layers of the site as well. A charcoal sample taken from a yellow sand horizon (52 m below surface) was contemporary with dates recovered from the yellow sand horizon at Tchissanga West (570 ± 60 B.C.E.), whereas the appearance of ceramic/lithic/iron assemblages took place in the fourth century B.C.E. (330 ± 70 B.C.E., 300 ± 60 B.C.E.).[62] Interestingly, no polished stone tools were uncovered at either of the Tchissanga sites.

This evidence led Denbow to conclude that Late Stone Age peoples of the Congo littoral were in contact with peoples or trade networks that carried ceramics (and later iron) by at least the fourth century B.C.E. The pottery at these sites most closely resembled that of the Okala and Ngovo traditions, these being late Stone to Metal Age ceramic styles found in Gabon and Congo, respectively, and dated to the second half of the last millennium B.C.E. (see following). When viewed in light of the linguistic hypotheses presented earlier, we can hypothesize that the inhabitants of the Tchissanga sites may have been in contact with ceramic-producing proto-Coastlands speakers, or alternatively, members of the proto-Kongo speech community located to the south.

From a broad perspective, the coastal Ceramic Late Stone Age sites parallel linguistic hypotheses in that they attest progressively later appearances of ceramics along the Gabonese and Congolese coasts. Although this study argues that the appearance of ceramics attests the presence of Bantu-speaking peoples within the region, it is important to recognize that we cannot unequivocally determine whether newly arrived Bantu speakers or older indigenous populations occupied a specific site. For example, it is generally assumed that Ceramic Late Stone Age sites were inhabited by indigenous fishing or hunting and gathering communities who entered into contact with newly arrived Bantu peoples. However, it is also possible that these sites represent an initial phase of settlement in which Bantu speakers took up the lifestyles of surrounding peoples. This possibility might also explain the relative paucity of polished stone axes and hoes in the coastal sites; subsisting on marine resource and hunted and gathered foods, early Bantu settlers to this region may have felt little need to clear forests and undertake an agricultural lifestyle. In such a case, the importance of agriculturally related technologies (such as the manufacture of stone axes/hoes and large quantities of pottery) would have declined.

Despite these ambiguities, the linguistic and archaeological data allow us to hypothesize that Bantu-speaking peoples settled the Gabonese littoral by at least the fourth millennium B.C.E. Trade and travel was an important aspect of these coastal dwellers lives, for both ceramics and raw materials used in the production of stone tools were passed up and down the coast. Although it is possible that some Bantu settlers carried out lifestyles similar to those of their hunting-gatherer or fishing neighbors for long periods of time, the appearance of a village settlement at Denis during the fourth millennium B.C.E. may indicate the earliest stages of sedentism and population growth. These phenomena would have allowed for the development of a Bantu language unique to this region alone—the proto-Coastlands speech community, which came into existence during the last half of the fifth millennium B.C.E.

The Early Stone to Metal Age

We now move on to compare linguistic hypotheses for Bantu settlement away from the coast with the archaeological record for the Early Stone to Metal Age. The data used are not generally highlighted in discussions of the central African archaeological record, largely because they provide isolated and exceptionally early dates for the appearance of ceramics at individual sites. As archaeological research has increased, however, the accumulation of dates for early appearances of ceramics—both at the coast and inland—has led scholars to posit that there may have been successive phases of the Bantu expansion.[63] This study works from an alternative notion, that such data do not attest distinct phases of expansion and settlement, but rather, the growth and maturation of earlier established Bantu-speaking communities as they came to prosper in the equatorial rainforest.

Beginning with the central regions of Gabon, the archaeologist Richard Oslisly has provided evidence for an early Stone to Metal Age (or as he terms it, Early Neolithic) on the middle reaches of the Ogooué River. Working from data uncovered at the Okanda 1 site, he has documented the earliest appearance of polished stone tools and ceramics in levels dated to 3560 ± 75 bp, or calibrated, between 2124 and 1730 B.C.E.[64] Although there is ample evidence of Late Stone Age peoples in this region (dated from c. 7700 bp in the savannas of the middle Ogooué river)[65], this site provides what might be the first indications of a sedentary lifestyle—deposit pits filled with fireplace cinders, charcoal, and ceramics. Oslisly indicates that these ceramics differ from styles associated with more recent Neolithic sites, comprising spheroid receptacles with uneven curvature, with annular bases and outward-beveled thickened lips and decoration in grooved patterns.[66]

The more recent Neolithic appears c. 2800–2300 bp (850–350 B.C.E.) and is characterized by the widespread diffusion of a distinctly different type of pottery (the Epona tradition) along 1,000 km of the Middle Ogooué River.[67] Associated with these ceramics are refuse pits that contain evidence of food processing (mortars and grinders, palm nuts, cola nuts, domestic charcoal) as well as polished stone axes/hoes. Despite his evidence for an early Stone to Metal Age assemblage, Oslisly associates the Epona assemblages with an "an initial migration from the north" although he does indicate "a process of neolithisation in situ cannot be ruled out."[68]

Working from the notion of an early and late Stone to Metal Age, Oslisly's evidence can be correlated with two different linguistic hypotheses provided earlier. The first relates to the proto-Okani speech community that was ancestral to the modern-day B-30 languages of Gabon. According to this classification, the proto-Okani language was developed among peoples who moved southwestward into central Gabon after diverging from the Sangha-Kwa language community of northern Congo. Because this divergence is postulated to have begun c. 2400–2000 B.C.E., we might propose that the earliest manufacturers of pottery along the Ogooué (2124 and 1730 B.C.E.) were members of the proto-Okani language community. It is also possible, however, that the earliest pottery from Okanda was produced by earlier Bantu-speaking settlers—groups whose existence is intimated by the divergence of proto-Mbaamba from the Nyong-Lomami community (c. 2700–2400 B.C.E.).[69] Whichever it was, the lack of polished stone tools at this earliest level likely indicates that the agricultural lifestyle was not fully developed; Bantu speakers would have subsisted on riverine food sources and hunting and gathering in much the same way as their indigenous neighbors. We do not see the florescence and expansion of the village lifestyle until the emergence of the Epona ceramic tradition six hundred to a thousand years later.

Early dates for the appearance of ceramics and polished stone axes/hoes have also been uncovered much farther to the south at the Sakuzi village site in the Bas-Zaire province of Congo-Kinshasa. These artifacts were found in levels dated to the sixteenth century B.C.E.[70] As was the case at Okanda, this earliest pottery is of an unknown style, clearly distinct from the later Stone to Metal Age tradition that appears in the region—the Sakuzi group (from the same site) dated between the fourth and second centuries B.C.E. and the Ngovo group, dated to the first and second centuries B.C.E.[71] Associated with these later Sakuzi and Ngovo assemblages are deposit pits, polished stone axes, ceramics of greater quantity and unique styles, flaked stone tools, mud wattle, and remains of oil palm nuts. At Sakuzi, therefore, we are once again presented with a period of at least one thousand years between the initial appearance of pottery and the emergence of the village lifestyle in its full florescence.

When viewed in light of the linguistic hypotheses presented earlier, the sixteenth century B.C.E. appearance of pottery and polished stone axes/hoes parallels evidence for the emergence of the proto-Kongo speech community, the earliest group of Bantu speakers to reach this region. The proto-Kongo society evolved, it appears, through settlements that settled downriver and away from the Sangha-Kwa speech community (on the Middle Congo), beginning as early as c. 2400–2000 B.C.E. By combining archaeological and linguistic data, we can propose that it took between four hundred and eight hundred years for members of this speech community to establish themselves in areas near the lower reaches of the Congo River.

The Late Stone to Metal Age

We next turn to evidence considered to represent a true Neolithic, that is, sites and assemblages that are firmly associated with Bantu-speaking peoples by archaeologists and historians alike. Archetypal examples of such sites include, for example, the assemblages associated with ceramics of the Okala tradition in the Gabon Estuary, the Epona tradition along the Middle Ogooué River, and the Sakuzi and Ngovo traditions of Bas-Zaire, Congo-Kinshasa. All of these sites produced evidence of the agricultural life in its full fluorescence (village settlements; deposit pits; large quantities of ceramics at the site; the presence of similar ceramics at numerous and geographically distant sites; the remains of palm nuts, cola nuts, and/or the fruit of *Canarium schweinfurthii;* and the presence of mortars and pestles). None, however, contained direct evidence of other domesticated animals or plants. The dates associated with all of these sites fall within the middle to late first millennium B.C.E. To supplement these data, we will focus on archaeological data from southern Cameroon and the Middle Congo basin.

Perhaps the most extensive excavations of Late Stone to Metal sites have been carried out in southern Cameroon at a series of locations near Yaoundé (Obobogo, Nkang, and Ndindan). All three of these sites attest the development of the agriculturalist life in its full complexity, and additionally provide evidence of domesticated plants.[72] Obobogo appears to have been the earliest inhabited; its dates cluster in the mid to late second millennium B.C.E.[73] There is one exceptionally early date of 3625 ± 165 bp, which in calendrical dates is roughly 2470–1534 bce. Although de Maret (the lead archaeologist) has rejected this date because of its association with iron slag, other authors have treated the slag as intrusive and used this date to mark the earliest stages of the Neolithic in southern Cameroon.[74]

Because the data from Obobogo so clearly attest village life in its full florescence, it is unlikely that the site represents an initial arrival of Bantu speakers into the southern regions of Cameroon. Linguistic data indicate that Bantu speakers were probably in these regions at much earlier dates, because the proto-Nyong-Lomami speech community had already begun to diverge by the mid third millennium B.C.E. If combined, linguistic and archaeological data might suggest that it took roughly one thousand years for communities in this region to develop the full village and farming lifestyle. Such hypotheses are only speculative at this point, however, because they are based on data from a very limited region of southern Cameroon. Further excavations will be necessary before we can extrapolate patterns identified in the Yaoundé region to the larger expanses of southern Cameroon.

The earliest pottery yet located in the Congo basin proper is that of the Imbonga tradition, situated on the left bank of the Congo in the Mbandaka area, as well as on the Ruki, Ikelemba, Lolonga, and Momboyo Rivers.[75] According to Eggert, who has discovered and described this pottery, its shape and decoration are similar to those found in the Sahara and Sahel regions of West Africa, as well as that found at Obobogo in southern Cameroon.[76] Although available Imbonga pottery does not appear in association with any polished stone tools, it was located in pits and accompanied by remnants of palm nuts (*Elaeis guineensis*) and the fruits of *Canarium schweinfurthii*. These associations, as well as its widespread distribution in the Congo basin, have led us to classify Imbonga-ware in the Late Stone to Metal Age.

As regards the dating of this ceramic horizon, Eggert has proposed that Imbonga-ware "first appeared and saw its florescence during the second half of the first millennium B.C.E."[77] This is based on a clustering of six dates which run from 800–390 B.C.E. to 375–100 B.C.E.[78] He has rejected, however, four earlier dates for Imbonga pottery (uncalibrated: 3775 ± 105 bp [1825 ± 105 bce], 3485 ± 220 bp [1535 ± 220 bce], 2860 ± 280 bp [910 ± 280 bce], and 2665 ± 110 bp [715 ± 110 bce]), stating that they are "rather far from the main trend," and that the lab that processed them (Hanover) "tends to furnish old dates."[79]

If we accept the earliest dates for Imbonga pottery—calibrating and adjusting them for the discrepancies made apparent at the Hanover lab—the two oldest would fall in the middle of the second millennium B.C.E.[80] They thus parallel the hypothesized eastward movement of peoples diverging from the proto-Nzadi speech community on the middle Congo between roughly 2000 and 1500 B.C.E. This hypothesis might also be supported by the fact that the earliest dates for Imbonga-ware are found closest to the Congo River (Imbonga and Bokuma sites) and get progressively older to the east (along the Ruki and Momboyo Rivers). It must be admitted, however, that this suggested parallel is more tenuous than those provided earlier, especially because it relies on dates that the lead archaeologist has rejected.

SUMMING UP

This chapter has presented linguistic and archaeological data to document the first two phases of the Bantu expansion into the equatorial rainforest. It covers a span of roughly three thousand years, c. 4500–1500 B.C.E., and is characterized by instances of relatively long-distance spreads of settlement—especially along the coasts and riverine routes of the interior. Although the locations and general characteristics of these two phases correspond in broad outline with those proposed by previous scholars, the history provided here differs significantly with regard to dating.[81]

For example, this classification indicates that the initial proto-Bantu divergence took place in the Grasslands region of western Cameroon between 5000 and 4000 B.C.E. Then, within a five-hundred-year period, proto-Bantu itself diverged to form the coastal Gabonese (Coastlands) and southern Cameroonian (Nyong-Lomami) speech communities. These dates are considerably earlier than those proposed in previous studies, which locate both of these events between 3000 and 2000 B.C.E.[82] These earlier dates are paralleled, however, by archeological evidence for the appearance of pottery and polished stone tools in the Grasslands region of Cameroon, in the coastal regions of Gabon, and along the Ogooué River of central Gabon.

Combined, linguistic and archeological evidence indicates that the earliest stages of Bantu expansion within the rainforest were exceedingly dynamic, characterized by long-distance settlement along rivers as well as in situ processes of language divergence in regions that had been inhabited by Bantu speakers for centuries on end. By the middle of the second millennium B.C.E., Bantu-speaking communities were established through many parts of the western equatorial rainforest, although their distribution probably concentrated especially in areas on and around the Sangha, Congo, and Ogooué Rivers and their numerous tributaries (Mambili, Likouala, Kwa, Aruwimi, Lomami, etc.). The evidence also indicates a recurrent pattern of roughly six hundred to sixteen hundred years elapsing between the initial appearance of ceramics (at either Late Stone Age or early Stone to Metal Age sites) and the later appearance and/or florescence of villages. This pattern occurred in the rainforest at various locations and in differing epochs of time.[83]

Although the coastal sites exhibiting this pattern document the existence of what were probably two distinct ceramic-using societies (Late Stone Age "campers" and early Stone to Metal Age "villagers"), archaeological evidence from more interior sites are more likely to represent the slow evolution of the farming lifestyle. This chapter proposes that it was during these intervals of time that Bantu immigrants undertook the initial phase of farming in the equatorial environment. Vansina has described this as a period when the West African root-crop planting complex was introduced in a very rudimentary form, and most Bantu societies were heavily reliant on fishing, hunting, and collecting for adequate nutritional sources.[84]

The archaeological record, especially along the coast, makes clear that exchanges between autochthonous and immigrant communities took place. Among the items traded were basalt and dolerite for the production of stone tools, sometimes coming from regions located 200 km away. Pottery was an important trade item as well, evidenced by its appearance in Late Stone Age sites dating from the fifth millennium B.C.E. Although two distinct lifestyles are often discernible from the archaeological record (i.e., mobile and sedentary), there is no evidence in these early eras to suggest that one was socially, culturally, or economically dominant over the other. As Vansina has noted, the only major advantage early Bantu settlers may have had was sedentism, a lifestyle that allowed for population growth and the absorption of autochthonous outsiders.[85]

Thus, the linguistic and archaeological data presented in this chapter have laid the groundwork for the history we seek to reconstruct. They provide a temporal and geographic template of the Bantu expansion, and, perhaps more important, document the emergence of the initial phase of the farming lifestyle at numerous locations in the rainforest. The data do little, however, to elucidate the nature of interactions between Bantu and Batwa during these earliest eras of settlement. Pottery and stone tools might serve well as indicators of economic and technological exchange, but what of the social, cultural, linguistic, and genetic exchanges that undoubtedly took place during these eras as well? For an understanding of that history, we turn to a different source of data, the vast body of oral and ethnographic data related to Batwa societies of the central African rainforest. As chapter 3 illustrates, such data goes a great deal further in uncovering the less tangible elements of early interaction between Bantu and Batwa.

NOTES

1. For a full accounting of these theories, see J. Vansina, "A Slow Revolution: Farming in Subequatorial Africa," in *The Growth of Farming Communities in Africa from the Equator Southwards,* ed. J. E. G. Sutton (*Azania* special vol. 29–30; London/Nairobi: British Institute of Eastern Africa, 1994–95), 17–22.

2. G. Sautter, "Carte des pluies au Congo et au Gabon" (hors texte), in *De L'Atlantique au Fleuve Congo: une gèographie du sous-peuplement,* (Paris: Mouton & Company, 1966).

3. A. Grainger, "Forest Environments," in *The Physical Geography of Africa,* ed. W. Adams, M. A. S. Goudie, and R. Orme (Oxford: Oxford University Press, 1996), 177.

4. D. Schwartz, "Les Sols de l'Afrique Centrale," in *Aux Origines de l'Afrique Centrale,* ed. R. Lanfranchi and B. Clist (Libreville, Gabon: Centre Culturel Francais CICIBA, 1991), 26–27.

5. Ibid.

6. D. Schwartz, "Les Paysages de L'Afrique Centrale Pendant le Quaternaire," in *Aux Origines,* 41–45.

7. B. Clist, *Gabon: 100,000 ans d'histoire* (Libreville: Centre Culturel Français/Sepia, 1995), 62–63.

8. Norman Myers, "Biodiversity and Biodepletion," in *Physical Geography,* 359.

9. A. Hladik, "Structure and Production of the Rain Forest," in *Food and Nutrition in the African Rainforest,* ed. C. M. Hadlick, S. Bahuchet, and I. de Garine (Paris: Unesco, 1990), 10.

62 "The Pygmies Were Our Compass"

10. T. C. Whitmore, *An Introduction to Tropical* Forests (Oxford: Clarendon, 1990), 9; cited by M. Meadows, "Biogeography," in *Physical Geography,* 166.

11. Meadows, "Biogeography," 166.

12. Ibid., 167.

13. Hladik, "Structure and Production," 8.

14. Ibid., 12.

15. The description of forest types and distributions is based on Grainger " Forest Environments," and C. de Namur, "Apercu sur la vegetation de l'Afrique Centrale Atlantique," in *Aux Origines,* 27–30.

16. de Namur, "Apercu," 28.

17. M. R. Hughes, "Wetlands," in *Physical Geography,* 271.

18. J. Vansina, *Paths in the Rainforest: Towards a History of Political Tradition in Equatorial Africa* (Madison: University of Wisconsin Press), 310, footnote 12. This approach can only elucidate the more recent past, however, because forests can regain their optimal conditions in as little as 140–200 years.

19. Grainger, "Forest Environments," 173.

20. B. Clist, "Traces de tres anciennes occupations humaines de la foret tropicale au Gabon," in *Challenging Elusiveness: Central African Hunter-Gatherers in a Multidisciplinary Perspective,* ed. K. Biesbrouck, S. Elders, and G. Rossel (Leiden: CNWS Press, 1999), 84.

21. Clist, *Gabon: 100,000 ans,* 127, 132.

22. Ibid., 127.

23. For data and interpretations regarding the reconstruction of the proto-Bantu terms that inform this brief overview, see M. Guthrie, *Comparative Bantu,* 4 vols. (Farnham, England: Gregg Press, 1967–71); C. Ehret "Linguistic Inferences about Early Bantu History," in *The Archaeological and Linguistic Reconstruction of African History,*" ed. Christopher Ehret and Merrick Posnansky (Berkeley and Los Angeles: University of California Press, 1982), 57–73; J. Vansina, *Paths*; and more recently, C. Ehret, *An African Classical Age: Eastern and Southern Africa in World History, 1000 B.C. to A.D. 400* (Charlottesville: University of Virginia Press, 1998).

24. Ehret, *An African Classical Age,* 299.

25. Vansina, "A Slow Revolution," 17.

26. K. Klieman, "Hunters and Farmers of the Western Equatorial Rainforest, Economy and Society, 3000 B.C. to A.D. 1880" (Ph.D. diss., University of California, Los Angeles, 1997), chap. 2.

27. These dates are based on comparative analysis of cognation rates for the Kalong (A52) language (used here as a representative of the Grasslands Bantu subgroup), which presents an internally consistent range of 5–17 percent cognation (median 14 percent) with the other 48 languages used in this classification. Historically speaking, these figures place the last divergence in the early Bantoid group of people—namely, the divergence of "Narrow Bantu" from its nearest Grasslands Bantu relatives—at around 6500–6000 bp, or 4500 to 4000 B.C.E. See Klieman, "Hunters and Farmers, chap. 2.

28. The core cognation range for this divergence is 24–29 percent. See Klieman, "Hunters and Farmers," chap. 2 and app. 3.

29. Vansina, *Paths,* 56–57.

30. Clist, "Traces de tres anciennes occupations," 75–87.

31. Clist, *Gabon: 100,000 ans,* 116.

32. The core cognation range for this divergence is 25–36 percent. See Klieman, "Hunters and Farmers," chap. 2 and app. 3.

33. The use of "Okani" as a reference to this family of languages is drawn from the work of linguist L. J. Van der Veen, who introduced the term in his Ph.D. dissertation,

"Etude comparée des parlers du groupe Okani, (B-30 Gabon)" (Ph.D. thesis, Université Libre de Bruxelles, Belgium, 1991). The family is also referred to as the B-30 group of languages in Guthrie's *Comparative Bantu*.

34. See, for example, Van der Veen, "Etude comparée," where oral traditions indicate that Pove and Okande speakers arrived along the Ogooué River by migrating down the Ivindo River. Also see A. Merlet (*Vers les Plateaux de Masuku: 1866–1890: Histoire des peuples du basin de l'Ogooué, de Lambaréné au Congo, au temps de Brazza et ses factoreries* [Libreville, Gabon: Centre Culturel Français St. Exupéry/Sepia, 1990], 100), who states, "les traditions orales unanimes de l'ensemble du groupe Tsogho et particulièrement celles des Apinji et des Okandè font du haut Ivindo le depart de leur migration."

35. The Bakolu language is today spoken by a community that lives in the interior parts of the Likouala Region, Congo Republic. Located along the Moungouma-Bai River, the inhabitants of this community are considered by agriculturalists of the region to be Pygmies. My sense—after working with a Bakolu informant (at Epena) who presented both physically and culturally as a Bantu—was that local inhabitants consider the Bakolu Pygmies because they had not relocated along riverine or automobile routes during the colonial era, and thus remained outside of more modern economic and exchange networks. They do however, live in very close association with a group of C-10-speaking forests specialists (I unfortunately failed to inquire as to which forest-specialist community this was). Hauser documented the existence of a "Bakolo" community in the same region (1953), noting that it comprised approximately one thousand "descendants de Babinga assez métissés."

36. P. R. Bennet and J. R. Sterk, "South Central Niger-Congo: A Reclassification," *Studies in African Linguistics* 3, no. 8 (1977): 241–265.

37. B. Heine, H. Hoff, and R. Vossen, "Neuere Ergebnisse zur Territorialgeschichte der Bantu," in *Zur sprachgeschichte und Ethnohistorie in Afrika,* ed. W. J. G. Möhlig, F. Rottland, and B. Heine, (Berlin: Reimer, 1977), 57–72.

38. Ehret, *An African Classical Age,* chap. 2.

39. C. Ehret, "Bantu Expansion: Re-Envisioning a Central Problem of Early African History," *The International Journal of African Historical Linguistics* 34, no. 1 (2001): 5–41.

40. A dialect chain can be formed when members of a single speech community settle along a corridor or linked zones of environmentally familiar lands. The members of the community living at the ends of this geographical distribution lose contact with each other, and over time, because of loss of contact, their manner of speaking the original language changes. In this manner, dialects and then languages come to be formed from the ancestral mother tongue. This definition is adopted from D. L. Schoenbrun, *A Green Place, A Good Place: Agrarian Change, Gender, and Social Identity in the Great Lakes Region to the 15th Century* (Portsmouth, New Hampshire: Heinemann, 1998), 44.

41. As was noted in the introduction, I recognize that it is oftentimes imprudent to correlate hypothetical speech communities with archeological remains, and that indigenous populations could have produced pottery as well. The correspondences that arise through this analysis, however, strongly support the long-standing notion that Bantu-speaking peoples introduced pottery.

42. As was discussed in chapter 1, the use of the Stone to Metal classificatory category has been proposed to eliminate confusion as to what the Neolithic symbolizes in the central African context. De Maret defines it as "a stage without metals but advanced technical traits, such as ceramics and polished stone, and sometimes possible indications of food production. (P. de Maret, "Pits, Pots, and the Far West Streams," in *Growth of Farming Communities,* 320. Lavachery has further refined the category by describing several

64

"The Pygmies Were Our Compass"

"phases" of the Stone to Metal Age, as discerned in the archeological record of the Shum Laka rock shelter of northwestern Cameroon (P. Lavachery, "De la pierre au metal: archéologie des dépots holocènes de l'abri de Shum Laka (Cameroon)" (Ph.D. thesis, Université Libre de Bruxelles, Belgium, 1997–98), 367.

43. Vansina, "A Slow Revolution," 20–30.

44. Lavachery, "De la pierre au metal," 367.

45. Ibid., 394.

46. Ibid., 395.

47. Ibid.

48. Ibid., 369; 376–377.

49. Clist, *Gabon: 100,000 ans,* 120.

50. See, for example, M. K. H. Eggert, "Central Africa and the Archeology of the Equatorial Rainforest," in *The Archaeology of Africa: Food, Metals, Towns,* ed. T. Shaw et al. (London: Routledge, 1993), 328, footnote 6. De Maret and Thiry, in a recent overview of central African archeology, cite the earliest evidence of pottery at the Estuary as that which is found at the Riviére Denis sites (i.e., not Sabliéres). See P. de Maret and G. Thiry, "How Old Is the Iron Age in Central Africa?" in *The Culture and Technology of African Iron Production,* ed. P. Schmidt (Gainesville: University Press of Florida, 1996), 30.

51. Clist, *Gabon: 100,000 ans,* 120, 137–38.

52. Ibid., 127; B. Clist, "Gabon," in *Aux origins de l'Afrique Centrale,* ed. R. Lanfranchi and B. Clist (Libreville, Gabon: Centres Culturels Francais/CICIBA, 1991), 167.

53. Clist, *Gabon: 100,000 ans,* 136.

54. Ibid., 138. The uncalibrated dates are 4810 bp at Denis 1 and 3400 bp at Denis 2.

55. Bernard Peyrot and Richard Oslisly, "Sites archéologiques associant pierres taillées, ceramique, coquilles marines, et outils en pierre polie a Tchéngue, Province de l'Ogooué-Maritime (Gabon)," *Nsi* 7 (1990): 13–19.

56. Ibid., 14. Clist, *Gabon: 100,000 ans,* 149.

57. Peyrot and Oslisly, "Sites archéologiques," 17.

58. Ibid. It must be noted that the authors use "BP" for all dates presented in this article, despite the fact that they are not calibrated dates. I have thus used lowercase to designate bp and bce.

59. J. Denbow, "Congo to Kalahari: Data and Hypotheses about the Political Economy of the Western Stream of the Early Iron Age," *The African Archaeological Review* 8 (1990): 139–76.

60. Ibid., 145.

61. Ibid., 147. These dates are indicated with "BC" in original article; I have changed them to B.C.E. for consistency and on the assumption that they are calibrated.

62. Ibid., 149–150.

63. Oslisly speaks of this in terms of initial and later phases of Bantu migration; see "The Middle Ogooué Valley: Cultural Changes and Palaeoclimatic Implications of the Last Four Millennia," in *Growth of Farming Communities,* 326. De Maret and Thiry are more circumspect, describing early and late appearances of pottery in the Gabon Estuary as "two Neolithic traditions." See P. de Maret and G. Thiry, "How Old Is the Iron Age?," 30.

64. R. Oslisly, "Archéologie et paléo environment dans la Réserve de la Lopé: Rapport final," Groupement AGRECO/C.T.F.T. (Unpublished manuscript, 1996) p. 25.

65. R. Oslisly and B. Peyrot, *L'Art Préhistorique Gabonais* (Libreville, Gabon: Rotary Club International Multipress, 1987).

66. R. Osisly, "Hommes et Milieux à l'Holocène dans la moyenne vallée di l'Ogoové (Gabon)," *Bulletin de la Souete Prehistorique Française* (95:1, 1998), 97.

67. R. Oslisly, "The Middle Ogooué Valley," 326.

68. Ibid.

69. This latter hypothesis is difficult to prove because recent migrations of the Fang have permanently altered the linguistic landscape of Ancient times. The unique nature of the earliest Okanda pottery might support this hypothesis, however. Because it is clearly distinct from that associated with the Epona group, agriculturalist communities of the last millennium B.C.E. might consider it a product of somewhat more isolated Bantu-speaking pioneers.

70. De Maret and Thiry, "How Old Is the Iron Age?," 30.

71. Kanimba Misago, "Zaire," in *Aux Origines,* 177.

72. Millet (*Pennisetum* sp.) has been found at the sites of Obobogo. Millet (*Pennisetum* sp.) and bananas (*Musa* spp.) have been found at Nkang. The latter are dated to between 790 B.C.E. and 370 B.C.E. See C. M. Mbida, "L'emergence de communautés villageoises au Cameroon méridional. Etude archéologique des sites de Nkang et de Ndindan." (Ph.D. thesis, Université Libre de Bruxelles, Belgium, 1995–96), 639.

73. The dates are Hv-10833:3055 ± 110 bp (or 1598–975 bce), Hv-10583: 3070 ± 95 bp (or 1580–1025 bce), Hv-10582: 2900 ± 110 bp (or 1429–830 bce), Hv-11045:2635 ±100 bp (or 1010–434 bce). The rejected date is Hv- 11046: 3265 ± 165 bp (or 2470–1534 bce). A. Holl, "Cameroon," in *Aux Origines,* 152.

74. For example, see Holl, 152.

75. Since 1977, Eggert has undertaken a wide-ranging survey of riverbank sites located along the middle reaches of the Congo, numerous rivers of the Congo basin (the Ruki, Momboyo, Tshuapa, Ikelemba, Lulonga, Mareinga, and Lopori), and the lower reaches of the Ubangi and Sangha Rivers.

76. Eggert, "Imbonga and Batalimo" 131.

77. M. Eggert, "Central Africa," 306.

78. Ibid., 308.

79. M. K. H. Eggert, "Imbonga and Batalimo: Ceramic Evidence for Early Settlement of the Equatorial Rainforest," *The African Archaeological Review* 5 (1987): 132–33. The laboratory numbers for these dates are Hv-11574, Hv-12627, Hv-12207, and Hv-12614, respectively.

80. Based on the dating results of samples that Eggert divided in two and sent to separate labs, there appears to be a four hundred year discrepancy between the dates from Hanover and other labs.

81. A detailed comparative analysis of this classification and those presented in Vansina, *Paths,* and Heine, Hoff, and Vossen, "Neuere Ergebnisse" can be found in Klieman, "Hunters and Farmers," 49–61.

82. These dates can be compared with Vansina, *Paths,* 53. Working from the results of the 1983 Tervuren Classification (Y. Bastin, A. Coupez, and B. de Halleux, "Classification lexicostatistique des langues Bantoues [214 relevés]," *Bulletin des Séances: Academie Royale des Sciences d'Outre Mer* 27, no. 2 [1983]: 173–199), he posits that these divergences took place between 3000 and 2000 B.C.E.

83. See comparative data and dates provided earlier for Sablières/Nzogobeyok and Rivière Denis (Estuary); Okanda 1 and the later Epona "tradition" (Middle Ogooué); the lower and upper levels at Sakuzi (Lower Congo River); and Tchissanga and Madingou-Kayes (Congolese coast).

84. Vansina, "A Slow Revolution," 17–22.

85. Ibid., 17–18.

3

OF INDIGENEITY AND INCORPORATION: IMMIGRANTS AND AUTOCHTHONS ON THE CENTRAL AFRICAN "FRONTIER"

Although chapter 2 presented evidence for Bantu settlement patterns and material culture before the Early Iron Age (c. 4500–1500 B.C.E.), this chapter applies primarily oral and ethnographic data to construct broader hypotheses about the nature of sociopolitical relations with the autochthons that the Bantu peoples met as they settled central African lands. A valuable interpretive tool in this analysis is provided by the concept of the "frontier process" in sub-Saharan Africa, a set of theories about "first-comer/late-comer" interactions laid out by Kopytoff in *The African Frontier: The Reproduction of Traditional African Societies.* In this collection of works, Kopytoff seeks to elucidate the manner in which the frontier experience has influenced the formation of African societies and contributed to a "pan-African political-culture" that is reproduced each time a new community is established on the borders of old.

Because he sought to construct a broad and specifically African theory of the frontier experience (somewhat on the model of Frederick Jackson Turner's "Frontier Thesis" for the U.S.), Kopytoff's analysis sometimes fails to acknowledge the cultural or historical specificity of the patterns identified. This is made apparent in his tendency to describe certain political and religious traits as pan-African in nature, when they are in fact particular to societies descended from the ancient Niger-Congo language community. As shown in this and following chapters, an understanding of the religious and cultural traditions that guide these societies can help us to develop an alternative to the evolutionist paradigm that currently dominates perceptions of the Bantu and Batwa past. Many of the political-cultural traits Kopytoff describes can be seen in both modern and historical observations of Bantu and Batwa interactions, suggesting that Niger-Congo belief systems have prevailed even in regions where centralized states did not always develop.

Thus, this chapter begins a process of model building, bringing together previous scholars' theoretical approaches, linguistic analyses, and ethnographic research. The hypotheses presented might best be considered acts of historical imagination at this point in the book, because they are drawn primarily from data pertaining to the last century alone. I posit, however, that by analyzing and identifying the widespread commonalities in ideas about first-comers, we can begin to discern elements of a politico-religious ideology that is as old as the Niger-Congo language family itself. This chapter presents the first step toward achieving that goal. It seeks to build upon Kopytoff's frontier thesis by illustrating that the sociopolitical dynamics he has identified in various sub-Saharan agriculturalist and pastoralist societies apply to Bantu and Batwa relations as well. Through this approach, and working from the notion that such dynamics are likely to have prevailed since ancient times, I construct a working model of first-comer/late-comer relations specific to the west-central African world. This model is used to interpret more historical types of data, presented in chapters 4 through 6.

ON THE AMBIGUITY OF BEING BATWA

In nearly all of the oral traditions told by agriculturalists of the forest region, Batwa peoples are represented as indigenous teachers and guides—individuals who led the new immigrants to favorable locations and taught them to survive in the unfamiliar rainforest environment. But their role as teachers does not end there; the Batwa are also considered to be the people who introduced civilization to agriculturalists, imparting the very skills and practices that separate humans from the animal world. The prohibition of incest, the use of fire, the cooking of food, the domestication of plants—even the techniques of weaving, potting, and metallurgy—have all been attributed to Batwa populations among various agriculturalist societies.

These traditions appear rather enigmatic to Westerners because our observations of Batwa societies are limited to a period when they have been treated with great disdain. In the nineteenth and twentieth centuries, the Batwa have occupied the lowest socioeconomic strata of central African societies, and they are often described as semi-human and savage by their Bantu neighbors. Intermarriage between the two groups remains heavily proscribed, and in many cases the simple act of eating with Batwa individuals is considered taboo. Although the severity of such discrimination varies according to historical eras and locations, most Batwa suffer some form of social stigmatization and economic exploitation at the hands of their agriculturalist neighbors today.

The harshness of this exclusionary discourse is universally tempered, however, by a respectful fear of Batwa peoples' mystical powers. Acknowledged everywhere as indigenous peoples, the Batwa are considered to have a special relationship to the land and its spirits. This notion derives from the "principle of precedence," a political-cultural doctrine found widespread in the Niger-Congo and Bantu-speaking world that accords autochthonous peoples ritual and/or political authority as intercessors with spirits of the land.[1] In the modern context, this notion is encoded in the special ritual role that Batwa people play in the institutions and ceremonies that agriculturalists deem integral to the prosperity and reproduction of their own societies. Thus, at various locations in the rainforest, Batwa participation is required to sanctify and legitimize rituals surrounding such events as the installations of kings, the smelting of iron, or the funerals of lineage heads and chiefs.[2]

These competing visions of the Batwa exemplify the rather ambiguous position they hold in modern central African societies. Although ostracized socially and dominated economically, the mythical remembrances of their role as teachers and their status as religious experts accords them a certain degree of power in patron/client relations that currently prevail. Although scholars generally attribute the positive aspects of this ideology to Batwa indigeneity and the purported role they played in aiding Bantu settlers, scholars are wont to explain the historical processes by which Batwa peoples came to be excluded, or why both images of the Batwa continue to exist today.[3]

This chapter begins to unravel this mystery by arguing that these seemingly contradictory visions of Batwa populations are in fact part and parcel of a single historical process, one in which immigrant populations have striven to establish new notions of precedence to legitimize their rule. When viewed through this perspective, many of the oral traditions and performative rituals can be seen as remnants of a more ancient political charter, originally designed to guide relations between immigrants and the original owners of the land. Furthermore, I argue that these charters are rainforest versions of a political-cultural model found widely within the history of Bantu-speaking peoples, one that required immigrant communities to incorporate indigenous peoples into their communities for politico-religious legitimacy during early periods of settlement and expansion.

It must be acknowledged that the assertion that ancient Batwa societies were somehow integrated into Bantu societies is by no means new. Since the 1970s, linguists have argued that the complete transfer of Bantu languages to Batwa societies had to have taken place under conditions of social contact that were much more intimate than those that prevail today.[4] This chapter, however, seeks to more fully explore this notion by developing hypotheses about the nature of these interactions during early periods of contact. Later chapters trace the transformation of these interactions through the watershed events of central African history, locating specific instances of interaction and separation in historical space and time.

CONSTRUCTING SOCIAL ORDER ON THE CENTRAL AFRICAN FRONTIER

As we saw in chapter 2, the majority of population movements in Africa have taken place on a very local scale, as families and larger communities sought to establish new settlements on or beyond the borders of old. Although some settlers may have joined preexisting communities as they moved into new lands, many proceeded to build new societies based on models of political culture and legitimate social order they brought with them. As Kopytoff sees it, the latter impulse has lent an air of conservatism and cultural-historical continuity to the frontier process in Africa, a fact that helps to explain the similarities in political culture exhibited among far-flung societies.[5] In parallel fashion, I argue that this phenomenon of cultural-historical continuity accounts for the striking similarity of equatorial oral traditions and performative rituals regarding the Batwa. Although their ancestors were undoubtedly involved in a variety of interactions throughout centuries of contact, the way that this history is remembered and retold has been shaped by the political idioms of agriculturalists, the people who eventually came to rule.

Before approaching this history, however, we must lay out a picture of how early Bantu societies were organized. To do this we will trace the histories of two very old root words, **-cúká* and **-gandá*. As will be shown, both suggest that the earliest Bantu settlers in the rainforest traced their ancestry and organized social relations around matrilineal systems of descent. Although previous scholars have acknowledged these root words, their full historical implications have not previously been taken into account.

Back to at least the proto-Sangha-Kwa period, we can reconstruct a root word (**-cúká*) that referred to the "matrilineage" or member of such a lineage. It occurs in the languages of at least three primary subbranches of the Sangha-Kwa branch of Bantu: in Wumbu of the Kota subbranch; all through the Mongo-Tetela-Bushong group (and probably in the Nzebi group) of the Nzadi subbranch; and in the Lega subgroup of the Savanna-Bantu subbranch. **-cúká* also occurs in Bantu languages of far eastern Africa, in Nyakyusa-Ndali of the Mashariki group of Savanna-Bantu. Interestingly, in Nyakyusa-Ndali, the root has narrowed in meaning to apply to one kind of lineage, the spirits of ancestors, members of the lineage who have passed into the afterlife.[6] The contiguous distribution of this term in the Mongo-Tetela-Bushong,

Lega, and Bobangi groups may in part reflect an areal spread.[7] But the geographically separate occurrences of the root in Wumbu and Nyakyusa-Ndali would seem to put it beyond doubt that this root traces back to the proto-Sangha-Kwa period and thus that unilineal descent of a matrilinear kind was already present at that period of history.

The derivation of *-cúká* provides important evidence about cultural history. In most of the places where *-cúká* refers to a lineage, it also has a concrete reference to a type of termite hill and, more metaphorically, to the "hearth." As Vansina sees it, this association arises from the fact that this kind of termite hill is used as a cooking support for pots.[8] Having assessed commonalities widely found in the cosmological systems of west-central Africa, however, I propose that a more incorporeal metaphor is at work—one that is rooted in the notion that termite hills serve as receptacles for ancestral first-comer spirits who control the fecundity and fertility of people and land.

Such associations are quite explicit in genesis stories told by peoples of the southwestern basin. The Bolia, for example, recount that the Supreme Creator—manifested on earth in the form of a primordial body of water—caused the female progenitor of all humankind to emerge from a termite hill. She in turn, gave birth to a series of twins, each set being the ancestors of neighboring chiefdoms and clans.[9]

Because the Batwa are considered the "original owners of the land," the Bolia myth asserts that their ancestors were the first to be born.[10] Elements of this theme appear widely in west-central Africa; although the earliest (Batwa) humans are sometimes said to have emerged from primordial waters, the progenitor is most often female, and termite hills are commonly considered locations where contact can be made with the world of spirits. As the following chapters reveal, termite hills are employed, variously, in initiation ceremonies of fertility cults, in altars dedicated to lineage ancestors, or as the shrines of religious specialists who provoke rain.

The association between first-comer spirits and termite hills is even more widespread, for a variety of peoples—located from the southern Central African Republic to Zambia in the south—recount that the spirits of first-comers sleep in termite hills. Based on these ethnographic and linguistic data, we can argue that the term *-cúká* developed during the Sangha-Kwa period of Bantu expansion and that it was a metaphor for unilineal kin groups. The direct evidence of this meaning of the term shows that it referred to matrilineal kin. This notion is supported by the fact that so many of the genesis stories of west-central Africa invoke an ancestral mother and by the continuing association of the term with anthills and hearths. The former serves as an emblem of the matrilineage, which for purposes of politico-religious legitimization is often reputed to hark back to primordial times. The hearth, on the other hand, provides a more abstract representation of this theme. Its association with matrilineality is intimated in the hearth's being a distinctly female domain.

A second term for the matrilineal kin group, *-gandá,* can be traced back at least as early and probably earlier than *-cúká.*[11] It occurs with the meaning "clan" or "lineage" of one kind or another in languages scattered from Gabon to Namibia to the Great Lakes region of Uganda.[12] Even more strongly than for *-cúká,* its distribution cannot be explained by borrowing spread, except possibly in one limited region, around the lower Congo River. It occurs in at least one language of the proto-Tanga-Bomwali subbranch of the Nyong-Lomami; thus, it probably traces back to earlier than *-cúká* to the Nyong-Lomami era. In that language, Kako, it has become the term for a patrilineage, and it now means "patriclan" in the Great Lakes subgroup of the Mashariki (Eastern Bantu). But everywhere else the social institutional meaning of this root is "matriclan." As Ehret has noted, the clinching evidence for its origin as a term for matriclan comes from the Herero, who have both matrilineal and patrilineal clans. There it applies specifically to a matriclan as opposed to a patriclan.[13]

The existence of two old terms for matrilineal descent groups suggests the possibility that these terms reflected the two levels of unilineal kin grouping among Bantu by the Sangha-Kwa period. According to this conjecture, *-gandá* would probably have been the term for matrilineage at the Nyong-Lomami period. At the Sangha-Kwa era, it would have become the term for an expanded grouping, the matriclan, while the new term *-cúká* took its place as the term for a matrilineage. Alternatively, *-gandá* may have been the collective Sangha-Kwa word for a lineage or clan as a collective, while *-cúká* designated a member of the matrilineage.

The linguistic evidence also makes clear that *-gandá* at the Sangha-Kwa period took on a second, more concrete reference, as the term for a settlement or part of a village. In modern-day languages, the reflexes of this meaning are varied; they range from "village" at one extreme, to "house" (a separate, later shift of meaning restricted to one isolated forest language and a few subgroups of the eastern Bantu languages) at the other extreme. The majority of meanings, however, fall in between, including "camp," "quarter of a village," and "chiefs compound." Combined with evidence relating to *-cúká,* this distribution of meanings suggests a possible historic scenario. We can propose that during Bantu expansions into the rainforest of the Sangha-Kwa period and afterward, Bantu settlement groups took the form of matrilineage- or matriclan-based communities, and thus the word *-gandá* began to refer to the new settlements as well as to the social grouping who made up their founding populations. When large villages emerged in later eras, it became possible for *-gandá* to take on different concrete meanings. In a few cases, it was applied to the whole expanded village. More often, however, it continued to denote a smaller settlement, such as a section of a village, in which one lineage group might predominate, or an outlying camp. In still other cases, it could be reapplied to a particular section of the village, the chiefs compound, inhabited by the putative founders of a settlement; in this way, the proposed original sense of *-gandá as a new settlement would be indirectly preserved.

These social historical reconstructions depart from ideas broached in other recent studies. In contrast to the views of Christopher Ehret, the evidence shows that *-gandá probably originally denoted a matrilineage or matriclan and took on its more concrete meaning only later, during the Sangha-Kwa stage. Contrary to the views of Vansina, our view is that we can reconstruct root words for unilineal kin group organization of Bantu societies, in all probability matrilineal, back to the Nyong-Lomami and Sangha-Kwa eras. The idea that the *-gandá was a "House"—comprising a "big man," his family, and various clients, dependents, and friends that reckoned relations according to bilateral ideologies of kinship—is not supported by the wider evidence of occurrence and varied meaning of *-gandá, both in the rainforest and beyond.[14] Likewise, the data do not support Vansina's argument that matrilineality was invented as a means of retaining wealth in the House in the eleventh or twelfth century C.E.[15] The distribution of *-gandá as "matriclan," "clan," and "patrilineage" are so widely and noncontiguously distributed in the Bantu world as to certify that we are dealing here with a Bantu social term going back to the second and third millennium B.C.E., the original application of which was to a community bound by ties of unilineal descent.

It must be noted that arguing for the existence of unilineal kinship ideologies in early Bantu cultures does not deny the later existence of the House. This book, however, works from the notion that it was the House, rather than the lineage, that was invented after Bantu societies began to accrue great surpluses of wealth. Accordingly, *-gandá should be associated with "frontier settlements" and "founders" during the pre-Iron Age era; only later, and in certain regions, did it come to be associated with the bilaterally reckoned kin relations of the House. Having laid out this background, we can now return to our task of building a model of first-comer/late-comer relations that can help us to discern the nature of early interactions between Bantu and Batwa.

Although we must work from recent ethnographic evidence and oral traditions to reconstruct pre-Iron Age periods of history, I argue that the first-comer model can provide an effective means of reading such data for clues regarding the more ancient past. As an alternative to evolutionist paradigms, it foregrounds the role of peoples deemed autochthons in politico-religious systems, allowing us to read Batwa data in an entirely new light. To carry out this task, however, we must move beyond strictly materialist interpretations of Bantu political development, focusing our attention on the religious and intellectual components of this process as well.

We can begin by reassessing theories of political development presented in Kopytoff's model of the frontier process. According to him, the founders of new settlements were initially faced with two problems: the necessity of attracting and retaining adherents to ensure the growth of the incipient polity, and the need to establish their independence by asserting their exclusiveness as first-comers on the land. Because both of these issues are conceptualized in terms of agriculturalist communities and competitive political spheres, we cannot project these same motives onto the history of early Bantu expansion. If the earliest Bantu settlers felt a need to attract adherents, it would not have been to build polities, per se, but to ensure the survival of the settlement itself. Furthermore, growth and survival must be conceptualized beyond the political sphere; in the case of early immigrants to the rainforest, economic, demographic, and religious concerns are likely to have been more important. Because each of these concerns may have provided different incentives for recruiting adherents, I will take a moment to describe them all.

Kopytoff notes that in the earliest stages of frontier settlement, founders were required to recruit followers from local populations. This phenomenon is likely to have prevailed wherever and whenever new settlements were established, be they among the early Bantu settlers or the expansion of Late Iron Age states. As Kopytoff points out, however, the recruitment of first-comers was no easy task. Immigrant populations had little to offer local populations because immigrants had little social, economic, or religious prestige upon arrival. At the same time, immigrant communities had to be careful not to incorporate too many outsiders, for they risked losing their own sense of political and cultural identity.[16] A widely adopted solution to this problem (both in Africa and other parts of the world) has been the use of the corporate kin group as an integrative mechanism. Rooted in notions of familial reciprocity, the corporate kin group seeks to control a body of resources (including people) by establishing relationships based on either real or fictive family ties. In the earliest phases of expansion, familial ties would have been literal because newcomers needed to establish enduring relations with the outsiders they sought to attract. As Kopytoff explains,

> The safest course . . . lay in expanding the kin-group internally, by acquiring adherents who could qualify as kinsmen rather than by bringing in mere followers, who, in time, might become competitors. Compared to the allegiance of strangers, rights over kinsmen were more reliable. At the same time, externally, one also sought alliances with other local groups, and these were best achieved through ties of kinship and marriage. In both instances, kinship provided a ready-made pattern for binding relations in a frontier area that otherwise represented an institutional vacuum for the newcomers. (44)

Rejecting evolutionist notions that Bantu societies were somehow superior (or saw themselves as superior) to central Africa autochthons, there is no reason to believe these same strategies were not employed in the early phases of Bantu expansion. The integration of autochthons would have been integral to the economic sustenance of early settlements because they were experts regarding the flora, fauna, and geography of the land. At the same time, their integration would have allowed for a growth in population in a relatively short period of time; demographic growth was equally integral to the survival of the community, especially in terms of increased productivity (agriculture, hunting, gathering) and perhaps also defense. Integrated autochthons are likely to have played an important role as intermediaries between first-comer and late-comer communities, paving the way for peaceful and enduring relations of exchange. Undoubtedly bilingual, they would have been the initial conduits through which language, culture, and technologies eventually came to be shared.

Although the need to increase population numbers and gain access to resources would have encouraged Bantu settlers to establish relations with autochthonous groups, it is likely that religious concerns would have long sustained such relations. This is because Bantu speakers entered into the region carrying a set of ideas derived from the ancient Niger-Congo cultural heritage, ideas that prescribed the type of relations they should establish with first-comers to ensure their own survival in the new land.

Key among these ideas, and certainly of great antiquity, is the notion that ancestor spirits are a central concern in religious observances.[17] Often accompanying this core concept is the idea that a society's land is its own because its ancestors are buried there. Ancestors are the link between past generations and the present, and their presence in the land legitimizes the right of the community to the land. In this worldview, every successive extension of Bantu groups into a new area was an intrusion into lands where the ancestors of other peoples held preeminence.[18] Bantu speakers also believed in another type of spirits, generally referred to as "territorial spirits." These lay in particular locales—usually bodies of water, caves, and so forth—and were considered to influence events that occurred on the land.[19]

As Bantu communities moved into new regions, autochthons would have been considered the most able intercessors with both types of spirits. This is because it was their ancestors who were originally buried in the land, and it was they who knew of existing spirits associated with the terrain. Thus, the beliefs that the Bantu brought with them necessitated giving religious respect to the autochthons and deferring to their knowledge if the Bantu communities themselves were to establish the right relations with existing spiritual power. Because right relations with local spirits are necessary to ensure fertility and fecundity of both people and the land, neglecting this responsibility would jeopardize the very existence of the communities that Bantu leaders sought to expand.

Kopytoff has identified this phenomenon among numerous communities of sub-Saharan Africa. He conceptualizes it in primarily political terms—as an example of the principle of precedence, whereby late-comers attempt to establish their exclusiveness as first-comers on the land. This book documents numerous instances of this process at work; from the start, however, I would like to focus on the religious implications of encounters with autochthons. Kopytoff, for example, cites instances of late-comers submitting themselves to the authority of autochthons, or immigrant leaders attaching themselves to local chiefs, ritual heads, or symbols of power.[20] When viewed through the lens of Niger-Congo beliefs, these tactics can be seen not only as a way of associating one's group with the prestige of first-comers, but also as an opportunity for immigrant leaders to gain knowledge of rituals that appease the ancestral/territorial spirits of the land. These acts of immigrant submission generally lead to the eventual appropriation of autochthonous ritual. Such appropriations can be seen as an attempt by immigrants to integrate autochthonous knowledge into their already-existing retinue of religious practices. In adopting these rituals, late-comers can attempt to influence local spirits without the aid of autochthonous intermediaries; by *controlling* these rituals, late-comers are able to assume the status of first-comers on the land.

This process makes explicit the ways that political and religious authority are deeply intertwined in Bantu political-cultural systems—and why it is illogical to try to separate the two. This duality is made evident in the etymology of the proto-Bantu term *-kúmú*, reconstructed by Guthrie as "chief" and/or "medicine man." The term is today used as a referent to the traditional doctor-diviner in the Great Lakes branch of Bantu (and some contiguous Takama dialects), as "chief-king" among languages of the Nyasa subgroup (Tumbuka, Sena, and Nyanja-Chewa), and as "chief" among numerous and widespread communities of the Bantu-speaking world.[21] The same word appears far away in Krobo, a Niger-Congo language of Ghana, as *okumo*, "ritual chief-priest." All of these forms are derived from an ancient verb, *-kúmu* "to be revered, respected."[22] Working from the entirety of these attestations, Ehret has concluded that the primary meaning of *-kúmu* was "person to whom reverence is due," and that the authority of these individuals was originally based on ritual power alone. As he sees it, early Bantu leaders played a role similar to those found among modern Bantu and Niger-Congo societies that have not developed formalized kingship systems. Like the *okumo* of the Krobo, these individuals serve as religious leaders of defined kin groups, interceding on their behalf with the ancestral or territorial spirits of the land.[23]

Conceptualizing early Bantu political authority in this way helps us to move beyond the "wealth in people" model commonly used to explain political development in Africa, but which can limit our understanding of early relations between immigrants and autochthons.[24] As Guyer and Belinga have noted, the central dynamic of this model is "one of numerical addition and control of pools of wealth in people—as producers and reproducers—analogous to the dynamics of capitalism."[25] As a result, kinship and marriage have been seen as the most critical components of "big man" strategies, and political/economic systems are analyzed primarily in terms of natalism, polygyny, servitude, or clientship.[26]

Guyer and Belinga argue that it is important to recognize the importance of *knowledge* as a key resource and "means of production" in the central African political sphere as well. "Ethnographic data from the equatorial region make clear that it was knowledge—knowledge of the forest, knowledge of things, knowledge that generated things and things that embodied knowledge—that constituted both the material and human basis of life in these societies."[27] Likewise, knowledge was integral to notions of leadership, for "no leader could succeed without powers derived from specialist knowledge," and leaders who did not possess it were required to attract individuals who did. Indeed, the ultimate leaders of central African societies were the ancestors, and they were considered to be the "embodiment of knowledge itself."[28]

Thus, the authors propose that historians begin to lift knowledge "out of the shadow" of accumulative theory by thinking in terms of compositional processes as well. This model works from the notion that human beings could be seen as assets by virtue of their knowledge alone, and that a key theme in central African history has been the aggregation and elaboration of such knowledge by political leaders. Accordingly, the "knowledge composition process" can be seen as a primary motive for Bantu recruitment of autochthons in the earliest stages of settlement because Niger-Congo religious beliefs required leaders to gain ritual knowledge through submitting to the original owners of the land.

The information so far presented suggests that we can envision early Bantu settlements as relatively egalitarian sociopolitical units based on the corporate kin-group model. Each of these units was likely headed by an individual who served as intercessor to the spirit world. Because autochthons were considered experts regarding the flora, fauna, and ancestral/territorial spirits of the land, it is likely that the establishment of relations with autochthons was one of the most important tasks of Bantu leaders after moving into new lands. It was the means of gaining new and necessary *knowledge* power. Although broader social organization may have been based on Bantu ideas of the lineage, the corporate kin-group model allowed for the integration of autochthons based on claimed family ties. It is through these mechanisms that autochthons may have been attached to or integrated into Bantu settlements. Through them, lasting relationships could also be established with other groups of autochthons living nearby, providing the possibility for further economic, religious, and cultural exchange.

Kopytoff's model of frontier relations stipulates, however, that the corporate kin-model could only work as an integrative mechanism when population densities were low. As the population numbers grew, factions could arise to challenge the authority of founders, and individuals might segment off to form frontier societies of their own. Once again, a common response to this problem is found in Africa and around the globe: the creation of a new type of hierarchy within the corporate kin group. Kopytoff's example of this phenomenon is based on observations made in incipient states; new hierarchies are created when blood descendants of the original founder, or alternatively, a line of elders, arrogate themselves to a position of authority over junior or lesser lines. This creation of inequality had to be carried out in very circumspect ways, however, because leaders ran the risk of losing adherents disgruntled at the loss of their "brother" status.[29] As a result, a new political model was developed, one that began to work from fictive notions of kinship while emphasizing interdependence between the rulers and the ruled.

Key to the working of the new political system was the integration of first-comers into the symbolic rituals of the newcomer populations.[30] Even in cases where political power was usurped, the ritual authority of first-comers remained intact; leaders were required to honor their expertise in spiritual matters to ensure the continued prosperity of the land. Thus, as Kopytoff puts it, late-comer leaders "co-opted their predecessors into the political rituals precisely because they were predecessors. And the predecessors agreed to their formally subordinate ritual status precisely because their participation in the ritual kept the memory of their original position publicly alive."[31] Once again, although Kopytoff's theory is geared toward an explanation of state formation among agriculturalist societies, similar dynamics are evident in modern-day relations between Bantu and Batwa. These dynamics help to explain the integral role that Batwa individuals play in agriculturalist rituals, yet who remain in most cases excluded from other aspects of village life.

Once newcomers had established hegemony over local peoples and lands, the notion of first-comer had to be altered to accommodate the new realities of political rule. Kopytoff cites a number of examples of how this was done. In some cases, newcomers portrayed themselves as the first population to "wrest civilization from a socio-political wilderness."[32] Under this type of thinking, autochthonous peoples are symbolically "deculturized," a process that renders them "precivilized" beings of a lesser status. In other cases, more accommodationist tactics are used. Among the Goba of the Zambezi, for example, distinctions were made between autochthonous "Tonga" inhabitants as "original owners of the land " and the conquering Korekore as "owners of the people."[33] Kopytoff also documents a technique described as "redefining the land." In this case, late-comers demarcate new conceptual or geographical boundaries, and often establish new territorial shrines as well.

A final element of Kopytoff's theory that is helpful in understanding first-comer/late-comer relations has to do with the manner in which the shift of political or ritual authority is remembered in oral tradition. According to Kopytoff, both first-comers and late-comers acknowledge this shift as a pivotal moment in their history. Late-comers often portray it as the first expansion of an already-existing frontier settlement—"the beginning of another stage in the process by which an original kin group, grown into a kin-like group, continues on its course toward founding a polity."[34] Those that have been subjugated, on the other hand, see it as the birth of an entirely new political order. Their narratives generally describe it as the moment when formerly meek immigrant societies began to let their true ambitions show, leading to a usurpation of power and a rupture in the sociopolitical relations that guided interactions in the past. As ethnographic data from this and later chapters show, this is a familiar theme in oral traditions told by Bantu and Batwa.

Drawing from the generalities described earlier, we can begin to discern that Batwa peoples have undergone somewhat similar processes of integration and exclusion as first-comer populations in sub-Saharan Africa. This history is so far only intimated, however, because examples of ancient respect and modern-day disdain serve as bookends to the frontier process itself. In an effort to glean more insight regarding the intermediate stages of this process, we turn to an analysis of oral and ethnographic data from the Aka and Ngbaka-Ma'bo societies of southern Central African Republic. Although these societies provide a modern example of the frontier process at work, I believe they can help us to understand earlier dynamics by going beyond evolutionist paradigms and beginning to envision knowledge as a key medium of exchange.

THE FRONTIER PROCESS AT WORK: THE AKA AND NGBAKA-MA'BO IN THE FORESTS OF CENTRAL AFRICAN REPUBLIC

The Aka forest specialists of the Central African Republic have been the object of French researchers' interest for nearly 30 years. As a result, there is large corpus of data to draw from regarding their languages, lifestyles, and interactions with neighbors. The discussion presented here draws primarily on the research of Serge Bahuchet and J.M.C. Thomas who, between them, have produced more than 12 volumes on the Aka communities alone. These detailed works provide a wealth of material for an analysis of the frontier process in the rainforest context because they combine linguistic, ethnographic, and historical data to paint one of most complete pictures of Batwa societies available today. Although Bahuchet and Thomas have never presented their work in terms of the frontier thesis, analysis of their ethnographic data provides ready evidence of its mechanisms at work.

More than one million Aka forest specialists inhabit the southern regions of the Central African Republic and northern Congo. Comprising both sedentary and nomadic communities, the Aka are found across an area approximately 70,000 km^2.[35] Although they all speak versions of the same Bantu C-10 language, Aka communities are in contact with more than 12 different Bantu- and Ubangian-speaking communities. Among these are the following:

Ubangian: Ngbaka-Ma'bo, Monzombo, Ngundi, Yangere, Mbanza, Gbaya;
Bantu C10: Pande (C-12), Mbati (Isongo) (C-13), Ngando, Bofi (C-10); and
Bantu A-80 and A-90: Mpiemo (A-86), Kako (A-93).

Although this work ultimately seeks to elucidate the historical nature of
Bantu and Batwa relations, we work with ethnographic data regarding Aka
peoples' interactions with the Ngbaka-Ma'bo—a Ubangian-speaking people.
Such an analysis is pertinent to our study because both Bantu and Ubangian
languages are derived from the Niger-Congo language group and share similar ideas about autochthonous peoples' relation to the spirits of the land. The
Ngbaka-Ma'bo might also be considered to resemble earlier Bantu communities in economic terms because they carry out very limited forms of agriculture (bananas, yams) and spend one half of the year in forest camps where
they organize along gender lines to hunt, trap, fish, and collect forest products.[36] Furthermore, the Ngbaka-Ma'bo are relatively recent settlers in the
rainforest region; oral traditions speak of an eighteenth-century arrival, and
migration accounts contain vivid remembrances of flora and fauna unique to
the savanna environment. [37]

Politically speaking, the Ngbaka-Ma'bo society is highly decentralized.
Authority is based on the power of village and lineage leaders alone, and conceptualizations of rights, responsibilities, and relationships remain rooted in
the idea of the corporate kin group.[38] This model is used to regulate relations
between villagers and their leaders, lineage heads, and associated Aka forest
specialists. Like other agriculturalists and fishing peoples of the region, the
Ngbaka-Ma'bo rely heavily on their Aka neighbors for provisions of meat
and honey. In return they provide the Aka with manufactured products such as
machetes, iron spearheads, and cultivated foods. Despite the economic
importance of these exchanges, Bahuchet argues that Ngbaka-Ma'bo relations with the Aka should be seen in a much broader sociopolitical context,
one in which the Ngbaka-Ma'bo strive endlessly to establish and maintain
alliances with local individuals, lineages, and families. Describing these
efforts as an ideology of *"appropriation humain,"* Bahuchet notes that the
Ngbaka establish such relations through the use of marriage alliances, gift
exchange, and the transfer of rights to Aka alliances between Ngbaka-Ma'bo
individuals.[39]

Thus, the Ngbaka-Ma'bo can be seen as relatively recent arrivals to the region
who are currently attempting to establish political and economic hegemony in a
region recognized as not their own. At the same time, however, the Ngbaka-
Ma'bo participate and contribute to a cultural complex that is as much Aka as it
is their own. As Thomas has noted, the interpenetration of the two cultures is so
intense that it is often impossible to determine the origins of religious and cultural traits they now share.[40] It is the nature of this interdependence, which coex-
ists with the Ngbaka-Ma'bo hegemonic agenda, that we focus on here.

The Ngbaka-Ma'bo recognize three social categories of Batwa peoples.[41] Those most distant to their lives are referred to as *beka,* Batwa peoples who live deep in the forest and with whom the Ngbaka have never established relations. They are reputed to practice very powerful magic and are generally considered elusive, "savage," and "bad." The Ngbaka-Ma'bo describe the *beka* as smaller and lighter-skinned than their more familiar Aka clients, whom they refer to as *Bambenga.* Because partnerships between Ngbaka-Ma'bo individuals and these Aka clients are passed from father to son, patron-client relations have in many cases endured for generations on end. Nonetheless, relations between the Ngbaka-Ma'bo and their Aka clients are today characterized by social distance, formality, and constraint. For example, the presence of these Aka clients is not tolerated in the village. If the Aka wish to commence a period of exchange, they install a camp on the outskirts of the village, entering only to announce their arrival or possession of game. All interactions are carried out in the Ngbaka-Ma'bo language, and in personal interactions, Aka individuals always present a reserved demeanor, "taking care not to let the smallest indication of their personal sentiments be known."[42]

The third category of Batwa individuals are Aka "cadets" or "lesser brothers," individuals who live in the village and are integrated into family lines. This occurs through either adoption or birth. As part of the ongoing process of *"appropriation humaine,"* Ngbaka-Ma'bo families are known to adopt Aka children in cases where both parents have died. Likewise, in instances where intermarriage occurs, Ngaba-Ma'bo men take Aka wives and their offspring are integrated into the father's family line. Although such intermarriage is rare today, it appears that this was not always the case in the southern regions of Central African Republic. Ngbaka-Ma'bo oral traditions recount episodes of agriculturalist women marrying Batwa men, an act that was accepted (at least in legend) as long as the couple resided in the village.[43] Administrative records further indicate that as many as 20 Mbati women married Aka men in the 1950s, and went to live with them in forest camps during this time.[44]

Because the Ngbaka cease to trace filiation after four generations (thereafter reckoning descent by the patrilineage alone), the descendants of integrated Aka are eventually absorbed into the Ngbaka-Ma'bo community. Until that point, however, their role as lesser brothers (or sisters) require that they serve as a companion to a Ngbaka individual. They are thus expected to assist this individual in all tasks, accompany him or her in travels, and generally protect his/her safety and well-being. Despite the subservient nature of this position, Aka cadets are not considered slaves. As Thomas has stated, "their lives are protected and their status as members of the lineage is never called into question."[45]

Although the Ngbaka-Ma'bo carry out less exploitative relationships with their Batwa clients than many neighboring societies,[46] their treatment of the

Aka makes clear that the process of symbolic deculturalization has already taken place. For example, in oral traditions the Aka are never mentioned by name. When they are referred to, they are described as "the person behind" or "the weak, inferior,"—a class of individuals who are expected to serve their Ngbaka "fathers" with loyalty and respect.[47] As Bahuchet and Guillaume describe it, the Ngbaka-Ma'bo view the Aka as deprived of culture, a people who lack the institutions and practices required for the reproduction of society itself. Among these institutions and practices are hierarchical or centralized systems of authority, strong social constraints on sexual and marriage relations, a sense of lineage or descent beyond a few generations, uxorilocal brideservice systems, and the stockpiling of food for later use. Such ideas have led to a general portrayal of the Aka as uncivilized and lax, a people destined to be dominated by outsiders.[48]

Despite this disdainful imagery, the Ngbaka-Ma'bo continue to attribute a civilizer status to Batwa peoples in general. Oral traditions recount that the Batwa introduced fire, cooked food, ironworking, and the domestication of plants, and migration accounts attest that the Ngbaka-Ma'bo were led to their present location by Batwa individuals. More important, the religious powers of Batwa peoples remain recognized as essential to the prosperity and continuance of the Ngbaka-Ma'bo community itself. Many village religious heads (*wama*) state that they obtained their supernatural powers through training with the Batwa,[49] and the participation of Aka individuals in certain ceremonial events is often required.

The latter phenomenon is most apparent at the funerals of village and lineage heads, when Aka clients are called upon to perform dances dedicated to *Ezengi,* the foremost spirit in Aka cosmology. As the first creation of the demiurge, *Ezengi* is considered to be the "master of the forest," responsible for the prosperity and fecundity of every Aka group.[50] He rules over the forest with a lesser spirit *Ziakpokpo,* "master of the hunt." Both *Ezengi* and *Ziakpokpo* guide the spirits of deceased Aka (*dio*) into the afterlife, and if appeased, allow for success during the hunt.[51] Although group elders and doctor-diviners pay homage to ancestors and such master-spirits alike, these supernatural beings are most influenced by individual comportment vis-à-vis the group. The Aka believe that if an individual commits a transgression against his or her own community, these spirits will rain terror on all. Calamities, famines, and epidemics can occur, oftentimes leading to the very extinction of the group. The importance attached to these spirits is made apparent by the fact the *Ezengi* dance is usually performed at initiation ceremonies that mark the passage of Aka youth into adulthood, thereby emphasizing each individual's newfound responsibility to the group.

In recent times, however, Ngbaka-Ma'bo individuals have begun to be initiated into the *Ezengi* cult as well. Contrary to the Aka, they view this initiation as an entrée into an exclusive brotherhood of hunters, one that can reveal the secrets of the forest world. [52] Through exposure to the religious systems of the Aka, the Ngbaka-Ma'bo have come to believe it is *Ezengi* who can assure the safe passage of Ngbaka-Ma'bo ancestors into the afterworld, a realm they consider to be ruled by *Ezengi* and the spirits of Aka ancestors alone.[53] Likewise, Ngbaka-Ma'bo patrons often impose themselves at Aka funerals, supplying large quantities of food and drink so that the spirit of the deceased client remains happy. If the spirit is satisfied, Ngbaka patrons believe that they will be assured success in all future endeavors—those carried out both in life and after death.[54]

These Ngbaka-Ma'bo beliefs provide a clear manifestation of Niger-Congo religious thought at work. By entering into the *Ezengi* cult, the Ngbaka-Ma'bo seek access to the ancestral and territorial spirits of the land, while concurrently altering the meaning of the ritual to fit their own economic and religious needs. Bahuchet has noted that the initiation of agriculturalist/fishing peoples into Aka ritual organizations is a common phenomenon throughout the region. Identifying the phenomenon outside of its specifically Niger-Congo context, Bahuchet states that it appears to be "a fundamental process of alliance" that occurs between the two types of population, and notes that it occurs in societies that have no prior history of contacts with the Aka.[55]

The Ngbaka-Ma'bo entrance into *Ezengi* initiations appear to be only the latest episode in an ongoing process of ritual appropriation. Arom and Thomas's studies of their religious practices suggest that one of the most important Ngbaka-Ma'bo ritual institutions—the veneration of *mimbo* trapping spirits—emerged during a period of contact with Batwa populations that occurred in the more distant past. At the same time, local Aka populations practice what appears to a variation of the *mimbo,* also altering it to fit their own needs. Because the divergent manifestations of this religious practice provide insight into the ways a common tradition can be altered to fit both Bantu and Batwa worldviews, we take a moment to consider them here.

The Ngbaka-Ma'bo pantheon is headed by a supreme being traditionally referred to as *Mungo.* Unlike *Ezengi* of the Aka, *Mungo* is an original creator spirit, considered to be present in all people, places, and things.[56] It is *Mungo* who created the sky, the earth, the water, and the forest. When he created humans, he also created their souls (*kulu*). Like a great many peoples who practice religions derived from the ancient Niger-Congo tradition,[57] the Ngbaka-Ma'bo conceive of *Mungo* as a very distant and abstract god, one that is too powerful for individuals to pray to directly. Instead they venerate a pantheon of lesser territorial and ancestral spirits, which serve as the focus of religious ritual, secret societies, and public performance as well.

Key among these are the *"mimbo,"* or spirits of the trap." The Ngbaka-Ma'bo consider *mimbo* to be the spirits of deceased Batwa individuals, in contradistinction to the spirits of their own ancestors, the *kulu-se.*[58] They say that these Batwa ancestors were "given" to them by the Batwa themselves, although no Aka individuals participate in the *mimbo* rituals that the Ngbaka-Ma'bo perform today. One of four different miniature humanoid spirits venerated by the Ngbaka, the *mimbo* are described as 30 cm in height and covered in fur, with long hair that falls to their knees.[59] They live exclusively in the forest, inhabiting trees and termite hills and moving about only at night. The *mimbo* do not eat meat, but prefer to feast on gathered forest products such as mushrooms and roots. Their main task is to aid Ngbaka-Ma'bo individuals in their efforts to capture game. They do this by attracting animals to the traps, or alternatively, if the hunt is carried out with a gun, by gathering animals together and guiding them toward the hunter. They are also said to aid the individual in combat, usually by carrying the human on their back and carrying out battle in his place.

To ensure the aid of *mimbo* spirits, the Ngbaka-Ma'bo must undertake an extensive array of ritual practices. An individual must first be initiated into the *mimbo* cult, an act that leads to spiritual "clairvoyance" and the right to call on *mimbo* spirits for help. Initiation involves the administering of special *loko,* or medicines, usually prepared by elders, or the village *wama.* Interactions with *mimbo* spirits must take place in forest camps alone, for they are considered very dangerous in the village realm. The adherents set up special altars, and wear ceremonial belts prepared by the *wama.* The Ngbaka believe that *mimbo* spirits can only be attracted by certain smells and sounds. For this reason, adherents are allowed only to bathe once a week, and after bathing, must rub their bodies with a perfumed bark supplied by the *wama.* They use a special whistle (*nzanza*) to call the spirit; the Ngbaka claim that this type of whistle originally belonged to the *mimbo* themselves. More important, adherents of the *mimbo* cult must play a one-stringed harp to attract these spirits. Called an *mbela,* this instrument was also given to the Ngbaka by the ancestral Batwa. It is played only when the Ngbaka are in their trapping and hunting camps; at the end of the season it is left in the forest, usually in a location where future hunters and trappers will be able to find and use it.

Arom and Thomas argue that an understanding of the *mimbo* is impossible outside the socioeconomic context of Ngbaka/Batwa relations. According to them, the *mimbo* are an idealized projection of Batwa clients, supernatural assistants whose sole aim and purpose is to serve the Ngbaka patron when he enters the forest domain. This sense of idealization seems all the more strange when one considers current Ngbaka-Ma'bo relations with their Aka clients, which are much more distant and constrained. This incongruity leads Arom and Thomas to propose that the *mimbo* might reflect Ngbaka remembrances of an earlier period of history, when contacts with Batwa communities were much more intimate and vital to their survival. They suggest that such relations were carried out with the Baka forest specialists of eastern Cameroon because it is they who speak the Ubangian language most closely related to Ngbaka-Ma'bo.[60]

When viewed in the context of the Niger-Congo religious thought, we might also argue that the *mimbo* are simply doing what the ancestral spirits of autochthons are supposed to do—aid supplicants in achieving prosperity in a new land. Seen in this context, there is no need to rely on the patron/client paradigm to interpret Ngbaka-Ma'bo religious beliefs. Indeed, Ngbaka-Ma'bo rituals appear to provide a classic example of late-comers' attempts to gain access to and influence the original ancestors of the land, although in this case they have fully appropriated such practices and excluded the people they deem first-comers in the present day. The fantastic descriptions of *mimbo* spirits suggest that the deculturalization process has been complete; rather than acknowledge any kind of connection between ancient or modern first-comers, the *mimbo* are rendered entirely nonhuman, a class of supernatural beings whose behavior is dependent on the actions of the Ngbaka-Ma'bo alone. Although we cannot identify the period in which this deculturalization occurred, it provides an excellent example of what Kopytoff has identified as the widespread "mythical solution" to the newcomers' dilemma of legitimacy. As an ideology designed to inculcate a new meaning of precedence, it "takes the notion of 'pre-civilized' predecessors to its logical extreme."[61]

Although neighboring Aka communities do not participate directly in the *mimbo* rituals of the Ngbaka-Ma'bo, they do practice what appears to be their own variation of the cult. It is dedicated instead to "*mbimbo*" spirits, who, like the *mimbo,* provide personal protection for Aka individuals. The *mbimbo,* however, accompany the Aka at all times, not simply when they are involved in the hunt. On one level, the *mbimbo* are considered to be the manes of deceased religious experts, spirits that can enter into the body of young religious apprentices and thus initiate their careers as ritual experts. At the same time, the *mbimbo* are considered to be the spirits of humans taken prematurely from the world: children, uninitiated youth, and apprentices who have not finished their training can all become *mbimbo* upon their death.[62] Bahuchet notes that the Aka have projected an image of their Ngbaka-Ma'bo neighbors into this latter category of *mbimbo* spirits; "for the Aka, the *mbimbo* are the immature spirits of humans who have not yet achieved their full social cycle. This is exactly what the Ngbaka are in the eyes of the Aka, because they are not initiated and are dependent on the Pygmies for the provision of forest products. Non-productive, they are like children."[63]

Like the *mimbo, mbimbo* are generally viewed as benevolent spirits— warning individuals of impending danger and stepping in to take their place when disaster is near. They can also be somewhat baleful, however, because they serve as monitors of individual behavior and inform the community when transgressions against the group are committed. Both of these characteristics are attributed to the Ngbaka as well. Although protectors, both the *mbimbo* and the Ngbaka are regarded as "omnipresent, suspicious, and endlessly surveying their partners," ready to profit at the slightest lapse of attention an Aka might make. Bahuchet cites such acts as the stealing of food or the abduction of women as examples of the treachery that these protectors have been known to commit.[64]

Because the *mbimbo* so closely resemble Ngbaka *mimbo* in function and form, and because the Aka offer domesticated foodstuffs to the *mbimbo* that they themselves do not produce (bananas and fowl), Thomas has suggested that the Aka borrowed the cult from their Ngbaka patrons.[65] Although this may be the case, there is a great deal of evidence to suggest that the original borrowing took place in the opposite direction—and that the ancestors of both groups practiced the rituals together in the past. This alternative borrowing scenario is initially intimated by the much more complex nature of the Aka *mbimbo* spirit, and the manner in which the projection of their Ngbaka-Ma'bo patrons appears to be grafted onto a preexisting set of religious ideas. It is also suggested by ethnographic data related to the *mbela,* the musical bow used by the Ngbaka to call upon the *mimbo* in forest camps. The name of the instrument is likely Batwa in origin because it is found among other Aka-speaking populations in the Mongoumba region and south of the Lobaye. Thomas shows that the Ngbaka borrowed the word for the bow along with the object, for they refer to it both as *mbela* and *ngangangongo,* the latter being an onomatopoeic term unique to them alone.[66] Furthermore, although the Ngbaka state that they received the *mbela* from the Batwa, they concurrently insist that no living Ngbaka has ever seen it played by neighboring Aka. A number of informants interviewed by Arom and Thomas even suggested that the Aka have entirely ceased to play the *mbela* because seven members of their community were killed after a *mbela* was accidentally broken. This latter assertion is not true, however, because the Aka do play the *mbela,* albeit in the privacy of their own camps. As the authors have noted, however, the Ngbaka version of this story is important in that it illustrates just how distant modern-day relations between the Ngbaka and Aka have become.[67]

Finally, if we view the veneration of *mimbo/mbimbo* as an originally Aka rite, it becomes apparent that the Ngbaka appropriated this set of religious beliefs in much the same way as the veneration of *Ezengi,* that is, by reinterpreting it to fit their own religious and economic needs. Although in modern-day religious practice the Aka do pay homage to ancestors, it is clear the veneration of *Ezengi* and the *mbimbo* spirits is focused on regulating individual transgressions against the group. Likewise, their rituals do not reflect a desire to regulate or control their neighbors in any way. As Thomas has noted, Aka religious practices are carried out as if the Ngbaka, as well as the goods they provided, were unessential to the well-being of Aka.[68] The Ngbaka-Ma'bo, however, have reinterpreted these rituals in a manner that allows them to focus specifically on individual achievement and supernatural control. Their religious worldview mandates that they appease the ancestors of the land—even if they are not their own. At the same time, they have transformed what was probably a set of ritual techniques learned in communal hunting expeditions into a religious cult that aids each individual in his success at the trap. Accordingly, those elements of the original *mbimbo* cult that dealt with group dynamics were simply left aside because the Ngbaka pray to their own ancestors (the *kulu-se*) to ensure group prosperity and accord.

Once we understand the different standpoints each society takes toward the different categories of spirits, it appears less likely that *mimbo* rites are a remembrance of interactions with the Baka of southeastern Cameroon. Instead, I suggest that they are likely to be the result of Ngbaka-Ma'bo interactions with ancestors of the Aka peoples who live in the region today. Although it is impossible to discern their precise origins in either agriculturalist or forest-specialist communities, the variant *mimbo/mbimbo* rituals make evident that a very deep interpenetration of cultures took place at some point in the past.

It is also possible that the Ngbaka-Ma'bo adopted *mimbo* rituals under the influence of neighboring Bantu groups, for, as chapter 5 illustrates, notions of dwarf-like benevolent forest spirits are widespread in the cosmological systems of west-central African peoples. Finally, the Ngbaka and Aka *mimbo/mbimbo* rituals illustrate the way that Batwa and Bantu societies can share institutions, yet simultaneously interpret them according to their own social, economic, and religious needs. Among the Aka, the *Ezengi* and *mbimbo* rituals are primarily focused on maintaining the stability and cohesion of their social groups. Even when rituals are geared toward protection of the individual (i.e., the *mbimbo*), the Aka interpret their role as monitors of individual behavior vis-à-vis the group. The Ngbaka-Ma'bo, on the other hand, practice both *mbimbo* and *Ezengi* rituals to fulfill the Niger-Congo religious mandate—gaining access to the territorial and ancestral spirits of the land. Because the control of these spirits is integral to their prosperity, the Ngbaka remain willing to enter into relations of religious subservience with peoples they portray as savage and uncivilized today. The veneration of *mimbo* spirits—as well as the manner in which these rituals are practiced without any participation of neighboring Aka—illustrates how autochthonous rituals can be deracinated from their cultural context in an attempt to establish hegemony over first-comers. As an extreme example of the deculturalizing process, it can be seen as a Ngbaka attempt to establish new notions of authority and politico-religious precedence in a land acknowledged to be not their own.

Although the deculturalization of Aka societies has played an integral role in Ngbaka-Ma'bo peoples' attempts to shift the cognitive meaning of precedence, it is not the only method they have employed. They have also relied on a redefinition of territory, today encoded in dichotomized conceptualizations of the forest and the village. Drawing once again on notions of the unordered and precivilized, the Ngbaka-Ma'bo view the forest as both a mystical and savage domain, an environment that houses a plethora of spirits largely out of their control. Integral to this imagery is the notion of the Batwa as uncivilized and semi-human, an idea reflected in oral traditions associating the Batwa with chimpanzees. Villages and hunting camps, on the other hand, are considered as superior and distinctly human cultural spaces. Thus, the Ngbaka-Ma'bo do not consider themselves to be forest dwellers, despite the fact that settlements are located within the forest and the greater part of their foodstuffs are obtained therein. This same type of environmental dichotomy, or division of the world, is found widely across the equatorial region. As Grinker has pointed out, it serves in every instance as "one of the most significant and basic markers of ethnic distinction" between Bantu and Batwa.[69]

Because of perceived similarities with the role of the Pygmy in our own racial and evolutionary paradigms, Western scholars have focused primarily on the denigratory aspects of this dichotomization, especially those that attribute a semi-human status to the Batwa.[70] As a result, the political and historical importance of this dichotomization is overlooked. Considered in terms of first-comer/late-comer relations, the establishment of a village/forest dichotomy might be seen as an integral step in the evolution of agriculturalist political institutions—one that was largely accommodationist in intent. By dividing the world in such a manner, late-comers are provided with a distinct space—both physically and conceptually—in which they can openly assert their hegemonic desires. At the same time, this dichotomy allows them to respectfully acknowledge the first-comer status of Batwa communities, albeit as masters of the forest environment alone. When viewed in this light, the dichotomization of forest and village can be seen as a division of religious/political responsibilities. Because this phenomenon is so widespread in the rainforest, I suggest that it constitutes a key element of the political charter applied as agriculturalists established political hegemony in the rainforest region. We return to this issue in chapter 5, where I argue that this new political charter was developed after the introduction of bananas and iron.

As Kopytoff's frontier thesis predicts, the establishment of agriculturalist hegemony is remembered in oral traditions as a distinct turning point when a new political order was set in place. This can be seen in versions recounted by both the Aka and their fishing neighbors, the Monzombo, Bantu-speaking fishing peoples that live along the Ubangi. According to versions collected by Bahuchet during the 1970s, the ancestors of the Aka originally invited Monzombo immigrants to live among them. Living together along the banks of the Ubangi River, it was during this period that the Aka taught the Monzombo how to use fire, cultivate plants, and forge iron. One day, however, upon returning from a lengthy hunting expedition in the forest, the Aka found that both the village and the forge had been taken over by the immigrants. The Aka were subsequently chased into the forest, and from this day forward divisions of culture, labor, and society were made complete. Similar traditions are found among Aka speakers located in the Likouala region to the south (Congo Republic); according to Hauser, who collected this tradition during the 1940s, the Babinga lost their former power and status after Bantu communities stole their ironworking tools. This occurred on a day when Babinga women delayed their husbands in the forest by searching too long for honey.[712]

These traditions provide archetypal examples of the narrative that Kopytoff identified as common to peoples subjected by late-comer rule, a history of interactions between an originally meek (or in this case uncultured) immigrant community that was unable to use fire, grow food, or produce iron. After a period of peaceful coexistence and tutelage however, the immigrants' true ambitions begin to show through, and they eventually assert authority over the society that both communities had helped to create. For the Aka who tell this story, this moment is seen as a clear rupture with the past, an era when their rights as members of the common society were reduced. This tradition also provides an example of a theme that is very widespread among peoples of the western equatorial rainforest—that Batwa societies were the first to produce or introduce iron. As illustrated in chapter 4, a number of oral traditions from the region indicate that it was the appropriation of this skill that led to societal ruptures between the Bantu and Batwa.

SUMMING UP

The primary goal of this chapter has been to illustrate that numerous elements of Kopytoff's frontier thesis are applicable to the history of relations between Bantu and Batwa. Working from his theories and ethnographic data related to the Ngbaka-Ma'bo and Aka, I have built a model of first-comer/late-comer relations in equatorial Africa, as well as hypotheses about the nature of relations between autochthons and Bantu immigrants during the initial stages of contact.[72]

The first-comer model is especially useful in that it provides an alternative to the evolutionary models and does not assume any kind of Bantu superiority from the start. It does, however, assert that first-comers are likely to have been considered experts regarding the flora, fauna, and territorial/ancestral spirits of the land. Accordingly, the model asserts that the ability to establish and maintain contacts with autochthons was one of the most important tasks required of early Bantu leaders; it was only through such contacts that local spirits could be appeased and the survival of the community ensured.

The Ngbaka-Ma'bo data have also provided an example of how immigrants might have categorized autochthonous peoples in earlier times: distant and dangerous, nearby and friendly, or individual integrated protectors whose religious knowledge helped assure the prosperity of individuals and the group. Those who served in the latter capacity may have held esteemed positions in early settlements, thereby being associated with the status accorded lineage heads. If such was the case, a dualistic system of politico-religious authority may have come to exist, with Bantu leaders focusing their religious efforts on appeasing the ancestral spirits of the lineage, while the task of supplicating local spirits (both ancestral and territorial) may have been the responsibility of autochthons alone.

Ethnographic data related to *mimbo* rituals confirm, however, that the leaders of immigrant societies eventually seek to assume control over religious practices dedicated to local territorial/ancestral spirits. Although this can be seen as an attempt to establish politico-religious hegemony over autochthonous societies, the successful completion of this task ultimately depends on economic independence as well as prosperity. In the case of the Ngbaka-Ma'bo such independence/prosperity has not yet been achieved. As a result, Ngbaka-Ma'bo hegemonic efforts remain focused on the control of lineage alliances and partnerships with various Aka communities, and they continue to seek entry into Aka rituals (i.e., *Ezengi* initiations) to influence the spirits of the land.

Finally, this chapter has provided readers with an initial exposure to a number of beliefs regarding the Batwa that are found widely in west-central Africa. As later chapters show, modern-day forest specialists are in many locations associated with dwarf-like spirits that reside in termite hills and the forest, aid agriculturalists in achieving prosperity and success, and roam the earth with the spirits of those who died a premature death. The widespread appearance of such notions suggests that we are dealing with an ancestral set of cosmological beliefs. The origins of this cosmology, as well as the oral traditions, rituals, and political charters it has engendered, are discussed chapter 5. Before approaching that topic, however, we must explore the social, economic, and political transformations that took place in central Africa as a result of the introduction of bananas and iron.

NOTES

1. Igor Kopytoff, "The Internal African Frontier: The Making of African Political Culture," in *The African Frontier: The Reproduction of Traditional African Societies* (Bloomington and Indianapolis: Indiana University Press, 1987), 52–54.

2. The Batwa participate in these activities in both centralized and noncentralized societies. Examples provided following include the Kingdom of Kongo, the Bolia and Ekonda of the central Congo basin, and the Ngbaka-Ma'bo societies of southern Central African Republic. These cases are documented in chapters 5 and 6.

3. See, for example, J. Vansina, *Paths in the Rainforest: Towards a History of Political Tradition in Equatorial Africa* (Madison, Wisconsin: University of Wisconsin Press), 56–57; and Eugenia Herbert, *Iron, Gender and Power: Rituals of Transformation in African Societies* (Bloomington: Indiana University Press, 1993), 137.

4. J. M. C. Thomas was the first to articulate this notion and document it with exacting studies of Aka phonologies, morphologies, syntax, and grammar. See, for example,

"Emprunte ou parenté? À propos des parlers des populations forestières de Centrafrique," 153 (1979). In more recent works, Bahuchet has suggested in *Pygmées de Centrafrique: Études ethnologiques, historiques, et linguistiques sur les Pygmées "Ba.Mbenga" (Aka/Baka) du Nord-Ouest du bassin Congolais,* ed. S. Bahuchet (Paris: SELAF, 1979), 153 that such transferals took place in a context of daily contact and bilingualism, a phenomenon that involved both children and adults alike. He argues that the children of both communities would have played together, because the complete disappearance of languages is only made possible when youth begin to speak only one language and bilingual elders pass away. See S. Bahuchet, *La rencontre des agriculteurs: Les Pygmées parmi les peuples d'Afrique Centrale* (Paris: Peeters, 1993), 17.

5. This tendency, of course, is not unique to Africa alone, but can be found in global societies as diverse as Polynesia and ancient Ireland.

6. Cymone Fourshey, "Agriculture, Ecology, Kinship, and Gender: A Socio-Economic History of Southwestern Tanzania, 500 B.C. to 1900 A.D. (Ph. D. diss., University of California, Los Angeles, 2002); for attestations of *-cúká,* see Table 5.1, 191; for discussion of meanings, see 189–191.

7. The term *-cúká* is found in Bobangi (C-32), Mpama (C30), Lingala (C36d), Libinza (C31), Mbole (D-11), Tetela (C71), Ngombe (C-41), Eso (C53), Bushong (C83), and Lega (D25). These attestations are provided by Vansina, *Paths,* 269. Attestations of *-cúká* also appear in a number of D-group languages (Mbole [D11], Lega [D25], and perhaps Kumu [D20]), all of which, according to the classification in this work, are descended from the proto-Nyong-Lomami speech community. As a result, one might conclude that *-cúká* is reconstructible to the proto-Nyong-Lomami stage. However, it seems more likely that *-cúká* spread to these few D-group languages as a result of societal contacts, because they are located on the peripheries of the Congo basin, where *-cúká* is widespread. Reconstructing *-cúká* to the proto-Sangha-Kwa period would also help explain why no attestations of the term are found among the A-group of languages (also descended from proto-Nyong-Lomami) of southern Cameroon.

8. Vansina, *Paths,* 269.

9. Ibid., 120.

10. E. Sulzmann, "Batwa und Baoto: die Symbiose von Wildbeutern und Pflanzern bei den Ekonda und Bolia (Zaire)," *SUGIA* 7, no. 1 (1987): 369–89; translated into French as "Batwa et Baoto: Symbiose chasseurs-ceuillers et planteurs chez les Ekonda et les Bolia (Zaire, region de l'Equateur et de Bandundu)," *Revue d'Ethnolinguistique (cahiers du LACITO)* 4 (1989), 39–57; cited in Bahuchet, *La rencontre,* 63.

11. This discussion draws from and builds upon Ehret's argument for the original meaning of *-gandá* in Christopher Ehret, *An African Classical Age: Eastern and Southern Africa in World History, 1000 B.C. to A.D. 400,* (Charlottesville, Virginia: University Press of Virginia, 1988), 151–55.

12. Presented here is a full listing of the distribution and associated meanings of *-gandá.* Readers may refer to this for the discussion that follows: *-gandá* is attested as "house" in Bongili (C15), Kikuyu (E 51), Rundi (D 62), Ruguru (G35), Bemba (M42), Ila (M63), and Nsenga (N41); "camp" in Bobangi (C32), Mboshi (C25), Koyo (C24), Leka (C30), Ekonda, Ntomba (C35), Lia , Mongo (C60), Lwankamba, and Lalia (C62); "quarter of a village" in Tio (B75); "surrounding of a village" in Angba (C45); "chief's enclosure" in Lwena (K14), Tetela (C71), Woyo, W. Kongo (H16d), and Lunda (L52); "village" in Iyaa (B73c), Yombe (H16c), Mbala (H41), Bushoong (C83), Bwendi (H16e), Lwena (K14), and Herero (R31); "kingroup/village" in Aka (C-18), Poto (C36a), and Ngombe

(C-41); "clan" in Tio (B75), E. Kongo (H16d), Herero (R31), Ganda (E15), Rundi (D62), Nyoro (E11), Nyankore (E13), Sukuma (F21), and Zulu (as "progeny," S42); "matriclan" in Mboshi (C25), Kongo (H16), Mbala (H41), and Tsong; and finally "patrilineage" in Kako (A93), Nyanga (D43), and Tembo (D53). These attestations are provided by Vansina in *Paths,* 269, and Guthrie, *Comparative Bantu,* 4 vols. (Farnham, England: Gregg Press, 1967–71), 207.

13. Ehret, *An African Classical Age,* 153.
14. For a detailed explanation of the "House," see Vansina, *Paths,* 75.
15. Ibid., 104–14.
16. Kopytoff, "The Internal African Frontier," 43–44.
17. Christopher Ehret, *The Civilizations of Africa: A History to 1800* (Charlottesville, Virginia: University of Virginia Press, 2002), 50.
18. This conceptualization of Bantu religious beliefs is outlined in Theo Schadeberg's article "Batwa: The Bantu Name for the Invisible People," in *Challenging Elusiveness: Central African Hunter-Gatherers in a Multidisciplinary Perspective,* ed. K. Beisbrouck, S. Elders, and G. Rossel (Leiden: CNWS, 1999), 21–39. There he provides a hypothesis as to why Fipa agriculturalists would attribute the founding of their kingdom to ancestral Batwa. As he states, "When a farming community establishes itself in a country which hitherto had been inhabited by hunters and gatherers, they have a problem: How can they reach the ancestors of the former inhabitants and get their blessings. The only way to do so is to form an alliance between their chief and the original population" (p. 30). I have sought to elaborate on this core idea by developing the first-comer model as it pertains to rainforest Batwa.
19. Ehret, *The Civilizations of Africa,* 50.
20. Kopytoff, "The Internal African Frontier," 55.
21. Ehret, *An African Classical Age,* 147.
22. C. Wrigley, "Review Article: The Long Durée in the Heart of Darkness," *Journal of African History* 33 (1992): 132.
23. Ehret's interpretation of the semantic evidence attached to *-kùmu* differs from that of Vansina, who reconstructs it as "leader, big man" during the proto-Bantu stage. See Vansina, *Paths,* 274.
24. As Guyer and Belinga have noted, this approaches Vansina's views of political development in equatorial Africa. It is ultimately rooted in Meillasoux's notions of accumulative processes. Jane I. Guyer and Samuel M. Eno Belinga, "Wealth in People as Wealth in Knowledge: Accumulation and Composition in Equatorial Africa, *Journal of African History* 36 (1995): 94, 106.
25. Ibid., 106.
26. Ibid., 118.
27. Ibid., 109.
28. Ibid., 113.
29. Kopytoff, "The Internal African Frontier," 47.
30. Here I transpose Kopytoff's theory slightly. Because he focuses on the formation of centralized polities, he suggests that locals had to be integrated into chiefly or kingly ritual. As we will see, however, in the noncentralized societies of the equatorial rainforest, Batwa peoples were integrated into numerous types of rituals, not only those related to authority figures.
31. Kopytoff, "The Internal African Frontier," 57.
32. Ibid., 56.

33. Ibid., 55.

34. Ibid., 50.

35. Bahuchet includes the Bambenjele, Bambenga, Mikaya, and Baluma, along with Aka proper, and therefore considers Aka speakers to inhabit a region of more than 100,000 km².

36. Because the Ngbaka-Ma'bo's semi-nomadic lifestyle is highly dependent on the cultivation of the banana (which requires little maintenance), the model may appear more pertinent to historical eras during and after the last half of the last millennium B.C.E., when the banana was introduced into the western equatorial rainforest. However, we assert that the semi-sedentary lifestyle was probably practiced during the earliest "rudimentary" stages of farming in the rainforest as well. For archaeology attesting the early presence of the banana, see Christophe M. Mbida, "L'emergence de communautés villageoises au Cameroon méridional: Étude archéologique des sites de Nkang et de Ndindan" (Ph.D. thesis, Université Libre de Bruxelles, Belgium, 1995–96). This work provides phytolithic evidence of banana (*Musa* spp.) cultivation c. 840–730 B.C.E. at the Nkang village site in southern Cameroon (p. 637).

37. Bahuchet, *La rencontre*, 32.

38. Simha Arom and J. M. C. Thomas, *Les Mimbo: Génies du piégage et le monde surnaturel des Ngbaka-Ma'bo (Republique Centrafricaine)* (Paris: Peeters/SELAF, 1974), 18–19.

39. Bahuchet, *La rencontre,* 28.

40. J. M. C. Thomas, "Relations sociales et projections ideologiques: Exemple des Ngbaka-Ma'bo et des Pygmées Aka d'Afrique Centrale, *Cahiers du LACITO* 2 (1987): 16.

41. The following descriptions of the *beka, Bambenga* (Aka clients), and Aka "cadets" are derived from Arom and Thomas, *Les Mimbo,* 42–46, and Thomas, "Relations sociales," 19.

42. Arom and Thomas, *Les Mimbo,* 46 (translated from French by the author).

43. Bahuchet, *La rencontre,* 34–35.

44. Arom and Thomas, *Les Mimbo,* 45.

45. Thomas, "Relations sociales," 19 (translated from French by the author).

46. As Arom and Thomas have pointed out, the nature of relationships between the Aka and their agriculturalist or fishing neighbors varies from place to place. Those of the Ngbaka-Ma'bo and Ngandu with their Aka are described as relatively egalitarian, because disdain for the Aka is not extremely severe and economic relations are based on simple relations of exchange. Among the Monzombo and Mbati, however, more exploitative interactions prevail, forcing the Aka into situations of economic dependence in which they are treated with contempt and disdain (e.g., the Mbati refer to their Aka clients as *mòɲà,* or "slaves"). Although variations in the nature of relationships probably existed in the past, Thomas suggests that the advent of colonialism permanently altered any "relationships of equality" that might have prevailed, because colonial administrations and economies created new conceptualizations of ownership that work to the disadvantage of the Aka (Arom and Thomas, *Les Mimbo,* 46, footnote 42). The nature of these transformations are addressed in the final chapter of this book.

47. Bahuchet, *La rencontre,* 34.

48. Serge Bahuchet and Henri Guillaume, "Relations entre chasseurs-collecteurs Pygmées et agriculteurs de la forêt du Nord-Ouest du Bassin Congolais," in *Pygmées de Centrafrique: Études ethnologiques, historiques, linguistiques, sur les Pygmées "BaMbenga" (Aka/Baka) du Nord-Ouest du Bassin Congolais* (Paris: SELAF, 1979), 116.

49. Arom and Thomas, *Les Mimbo,* 43–44.

50. Thomas, "Relations sociales," 21.

51. Ibid. *Ezengi* and *Ziakpokpo* are believed to provide supernatural powers that allow them to become invisible or to metamorphose into an animal when danger is near.

52. J. M. C. Thomas, "Organisation sociale," in *Encyclopédie des Pygmées Aka: La Société,* ed. J. M. C. Thomas and S. Bahuchet (Paris: SELAF, 1991), 37.

53. Bahuchet, *La rencontre,* 57–58.

54. Ibid., 58.

55. Bahuchet cites as an example the Kaka and Pomo peoples' relations with the Bambenjele in the Sangha region of the Congo Republic, and the Bangango (Ubangian), Mboman (Bantu A-80), and Konabem (Bantu A-80) peoples' relations with the Baka in the eastern regions of Cameroon. Bahuchet, *La rencontre,* 28.

56. Arom and Thomas, *Les Mimbo,* 26–29.

57. Ehret, *The Civilizations of Africa,* 50.

58. Thomas, "Relations sociales," 17.

59. The following description of *mimbo* spirits and rituals is drawn from Arom and Thomas, *Les Mimbos,* 48–64.

60. Arom and Thomas, *Les Mimbo,* 95–96.

61. Kopytoff, "The Internal African Frontier," 57.

62. Thomas, "Relations sociales, 15–30, as cited and translated from Bahuchet, *La rencontre,* 60.

63. Bahuchet, *La rencontre,* 60.

64. Ibid.

65. Thomas, "Relations sociales," 28.

66. Arom and Thomas, *Les Mimbo,* 78.

67. Ibid., 85. Although not directly mentioned, it seems that Thomas is referring to the development of colonial and postcolonial economies that she previously mentioned as working to the disadvantage of Batwa societies.

68. Thomas, "Relations sociales," 26.

69. Roy Richard Grinker, *Houses in the Rainforest: Ethnicity and Inequality among Farmers and Foragers in Central Africa* (Berkeley: University of California Press, 1994), 77.

70. Recent work by the anthropologist Jerome Lewis has shown that the Bambenjele, forest specialists of the northern Congo Republic, describe their agriculturalists neighbors as "gorillas," because they are both "large animals" with lots of meat/wealth, are especially "fierce and dangerous to hunt," and are "preoccupied with demarcating and aggressively claiming areas of forest as their own, to the exclusion of all others." This insight shows the importance of identifying the cultural idioms of both forest specialists and agriculturalists before assuming the latter work from the same evolutionist paradigms that Westerners do. J. Lewis, "Forest Hunter-Gatherers and Their World: A Study of the Mbenjele Yaka Pygmies of Congo-Brazzaille and Their Secular and Religious Activities and Representations" (Ph.D. thesis, London School of Economics and Political Science, 2002), 210.

71. A. Hauser, "Les Babinga," *Zaire* (Brussels) 7, no. 2 (1953): 163.

72. It must be remembered that there are no archeological, linguistic, or biological data that can definitively link modern-day Batwa societies to the Late Stone Age inhabitants of central Africa. As a result, the theories put forth regarding ancient autochthons and immi-

grants should not necessarily be seen as interactions between peoples of a different physical type. Although short-statured forest specialists are considered to be the "original owners of the rainforest" today, the theories put forth in this chapter apply to all populations the Bantu found upon their arrival in the rainforest regions—be they fishing peoples or hunter-gatherers, short in stature or tall.

4

NEW ECONOMIES, NEW COMMUNITIES: THE IMPACT OF BANANAS AND IRON

The previous chapters proposed a history of interactions for Bantu and Batwa societies before the introduction of bananas and iron. They used archaeological evidence to argue that the subsistence practices and technologies of the two types of communities were in many ways similar, with hunting and gathering supplying the majority of food. I have also argued that Bantu leaders consciously sought to integrate autochthonous peoples into their settlements during these early periods. In the initial stages of frontier settlement, the integration of local populations would have aided late-comers in gaining knowledge about local resources and the geography of the land. As the centuries passed, however, these types of interactions were primarily guided by religious concerns. The politico-religious beliefs of Bantu peoples required that they honor the ancestors of peoples deemed first-comers because it was they who influenced the fertility and fecundity of both people and land. As a result, Bantu leaders encouraged alliance and intermarriage with the Batwa, and strove to increase their own politico-religious prestige by entering into and adopting ritual practices unique to the Batwa.

This chapter employs linguistic and archaeological evidence to document the drastic transformations that occurred in central Africans' lifestyles after the introduction of both bananas and iron. It illustrates how economic and technological practices began to diverge, with Bantu populations beginning to focus on agriculture and iron production as sources of subsistence and wealth. Linguistic evidence is used to argue that numerous Batwa societies began to lessen their contacts with agriculturalists during this period, developing a unique economic niche as specialist procurers of forest products that could be entered into burgeoning systems of regional trade. It was during the Late

Stone to Metal Age (c. 1500–500 B.C.E.) that this differentiating process began, and during the Early Iron Age (c. 500 B.C.E.–1000 C.E.) that economic and ethnic distinctions between the two types of societies became complete. As shown following, the introduction of bananas and iron led to demographic growth and increased wealth among Bantu agriculturalists. This change, in turn, allowed them to predominate over autochthons in new social, political, and religious ways. This chapter focuses on the economic aspects of this transitional era, whereas chapter 5 details the political and religious transformations that altered former patterns of interactions between Bantu and Batwa.

BANANAS AND PLANTAINS IN WEST-CENTRAL AFRICA

Although Westerners are accustomed to conceptualizing the introduction of iron as a revolutionary event, it is much harder to imagine how the banana could have engendered a drastic transformation in central Africans' lifestyles. Vansina has provided the most apt explanation of this phenomenon:

> The yield of bananas exceeds that of yams by a factor of ten, and is equaled only by the yield of manioc. Unlike yams or oil palms, bananas are ideally adapted to evergreen rainforests. Unlike yams, the absence of a dry season does not hurt them. One needs to clear only about two-thirds of the trees on the field, rather than clear it completely as is necessary for yams. That produces a microenvironment freer of *Anopheles* and hence of malaria, helps the forest to regenerate faster on the fallow field, and saves labor. Compared with yams, the crop requires less care after planting and its preparation for food saves much time. It was the ideal staple crop for agriculture in the rainforests, and it allowed farmers to colonize all of its habitats everywhere.[1]

Thus, the introduction of bananas not only benefited Bantu agriculturalists in terms of food output, but it also reduced the amount of labor required throughout the planting cycle. By generating an agricultural surplus, reducing labor, and creating healthier, mosquito-free environments, the banana allowed for substantial demographic increases among agriculturalist populations; indeed, it is generally believed that high population densities were impossible to achieve in the rainforest before the banana arrived.[2] Herein lies the revolutionary nature of the banana in central Africa; by allowing for substantial economic and demographic advances, agriculturalist populations were able to develop much more complex sociopolitical networks and regional systems of trade.

Despite their widespread usage in Africa, bananas are not indigenous to the continent. Botanical studies indicate that they were originally domesticated in southeast Asia. Wild species, which are characterized by little pulp and a large number of seeds, are found across a region that stretches from Papua New

Guinea to India.[3] Edible bananas, on the other hand, are characterized by plentiful pulp and a lack of seeds, and are found all over the world. Their presence outside of Asia must be explained by human intervention because seedless varieties can only be spread through the transplanting of rhizomes—the small shoots or suckers that emerge at the foot of mature plants. The exact point of entry onto the African continent remains a historical enigma, although Egypt, Ethiopia, the southern Somali/Kenya coast, and Madagascar have been proposed.[4]

The edible varieties of bananas are believed to be derived from two wild species—*Musa acuminata* (AA) and *Musa balbisiana* (BB).[5] Both of these are diploid, that is, contain two sets of chromosomes. As humans domesticated and transplanted these varieties, triploidy and hybridization took place. These processes are attested by the cultivar groups that exist today, referred to as the AA, AAA, AB, AAB, and ABB species. Only the AAA and AAB *Musa* spp. are found in Africa, and each has its own subset of cultivars.[6] The AAB cultivars of *Musa* spp. are commonly referred to as plantains. Although they comprise less than 1 percent of the banana population in the eastern regions of Africa, plantains predominate in the rainforest regions of central Africa. They are roasted, boiled, baked, or pounded, providing a starchy staple to be eaten with meat and vegetable stews. Their genetic variation in central Africa is unique to the world; more than 120 different cultivars have been identified. This is more than 10 times the amount of cultivars found in Asia—an excellent testimony to the agricultural skills and innovative capabilities of ancient rainforest inhabitants.[7]

Ecological, cultural, and demographic factors can all contribute to the development of species diversity. However, the large number of central African plantain varieties is generally considered to be the result of a long history of cultivation characterized by a large number of trees and a great deal of human selection.[8] Using estimations of in vitro mutation rates, de Langhe and his colleagues hypothesized that it would take approximately sixteen hundred to two thousand years to produce 120 cultivars.[9] Their estimates appear to be supported by the recent discovery of *Musa* spp. phytoliths (cellular silica bodies) at the archaeological site of Nkang (southern Cameroon). Extracted from a carbon deposit on pottery found in a refuse pit, these phytoliths were associated with levels dated between 840 and 370 B.C.E.[10] In terms of the history of bananas in Africa, this is a groundbreaking discovery. It provides the first and earliest evidence of banana cultivation in Africa, linking it to a time period much earlier than scholars have previously supposed.[11] Furthermore, if the earlier end of this dating range is reflective of historical reality, the data from Nkang serve as the earliest evidence of any domesticated food plant—and thus a truly agricultural lifestyle—within the rainforest. Until now, such evidence has only been available for the last few centuries of the last millennium B.C.E.[12]

Although it is difficult to determine exactly where and when *Musa* spp. originally entered Africa, distributional analyses of species types suggest that plantains (*Musa* spp. AAB) arrived first, and other types of bananas were introduced onto the continent in successive waves.[13] Similar analyses, based on botanical, linguistic, and ethnographic alike, have allowed for the development of hypotheses regarding the diffusion of plantains into central Africa as well. The most comprehensive is that of Gerda Rossel, whose conclusions I synthesize here.

The most widespread generic name for plantain in Africa is *-konde*.[14] It is found in nearly all of the languages of the western equatorial rainforest, and is used in reference to different banana species in other regions of sub-Saharan Africa as well. Rossel argues that this term is reconstructible to the proto-Bantu language, but that it was originally used in reference to the soft bast or bark of certain plants, trees, and shrubs.[15] Combining this information with an extensive ethnographic record attesting the utilitarian, medicinal, and ritual use of banana plants, she hypothesizes that Bantu speakers originally adopted *Musa* spp. as a useful nonfood plant. This introduction most likely took place in the northeastern reaches of the equatorial rainforest, because this is the only area of the Bantu-speaking world where *-konde* continues to be used in reference to the stems of *Musa* spp. alone.[16]

From the northeastern regions, plantains spread across the northern rainforest edge, into the central and coastal regions of southern Cameroon, down the Congo River, and along a number of its western tributaries. There are two regions where the initial diffusion of the plantain seems to have been impeded: the Bateke plateau and the Mayombe mountain range.[17] Rossel suggests environmental conditions as the cause of this phenomenon because neither location receives enough rain to provide the humid climate best suited for plantain cultivation. It is also possible, however, that Bantu agriculturalists had not yet settled in these regions during the first half of the last millennium B.C.E.[18] Because the standard *-konde* form is found in languages spoken in the central and coastal regions of Gabon (Itsogho, Himba, Punu, Mpongwe, etc.), and the lower reaches of the Congo River (western and central Kongo), it is likely that the plantain spread in a southward direction through the forests of Gabon.[19] Interestingly, each of the paths of diffusion Rossel has proposed parallels those used by Bantu settlers upon their initial entry into the equatorial rainforest.

Although the phytolith evidence from Nkang attests that *Musa* spp. was being cultivated in southern Cameroon by the middle of the last millennium B.C.E., there is as yet no information as to the era when bananas were initially introduced. Until this discovery, scholars generally assumed that the diffusion began in the first few centuries C.E. through trading contacts with Arabs and Persians along the coast. As a result, the dramatic changes in the archaeological record of the last millennium B.C.E. have generally been attributed to the arrival of Bantu-speaking populations and/or the introduction of iron. The data from Nkang now allow us to propose another scenario, one that sees bananas and plantains as crucial to the early spread of iron. By reducing the amount of labor required for day-to-day sustenance, the cultivation of bananas was likely to have provided central Africans with their first opportunity to undertake specialized, more labor-intensive tasks, key among them the mining, smelting, and forging of iron.

THE INTRODUCTION OF IRON

Unlike other regions of the Old World, sub-Saharan Africa did not have a unique Bronze Age or Copper Age that preceded the introduction of iron. Bronze was produced only in Egyptian and other north-African societies, and archaeological evidence indicates that the working of copper south of the Sahara began at the same time or slightly later than the introduction of iron.[20] Sub-Saharan Africa is also unique in that stone-tool use often continued after the introduction of iron; one instance is found along the middle Ogooué River in Gabon, where the coexistence of stone and iron-using societies is documented for periods of at least three hundred years.[21] This phenomenon might be explained by the fact that the earliest iron objects may have been small prestige items or currencies rather than implements for use in daily tasks. Once central Africans began to produce and use iron tools, however, the efficacy of their subsistence strategies was amplified; the clearing of forests, the cultivation of plants, the harvesting of crops, the hunting and slaughtering of animals—all could be carried out more effectively by people who used iron.[22]

In sub-Saharan Africa, the earliest archaeological evidence for ironworking has been found at Taruga in northwestern Nigeria and in the African Great Lakes region (Rwanda and Burundi) (see Map 4.1). Radiocarbon dates from furnaces uncovered at Taruga cluster between 850 and 400 B.C.E., leading archaeologists to suggest a commencement of ironworking by at least the sixth century B.C.E.[23] The evidence from the Great Lakes region is not quite as definitive. Although radiocarbon dates from sites located in Rwanda and Burundi tend to cluster in the last seven centuries B.C.E., there are outlier dates from Burundi that suggest ironworking began two to five centuries earlier.[24] Such data have led some scholars to suggest an independent invention of ironworking in sub-Saharan Africa.[25] More pertinent to our analysis, however, is the fact that both Nigeria and the Great Lakes have been put forth as the source of ironworking knowledge that entered the western equatorial regions a few centuries later.

At present the earliest evidence of ironworking in west central Africa is found along the middle reaches of the Ogooué River, deep in the rainforests of central Gabon. Excavations on the Otoumbi massif (Otoumbi 2, located at the confluence of the Ogooué and Okano Rivers) and the Lopé Reserve (Lope

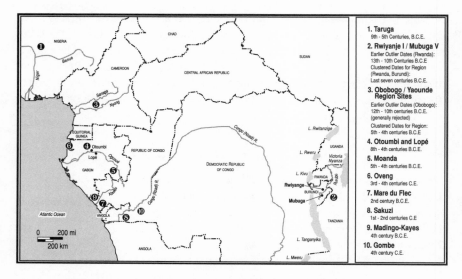

Map 4.1. Early Ironworking Sites in West and Central Africa

5, 60 km upriver) have provided evidence of ironworking between the ninth and fifth centuries B.C.E., although widespread evidence of smelting does not appear throughout the region until the last few centuries B.C.E.[26] A series of four anomalously early dates associated with furnaces at Obobogo (southern Cameroon) might suggest an even earlier introduction to the north (seventeenth to tenth century B.C.E.[27]), although radiocarbon dates from this and other sites in the Yaoundé Region (Ndindan, Nkoumeto, Okogo, and Okiga) tend to cluster between the fifth and fourth centuries B.C.E.[28]

Peoples living on the coast and its hinterlands appear to have been the last to adopt iron-production techniques. Although small iron fragments were found at Tchissanga in the coastal regions of the Congo Republic, the earliest evidence for production in this region is dated to the first few centuries C.E. (Madingo-Kayes).[29] Excavations carried out in the Gabon Estuary (Oveng), the Mayombe mountain range (Mare du Flec), and along the lower reaches of the Congo River (Kay Ladio, Bas Zaire; Gombe, near Kinshasa) attest later dates as well; ironworking appeared in these regions between roughly 200 B.C.E. and 400 C.E.[30]

Although archaeological data can provide chronologies for the appearance and locations of iron production, the data provide no information regarding its origin and initial paths of diffusion. For this history, we can turn to linguistic methods and data, combining hypotheses recently put forth by Christopher Ehret with data from languages spoken in the interior regions of Congo Republic and Gabon.[31]

Ehret argues that the first appearance of iron among Bantu speakers took place in the Great Lakes region, where proto-Eastern Bantu speech communities learned of iron and ironworking from Sudanic-speaking peoples.[32] From there, knowledge of iron and ironworking spread in two directions. One was westward across the northern equatorial rainforest, extending to the Atlantic coast of Cameroon and also descending down the middle reaches of the Congo River. The other spread was southward, into the more southerly proto-Eastern Bantu societies. During the latter half of the first millennium B.C.E., knowledge of iron and ironworking spread into the lower Zambezi through the movement of Bantu-speaking peoples, as well as across the southern savanna zones. This latter extension took place along three distinct paths: (1) from the Lake Tanganyika region to the early Luban peoples (southeastern Democratic Republic of Congo) and southwestward into Zambia, (2) from the lower Zambezi basin through Zambia to the Atlantic coast and northwestward to the lower Congo River, and (3) west along the northern fringe of the Kalahari.

Understanding these patterns of diffusion help us to reconstruct both Bantu and Batwa histories because both the northern and southern routes of introduction are associated with particular sets of words. By identifying which words that specific speech communities employed, information is provided as to where their original knowledge of iron and/or ironworking came from. The terms associated with the northern route of introduction are *-gèla/yeli*, "iron," *-gùbà*, "smithy/blacksmith," *-túl-*, "to forge," *-pàgá/*-bàká*, "knife," and *-kúngù/gúngù*, "hoe." In many instances, these terms are found among languages spoken in the interior regions of Gabon as well (Itsogho, Nzebi, Mbaamba, Kota), suggesting a subsequent diffusion southward through the central forest regions of Gabon. The southern route of introduction is associated with a smaller set of words: *-tálè*, "iron," *-túl-*, "to forge", *-túli*, "blacksmith, and *-bièlì*, "knife."[33]

The term *-bièlì* can be shown to be a Teke innovation (from the proto-Bantu *-bèèlì*, "knife").[34] Because of this origin and its distinctive phonology and form, the modern-day distribution of *-bièlì* must be considered the result of a loanword spread that accompanied a trade in Teke-produced knives. Its distribution indicates the extent of the Teke trading sphere at its height, that is, sometime after the twelfth century C.E. Likewise, the Nzebi, Bobangi, and Nduumo languages have double attestations (of both northern and southern words) for words such as "iron," "blacksmith," and "knife." Because the Nzebi and Bobangi became middlemen carriers of local trade in more recent times, we can attribute their use of southern words to the influence of contacts with Teke or Kongolese trading spheres after the initial introduction of iron. Aside from these cases of double attestations, none of this southern set of words appears in the central regions of the Gabonese rainforest.

The broad picture that seems to emerge from these data is a meeting up of two separate iron-trading networks in the western equatorial rainforest, one from the north and one from the south. To the west of the rivers a distinct frontier appears, that is, an expanse of land where northern and southern sets of vocabulary meet. This region is defined on an east/west axis located roughly between one and two degrees latitude, a large swath of land that includes the du Chaillu massif and the Teke plateau. It is possible that these topographical obstacles slowed the original diffusion of ironworking from the north. As was the case with the plantain, however, we must also consider that Bantu-speaking peoples had not settled these regions during the period when iron was introduced.[35]

There are three regions where neither northern nor southern terms for "iron" appear, suggesting that they were bypassed during the original introduction of iron. These regions are the Congo panhandle (C-10 languages), southeastern Cameroon (A-80 and A-90 languages), and the coastal regions of Gabon (B-30 languages). All of the C-10 languages of the Congo panhandle attest *-bɛnde, "iron." This term is found in very limited distribution within the Bantu-speaking world; outside of the Congo panhandle, it is attested only in the Ngiri (C-30 and C-40) and a number of Ubangian languages spoken in northwestern Democratic Republic of Congo. Among the A-80 and A-90 languages of southwestern Cameroon, an alternative term, *-ngonzo, "iron" is used.[36]

The majority of Gabonese coastal languages attest *-uanga, "iron."[37]As I have argued elsewhere, it is likely that this term was innovated among proto-Okani-speaking peoples of the Middle Ogooué River, who passed it to coastal populations as they introduced them to iron.[38]

Although future archaeological discoveries might drastically alter these hypotheses about the introduction and spread of iron, the data available at present provide a number of important insights into the nature of rainforest societies during the last millennium B.C.E. First, the relatively rapid diffusion of iron and ironworking suggests well-established systems of communication, travel, and trade, especially along the routes that Bantu speakers originally used to settle the region. Second, it appears that nearly all peoples of the equatorial rainforest were familiar with iron by the middle of the last century B.C.E.; although each and every settlement may not have smelted, forged, or even traded iron, most would have been familiar with the benefits of iron tools.

Finally, the fact that central Africans were able to adapt the very complex technologies of iron production to their specific environments—this without a prior knowledge of copper or bronze metallurgy—attests an extraordinary capacity for technological innovation and change. This fact, along with the evidence for experimentation and manipulation of plantain species, should be viewed as a testimony to the intellectual and innovative capabilities of central African peoples. They were undoubtedly some of the most dynamic populations to exist on the globe, especially during the last millennium B.C.E.

THE IMPACT OF BANANAS AND IRON

The archaeological record of the Late Stone to Metal Age (1500–500 B.C.E.) and the Early Iron Age (500 B.C.E.—1000 C.E.) clearly attests the impact that plantains and iron had on central Africans' lives. The most striking innovation is the simultaneous appearance of large villages throughout the region, documenting both an increase in population numbers and a transition toward more sedentary lives. The increase in sedentism is especially indicated by the appearance of numerous earth pits in villages. Although the original motive for digging these pits is not yet clear, they were always filled with village refuse, allowing modern archaeologists a glimpse into the ancient inhabitants' lives.[39] Ceramics, mortars, pestles, and the remains of oleaginous nuts (palm, cola) are the most common items found. In southern Cameroon, evidence for domesticated plants and animals has also been obtained (bananas, millet, sheep, goat), generally dated to the middle of the last millennium B.C.E.[40]

Also striking is the vast increase in amounts and styles of ceramics produced. Both the Late Stone to Metal and Early Iron Ages see new styles of ceramics, oftentimes found at multiple sites across vast expanses of land.[41] This phenomenon is considered to attest an increase in economic specialization and regional trade. Although there is evidence of iron production during this time, the Late Stone to Metal Age is transitionary, for a great many communities continued to produce and use stone tools. De Maret and Thiry have described it as a "long period where a mosaic pattern prevailed with various groups exploiting ecosystems at various technological stages, prefiguring the complex situation of iron metallurgy that we see from ethnographic observations."[42] The Early Iron Age, on the other hand, was characterized by the widespread production and use of iron; iron implements and currencies were manufactured in the majority of villages, and the use of stone tools became obsolete.

Linguistic data also provide evidence of the drastic social and economic changes that took place after the introduction of bananas and iron. The Late Stone to Metal Age is characterized by a filling-in tendency, whereby new speech communities began to be formed in more interior regions, that is, those that had been circumscribed by earlier settlements along rivers. Banana cultivation is likely the cause of this phenomenon because it made forest dwelling (away from the rivers) a much more viable way of life.

Our language classification provides evidence of this filling-in tendency in three distinct regions: (1) in the far northeastern reaches of the Congo Republic, leading to the formation of proto-C-10 and C-30 speech communities; (2) in the central Congo basin, where proto-Mongo, proto-Tetela, and proto-Bushoong came to be formed; and (3) in southern Congo Republic/Gabon, among the proto-Nzebi-Vili speech community. Table 4.1 provides a thumbnail sketch of these divergences.

Table 4.1 The Formation of New Speech Communities, c. 1500–500 B.C.E.

Central Congo Basin: (1500--500 B.C.E.)
Through a succession of settlements eastward along the tributaries of the Congo River, **proto-Mongo-Tetela** diverges to form:
  -Proto-Mongo
  -Proto-Tetela
  -Proto-Bushong

Northern Congo (1000--500 B.C.E.)
Through a succession of settlements toward the east (Congo/Ubangi confluence), **proto-Sangha** diverges to form:
  -Proto-Babinga
  (a language ancestral to modern-day Babenzele, Bambenga, Aka)
  -Proto-Bobangi
  (or, language ancestral to C-30 languages)
Remaining centered on and around the Sangha River:
  Proto-Mikaya-Bambomba
  (a language ancestral to modern-day Bongili, Bakolu, Bambomba, Inyele, etc.--C-10 languages) and perhaps also Mikaya, Baluma (Batwa C-10 languages)

Southern Congo/Gabon (1000--500 B.C.E.)
Through a succession of settlements westward (valleys of the Louessé and Kouilou Rivers), **proto-Nzebi-Vili** diverges to form:
  -Proto-Igama-Vili (westernmost)
       (a language ancestral to modern-day Igama (Btw.) and Vili
  -Proto-Irimba-Ipunu (central)
       (a language ancestral to modern-day Irimba (Btw.) and Ipunu
  -Proto-Nzebi-Ibeembe (between Congo R. and Massif du Chaillu
       (a language ancestral to modern-day Nzebi, Ibongo-Nzebi (Btw.),
       Ilaali and Ibongo-Ilaali (Btw.), Iyaa and Ibongo-Iyaa (Btw.),
       Ibeembe, and Ibongo-Ibeembe (Btw.), as well as other Teke
       dialects.

The appearance of these new speech communities can in many cases be associated with the appearance of new types of ceramics. Although we have already suggested that the earliest dates of the Imbonga-ware might correspond with an initial era of settlement along the Congo River (see chapter 2), the majority of dates associated with this tradition cluster in the last eight centuries B.C.E.[43] We might thus associate these later dates with the formation of the proto-Mongo speech community, c. 1500–500 B.C.E. The locations of Imbonga-ware suggest that members of common ancestral community fanned

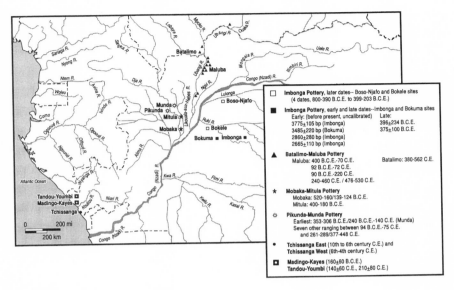

Map 4.2. New Pottery Traditions, 1500–500 B.C.E.

out from the Ruki, Momboyo, and Ikelemba Rivers to the Lulonga and Loile Rivers to the north and south, respectively (see Map 4.2). It is perhaps this phenomenon, along with a history of close contacts and continued inter-actions, that accounts for the deep cultural and linguistic cohesion of Mongo-speaking peoples that inhabit the entire central basin today.

In his reconnaissance survey of the Congo basin, Eggert also identified a more refined ceramic tradition toward the north—primarily along the lower reaches of the Ubangi River and at numerous sites between the Ubangi and Congo bends. At Maluba (lower reaches of the Lua River), this pottery was found in association with oil palm nuts and a burial that contained human bones. Although Eggert judged it to be derived from a common ceramic antecedent with Imbonga, this pottery holds its greatest affinities with pots discovered at Batalimo in the southwestern corner of the Central African Republic.[44] Accordingly, Eggert has termed it the "Batalimo-Maluba Hori-zon," and considers pottery from the two sites to be of the same tradition. The earliest radiocarbon date associated with Maluba-ware is 400 B.C.E.–70 C.E.; two others are located near the turn of the era (92 B.C.E.–72 C.E., 90 B.C.E.–220 C.E.), and one is dated to between 240 to 460 C.E. and 476 to 530 C.E. Com-bining the later dates with that found at Batalimo (380–562 C.E.), Eggert sug-gests that the Batalimo-Maluba traditions should be considered a product of the first half of the first millennium C.E.[45]

The appearance of Batalimo-Maluba ceramics at a more northern location and later date than Imbonga parallels the linguistically derived hypothesis that Bantu speakers initially migrated down the Sangha and Congo Rivers and only later moved into regions toward the east. Linguistic data suggest that peoples descended from the proto-Sangha speech community began to move toward the Ubangi between 1000 and 500 B.C.E., leading to the formation of the proto-Babinga (Batwa) and proto-Bobangi (C-30) speech communities. If we accept the earliest dates associated with Batalimo-Maluba pottery as valid (i.e., 400 B.C.E.–70 C.E.) its appearance parallels the movement of proto-Babinga and proto-Bobangi/C-30 speakers into regions toward the east. Maluba-ware might be associated with the latter because it is found in the regions where C-30 and C-40 languages are spoken today. Because the ceramics at Batalimo resemble those of Maluba, we must also conclude that the peoples who occupied this site were either closely associated with Bantu speakers or were Bantu speakers themselves. A large quantity of stone axes (226, with only a few polished) and flakes (6,824) were found along with the pottery (shards to equal 36 receptacles); this finding has led archaeologists to conclude that the site served primarily as a workshop for stone-tool production.[46] Given the fact that proto-Babinga speakers were formerly associated with Bantu speakers in regions to the south—and thus would have been familiar with the use and/or production of pottery—there is no reason to assume that the Batalimo site was not occupied by descendants of the proto-Babinga speech community. This may have been how the Aka speech community later came to be formed; its modern-day distribution is centered on the regions where the Batalimo site is found (southern Central African Republic).

Eggert also carried out a very limited reconnaissance survey within the Congo panhandle itself. His interpretations are based on data from only five sites, making it difficult to come to solid conclusions. Nonetheless, the earliest pottery was found at Mobaka and Mitula on the lower Sangha, dated to between 520 and 180 B.C.E.[47] Although contemporaneous with Imbonga-ware, this pottery was of distinct style. Another distinctive style of pottery was identified at Pikunda on the Sangha River and Munda on the Likouala-aux-Herbes; Eggert has thus termed it the "Pikunda-Munda" horizon. The earliest date for Pikunda-Munda falls between 353 B.C.E. and 140 C.E.; seven others cluster between 200 B.C.E. and 400 C.E.[48] Slag appears at the Munda site, suggesting the production of iron. An iron tool was also found at Pikunda; Eggert describes it as having "one end worked into a spatula-like blade" and the other in the shape of "a badly corroded handle."[49]

As Eggert has noted, the Pikunda-Munda data do not support the linguistic analyses that suggest the Sangha River was an initial route of Bantu expansion, because the ceramics are associated with rather late dates.[50] There are, however, indications that earlier groups of ceramic-producing peoples lived in the region. At Pikunda, for example, Eggert found an unidentifiable type of pottery in the lower part of the shaft.[51] Although undated, its nonhomogenous style (no clear defined boundaries of shape, decoration, or fabric) might suggest it was the product of communities whose economies had not yet developed to the point where an occupational specialization in pottery manufacturing had come to exist. A great deal more archaeological work is needed in this region before solid conclusions about Bantu settlement can be made; as Eggert has noted, work so far carried out should be considered a "drop in the bucket" for a region so vast.[52]

Linguistic data further correlate Eggert's findings in that they suggest that the earliest iron tool to be used in this region was an indigenous razor. This can be discerned from the fact that the only iron-related terms common to the C-10 and C-30 languages of the region are the words for iron itself (*-bɛnde*) and the razor that is used for shaving the head and scarification (*-tebu*). All other terms, such as those that refer to techniques of production or other types of tools, differ from group to group. They are usually found in limited areal distributions that involve Bantu and Ubangian languages alike. These data suggest that iron and indigenous razors were introduced while the members of the proto-Sangha speech community remained in close contact on and around the Sangha River, that is, sometime before or during the fifth century B.C.E. Furthermore, it is possible that the iron tool discovered at Pikunda (fourth century B.C.E.) was an indigenous razor as well because Eggert's description of the tool resembles the form of indigenous razors that are used by local populations today.

Because of a real lack of archaeological work in the surrounding regions, we have no indication as to where iron may have earliest been produced. There are, however, a series of iron-rich deposits along the northern edge of the Great Bend in the Ubangi. Linguistic data indicate that proto-Ubangian speakers inhabited these regions from as early as 2000 B.C.E.;[53] they may have produced iron and introduced the term *-bɛnde* as well. Evidence from the nineteenth century also indicates that important centers of production were located among Bantu speakers to the immediate east—the Mongo of Ikelemba, the Ngombe of Maringa-Lopori, and the Lukani of Lake Tumba.[54] Although observations made at such late dates do not guarantee that production occurred in the last millennium B.C.E., there is evidence to attest production for comparable lengths in other iron-rich regions, such as the Kukuya plateau (western Congo Republic) and Haut Ogooué (southwestern Gabon).[55] If iron was being produced in the northwestern regions of Congo-Kinshasa at these early dates, it is possible that proto-Bobangi (C-30) and proto-Babinga (C-10) moved eastward to take part in newly developing systems of regional trade.

Finally, the westward expansion of proto-Nzebi-Vili speakers can be correlated with archaeological evidence for early iron-using villages along the Congolese coast. As was mentioned in chapter 2, Denbow uncovered evidence of ceramic-using Late Stone Age populations at Tchissanga West and East (15 km south of the Kouilou River), dated between the tenth and fourth century B.C.E.[56] In the upper levels of the latter site, small pieces of iron were discovered, suggesting contact with iron-producing populations somewhere nearby. Subsequent excavations at Madingo-Kayes (at the mouth of the Kouilou River) revealed the presence of an ancient village, with a surface extension of nearly 20,000 m². Ceramics of a style distinct from those at Tchissanga were discovered, along with iron slag and numerous iron artifacts (leg bangles, beads, rings, and a barbed arrow point). Eight kilometers to the north another village site was discovered (Tandou-Yombi); it contained pottery of the same tradition as Madingo-Kayes, as well as a polished stone axe.

Charcoal samples provided radiocarbon dates of 160 ± 60 B.C.E. at Tandou-Yombi, and 140 C.E. ± 60 C.E. and 210 ± 80 C.E. at Madingo-Kayes. Because the ceramics at these sites are so clearly distinct from those at Tchissanga, Denbow has suggested that they represent the "manifestation of a new cultural tradition which moved into this stretch of the Atlantic coast from the north or east during the last few centuries B.C.E."[57] These data parallel linguistic evidence for the formation of a proto-Vili-Igama speech community c. 1000–500 B.C.E. Formed at the westernmost extension of the ancestral proto-Nzebi-Vili speech community, this language was ancestral to both proto-Vili and proto-Igama, the latter being spoken by the Bagama, a group of Batwa forest specialists that now live in association with both Lumbu and Vili societies.

Because our classification only provides evidence as to when Igama speakers lessened contacts with Vili speakers to form their own speech community (c. 1500 B.C.E., see chapter 6), we have no evidence to attest exactly when the two societies first met. However, the linguistic data do indicate that proto-Vili-speaking peoples entered into the region toward the end of the last millennium B.C.E. If we work from the assumption that indigenous hunter-gatherers inhabited the Tchissanga sites, we might suggest the appearance of iron at Tchissanga West attests a history of contacts between the ancestors of proto-Vili and (autochthonous) proto-Igama speakers from as early as the fourth century B.C.E. Although this scenario does provide a convenient fit between archaeological and linguistic data, it must be recognized that it is dependent on the assumption that Late Stone Age sites were actually inhabited by indigenous hunting and gathering people. As was argued in chapter 2, however, we might also assume that indigenized Bantu speakers occupied Late Stone Age sites. I make this point not to argue for an alternative interpretation of the data, but to illustrate the great degree of ambiguity that arises when attempting to reconstruct a Batwa history from archaeological data alone.

Although we can document parallels in linguistic and archaeological data—and use them to help us reconstruct the ancient past—it remains impossible to establish direct links between ancestral speech communities and archaeological traditions or artifacts. We can, however, gain insight into the lifestyles of ancient speech communities by reconstructing lexicon for the language they once spoke. In this case we are fortunate to have three sister languages to work from—Bambenjele, Bambenga, and Aka—all spoken by Batwa communities of northern Congo Republic. We now turn to an analysis of this kind of linguistic data.

THE PROTO-BABINGA OF NORTHERN CONGO:
c. 1500–500 b.c.e.

The Late Stone to Metal Period provides us with our first evidence for a Bantu-speaking Batwa community. It is found in the formation of the proto-Babinga speech community (c. 1000–500 B.C.E.), ancestral to modern-day Bambenjele, Bambenga, and Aka—and probably Mikaya and Baluma as well. The common ancestry of these five forest-specialist languages is attested not only through lexicostatistical analyses, but also by evidence of shared language traits (i.e., sound changes, lexical items) that are unique to them alone.[58] Because many of these traits appear only sporadically in Mikaya and Baluma, we might envision that the proto-Babinga divergence began to take place in situ, or that contacts between the various Batwa communities carried on for quite a long time. The "least moves" principle suggests that the proto-Babinga speech community eventually came to be centered in regions to the northwest of the Sangha River, although we cannot tell exactly when.

The classification indicates that proto-Baluma and proto-Mikaya, also ancestral to modern-day Batwa languages, were formed as distinct communities roughly half a millennium later. They developed as part of a five-way divergence that included the formation of other fishing/agriculturalist communities in the region, including proto-Bongili (C15), proto-Inyele (C-10s), and proto-Bambomba (C14b). It is possible, however, that the higher rates of cognation with these three agriculturalist languages are due to a recent history of close contacts. The Baluma currently live together with the Bongili in the villages of Pikunda and Bokibo, and certain Mikaya were living with the Bongili during the 1950s as well. Thus, although I will here use the term proto-Babinga as a referent to a language that is clearly ancestral to modern-day Bambenjele, Bambenga, and Aka, it must be remembered that it is likely ancestral to other C-10 languages spoken by Batwa people in the region as well.

Recent research by Serge Bahuchet has indicated that the ancestors of Ubangian-speaking Baka forest specialists are likely to have been members of this ancient C-10 speech community as well. In a comparative analysis of forest-related vocabularies in the Aka and Baka languages, Bahuchet identified as many as 600 words (from a 3,000-word corpus) shared between the two.[59] Although it is not unusual for geographically contiguous speech communities to share a great deal of vocabulary items, this is an unusually high amount for languages of different families. Although Bahuchet attributes more than half of the shared lexicon to an original Pygmy language, his research showed that the majority of terms remaining were found in nearby Bantu C-10 languages.[60] More important, he also identified a number of deeply embedded Bantu grammatical traits in the Baka language (fossilized class prefix and noun/verb derivation systems) that are not easily explained by borrowing. Because the fossilized prefixes found in Baka are of the same forms used by Bantu C-10 speakers of the region, Bahuchet has suggested that the linguistic ancestors of both Aka and Baka communities originally comprised a single community (the *Baakaa), and that this community had extensive contacts with C-group speakers in the distant past. Thereafter came a period of divergence, during which the ancestors of modern-day Baka speakers came into contact with Ubangian-speaking communities of the proto-Gbandzili-Sere subgroup. After adopting this language, they eventually began to develop an Ubangian language unique to them alone (i.e., Baka).[61]

Although Bahuchet's results help to confirm that the ancestors of Batwa peoples in Cameroon, Congo, and Central African Republic originally spoke a Bantu C-group language (and thus accord with my own results), I am not as quick to consider terms common to Aka and Baka as substrate evidence of an original Pygmy language. Their phonologies and structures are entirely in line with Bantu systems, and as shown following, many of the proto-Babinga terms I have been able to reconstruct are derived from ancient Bantu roots. It should be recognized that there are a number of irresolvable problems encountered in any attempt to reconstruct an original Pygmy language.

First, if interactions between immigrant and indigenous communities took place from the earliest stages of Bantu expansion, we cannot assume that the latter did not make considerable contributions to the development of the very phonologies, morphologies, and grammatical systems we deem quintessentially Bantu today. The identification of such elements will forever be impossible to identify, given that all societies of the region speak Bantu or Ubangian languages. Second, the confirmation that certain lexical items can be traced to a primordial Batwa language will not be verifiable until equally specialized vocabularies have been collected across the entirety of the Ubangian- and Bantu-speaking world. Although both Bahuchet and myself have identified a number of terms we consider unique to the Batwa languages of the region (he, the "*Baakaa," I, the "proto-Babinga"), I suspect the etymological origins of these terms will be discovered as we continue to amass data from the broader Niger-Congo field.

Given these caveats, how can we interpret the evidence for an ancient group of C-10 language speakers that was ancestral to modern-day Bambenjele, Bambenga, Aka, and Baka? We must speak of a long period of close interactions between agriculturalists' and forest specialists' linguistic ancestors—one that eventually led not only to the sharing of languages, but probably also cultures, technologies, and genes. This scenario is supported by genetic evidence as well; as Cavalli-Sforza has noted, Batwa populations from southern Central African Republic (the Aka), Cameroon, and Rwanda are "indistinguishable, genetically, or hardly distinguishable, from some groups of farmers."[62]

Because the proto-Babinga speech community was formed through divergence from an agriculturalist community between 1000 and 500 B.C., we must presume that these interactions began much earlier. The linguistic data suggest they occurred during a period in which an undifferentiated version of the Bantu language was spoken across vast areas of land; this may have been the proto-Nyong-Lomami period (c. 2700–2400 B.C.E.) or, more likely, the subsequent proto-Sangha-Kwa era (2400–2000 B.C.E.) because the latter eventually diverged to form proto-Babinga and its two sister languages (proto-Bobangi and proto-Sangha). Bahuchet's identification of C-10 group grammatical structures in the Baka language also supports this latter scenario, suggesting that the proto-Sangha-Kwa language may have earlier been spoken in the regions of southeastern Cameroon as well.

This is critical information because it affirms that peoples linguistically ancestral to modern-day Batwa peoples were in contact with Bantu agriculturalists before the introduction of bananas and iron. We might imagine the types of relations were based on those described in chapter 3, whereby essentially egalitarian relations existed between autochthons and immigrants, and leaders of Bantu settlements consciously strove to establish alliances with the people they deemed first-comers on the land. This historical scenario is supported by the proto-Babinga term for non-Batwa populations, *-mílô/bilô*. In the modern-day context, this term is translated variously as "friend/trading partner" (Bambenjele), "village dweller" (Aka and Bambenjele), or "slave-owner" (Bambenga). Its literal definition, however, is simply "the uninitiated."[63] This ancient sobriquet attests that Batwa people of early eras defined their relations with agriculturalist/fishing peoples primarily in terms of religious and ritual practices; when viewed in light of the first-comer paradigm, it suggests that the Batwa were called upon to initiate their neighbors in much the same manner as they do for newcomers to the region today.[64]

Finally, it must be remembered that linguistic evidence is just that—it cannot provide any information regarding the body size, height, or other physical characteristics of these ancient Batwa. Because the modern-day sobriquet, *-mílô/bilô*, makes no reference to physical stature,[65] we have no evidence to confirm or deny that the proto-Babinga were short-statured peoples when the proto-Babinga language was spoken. Likewise, proto-Babinga vocabularies refer only to the periods when the language existed, i.e., between 500 B.C.E. and 1000 C.E. Although they might reflect historical realities of periods just prior to the divergence of proto-Babinga, they cannot be extrapolated to "primordial" times.

As was mentioned earlier, proto-Babinga was formed as part of a three-way divergence that occurred in the proto-Sangha-Nzadi speech community.

Table 4.2a Proto-Babinga Vocabulary

Proto-Babinga	Gloss	Attestations in other F/S Languages	Source or Possible Source	Distribution in wider Bantu or Ubangian langs.
Certain proto-Bantu Origin:				
1. *-cuoko	"head"	-------	ps. 119 *-cóókò "head" BLR2 #649 (f. 5)	Zone S (SE)
2. *-panga	"to track, hunt by tracking"	Baka [bopanga]	BLR2 # 8705 *-pang- "to chase" (f. 5)	Zones K, L (Angola, Congo-Z, Zambia)
Possible Proto-Bantu Origin (through processes of semantic shift)				
3. *-tukuma	"hot"	-------	BLR2 5334 *-tùkum- "to be swollen, aching"	Zones L, M, S (Congo-Z ,SE, S)
4. *-kan-	"to bury"	-------	BLR2 8297 *-kàn- "to bind tightly, tighten"?	Zone J (Great Lakes, E)
			C.S. 8268 *-gàn- "to praise, eulogize"?	Zones D, L (Congo-Z)
5. *-yobe/*-yebe	"knife"	-------	C.S. 388 *-yob- "to skin" ?	Zones A (Duala, Oli), C (Bambenjele)
6. *-puma	"house" (rectangular var.)	-------	C.S. 1600 *-pùùm- "to breathe, rest"?	Zones B,C,D,E,H,L M,N,P,S
7. *-yángò	"camp"(quotidian)	-------	C.S. *-yáng- "to dance about"?	Zones A,B,H,M,N,P,R

Table 4.2a (continued)

				Ngando (C19)
8. *-pɑnɑ	"digging stick" (w/pointed end)	--------	???	
Unknown Origin				
9. *-sↄpↄ	"earth"	--------	???	???
10. *-bole~bwe	"big, large"	--------	???	???
11. *-sɔ́lɔ̀	Ongokea gore (tree sp.)	Baka, Mik.	???	???
12. *-páyó	Irvingia excelsa	Baka, Mik.	???	Inyele (C-10), Bomwali (A87) Bomassa (Ub.)
13. *-pɑnge	"wild yam sp."	Baka, Bngb., Bal.	???	Bongili
14. *-kenjo	"stinger" (of bee)	Baka, Bngb.	???	Bomassa (A-87)
15. *-pɛ̀ndí	"basket for collecting honey"	Baka	???	Inyele, Kabunga (C-10's) Bekwil (A 85), Bomassa (U.)
16. *-lepɑ	"to throw spear"	--------	???	???
17. *-mbὲmbó	"trail made by passing of elephants"	Baka, Bngb, Mik, Bal.	???	Kabunga (C-10), Bomassa (U.)

Note: Found in all three descendants of proto-Babinga language: Bambenjele, Bambenta, Aka. C.S. (Comparative Series) and ps. (partial series) refer to Guthrie's Reconstructions (1967–71). BLR2 refers to Bantu Lexical Reconstructions (Coupez et al., 1998).

Table 4.2b Probable Proto-Babinga Vocabulary

Certain proto-Bantu Origin

	Aka, Bbzl, Mik., Baka, Bngb.	ps.292 *-kééngé "skill" C.S. 1043 *-kéngid- "to become clever"	Zones A, B (Cameroon,Gabon) Zones M, N, S (SE, S)
18. *-kenga (v.) "to kill first animal" *-kengo (n.) "first animal killed"			???

Unknown Origin

19. -njene Tetrorchidium didymostemon (tree sp.)	Aka, Bbzl.,Baka	???	
20. *.-so "multi-pronged cone-shaped tool for unearthing yams"	Aka, Bbzl., Mik.	???	Inyele (C-10) "iron tipped digging stick" (used by "ancestors")
21. *-pim̩ "to dig"	Baka *mopimo* "unearthed yam"	???	???
22. *-beleko "honey guide" (bird species)	Bbzl., Mik., Baka, Bngb.	???	Bomwali (A-87)
23. *-lenga "trail made by small animals"	Bbzl., Bamb., Mik., Bal.,	???	Kabunga (C-10)
24. *-sɛ̀ndɔ̀ "1-day hunt"	Aka, Bbzl, Mik., Bal., Baka, Bngb.	???	Bomassa (Ubangian)
25. *.- longo "3-month hunt"	Aka, Bbzl, Mik., Bal., Baka	???	Bomassa (Ubangian)

Note: Found in two of the three confirmed descendants of proto-Babinga (Aka, Bambenjele, Bambenga) as well as other forest-specialist languages of northern Congo.

Because of this, it shares the majority of its vocabulary with other C-30 and C-10 languages of the region. I have identified, however, a small subset of proto-Babinga words that other members of other C-group languages do not use.[66] The terms are listed in Table 4.2 and classified into two categories: "proto-Babinga terms" (Table 4.2a) and "probable proto-Babinga terms" (Table 4.2b). The latter category contains words that are attested in Aka, Bambenjele, and a number of other Batwa languages of the region (Bantu and Ubangian alike), but not among the Bambenga who live farthest to the east.[67]

Many of the proto-Babinga terms—though unique to Batwa communities of northern Congo—can be traced to more ancient proto-Bantu origins. Two very clear examples are the words for "head" (*-soko) and "to hunt by tracking"(*-panga). The former is derived from the same proto-Bantu term that produced *-cóókò (p.s. 119), a word that refers to "head" in the S-group Bantu languages of the far southeast (Venda, Sotho, Xhosa, Zulu, Tswa).[68] The verb *-panga is likely derived from the same proto-Bantu term that produced *-pang, "to chase" (BLR2 # 8705); like *-cóókò, this term is so far documented only among languages beyond the equatorial rainforest.[69] These wide-ranging distributions indicate that the terms are of a very ancient Bantu origin, derived from proto-Bantu or proto-Nyong-Lomami. Their common retention in the Aka, Bambenjele, and Bambenga languages confirms that the proto-Babinga stood apart from other speech communities after their divergence because they did not drop these terms or adopt others used by neighboring communities of C-group languages.

The proto-Babinga also created a number of their own words through the process of semantic shift, that is, slightly altering and/or adding to the meaning of preexisting proto-Bantu terms. For example, the adjective *-etukuma, "hot," was likely derived from the proto-Bantu adjective *-tùkum, "to be swollen, aching." This origin is suggested not only by its similarity in form, but also by a widespread association between heat/sickness and coolness/health in the Bantu world. As such, we are provided with an interesting bit of intellectual history among ancient Babinga speakers—the innovation of a word that reflected their feelings about the changing environment.

The term *-gan, "to bury," might reflect cultural preferences as well; I suggest that it is possibly derived from the proto-Bantu term *-kàn, "to bind firmly or tightly," or, alternatively, *-gàn, "to praise, eulogize." This etymology must be considered tentative because it is based on an assumption that wrapping cadavers and praising the dead might be human universals. As Bahuchet has noted, however, funerals and coming-of-age ceremonies are today the two most important rituals among Batwa societies of the region, and each is characterized by ceremonies that are unique to Batwa societies alone.[70] The Aka and Baka also share a word for "tomb" (*-mbìndò) that does not appear in other C-10 or Ubangian languages of the region; it is likely, however, that *-mbìndò is derived from *-bį́ndò (C.S. 150), a proto-Bantu word for "dirt." Regnault noted in 1911 that the Babinga of the Sangha region buried their dead in the bush next to a termite hill; perhaps this is the dirt that *-mbìndo refers to.[71] As we see in the following chapter, associations between Batwa, termite hills, and nature spirits are a widespread phenomenon in central Africa.

Proto-Babinga speakers are likely to have innovated the term *-yobe (or perhaps *-yébe) in reference to knives. Bambenjele attests yobe/biobe, "knife," Aka speakers use yébé/biébé, "knife," and Bambenga speakers use yobe/biobe in specific reference to daggers or double-sided knives. The exact etymological origins of these forms are unknown; however, it is possible that they were formed through a semantic extension from the proto-Bantu *-yob, "to skin" (C.S. 388). Although the Aka, Bambenjele, or Bambenga do not use this verb today, its nominal derivative does appear in Bambenjele as yobo/biobo, "skin." [72] Similar attestations appear in the Douala and Oli (A-20) languages (obo/biobo, "skin"). The latter are spoken in the coastal regions of Cameroon, suggesting that obo/biobo was current in the proto-Bantu or proto-Nyong-Lomami stage. If the term was developed in reference to a tool used to skin animals it is likely to have originally meant "dagger" because double-sided knives are more effective in slaying and slaughtering prey. This hypothesis is partially supported by the fact that the Bambenga (of the far northeastern Congo panhandle) later adopted their neighbors' generic term for "knife" (mbao/mambao), which they continue to distinguish from double-sided knives.

Because the proto-Babinga language was spoken during the Late Stone to Metal Age, it is impossible to discern whether *-yobe/*-yébe originally referred to stone or metal knives. Both were likely to have been in use by the end of the period, and it is possible that the proto-Babinga simply applied an older term to iron knives as they were introduced.[73] We must also consider that the use of stone tools in southern Central African Republic did not die out until a relatively late date: as indicated earlier, the site of Batalimo in southern Central African Republic (on the Lobaye River) provided evidence of stone-tool production as late as the fourth century C.E. The entirety of this data might be read as an indication that the use of stone tools continued in the region until an exceptionally late date, and therefore, that *-yobe is a retention from such times.

Another term the proto-Babinga are likely to have innovated is *-puma, "house." In the Bambenjele and Bambenga languages, this term refers specifically to mud and wattle houses of rectangular shape that are associated with the village lifestyle. In French collections of Aka data this term has been glossed as both "hut" and "house."[74] I posit that this term might be derived from the proto-Bantu term *-pùùm, "to breathe, rest" (C.S. 1600). Again, this is only a tentative etymology at present because a similar innovation has not yet been identified in the broader Bantu-speaking world. The term becomes especially intriguing, however, when we consider the fact that a word for dwellings assumed to be traditional to Batwa societies (small hemispherical huts) cannot be reconstructed to the proto-Babinga language. Each of the three descendent languages has its own word for these dwellings: *mangulu/mingulu* in Bambenjele, *ekuta/bikuta* in Bambenga, and *mopiko/mepiko* in Aka. As a result, we cannot be sure that such dwellings were part of the proto-Babinga lifestyle. Taken together, these data suggest that proto-Babinga society may have been more sedentary than the Batwa societies of today.

The etymology of the proto-Babinga term for "camp" (of the quotidian variety) can be considered to substantiate a formerly more sedentary life as well. It is attested as *lángò/nzángo* in Aka, as *lango/malango (~mandʒango)* in Bambenjele, and as *lango/malango* in Bambenga. The alternate forms in Aka and Bambenjele (those attesting *[z/dʒ]* in the initial consonant position) indicate that the original form of this term was **-yángo,* to which the singular class 5/6 prefixes [**-lį́/*-ma*] were applied.[75] In the Aka language **-yáng-* is the verb for "to call," and Guthrie has reconstructed an identical form (**-yáng-* C.S. 1936) as "to dance about (especially as a sign of joy)" from attestations found in the wider Bantu-speaking world.[76] These meanings suggest an original connotation of a gathering, or coming together, perhaps for the purposes of ritual, celebration, and dance. If proto-Babinga peoples did live more sedentary lifestyles in the past, it is possible that forest camps were originally conceived of as the locations where these activities were carried out; likewise, it would have been in later times that they came to be associated with their habitual dwelling place.

Words for the tools used to unearth tubers also suggest that the forest-specialist lifestyle may have developed over time. One is *mopana/mipana* used in Aka, Bambenjele, and Bambenga and thus reconstructible to the proto-Babinga language (**-pana*). It is a piece of wood sharpened at one end, used primarily to unearth wild yams. Numerous hunting and gathering peoples on the continent use this type of tool. The second type of digging stick is unique to Batwa societies of northern Congo Republic alone. It is distinguished by a conical probe, which is formed by splitting the end of the stick into four or eight pointed teeth. As Bahuchet has noted, this tool is a testament to the technical ingenuity of Batwa peoples in the Central African Republic and southwestern Cameroon, for it was developed to extract *esuma* (*Dioscorea semperflorens*), a type of yam whose tubers grow as long as five meters long and root exceptionally deep into the ground.[77]

Among the Aka, Bambenjele, and Mikaya, this cone-shaped tool is referred to as *dìsó/madìsó*. We see in the plural form of this word a fossilization of the class five singular prefix *(*-lį́),* which in the C-10 languages of northern Congo became [**dį́*] because of the high vowel. Because the loss of [l] between vowels appears regularly among the Batwa languages (and a number of agriculturalist/fishing peoples languages as well), that root of the word *(-só)* must be seen as originally derived from the proto-Bantu **-còdò* (C.S. 369), "tip of something."[78] This same shortened form is found among the Inyele, who state that their ancestors used an iron-tipped digging stick called *mosu/mesu.* It also appears among Luba speakers of Katanga (L-33, southeastern Democratic Republic of Congo), where digging sticks are referred to as *musolo/misolo.* The fossilized prefix suggests that the ancestors of modern-day Batwa may have borrowed the word originally, even though it now refers to a tool used by them alone. This same cone-shaped tool is referred to as ŋ*gbápa* among the Baka of Souanké district and the Bangombe of Bomassa (Ubangian speakers), *bòndùngà* among the Baka of southeastern Cameroon, and *ndaba* among the Bambenga to the far east. The great variety of names for this tool again suggests that it may have entered into use after the proto-Babinga diverged into its own descendent speech communities, i.e., after c. 1000 C.E.

There are a number of terms that attest the social and economic significance of hunting for proto-Babinga speakers. The first of these is **-kenga,* "to kill one's first animal," and its noun derivative **-kengo,* "first animal killed by a youth." These terms make reference to a broader set of ritual practices and/or celebrations that take place when a Batwa youth kills his first large prey. Although they are used exclusively by the Aka, Bambenjele, Mikaya, Baka, and Bangombe, they are clearly derived from the same roots as proto-Bantu **-kééngé,* "skill," and **-kengid,* "to become clever." **-kenga* is not used, however, by the Bambenga near Dongou; they may have stopped practicing the ritual as they became more enmeshed with Inyele-speaking communities. Alternatively, **-kenga* may be a term that developed after the proto-Babenga divergence (c. 1000 C.E.); if such is the case, its widespread distribution among forest specialists to the west might be considered evidence of a later areal spread.

Proto-Babinga speakers also relied on ritual specialists in their hunting pursuits. This can be seen in the widespread use of **-túmá,* "master-hunter" or "magician," an individual whose hunting and supernatural skills help to ensure a successful hunt. In northern Congo this term is found in all of the forest-specialist communities (Aka, Bambenjele, Bambenga, Baka, Bomassa, and Bangombe) and a number of agriculturalist/fishing communities as well (Bomwali [A-80], Bongili [C-15], and Ngando [Ubangian]).[79] As Bahuchet has noted, this term also has a wide distribution among Bantu-speaking societies of equatorial Africa. The Mongo of the central Congo basin have a verb *-túmà* that means "to indicate, show a path." The Kumu (D37) and Budu (D35) of northeastern Democratic Republic of Congo also refer to specialist elephant hunters as *bàtúmá;* these individuals participate in a brotherhood of hunters (*bòtúmá*) that has its own rituals and initiation ceremonies. Farther to the east in the Ituri forest, Bila-speaking Mbuti forest specialists refer to respected elephant hunters as *tuma* as well. These attestations suggest that elephant hunting has been an esteemed activity since the earliest eras of Bantu expansion across the rainforest (i.e., the proto-Nyong-Lomami period). These forms are likely derived from same root that produced the proto-Bantu *-tṵm*, "to stab" (C.S. 1866), and *-tṵmò* or *-tṵmù*, "spear" (C.S. 1867, 1868).

There are a number of proto-Babinga terms whose etymologies cannot yet be traced. Nearly all are related to forest products and the techniques or tools used to procure them, such as honey-indicator birds, baskets for collecting honey, one- and three-day hunts, and trails made by the passage of elephants and small animals. My limited survey identified the names of three species of trees unique to Batwa languages alone: *Tetrorchidium didymostemon, Ongokea gore,* and *Irvingia excelsa.* The fiber, bark, and fruit of these trees, however, are used throughout the rainforest region by Bantu and Batwa societies alike.[80] Interestingly, Bantu, Ubangian, and Batwa speech communities of the region often share the same terms for hunting nets and animal traps. Although working from an absence of data cannot be considered historical proof, the lack of distinctly proto-Babinga terms for these techniques substantiates what Bahuchet has long argued from ethnographic evidence: that the use of nets and traps are recent additions to the Batwa repertoire of subsistence techniques.[81]

Although the etymological origins of all of the proto-Babinga terms are not clear, many provide us with valuable insight into the lifestyles that the linguistic ancestors of the Bambenjele, Bambenga, and Aka led. They suggest that the proto-Babinga began their existence as a distinct speech community living a somewhat sedentary lifestyle, and that their role as specialist procurers of forest products developed over time. This evidence correlates linguists' proposals that Bantu and Batwa communities formerly carried out much more intimate interactions, because the transferal of Bantu languages was so complete. These types of interactions were disrupted during the first half of the last millennium B.C.E., when the peoples linguistically ancestral to modern-day Batwa communities began to lessen their contacts with the Bantu peoples with whom they formerly shared languages. As a result, they began to develop C-group languages that were unique to them alone.

Given the widespread evidence for lifestyle changes and the formation of new speech communities that occurred in central African at this time, I argue that the proto-Babinga separation was engendered by the introduction of bananas and iron. Like the peoples around them, the proto-Babinga may have begun to develop an economic specialization based on the resources they had at hand. As first-comers they were already considered experts regarding the geography and spirits of the rainforest; by focusing on the procuration of forest products, they may have sought to build upon this reputation and develop their own economic specialization that would allow them to enter into newly expanding systems of regional trade.

What type of forest products did the proto-Babinga procure? The lexical reconstructions suggest that honey, wild game, and elephant products (probably ivory, elephant tails, and elephant meat) were important items of proto-Babinga trade. Linguistic data from another group of Batwa in central Gabon (the proto-Ebongwe; see chapter 6) indicate that their ancestors traded civet skins, cache-sexes made of animal skins, and natural dyes (derived from plants and tree barks) during the early second millennium C.E. Finally, in the modern-day context, Batwa communities are often commissioned by agriculturalists to procure medicinal tree barks and plants. It is likely that all of these products, as well as others still unidentified, were carried by early forest specialists in emerging systems of regional trade.

It must be recognized that the proto-Babinga and others like them did not make a direct transition from the hunter-gatherer lifestyle to forest specialization. They already lived in very close contact with Bantu agriculturalists, and had probably been integrated to some degree. For this reason, they would have been familiar with the benefits of agricultural foodstuffs as well as iron, and thus continued to rely on these products in carrying out subsistence strategies. Likewise, the transition toward forest specialist would have required longer periods of forest dwelling and increased mobility—the latter to carry forest products to villages and regional centers of trade. As a result, the proto-Babinga were required to develop new types of housing, hunting rituals, and tools, all of which are made evident by the linguistic innovations presented earlier.

Furthermore, I am not proposing that this shift in lifestyle took place among each and every autochthonous community after the introduction of bananas and iron. There were undoubtedly a large number of autochthons that chose not to establish close relations with immigrant Bantu societies, and who therefore did not find it necessary to lessen their contacts with agriculturalists as the proto-Babinga did at this time. These communities would have continued to practice hunting and gathering, a lifestyle substantially different from one focused on procuring rainforest products for trade.

If we are to accept this scenario, we must envision the Late Stone to Metal Age and Early Iron Age as an era when agriculturalists, forest specialists, and hunter-gatherers existed in rainforest regions. Contacts between the former two groups may have increased in the earliest stages, with instances of intermarriage and assimilation occurring both ways.[82]

However, as Bantu populations grew and their polities expanded, increasingly larger numbers of hunter-gatherers were undoubtedly affected by the frontier dynamic. In this context, the spread of the fully agricultural lifestyle can be seen as an antecedent for the transition toward forest specialization; each founding of a new Bantu settlement initiated a period of transition for autochthons, in which forest-specialist communities began to be formed. As the centuries passed and rainforest economies became increasingly integrated, it is likely that hunter-gatherers assimilated into nearby forest-specialist communities as well. This assimilation would explain why there are no Batwa peoples who speak autochthonous (i.e., non-Bantu, Ubangian, or Central Sudanic) languages today, and why no Batwa society has ever been observed subsisting on rainforest resources alone.[83]

This history thus proposes that the spread of the fully agricultural economic systems engendered processes of both assimilation and social distancing between Bantu and Batwa, with the latter leading to the development of forest specialization as a viable economic pursuit. There is insufficient evidence to determine whether the ancestors of modern-day forest specialists took up this lifestyle entirely of their own choice. As chapter 5 suggests, it is possible that the distancing phenomenon was a reaction to social transformations that occurred within Bantu societies at this time. As they gained a demographic and economic advantage over the autochthons they had long associated with, Bantu communities developed numerous techniques to reduce political and ritual powers of the original owners of the land.

Thus, in contrast to many regions of the globe where hunter-gatherers were entirely assimilated into agriculturalist economies, those of the equatorial rainforest had another option to choose. Because of a continued demand for forest products (well into the nineteenth century), hunter-gatherers could become forest specialists, thereby arresting the processes of assimilation that would have occurred if they remained in contact with one agriculturalist community alone. This history explains how Batwa societies of the equatorial rainforest have been able to maintain a distinct cultural and economic role in central African for centuries on end.

Admittedly, these are grand conclusions to be made from the evidence from one set of speech communities alone! However, linguistic and archaeological evidence from the Middle Ogooué River regions suggest that similar dynamics prevailed among proto-Okani-speaking peoples during the Early Iron Age. Because I have documented this history elsewhere,[84] I provide a brief summary of this evidence here.

THE PROTO-EBONGWE OF THE MIDDLE OGOOUÉ, c. 500–1000 c.e.

As we learned in chapter 2, archaeological evidence attests the presence of hunting and gathering peoples in the central regions of Gabon from as early as 7700 B.C.E. The first evidence of an agriculturalist lifestyle (deposit pits, ceramics, polished stone tools) identified along the Ogooué River (Okanda 1) dates to between 2124 and 1730 B.C.E. Linguistic data suggest that the inhabitants of this region were proto-Okani speakers—a language ancestral to modern-day Itsogho, Himba, Pove, Okande, Gevia, Pindji, and Ebongwe, the latter being a Batwa language most closely related to Itsogho. The proto-

Okani speech community formed as a western offshoot of the proto-Sangha-Kwa divergence that had taken place by c. 2400–2000 B.C.E.

The full florescence of the village lifestyle is not seen until roughly a thousand years later (850–390 B.C.E.), with the appearance of Epona ceramics at numerous sites along a 35-km stretch of the Middle Ogooué River (and possibly in the Gabon Estuary as well).[85] This period corresponds to the introduction of bananas and iron, and initiates an era of intense social differentiation between peoples already living along and/or migrating to the middle Ogooué River. Within the next six hundred years, four new types of ceramics appear in the regions of the modern-day Lopé Reserve alone; between 400 B.C.E. and 400 C.E., all four were manufactured contemporaneously.[86]

Although the classification cannot provide evidence to suggest when initial contacts between the ancestors of modern-day Ebongwe speakers and proto-Okani speakers began, phonological data suggest that their initial contacts with proto-Okani speakers were made quite early on; the Ebongwe language attests an archaic grammatical trait (the use of pre-prefixes) that, although reconstructible to the proto-Bantu stage, is no longer present in the Okani languages of today. Throughout central Gabon, oral traditions also report that it was Batwa peoples who introduced *iboga* to late-comer populations, a hallucinogenic derived from the bark of the *Tabernanthe iboga baill* tree species that plays a central role in the widespread *bwiti* ancestral cult. If such traditions are considered to reflect a historical reality (see chapter 5), we might posit initial contacts by at least the turn of the era, for remnants of the plant have been identified at the village site of Okanda 6 dated to between 40 B.C.E. and 150 C.E.[87]

Our language classification does, however, reveal a sequence of linguistic divergences that took place after the introduction of iron. In the last millennium B.C.E., peoples linguistically ancestral to Itsogho, Himba, and Ebongwe (the proto-Itsogho-Himba) speakers were living in forested regions to the south of the Ogooué River. Then, during the first few centuries C.E., proto-Himba speakers diverged from the ancestral speech community and began to move north. A geographical movement of people is implied not only by the "least moves" principle but also the presence of a large number of words from the Coastlands languages in the core vocabulary of Himba. This phenomenon can only be explained by a history of very close interactions, such as the Himba incorporating numerous Coastlands speakers into their communities at some point in the past.

A second divergence involves the proto-Ebongwe speech community, which began to lessen its contacts with proto-Tsogho speakers sometime between c. 500 and 1000 C.E. Thereafter it began to develop a unique version of the Tsogho language (72 percent cognation in the modern day) with a number of sound changes unique to it alone.

To tease out elements of proto-Ebongwe history, we can carry out a comparative analysis of vocabularies for the Itsogho, Ebongwe, and Himba languages. This aids in identifying words and histories unique to Ebongwe speakers alone, as well as the trade networks that each of these communities contributed to in the past. However, because the proto-Ebongwe diverged from proto-Itsogho between 500 and 1000 C.E., we have no way of confirming that the unique proto-Ebongwe terms were not adopted sometime during the second millennium B.C. For this reason, we analyze the majority of uniquely Ebongwe terms in chapter 6, which deals with the period between 1000 and 1900 C.E. Here, I briefly assess vocabularies related to iron and the production of iron alone, working from an assumption that peoples of this region have retained the same words since the era of the introduction of iron.

Modern-day Ebongwe speakers share the majority of iron-related lexicon with their Itsogho and Himba neighbors, suggesting that they were deeply embedded in the proto-Itsogho-Himba speech community when iron was introduced. All three languages attest a regional innovation for "iron" (*-uanga*), found only in the Okani and Coastlands languages. This term may have been derived from an earlier proto-Okani verb, *-uang-*, "to chop down a tree" (attested in Itsogho, Ebongwe, Himba); it is also the source of the nominal derivative, *-uangeo*, "ax" (Itsogho, Ebongwe).[88] Himba speakers attest an alternative for "ax" (*-goba*). This may have been a term used along the Ogooué–Ivindo trade route, for it is found in the Ubangian languages spoken around Ouesso as well (Baka, Bangombe, Bomassa).

There is only one piece of evidence to suggest that proto-Ebongwe speakers had contacts beyond the Itsogho and Himba cultural spheres; the Ebongwe language attests the northern-introduced term, *-baga*, "knife," although it is used uniquely in reference to daggers (double-sided knives). Neither the Itsogho nor Himba languages attest this term; in fact, the Mitsogho currently make no distinction in their terminologies between two-bladed and one-bladed knives. The unique use of this term by Ebongwe speakers suggests that their ancestors had trading contacts beyond the proto-Itsogho-Himba linguistic sphere. It can also be seen as evidence, much like the unique proto-Babinga term *-yebe/yobe*, "dagger," for a specialization in hunting because daggers are especially effective in slaying and skinning game.

SUMMING UP

This chapter has used archeological and linguistic evidence to document the drastic changes that occurred in west-central Africa after the introduction of bananas and iron. Bantu populations grew in number, settled into larger more sedentary villages, and began to produce larger quantities and more diverse styles of ceramics. Iron tools and banana cultivation also allowed Bantu villagers to move into forested regions away from the original riverine routes of settlement. This phenomenon resulted in the formation of numerous new speech communities, especially during the Late Stone to Metal Age (c.

1500–500 B.C.E.). As was the case in other parts of Africa, the introduction of iron engendered a greater centralization of local economies and an increase in economic specialization.

Linguistic evidence indicates that Batwa populations were affected by these historical developments as well. During the latter half of the Late Stone to Metal Age, proto-Babinga speakers of northern Congo began to lessen their ties to the agriculturalist communities they formerly shared languages with, and began to develop a more forest-oriented lifestyle. A similar distancing phenomenon occurred during the latter half of the Early Iron Age (c. 500–1000 C.E.) among proto-Ebongwe speakers, the linguistic ancestors of Batwa populations currently living in the du Chaillu massif of central Gabon. Based on this evidence, as well as reconstructed proto-Babinga vocabularies, I have argued that the ancestors of modern-day Batwa populations developed their own form of economic specialization during this time, serving as specialist procurers of forest products for entry into expanding systems of regional trade.

This historical scenario appears to support what have been considered revisionist theories regarding the origins of the central African Batwa—that the lifestyle we associate with these societies today is the result of a Neolithic adaptation, a phenomenon that accompanied the rise of agriculture within the rainforest proper. I depart from such theories, however, by arguing that true hunter-gatherer communities existed both prior to and after the period when bananas and iron were introduced. Such societies would have lived autonomously, relying on the subsistence strategies all autochthons used before the Bantu arrived. However, as Bantu communities expanded and regional economies became increasingly complex, these remnant communities were encountered and eventually assimilated into either forest-specialist or agriculturalist societies. This history explains why no Batwa societies have ever been observed using stone tools, subsisting on exclusively rainforest food sources, or speaking an indigenous language unique to them alone. They are not the descendants of Late Stone Age hunter-gatherers, but rather, of forest specialists, communities that had undergone long periods of intimate interactions with agriculturalists, thereby developing a lifestyle dependent on access to cultivated foods and iron.

The transformations wrought by the introduction of bananas and iron eventually allowed Bantu populations to assert hegemony over peoples they deemed first-comers on the land. The following chapter further documents this history, drawing on oral and ethnographic evidence to reconstruct a history of altered social, political, and religious relations between Bantu and Batwa.

NOTES

1. J. Vansina, *Paths in the Rainforest: Towards a History of Political Tradition in Equatorial Africa* (Madison, Wisconsin: University of Wisconsin Press, 1990), 61.

2. M. Posnansky, "Bantu Genesis," *Uganda Journal 25*, no. 1 (1998): 86–93; cited in Gerda Rossel, *Taxonomic-Linguistic Study of Plantain in Africa* (Leiden: CNWS, 1998), 1.

3. E. de Langhe, R. Swennen, and D. Vuylsteke, "Plantain in the Early Bantu World," *Azania* 29–39 (1994–95): 147–60.

4. Arguments for an introduction through Egypt are usually couched in terms of diffusion from the Upper Nile; see Vansina, *Paths,* 61–65 for an example of this approach. For theories on an introduction from Ethiopia, see D. Kervegant, *Le bananier et son exploitation* (Paris: Societé d'Édition Géographiques, Maritimes et Coloniales, 1935). Rossel proposes the southern Somali/northern Kenya coasts in *Taxonomic-Linguistic Study,* 120. References to an introduction via Madagascar can be seen in G. P. Murdock, *Africa: Its Peoples and Their Culture History* (New York: McGraw-Hill, 1959); N. W. Simmonds, *Bananas* (London: Longman, 1966); J. W. Purseglove, "The Origins and Migration of Crops in Tropical Africa," in *Origins of African Plant Domestication,* ed. J. R. Harlan, Jan M. J. de Wet, and Ann B. L. Stemler (Paris: Mouton, 1976); and D. A. Livingstone, "Interactions of Food Production and Changing Vegetation in Africa," in *From Hunters to Farmers: The Causes and Consequences of Food Production in Africa,* ed. J. Desmond Clark and Steven Brandt (Berkeley: University of California Press, 1984), 22–25.

5. N. W. Simmonds and K. Shepherd, "Taxonomy and Origins of Cultivated Bananas," *The Journal of the Linnean Society of London* 55 (1955): 302–12; N. W. Simmonds, *The Evolution of the Edible Banana* (London: Longmans, 1962), 134–41, as cited in Rossel, *Taxonomic-Linguistic Study,* 11.

6. de Langhe, Swennen, and Vuylsteke, "Plantain in the Early Bantu World," 148.

7. Ibid.

8. Simmonds, *Bananas,* as cited in de Langhe, "Plantain in the Early Bantu World," 150.

9. Ibid., 156.

10. Although these dates represent the radiocarbon dating results of one charcoal sample, they encompass the entire range of dates found in the pit at Nkang (pit #9). Dates were obtained at three different depths: (1) 200–250 cm: 2400 ± 60 bp, or 770–380 BC (Lv-1942); (2) 250–300 cm: 2490 ± 80 bp, or 790–400 BC (Lv-1943); and (3) 300–350 cm: 2490 ± 110 bp, or 840–370 BC (Lv-1944). See C. M. Mbida, "L'emergence de communautés villageoises au Cameroon Méridional; Étude archéologique des sites de Nkang et de Ndindan (Ph.D. thesis, Université Libre de Bruxelles, 1995–96), 639.

11. Estimations of when the banana was introduced have generally been based on historical evidence for its appearance on the East African coast. The oldest source attests the presence of the banana at the Ethiopian port of Adulis during the sixth century C.E. Thus, scholars have supposed an introduction during the first few centuries of the first millennium C.E. See Vansina, *Paths,* 64 for a more detailed discussion.

12. C. M. Mbida et al., "Evidence for Banana Cultivation and Animal Husbandry during the First Millenium B.C.E. in the Forest of Southern Cameroon," *Journal of Archaeological Science* 27 (2000): 151.

13. Rossel, *Taxonomic-Linguistic Study,* 198; de Langhe, Swennen, and Vuylsteke, "Plantain in the Early Bantu World," 150.

14. Rossel, *Taxonomic-Linguistic Study,* 114.

15. Ibid. Guthrie reconstructed *-konde* to the proto-Bantu language as "banana" (C.S. 1144). Later historians, however, considered it a loanword because *Musa* spp. are not indigenous to Africa and *-konde* is found in contiguous distribution across large expanses of land.

16. Ibid., 117. The languages she cites are Amba/Isi (D32), Tooro (J11), Konjo (J41), Kabwari (J56), and Rwanda (J61).

17. It is the use of alternative terms in these regions (*-kò* and *-tiba*) that suggests the original diffusion of plantains was impeded. Rossel's analysis of the distribution and etymology of *-kò* helps to reconstruct the history of plantains on the Teke plateau. She notes that *-kò* is used exclusively in languages that are today spoken on and around the Teke plateau (e.g., Tio, Tsaayi, Ngungwel, Mongo, Loi/Ngiri, Iyaa, Ilaali, Nzebi, Mbete, Beembe, and Bwende). In contrast to Guthrie—who considered *-kò* a shortened version of *-konde*—she suggests that the term is derived from the proto-Bantu *-gòngò* which enjoys widespread use in the Bantu world as a referent to plants with large leaves (for examples, see Rossel, *Taxonomic-Linguistic Study*, 110–11). Because the Teke languages regularly lose [*ng*] in the second consonant position, she suggests that the use of *-kò* as a referent to plantains developed among the proto-Teke (where $*g > k$ is regular), and that their initial exposure to the plantain was through the use of its leaves. The term, and perhaps the plant as well, is likely to have been introduced into nearby regions in slightly later eras, when peoples linguistically ancestral to the Teke came to dominate local systems of trade.

18. As discussed following, the Bantu speech communities that later came to inhabit these regions (Teke, Lumbu, Vili) were just beginning to be formed during this time, and evidence of village settlements is not found in either the Bateke Plateau or the Mayombe mountain range until the last few centuries B.C.E. See data regarding Madingo-Kayes (fourth century B.C.E.) and also that of Djambala (third to fourth centuries B.C.E.), following.

19. Arguing from evidence of what they see as successive phonological shifts, de Langhe, Swennen, and Vuylsteke have suggested this same path of diffusion, with a subsequent introduction into southern/southeastern Africa via Angola and Luba speakers of southeastern Congo-Kinshasa. See "Plantain in the Early Bantu World," 156–57.

20. D. Phillipson, *African Archaeology* (Cambridge: Cambridge University Press, 1993), 159. For a full analysis of the role of copper in sub-Saharan history and societies, see Eugenia Herbert, *Red Gold of Africa: Copper in Precolonial History and Culture* (Madison: University of Wisconsin Press, 1984). Although copper played an integral part in the development regional economies in west-central Africa, archaeological evidence suggests that "it filled the role of ritual, ornamental, and status metal with almost no hint of utilitarian use—for which ample supplies of iron were available" (Herbert, *Red Gold*, 110). Because this chapter focuses on the transformations that ironworking engendered in central African agricultural systems, copper is not treated here.

21. This phenomenon has been observed on the Otoumbi massif and in the Lopé Reserve, where sites containing polished stone axes/hoes and ceramics of the Epona style (Otoumbi 13, Lope 12) are dated to between 800 and 300 B.C.E. Nearby are sites containing the earliest evidence of iron smelting in west-central Africa (Otoumbi 2 and Lope 5), dated to the seventh and sixth centuries B.C.E. (R. Oslisly, "Archéologie et Paléoenvironnement dans la Réserve de la Lopé: Rapport Final" [Groupement AGRECO/C.T.F.T., unpublished manuscript, 1996]). It must be noted that stone tools continue to be manufactured for ritual and utilitarian uses in a number of sub-Saharan societies today. See P. Lavachery, "De la pierre au metal: Archéologie des depots Holocenes de l'abri de Shum Laka (Cameroon)" (Ph.D. thesis, Université Libre de Bruxelles, 1997–98), 440–43. Stone is also used in gross smithing procedures (Eugenia Herbert, personal communication, 3 April, 2002).

22. Other early uses may have been the production of tools for fishing, woodcarving, and boat making, as well as the manufacture of new types of arms.

23. For Taruga, see B. Fagg, "The Nok Culture: Excavations at Taruga," *West African Journal of Archaeology* 1 (1968), 27–30; A. Fagg, "A Preliminary Report on an Occupation Site in the Nok Valley, Nigeria: Samun Dukiya," *West African Journal of Archaeology* 2 (1978), 75–79; T. Shaw, *Nigeria: Its Archaeology and Early History* (London: Thames and Hudson, 1978); and D. Calvocoressi and N. David, " A New Survey of Radiocarbon and Thermoluminescence Dates for West Africa, *Journal of African History* 20, no. 1 (1979): 1–19.

24. These earlier dates were identified at the sites of Rwiyanje I (1230 ± 155 B.C.E., 905 ± 285 B.C.E.) and Mubuga V (1210 ± 135 B.C.E.) in Burundi. See M. C. Van Grunderbeek, E. Roche, and H. Doutrelepont, "Le premier âge du fer au Rwanda et Burundi; archéologie et environnement," *Journal des Africanistes* 52 (1982): 55.

25. B. Clist, *Gabon: 100,000 ans d'histoire* (Libreville: Centre Cultural Français Saint-Exupery/Sepia, 1995), 220; C. Ehret, "The Establishment of Iron-Working in Eastern, Central, and Southern Africa: Linguistic Inferences on Technological History," *Sprache und Geschichte in Afrika* 16–17 (1995–96): 1–47.

26. Oslisly, "Hommes et milieux à l'Holocène dans la moyenne vallée de l'Ogooué (Gabon), *Bulletin de la Société Préhistorique Française* 95, no. 1 (1998): 98.

27. P. de Maret and G. Thiry, "How Old Is the Iron Age in Central Africa?" in *The Culture and Technology of African Iron Production*, ed. Peter R. Schmidt (Gainesville, Florida: University Press of Florida, 1996), 31.

28. Mbida, "L'emergence de communautés."

29. J. Denbow, "Congo to Kalahari: Data and Hypotheses about the Political Economy of the Western Stream of the Early Iron Age," *African Archaeological Review* 8 (1990), 155.

30. For an overview of the evidence associated with these sites, see R. Lanfranchi and B. Clist, eds., *Aux origines de L'Afrique Centrale* (Libreville: Centre Culturel Francais Saint Exupery/CICIBA, 1991), 205 (Oveng), 210 (Mare du Flec), 213 (Sakuzi and Gombe).

31. C. Ehret, "The Establishment of Iron-Working," 1–47. What is presented here is a modified version of that history, for it integrates linguistic data I collected in the field (Congo Republic and Gabon). For a more detailed accounting of this history, see K. Klieman, "Hunters and Farmers of the Western Equatorial Rainforest, Economy, and Society, 3000 B.C. to A.D. 1880" (Ph.D. diss., University of California, Los Angeles), chap. 4.

32. Linguistic evidence places the proto-Eastern Bantu community along the western reaches of the Great Lakes Region during the first half of the last millennium B.C.E., and Central and Eastern Sudanic communities were located to their north and northwest.

33. Of these, only the generic word for "iron" (*-tále*) shows clear links with the savanna regions to the south. Both *-túli,* "blacksmith," and *-bèlì* "knife," show clusterings of attestations in the Teke languages or those to their immediate north or west, but they are additionally used in languages spoken along the Congo, Ubangi, and Sangha Rivers. Attestations of the term *-tul,* "to forge," are exceptionally widespread within west-central Africa. As with the other terms, there is a clustering of attestations in Teke languages, but *-tul* is also present in a large number of languages spoken up the Congo, Ubangi, and Sangha Rivers, as well as across the entirety of southern Cameroon. This widespread distribution—so different from the related *-túli,* "blacksmith"—makes it difficult to agree with Ehret in assigning it a southeastern source.

34. Klieman, "Hunters and Farmers," 208–10.

35. As linguistic data illustrate following, Bantu expansion into the southern regions of Congo and Gabon appear to have initially proceeded westward along rivers situated toward the south (the Niari and Louessé), where the land was characterized by a forest-savanna mosaic.

36. This term is also found in languages of the Cameroonian coast (A-30), at the confluence of the Sangha and Congo Rivers (Pama C-30), and near the confluence of the Congo and Kwa Rivers (Yans B-85) to the south. These isolated attestations are best described as a relict distribution, suggesting that the word is reconstructible to proto-Bantu. Perhaps *-ngonzo* was associated with iron ore or other types of stones. It might also represent an earlier spread of an Ubangian word for iron. The resolution of this issue will require continued research among Bantu and Ubangian languages; as yet, I have not been able to find any attestation of this word beyond the rainforest regions.

37. This term is found in Nkomi, Galwa, Orungu, and Mpongwe, as well as among peoples to the south of the Ogooué.

38. K. Klieman, "Towards A History of Pre-colonial Gabon: Farmers and Forest Specialists along the Ogooué, c. 500 B.C.–1000 A.D.," in *Culture, Ecology, and Politics in Gabon's Rainforest,* ed. Michael C. Reed and James F. Barnes (Lewiston, New Jersey: Edwin Mellen Press, 2003).

39. Some scholars have proposed that such pits were originally used for the storage of surplus goods or defensive purposes (Mbida, "L'emergence de communautés"); however, it is generally considered that they are simply the result of people extracting soils for house construction.

40. Mbida et al., "Evidence for Banana Cultivation," 151.

41. Among the best known of these new traditions are the Obobogo group of southern Cameroon, the Okala group in the Estuary, the Epona and Okanda traditions of the middle Ogooué, and the Sakuzi group of the lower Congo.

42. De Maret and Thiry, "How Old Is the Iron Age?," 30.

43. For a full accounting of these dates, see M. K. H. Eggert, "Imbonga and Batalimo: Ceramic Evidence for Early Settlement of the Equatorial Rainforest," *The African Archaeological Review* 5 (1987): 132–33, as well as M. K. H. Eggert, "Central Africa and the Archaeology of the Equatorial Rainforest; Reflections on Some Major Topics," *The Archaeology of Africa,* ed. Thurstan Shaw et al. (New York: Routledge, 1993), 306.

44. See R. de Bayle des Hermens, "Résultats d'ensemble des missions de recherches préhistoriques effectuées en 1966–1967 et 1968 en Republic Centrafricaine," *Bulletin de la Société Royale Belge d'Anthropologie et de Préhistoire* 80 (1968): 5–20.

45. Eggert, "Central Africa," 311.

46. de Bayle des Hermens, "Résultats d'ensemble," 5–20.

47. Eggert, "Central Africa," 314.

48. Ibid.

49. Ibid., 326.

50. Ibid., 322.

51. Ibid., 314.

52. Eggert, "Central Africa," 319.

53. D. E. Saxon, "Linguistic Evidence for the Eastward Spread of Ubangian Peoples," in *The Archaeological and Linguistic Reconstruction of African History,* ed. C. Ehret and M. Posnansky (Berkeley: University of California Press, 1982).

54. R. Harms, *River of Wealth, River of Sorrow; the Central Zaire Basin in the Era of the Slave and Ivory Trade, 1500–1891* (New Haven, Connecticut: Yale University Press, 1981), 67.

55. B. Pincon, "L'archéologie du Royaume Teke," in *Aux origines de l'Afrique Centrale,* ed. R. Lanfranchi and B. Clist, (Libreville, Gabon: Centres Culturels Français CICIBA, 1991).

56. This dating, as well as all details to follow in the next two paragraphs, can be found in Denbow, "Congo to Kalahari," 139–76.

57. Ibid., 155.

58. The most consistent of these shared sound shifts can be seen in the pronoun class eight noun prefix from [*bi-] to [be-]; this shift is not apparent in any of the C-10 or C-30 Bantu languages of the region (i.e., Pande, Ngando, Mbati, Inyele, Bongili, Bambomba, Bakolu, Kabunga, Ingundi, Bobangi). For details and more examples of shared traits, see Klieman, "Hunters and Farmers."

59. S. Bahuchet, "Les Pygmees Aka et Baka: Contribution de l'ethnolinguistique a l'histoire des populations forestièrs d'Afrique Centrale" (Thèse de Doctorat d'Etat, Université René Descartes, Paris, 1989).

60. Of the 600 words identified as common to Aka and Baka, Bahuchet suggests that 365 are unique to them alone, 145 are found in Ngando (Bantu C-19), 64 are found in Ngbaka-Ma'bo (Ubangian), and 70 are found in Ngando and Ngbaka-Ma'bo both. Although he did search out these terms among rather extensive collections of data for languages spoken in the Lobaye region (i.e., Ngbaka-Ma'bo [corpus of 8,000 words], Monzombo [3,000 words], Gbanzili [3,000 words], Bantu languages [Mbati and Ngando, 3,000 words each], and Pande [227 words]), I have extended the analyses by searching out these vocabulary items among the C-10 languages of the panhandle region. Of 145 comparable terms, only 13 were determined to be unique to Batwa languages alone. These have been included in the list of proto-Babinga vocabulary, Table 4.2(a) following.

61. The Baka language, along with Ngbaka-Ma'bo, Monzombo, and Gbanzili, form the western branch of the Gbanzili-Sere subgroup of the western branch of Ubangian languages. L. Bouquiaux and J. M. C. Thomas, "Le peuplement oubanguien: Hypothèse de reconstruction des mouvments migratoires dans la région oubanguienne d'après les données linguistiques, ethnolinguistiques, et de tradition orale," in *L'Expansion Boantoue,* ed. L. Bouquiaux (Paris: SELAF, 1980), 807–824. Although the arrival of members of this western branch (into southeastern Central African Republic) is considered to be a relatively recent event, classifications of the wider Ubangian family indicate that western Ubangians were present in regions to the north and west of the bend in the Ubangi from at least 3000 B.C.E. (see Saxon, "Linguistic Evidence"). There they carried out lifestyles similar to the Bantu populations of the time. They lived in villages, produced ceramics, raised goats, and fished. Their cultivation systems, however, were based on slightly different crops (cowpeas, sesame seeds, yams, and calabashes).

62. L. Luca Cavalli-Sforza, Paolo Menozzi, and Alberto Piazza, eds., *The History and Geography of Human Genes* (Princeton: Princeton University Press, 1993), 178. These conclusions are drawn from the analyses of Ellen M. Wijsman, who states "the estimates of admixture indicate that the proportion of genes in these populations derive mostly, if not entirely, from the Bantus or a similar population. Thus, it seems . . . that the ancestors of the Pygmies in these areas were related primarily to the ancestors of the Bantus, and that perhaps some gene flow occurred from the original Pygmy population" ("Estimation of Genetic Admixture in Pygmies," in *African Pygmies,* ed. L. Luca Cavalli-Sforza [New York: Academic Press, 1986], 357–58). Although there are a number of issues to be dealt with before accepting the conclusions of such genetic research wholeheartedly (especially the premise that "pure" or "original" "Pygmies" ever existed at all), these data seem to me

to be relevant, because in the Central African Republic case, genetic samples were collected directly from the Aka and their neighbors and not based on a cumulative pool of data comprising genetic samples from various peoples deemed "Bantu" or "Pygmy" across the continent.

63. J. Lewis, "Forest Hunter-Gatherers and Their World: A Study of the Mbenjele Yaka Pygmies of Congo-Brazzaville and Their Secular and Religious Representations" (Ph.D. thesis, London School of Economics and Political Science, 2002), 210.

64. See discussion in chapter 4.

65. J. Lewis, "Forest Hunter-Gatherers," 51, footnote 45.

66. These terms have been identified through an analysis of 250 lexicon, both cultural and core alike. "Unique" in this instance refers to words that are commonly found in all five of the C-group Batwa language communities (and oftentimes Baka and Bangombe as well), but not in those of Bantu- or Ubangian-speaking communities of the region. In some instances, a single term appears in just one of the agriculturalist/fishing peoples' languages. This is likely due to a more recent history of cohabitation or symbiotic relations between Batwa and neighboring groups, such as can be seen between Ngando speakers and certain Aka, Inyele speakers (at Dongou) and the Bambenga, Kabunga speakers and the Bambenga east of the Likouala-aux-herbes, Bomwali and Bongili speakers with Baluma and Mikaya near Ouesso and south along the Sangha, and Bomassa (Ubangian) speakers with Bangombe and Bambenga in Bomassa village. With the exception of the Ngando and Kabunga, these associations are modeled on hierarchical patron/client models of interaction. In many instances, these agriculturalist/fishing communities openly acknowledge the Batwa origin of the shared term, stating that the word (or object/ technique it refers to) has its origin in Pygmy societies alone.

67. The loss of vocabulary in this version of the Bambenga language may be due to a more recent history of intensive contacts with riverine Bantu-speaking communities. For example, I collected data among a group of Bambenga speakers who lived in close association with Inyele peoples living in Dongou. Research carried out in the interior regions might indicate that these words continue to be used among more autonomous groups. The linguist William Gardner identified six such communities in 1990, all located in the northern and northeastern reaches of the Epena district (Molembe [outside Mbanza], Mobangui, Mossombo [near Minganga], Mbili, Zelo, and Yecola); see William C. Garder, "Language Use in the Epena District of Northern Congo" (master's thesis, University of North Dakota, 1990).

68. Malcolm Guthrie, *Comparative Bantu,* 4 vols. (Farnham, England: Gregg Press, 1967–71), 110.

69. Languages spoken in Angola, southeastern Congo-Kinshasa, and Zambia, for example. This distribution has been identified through the use of the linguistic database *Bantu Lexical Reconstructions II,* created by A. Coupez, Y. Bastin, and E. Mumba (Tervuren: Musée royale de l'Afrique Centrale, 1998), which does not provide information as to the specific language where attestations are found—only the linguistic "regions" as based on Guthrie's categorization (*Comparative Bantu,* 1967–71).

70. S. Bahuchet, *La Recontre des agriculteurs: Les Pygmées parmi les peuples d'Afrique Centrale* (Paris: SELAF, 1993), 57–58.

71. M. Regnault, "Les Babinga: Negrilles de la Sangha," *L'Anthropologie* 22 (1911): 283.

72. This term is derived from the proto-Bantu **-gubo,* "skin" (C.S. 874).

73. Roger Blench has suggested that this term is derived from the proto-Voltaic form **-gbeN,* which would trace it back seven thousand years as a referent to stone-bladed

knives (personal communication, 14 October, 2000; R. Blench, "The Niger-Congo Languages: A Proposed Internal Classification" [Internet communication, 2000]). Although this may be the case, the **-gbe* of Niger-Congo languages most regularly appears as *–gue* in Bantu languages (not *–be*). Given the fact that proto-Babinga and modern forest-specialist languages of northern Congo/southern Central African Republic so closely follow Bantu phonologically, I do not consider this the most likely etymology for the **-yobe/*-yébe* form.

74. Because I did not collect the Aka data myself, I cannot confirm whether it refers to semi-permanent or permanent types of housing.

75. The phonological sound shift took place through the following process: **-lį +
-yángo > liángo > lángo. The high vowel [į] causes **y>nz* in Aka and **y>dȝ* in Bambenjele, thus producing the more archaic forms of *nzángo* and mandȝango.

76. Guthrie cites attestations in Duala (A24), Yaa (B73c), Bemba (M42), Nyoro (E11), and Mbundu (R11), among others. Guthrie, *Comparative Bantu*, 150.

77. S. Bahuchet, "Les Pygmees Aka et Baka," 278.

78. The derivation process is **-còdo > *-cò0 > *-có* (shift from low to high tone as a result of syllabic reduction).

79. I argue that the use of this term among agriculturalist/fishing communities is the result of Atlantic era trade dynamics; see chapter 7 for full discussion.

80. The *Tetrorchidium* sp. is often referred to as a "soap tree," for its bark, when crushed, is used to wash clothes. In languages of central Gabon (Fang, Itsogho), this tree is specifically referred to as "soap of the Batwa" (*ntsap-beku* and *tsavo-a-abongo*, respectively), suggesting that it may have been introduced to Bantu agriculturalists by indigenous peoples. The bark of this plant is also used in gargles against toothache and added to infusions that are applied to infections. The bark of *Ongokea gore* is used throughout Congo and Gabon as a purgative for infants and children. It is either made into an infusion and imbibed, or the freshly scraped bark can be rubbed on the tip of a mother's breast to help deconstipate an infant. Finally, the cotyledons of *Irvingia excelsa* are today eaten by numerous Batwa peoples of the Sangha region. If gathered in large quantities, they are grilled and pounded into a hot waxy mass and saved for consumption at a later time. See A. Bouquet and A. Jacquot, "Essai de géographie linguistique sur quelques plantes médicinales du Congo Brazzaville," *Cahiers Orstom* 5, no. 3–4 (1967): 5–25; A. Raponda-Walker and R. Sillans, *Les plantes utiles du Gabon* (Paris: P. Lechavalier, 1961; reprint Sepia, 1995).

81. Bahuchet, "Les Pygmees Aka et Baka," 325.

82. A somewhat similar historical scenario has been identified in the south-central regions of Africa (Malawi), where archaeological evidence indicates that for a few centuries after the advent of agriculture, farmers and hunter-gatherers entered into a period of increased interactions. See for example, G. G. Y. Mgomezulu, "Food Production: The Beginnings in the Linthipe/Cangone Area of Dedza District, Malawi (Ph.D. diss., University of California, Berkeley, 1975); D. Crader, "Faunal Remains from Chencherer 2 Rock Shelter, Malawi," *South African Archaeological Bulletin* (1984): 37–52; S. Davison, "Namaso and the Iron Age Sequence of Southern Malawi," *Azania* 26 (1991).

83. This observation was originally made in an article by R. C. Bailey et al. ("Hunting and Gathering in the Tropical Rainforest: Is it Possible?" *American Anthropologist* 91, no. 1 [1989]: 59–82). The notion that human beings could not live on rainforest resources alone was vigorously rebutted by ecologists and anthropologists alike (see, for example, H. Terashima, M. Ichikawa, and M. Sawada, "Wild Plant Utilization of the Balese and the Efe of the Itori Forest, the Republic of Zaire [Kyoto: Center for African Area Studies, 1988];

H. Terashima and M. Ichikawa, *Afora Catalog of Useful Plants of Tropical Africa* [Kyoto: Center for African Area Studies, 1991]; S. Bahuchet, D. McKey, and I. de Garine, "Wild Yams Revisited: Is Independence from Agriculture Possible for Rainforest Hunter-Gatherers?" *Human Ecology* 19, no. 2 [1991]: 213–243; H. Sato, "The Potential of Edible Wild Yams and Yam-like Plants as Staple Food Resource in the African Tropical Rain Forest," *African Study Monographs* [Kyoto], no. 26 [2001]: 123–134). Although these studies did show that there were sufficient nutrients in rainforest foodstuffs to survive without agricultural products, they did not invalidate the original observation that no central African societies have ever been observed living on rainforest resources alone.

84. See K. Klieman, "Towards A History."

85. Sites containing Epona-ware are Okanda 5, Okanda 6, Epona 1, Epona 2, Otoumbi 13, Otoumbi 12, Ndjole Pk. 5, and Lalala, in the Gabon Estuary. For the first two, see A. Assoko Ndong, "Archéologie du peuplement Holocene," 450–455. For the remaining, see Oslisly, *Préhistoire de la Moyenne Vallée de l'Ogooué (Gabon)* (Paris: ORSTOM, 1992), chap. 4. There is some disagreement as to whether the ceramics found in the Estuary regions (at Lalala) should be classed in the Epona tradition. Although Assoko-Ndong argues that they should, Clist considers them to be part of an earlier Okala Neolithic tradition that is found in the estuary region alone.

86. The four new types of pottery to appear are Yindo-ware (750–400 B.C.E.), Okanda-ware (from c. 400 B.C.E.), Lindili-ware (20–800 C.E.), and Otoumbi-ware (100–400 C.E.). Oslisly previously documented the presence of Okanda- and Otoumbiware. Yindo and Lindili were more recently discovered by Assoko Ndong, "Archéologie du peuplement Holocene."

87. See Assoko Ndong, "Archéologie du peuplement Holocene," 449, 167.

88. There are a series of words referring to smiths among the Bakongo that appear to have -*ang*- or -*gang*- as their root: *mpangulu* appears as a referent to "blacksmith" in a seventeenth-century dictionary by a certain Father Gheel; in a more modern dictionary (P. Swartenbroeckx, *Dictionnaire Kikongo et Kituba-Francais* [Kinshasa: CEEBA, 1973]) *mpangulu* refers to "creation, fabrication," whereas "blacksmith" is *ngangula*. These might somehow be related to the proto-Okani forms, but I have not yet figured out how (Kikongo attestations are cited in de Heusch, *Le roi de Kongo,* 107).

5

BANTU SOCIETIES AND THE IDEOLOGY OF THE PRIMORDIAL BATWA

In this chapter we return to the oral and ethnographic sources and what they reveal about politics, ideology, and relations between Bantu and Batwa after the introduction of bananas and iron. Although the evidence used reflects the circumstances of the last three to four hundred years, it retains earlier layers of social discourse that are at a variance with the modern vision of the socially subordinate Batwa. When viewed through the lens of the first-comer paradigm, these data show that from very early times the Bantu societies of west-central Africa held a common set of beliefs about Batwa supernatural powers. Furthermore, their beliefs about these supernatural powers played an integral role in the development of central African notions of politico-religious leadership. Although these beliefs manifested themselves in different ways during the Atlantic era, I argue that they were originally derived from a common and ancestral political-cultural model that posed first-comers as experts in the religious sphere. Elements of this model have already been presented in chapter 3; here we focus on the cosmological implications of such ideologies, and the ways that they were transformed after the introduction of bananas and iron.

The chapter begins by arguing that west-central Africans long ago created their own Ideology of the Primordial Batwa, long before contact with Europeans and exposure to the ideas of the Western Pygmy Paradigm. The core elements of this ideology are unusually clear among the Mitsogho, especially in genesis accounts and traditions about the origins of *bwiti,* their most important ancestral cult. Accordingly, I begin with these traditions and their image of the primordial Batwa. This approach provides us with a template for recognizing similar cosmological associations and beliefs among other west-central African societies, where they tend to persist in more veiled or disjointed forms.

Because religion and politics are so closely intertwined in central Africa, it follows that these cosmological beliefs would have important repercussions in the political sphere. The second section of this chapter illustrates that this is in fact the case. It argues that the Ideology of the Primordial Batwa played a central role in the development of notions of leadership within the central African world, but that a new political-cultural model was developed after the introduction of bananas and iron. This was engendered by the rise of territorial chiefs, new owners of the land who in essence usurped the status of first-comers. In an effort to legitimize their own rule and continue to honor the first-comer status of the Batwa in purely symbolic ways, a whole new set of myths, rituals, and oral traditions were developed. Because they are employed widely across the central African world, I argue that these myths, rituals, and oral traditions are the remnants of an ancient political charter, one whose central tenets spread widely across central Africa during the Early Iron Age (c. 500 B.C.E.–1000 C.E.).

MITSOGHO VISIONS OF THE PRIMORDIAL BATWA

The Bokudu Narrative

Chapter 2 illustrated that the Tsogho language is part of a more widespread Okani language group (including Okanda, Pinji, Himba, and Shake), whose linguistic ancestors lived around the middle regions of the Ogooué River by as early as 2000 B.C.E. Although a number of the communities that speak languages derived from proto-Okani still reside in regions close to the Ogooué, the Tsogho are today located much farther south. Numbering fewer than 13,000 people, they live in the mountainous regions of the du Chaillu massif, primarily between the Ngounié and Lolo Rivers. Despite their low population numbers, the Mitsogho are known throughout Gabon as a people with exceptionally powerful supernatural skills. They are reputed to be the source of the Bwiti ancestral/prosperity cult, an initiation society that has been adopted by numerous societies of central and eastern Gabon over (at least) the last two hundred years.[1] There exist today numerous versions or branches of the Bwiti cult; these branches are practiced by different ethnic groups and many have been heavily syncretized with Christian religious practices. Each of these groups, however, relies on a liturgy performed in an archaic form of the Tsogho language.

Although we look at myths surrounding the origins of the Bwiti society in the following paragraphs, we must begin with an analysis of the Bokudu narrative to understand the cosmology that informs Mitsogho religious and political thought. As Gollnhoffer and Sillans have explained it, the Bokudu is a mythico-religious narrative that recounts Mitsogho history from the origins of the universe to present day.[2] It can only be told by *evovi* (judges), lineage heads who serve as intermediaries between their community and the supernatural world. These individuals are also referred to as *kumu-a-mbuku* (owner of the village); they occupy the highest position of political authority among the Mitsogho, who have no traditional chiefs of clans or districts. When a *ghevovi* ("judge") is near death, he passes his knowledge of the Bokudu to his legitimate heir, that is, his sister's eldest son. The sacredness of this narrative is evident in the fact that it must be recounted in an idiomatic form of the Tsogho language, one that is unique to the *evovi* alone. Likewise, the *evovi* are required to make supplications to the supreme nature spirit Ya Mwei (mother *mwei*) before commencing the narrative. It is said that if these ritual acts are not performed, both the *ghevovi* and his audience might be swallowed into a nearby river, or alternatively, a hole that suddenly appears in the ground.

The Bokudu narrative begins with an account of genesis. Before the world existed, there was the Supreme Being Muanga.[3] Because it is he who created the universe, Muanga is also referred to as Koko-Akanza (grandfather of the universe), Ghevanga-danga (he who endlessly organizes), and Kumu-atsenge (owner of the land). Muanga lives at Mobumate, located where the earth meets the sky, and surrounded by a vast river called Mubu. The ancestors of all humans originally lived in Mobumate. They were primordial beings that lived in the shadows and darkness. Enclosed in packets, they could not open their eyes or speak. Because there was no room for them to move, Muanga used the turtle to split the earth from the sky.[4] As a result, the primordial beings were required to travel in pirogues along the Mubu River to reach the upper world. However, because Muanga had separated the earth from the sky, the sun began to shine into the upper world, and the primordial beings got hot. Muanga blew on them, causing the waters of the Mubu to cool and moisten them. It was this combination of wetness and air/wind that led to the original creation of humanity. As the Mitsogho see it, the first human beings were "engendered by the wind; nourished by water."[5]

The imagery surrounding ancestral beings in Mobumate acts as an obvious metaphor for the fetus in utero. The imagery also serves as the source for a great deal of symbolism that is employed in Mitsogho thought and religious practices. For example, both water and wind are seen as forces of fecundity and creation. The importance of the former is associated with Ya Mwei, who is considered to live in the bottom of rivers. As the *ghevovi* Ghebonzwe Sekwae stated, "The mother of us all is Ya Mwei, that is, the water. We all came after. We all are humans, we all are water. She nourished the trees, the animals, you. The water, that is the human." Ya Mwei is also the focus of one of Mitsogho men's most important initiation societies. Considered to have an influence over the maintenance of social order, this society requires that young initiates (age 7–8 years) undergo a series of often painful proofs at an initiation camp in the forest. It is there that they begin to receive her knowledge, although they will not be able to hear messages until later in life. Following the precepts of Niger-Congo religious beliefs, each clan and lineage associates Ya Mwei with a particular cascade or waterfall. Adepts frequent this location to interpret the messages that she sends. As the supreme symbol of fertility, Ya Mwei is often assimilated with the earth as well.[6]

The wind, on the other hand, is especially associated with the Supreme Being. The Mitsogho use the word *opunga* to refer to this creative aspect of his power, which is translated variously as "air, wind, whisper, speech, voice."[7] Thus, Muanga is also referred to as Nzambe-apongo (Nzambi the wind) and Muanga-benda (Muanga who speaks, i.e., creates). Through whistling, Muanga is said to have engendered three supernatural siblings: Kombe, the sun (and male principle of the universe), Ngonde, the moon (and female principle of the universe), and Dinzona/Disumba, the being from which all supernatural phenomena emanate.[8] Likewise, *opunga* is seen as the source of all animal, plant, and human life. "Even if you see us planting manioc and taro," the *ghevovi* Mboña-a-Moñepi indicates, " it is nonetheless the wind that makes these food plants grow." The same can be said of human conception, for 'if the wind has not entered into the girl and boy, it is not the boy who can cause the pregnancy, it is not in that (the sex act) that the human appears."[9] As is the case with numerous societies around the globe, the Mitsogho also associate breath or *opunga* with the human soul (*ghedidi*). The reflection of the soul can be seen in the shadow (*ghedinadina*); both *ghedidi* and *ghedinadina* leave the body when a person dies.

The Mitsogho genesis account provides a particular version of cosmological beliefs that are found among numerous societies of central Africa. The notion of a primordial water—one that separates the world of terrestrial and celestial beings—can be seen among the Mpongwe, Vili, Kongo, Yaka, southern Mongo, and even the Kuba and Luba to the east. Kuba traditions associate this water with the original creator Mboom (The Great Water) who engendered nine children (all named *Woot*). It was these children, in turn, who created the world. Other Kuba myths speak of a primordial marsh that gave birth to Mboom himself.[10] Nkongolo, the founding hero of the Luba dynasty, is associated with the rainbow. He represents the unification of the celestial "fire" (i.e., sun) and the wetness of terrestrial rivers or swamps, paralleling the theme of celestial heat and water in the Bokudu narrative.[11] We encounter these same themes among the Vili, Kongo, Yaka, and southern Mongo speakers, following. All of these societies have myths that speak of an ancestral mother emerging from water to engender either the first human beings or a dynasty's founding king.

The association between wind/breath and creation recurs widely in west-central Africa as well. The Bafut of central Cameroon believe that the "breath-life" of humans is released upon death. Thereafter it wanders about seeking out a humid environment where it can be reborn in the form of another soul. Like the Mitsogho, the Nso (central Cameroon) consider a child to be conceived when divinity breathes life into the woman's womb. This takes place during the sixth month of pregnancy, when the fetus begins to move. Peoples of the Kongolese cultural sphere also associate winds, tempests, or whistling sounds with nature spirits (*simbi* or *nkita*)—the supernatural powers that control the fertility and fecundity of people and land.

The Mitsogho Bokudu narrative goes on to recount that after living at *Mobumate* for some time, the primordial beings began to complain of too much water and heat. Because of this, their chief—a Pygmy named Motsoi—went to Muanga to ask if his people could descend to the earth. Muanga was not happy, but he obliged. According to some versions, he used a long wooden pole to pierce the sky; he then gave Motsoi a chain that enabled him to descend. Other versions recount that this pole was made of iron. Motsoi surveyed the New World, found it pleasing, and reported back that all the others should come as well. After surveying the earth, Motsoi named all things ("this is the river, this is the house, this is the banana") and instructed others on how to use the resources of the land. In some versions, his wife Madombe accompanies him, or alternatively, his son Ghebangoa provides the names.

The description of *Mobumate* as too wet and hot has associations with pregnancy and impending birth because, in many Bantu societies, pregnancy is conceived of as an "internal fire."[12] The use of a chain or pole to descend from the heavens appears in numerous oral traditions as well. Baumann refers to it as the theme of the "heavenly ladder."[13] It appears among the Kuba, who recount that a rope, or alternatively, a spider web, was employed.[14] Luba traditions refer to the spider web alone. Finally, the pioneering role of Motsoi and his family clearly reflect the Mitsogho belief that Batwa peoples were the original owners of the land. Especially notable are their links to the Supreme Being and upper world. The Mitsogho reiterate this association today by referring to Batwa peoples as "those who fell from the sky."[15]

After living on the earth, Motsoi impregnated Madombe, thus engendering all the races that exist in the world. In her role as the ancestral mother, Madombe is assimilated with Ya Mwei, the primordial waters, and accordingly, the earth.[16] In some versions of the Bokudu narrative, early life on earth is seen as a period when all of the races lived together without conflict. Others describe it as a period when all beings (human and animal) were in a state of confusion, that is, incest and bestiality. All versions of the Bokudu narrative credit the Batwa with remedying this situation, through the introduction of fire, dogs and dog bells, or the *tsenda,* an iron razor of indigenous origin.

One version recounts that Motsoi and his son Ghebangao descended from Mobumate with fire. Although the other beings originally possessed fire as well, they spent all of their time eating fruit and their fires eventually went out. Because Motsoi and Ghebangoa maintained their fire, they were able to chase all the animals into the forest, and thus establish proper order on earth. Another version indicates that God told both the Blacks and Whites to fetch fire, but both refused to go. The Pygmies however, followed this order, and returned with both fire *and* dogs. The dogs wore bells that made such great noise that all of the animals were frightened and fled into the forest. The *ghevovi* Nzondo-a-Mighino recounts this version of the narrative, additionally indicating that it was the Batwa who introduced the *tsenda,* the first iron tool:

> If the Pygmy had not brought the dog bell, we would live, until present, together with the animals. Because we were all in the same place. If they had not hid themselves we would not eat them. It was from that moment that we were separated and the animals and men couldn't see one another. Before we were all furry (like the animals). It is since they gave us the knife (*tsenda* "indigenous razor") and said "shave yourselves of all the fur." (141)

As we learned in chapter 3, the notion that Batwa peoples introduced fire, iron, or iron tools is widespread in the central African region. Oral traditions of the Aka and Monzombo credit the Batwa not only with the introduction of fire and iron, but with cooked food and prohibitions against incest as well. These myths have perplexed Western scholars for decades on end. For lack of a better explanation, they have been interpreted as remembrances of the crucial role that autochthonous people played in the earliest stages of Bantu expansion.[17] But these are the very same themes that appear in myths about founding heroes and kings among centralized societies of the central African region. In both instances, these myths refer to individuals who were considered to hold extraordinary supernatural powers, especially regarding the spirits of the land. Given the widespread appearance of this Batwa as "civilizing hero" theme, it seems probable that the myths reflect the same kind of political impetus as those surrounding the origins of dynasties and kingdoms—the need to legitimize late-comer rule. We return to this issue in the concluding section of this chapter, where were will consider the origins of "civilizer" myths as they relate to the Batwa.

In the meantime, it is important to understand why central Africans often associate civilizing heroes and first-comers with the introduction of fire, iron, or cooked foods. Although the introduction of iron may be seen as an event that initiated the start of a new civilization among central African societies, the mention of fire, cooked food, and Batwa civilizers suggests that such associations are derived from a much more symbolic system of thought. This is indeed the case, for these associations are derived from Bantu conceptualizations about the transformative properties of heat. In the physical world, heat can change one substance into another, producing a new type of material that can never be reverted to its original state.[18] This process can be observed with the cooking of food, smelting of iron, and manufacturing of pottery. Numerous Bantu societies conceptualize the gestation and birth of a child through this symbolism as well; thus can be explained references to an internal heat during pregnancy, as well as the widespread tendency to associate iron smelting with the process of birth. The Bokudu narrative refers to this metaphor in its account of the peopling of the earth. The heat of the sun made the primordial beings of Mobumate too hot; as a result, they emerged from their packets and descended to the earth, never again returning to the upper world.

Monica Wilson and Luc De Heusch have documented the manner in which Bantu societies of southeastern Africa apply the metaphor of an irreversible heat-mediated transformation to the social realm.[19] The Luba and Nyakyusa (south-central Africa) use fire and cooked food to differentiate cultured people from wild. In this context, the metaphor "provides a cultural solution to the crossing of boundaries."[20] It is this same imagery that informs rainforest traditions about Batwa first-comers who introduced fire, cooked food, or iron. Although such myths tend to be read as references to individuals who were able to usher in a new era of history, their underlying message is that these individuals possessed formidable transformative powers themselves. Derived from their close association with nature spirits, it is these powers that Bantu peoples attributed to both Batwa peoples and chiefs/kings: both were considered people who could act upon and change the world.

Returning to the Bokudu narrative, the Mitsogho today conceptualize humanity in terms of three races: the Pygmies, the Blacks, and the Whites. Although all are said to be descended from the original mother Madombe, a number of informants explained the origins of these races according to the order in which they descended from the upper world. In every case—even those in which the *evovi* insist that there were no races in the other world—the Batwa are reported as the first to descend.[21] Following the account of the peopling of the earth, most *evovi* recount that it was Blacks who followed them, although a few also recount that the Pygmies were followed by the Whites. This latter version relies on the principle of precedence to explain European domination over Africans because in Bantu thought elder siblings have the right to demand subservience from younger. This version is also used to explain why Europeans did not demand labor or taxes from the Batwa during the colonial era. As the younger brothers of the Batwa, such a request would be inappropriate by all accounts.

Another account of the origins of races focuses on the perceived economic specializations of each group. After a long period of living together in peace, Muanga called Motsoi back to Mobumate and asked him to carry two trunks down to earth. Motsoi did so, and after arriving, began to open the largest trunk. A Black man saw him inserting the key and pushed him away. He opened up the trunk and found machetes and axes. He called all of the Blacks, exclaiming "take these good things, clean our paths!" The Blacks were very happy, for they felt that this was the best gift Muanga could give anyone.

They began to clear many fields, building houses everywhere they went. Meanwhile, the Whites just stood by. One day, a White child said, "I'm not going to stay here doing nothing, I'm going to open the small package." He took the keys and opened it, and found piles of paper and lots of pens. The White child said, "I have therefore nothing more to do than write—paper will be my work."

According to the Mitsogho, this was the beginning of a world where Blacks are relegated to a life of hard labor, and Whites one of ease. Whites do not suffer in their work; "their plantations are on their tables."[22] The Whites lacked houses, however, and eventually tried to move into those of the Blacks. They were chased away, and cried "What will we do?" The Blacks told them, "stay like you are—you accepted the paper and pen." This angered the Whites, who stated that they would get other Blacks to come and build their houses. At this point, all of the houses fell down. As a result, the Whites got all the riches, and the Blacks were left with only manual labor. In a slightly different version, Muanga showed writing to the Whites, who were the younger brothers of Blacks. This led to a division of labor ("Blacks fabricate; Whites correct") that reversed what should have been the primacy of the Blacks over Whites. The *ghevovi* Mboña-a-Moñepi indicates that the Whites told the Blacks, "You don't know how to write, stay behind." "This is why we left our younger brother who always wanted to command," he explains, "this is why we don't have things."[23]

As regards the Batwa, one account reports that the Blacks told the Pygmies to stay in the village. They refused, however; they wanted to go in the bush. Other versions recount that Muanga sent down not two but three trunks; the largest with iron for the Blacks, a smaller with paper for the Whites, and the smallest for the Pygmies, who refused to open it up. They are thus considered to have no tools, providing another explanation of why the Whites do not demand labor or taxes from Batwa communities. This version goes on to state that it was after this period that the Pygmies began to move into the forest, where they chased the animals that had fled at sound of dog bells (and/or sight of fire.)

In its attempt to explain the injustices of colonial rule, this latter section of the Bokudu myth provides an eloquent example of the way oral traditions can be amended to explain the realities of modern day. Having only recently emerged from the colonial experience when these myths were collected, the Mitsogho *evovi* tended to highlight stories about the origins of races and conflicts between Black and White. The lack of clarity regarding the origins or even existence of races in primordial times suggests that this mode of social categorization is the product of more recent times—and that the Mitsogho as a culture had not yet come to a consensus as to which version of the story should prevail. Remaining constant throughout all versions of the Bokudu narrative, however, is the principle of precedence. It appears as the most fundamental mode of social classification, although distinctions based on economic specializations rise in importance after mention of the introduction of iron. Likewise, the narrative also works from two themes found in the oral traditions of a great many west-central African societies: (1) the idea that Batwa first-comers introduced iron and (2) the notion that late-comer appropriation of this material led to a societal division, whereby Batwa peoples began to live in the forest on their own. Chapter 3 provided evidence of these themes among the Aka, Ngbaka-Ma'bo, and Monzombo of southern Central African Republic; in the following sections we encounter these same themes in the oral traditions of societies located farther to the south.

The Bwiti Ancestral Cult of Central Gabon

The Mitsogho have a number of different religious societies dedicated to the ancestors or spirits of the dead. Among these are the men's initiation societies Bwiti and Ya Mwei, as well as Omberi and Boo (also called Ndjembe) for women.[24] Although the Bwiti society is said to have originated among the Mitsogho proper, it is practiced by peoples throughout central and western Gabon. Likewise, the Omberi cult is said to have originated among the Mpongwe (where it is called the Ombwiri cult), but the Mitsogho and Fang practice it as well. Nearly all of these religious societies rely on *iboga* to induce a trance state. Likewise, most branches of Bwiti tell a similar myth about the coming of *iboga,* stating that it was a "gift" from the Batwa.[25] Presented following is a shortened Fang version of this myth, considered by Fernandez to be one of the more central versions he collected. He gathered it in the villages of Sougoudzap and Ayol (northern Gabon) among members of the *Asumege Enging* (New Life) Bwiti church.

Zame ye Mebege (the last of the creator gods) saw the misery in which the Blackman was living. He thought how to help him. One day he saw a Blackman, the Pygmy Bitumu, gathering fruit in the *atanga* tree. Zame made him fall, and then brought his spirit to him. He then cut off the fingers and little toes of the cadaver and planted them in the deep forest. These sprouted and turned into *eboga* [sic] plants. Some time later Bitumu's widow was fishing in the forest and she came upon a pile of bones in the river. Suspecting that they were the bones of her deceased husband, she took them out and put them on the riverbank to take home. While she was fishing, however, a wildcat came and took them away. On her way back home she got lost in the forest, but came across a cave. Her husband's voice called to her from inside the cave, so she entered. Inside she found the missing bones. The voice directed her to an *eboga* plant, and told her to eat it. She did, and she was able to see her husband and other dead relatives. They talked to her and gave her the name Disumba. They told her that she had found the plant that would enable men to see the dead. This was the first baptism into Bwiti and that was how men got the power to know the dead and have their council with the dead.

This myth provides a counterexample to the Bokudu as regards the social classification of Batwa peoples, for in this context they are not considered a different race. It also refers to locations where Niger-Congo speaking peoples consider nature spirits to dwell—the forest, rivers, and caves. The presence of the wildcat has religious symbolism as well; when undergoing initiation, Bwiti initiates are required to eat *iboga* off a wildcat skin placed between their legs. The symbolic importance of this skin lies in its mottling of red and white, the basic colors of the cult.[26] These colors are also seen in a line traced from a wooden pole in front of the Bwiti temple to its center, where candidates sit. The pole is associated with the newborn (i.e., Motsoi's original descent to the earth), whereas the red and white lines (drawn in ochre and kaolin) represent an umbilical cord that will be ruptured when Bwiti initiates are reborn into the world of the dead.[27] Like numerous peoples of west-central Africa, the Mitsogho consider white the color of the dead. The bodies of Bwiti candidates are painted with kaolin once they come under the influence of *iboga;* during this phase of the initiation process, they stare intently out of the chapel, waiting for the ancestors to arrive.[28]

As we see following, most west-central Africans work from the same sort of color symbolism as the Mitsogho. Perhaps the most important and common theme to be drawn from the Bwiti origin myth, however, is the posing of Batwa peoples as the original mediators between humans and the spirits of the dead. At its most basic level, this notion can be said to derive from the first-comer paradigm; Batwa peoples are considered religious experts because their ancestors were originally buried in the land. But also important is the assimilation of a primordial Batwa figure with a supreme nature spirit, referenced in the ancestors act of naming Bitumu's wife Disumba. In Mitsogho religious systems, Disumba is one of the three children of the Supreme Being (along with the sun and the moon) and originator of all supernatural phenomena. Because of this, both the Fang and the Mitsogho call the original branches of the Bwiti religion Bwiti-Disumba.

Although the Fang retain a reference to Disumba in their version of the Bwiti origin myth, this female principle of the universe is referred to as Nyingwan Mebege. Fernandez notes that among the Fang, the Bwiti religion "directs itself, in relation to the great gods, and in distinction from the ancestors, to Nyingwan Mebege, the author of procreation and the guarantor of a prosperous life."[29] Thus, we once again see the symbolic association of a primordial Batwa figure with the supreme nature spirit, in the same way that the Mitsogho associate Madombe, Motsoi's wife and the mother of all humanity, with the supreme nature spirit of the Mitsogho, Ya Mwei.

Fernandez has noted that Fang forms of Bwiti are in many ways syn-cretized with Christian beliefs, especially those of the Catholic religion. This is best seen in the eucharistic act of eating *iboga,* a substance sprouted from the flesh of a primordial Batwa. Indeed, *iboga* is seen as the sacrament of the Bwiti church; its members "boast of the efficiency of *iboga* over bread in its power to give visions of the dead." Some branches of the Bwiti church, espe-cially those not cognizant of the origin tradition, even go so far as to state that *iboga* is "a more perfect and God-given representation of the body of Christ."[30] All of this leads Fernandez to conclude that the Batwa are seen as the saviors of the Fang. This is made apparent not only in the context of Bwiti myths, but also by their role in migration traditions. In the legend of Adzap Mboga, for example, the Batwa save the Fang by guiding them past a giant tree that blocked their entrance into the rainforest and teaching them to sur-vive once they made it in.[31]

Although there is most assuredly a great deal of syncretism at work, one must be careful not to attribute the entire ideological complex of the primor-dial Batwa to Christian influences alone. What we see in Fang traditions is another version of the civilizing or heroic Batwa theme. Posed as first-comers, they are considered not only the most capable intercessors to the supernatural world, but are attributed supernatural powers themselves. Chris-tian symbolism has been superimposed on a more fundamental set of beliefs about first-comers; accordingly, eucharistic rituals have been modified as well. We might also suggest that a similar dynamic is at work in the Bokudu narrative, in which the Batwa are posed both as the original humans and as saviors by virtue of their introducing fire, dogs, and iron. Although it is possi-ble that this myth has been influenced by Western ideas about the primordial-ity of Pygmies (i.e., the Pygmy Paradigm), there is no denying that it is rooted in beliefs about the religious powers of first-comers on the land.

Accordingly, I argue that Bwiti myths and rituals provide an example of a cosmological phenomenon that is common to the majority of peoples of west-central Africa. In paying homage to the Supreme Creator or nature spirit, Bwiti practitioners also fulfill their obligations to the ancestral spirits of peo-ple they deem the original owners of the land. This is possible because they have fused the notion of the Supreme Being/nature spirit with that of the first-comer on the land—commonly envisioned as a primordial Batwa. In Niger-Congo religious thought, both of these categories of spirits must be supplicated to ensure the fertility and fecundity of people and land. As was the case with the Ngbaka-Ma'bo—who were given *mimbo* rituals by the ancestors of Aka—it is the gift of *iboga* that allows Bwiti initiates to enter into contact with the spirits that can most affect their success on earth. Encoded in this theme of gift giving is the notion that Batwa first-comers sanctioned the ritual appropriation of their own ancestors, thereby alleviating the awkward situation that late-comers often find themselves in, that is, the necessity of supplicating ancestors that are not their own.

This detailed analysis of Mitsogho cosmology and religious practices has served two important purposes. First, by pointing out similarities between Mitsogho religious thought and that of other west-central Africans, this discussion has helped to substantiate the notion that the societies of this region participate and draw from a common cultural sphere. Second, by documenting and explaining the cosmology of the primordial Batwa, I have introduced an important new category of analysis for understanding west-central African religious and political system—one that has been entirely overlooked in the past. Because the Mitsogho tend to forefront this cosmology in their oral traditions and religious beliefs, it can serve as a kind of blueprint for discerning similar elements among other peoples. As shown in the section to follow, numerous west-central African societies work from the cosmology of the primordial Batwa, although references to this ideological complex tend to be presented in much more enigmatic or discrete forms.

THE COSMOLOGY OF THE PRIMORDIAL BATWA: EXAMPLES FROM THE WIDER WEST-CENTRAL AFRICAN WORLD

The Beti

The Mitsogho have created a genesis myth that poses Batwa peoples as primordial to all humankind, thereby justifying their attempts to supplicate ancestors that are technically not their own. There are, however, other ways that late-comers have posed Batwa as primordial to achieve the same end. Perhaps the most common is the tendency to place Batwa figures at the origin of late-comer lineages. This phenomenon is widespread in west-central Africa, appearing in centralized and noncentralized societies alike. For example, the Beti of central Cameroon derive a number of their lineages from Pygmy ancestors, and say that their own ancestors underwent initiation into Pygmy religious cults. These rituals required an individual to stay underwater (in the bed of a river) for a period of nine days.[32] The Beti also attribute a number of their dances to Pygmy origin, especially those designed to bring forth spirits and initiate young males. These mythologized remembrances continue to be told today, even though very few Beti communities live in association with Batwa groups. As was the case among the Ngbaka-Ma'bo, these ancient associations are cast in a very positive light. This outlook contrasts with modern-day descriptions of Batwa peoples, such as the Bagyielli and Bakola, who live to the southwest; the Beti refer to these populations with a great deal of disdain.[33]

In these Beti stories, we see preserved elements of the cosmology of the primordial Batwa. The references to underwater initiations suggest that, like the Mitsogho, the Beti work from a notion of nature (water) spirits that has been assimilated with the spirits of deceased first-comers. Likewise, their use of Pygmy dances to call forth spirits suggests that they, too, see Batwa societies (at least the ancient ones) as expert intercessors to the supernatural world. The incorporation of such dances may have been due to a period of interaction much like that described by Bahuchet for the southeastern region of Cameroon (see chapter 3): late-comer leaders voluntarily enter into the ritual practices of the autochthonous societies to appropriate their ritual expertise regarding spirits of the land. Although the full implications of Beti references to ancestral Batwa have not yet been flushed out, the data provide an indication that associations between the primordial Batwa figures and water spirits can be found as far north as the central regions of Cameroon.

The Yaka

The Yaka retain a more complete set of elements of the cosmology of the primordial Batwa. They are a Bantu-speaking people living in the forest/savanna mosaics of the Kwilu River valley (southwestern Democratic Republic of Congo). Their religious and political systems in many particulars follow the same model as that of the Bakongo; indeed, Yaka societies border the easternmost societies of what was formerly the Kongo Kingdom. During the eighteenth century, however, they came under the sway of the Lunda Kingdom, which conquered from the east. Lunda rulers allowed the Yaka to retain their traditional system of territorial chiefs or *bakaalamba,* lineage and clan heads who serve as intercessors to nature spirits on behalf of the clan.[34]

Although the *bakaalamba* are referred to as the "original owners of the land," the Yaka recount numerous stories about the Bambwíiti—short-statured first-comers who formerly inhabited the region. The Jesuit priest Hubert Van Roy collected numerous traditions about the Bambwíiti during the 1960s and 1970s. He noted that it was the *bakaalamba* who provided the most detailed accounts of these societies, and suggested that it was due to their ancestors' experiences as first-comers to the region.[35]

However, their descriptions of Bambwíiti populations are so replete with cosmological symbolism that it seems more likely that the *bakaalambas'* expertise derives from their role as religious specialists for their clans.

Although only one account of genesis has been documented among the Yaka, it works from a theme strikingly similar to that of the Mitsogho. In the 1960s, an elder of the Tsaamba clan recounted to De Beir that the first humans created by God were incomplete; they had only one eye, one ear, one breast. To remedy this problem, God carved a complete female form out of stone. This form was called Issimbi, the female ancestor of all humanity. God threw the Issimbi figure into water, and a lake began to be formed. Then the water surged, and the first two ancestors were born; these were Bambaka, described as either Pygmies or dwarfs.[36] As we see following, "simbi" is a general term for water spirits within the Kongo Kingdom proper. The Yaka Issimbi parallels Mitsogho Ya Mwei, however, in that it is seen as a female force that gave life to the original human beings.

None of Van Roy's *bakaalamba* informants provided genesis myths of the same sort. However, their descriptions of ancient Bambwiiti populations work from religious symbolism commonly associated with nature spirits and their manifestations on earth. For example, numerous *bakaalamba* indicated that the ancient Bambwiiti spoke in two tongues. One was a normal (voiced) language, and the other was whistled. Only the Bambwiiti could understand the whistling language, for, as the chief Kasongo-Luunda stated, "their language was as incomprehensible as the language of the birds."[37] Although Van Roy interpreted this statement as reference to a tonal language, it is likely that the notion of a whispered language is derived from associations between nature spirits and breath/wind.

We saw this theme among the Mitsogho, and it is made apparent among the Mbata peoples (of Bakongo Kingdom proper) directly to the west. They describe *simbi* nature spirits as the *"ancêtres du debut"* who have been transformed into water spirits. These spirits are known to whistle over the water to bring forth *nkita,* their manifestations in the physical world. Likewise, across all of the Kongolese cultural sphere, birds are associated with nature spirits through the wind they produce when flapping their wings. They are also said to resemble *simbi* because they fly about and perch in trees.[38]

Allusions to water and nature spirits can also be seen in accounts of where the ancient Bambwiiti lived. Van Roy's *bakaalamba* informants indicated that their habitual dwelling place was in the forest, and that they always established their settlements near rivers, ponds, or in well-watered valleys. When they went on a hunt, they lived in the crevices of rocks, caves, hollowed-out logs, or in the roots of large trees. If these places could not be found, they slept in the branches of trees, or, alternatively, termite hills that had been emptied of their soil. The associations with water and humid areas make reference to primordial origins; all of the other locations mentioned (crevices of rocks, caves, etc.) are commonly associated with territorial spirits in Niger-Congo religious thought.

The reference to termite hills is especially indicative of religious symbolism at work. Like numerous central African societies, the Yaka see termite hills as the abodes of supernatural spirits and incorporate them into ritual practices. Before embarking on a hunt, Yaka men build small semicircular huts at the bifurcations of roads near their villages. According to Van Roy, these structures resemble those built by forest specialists in the rainforest regions to the north. Inside each of these huts is placed a small termite hill referred to as Issimbi (the supreme nature spirit) and said to represent the ancestors who can ensure a successful hunt. Van Roy also documents an encounter with a land-chief who placed a termite hill among the protective objects in front of his house. When asked if it was an offering to Issimbi the chief replied, "yes, because it is our ancestor." Upon further questioning, the chief made clear that he was not referring to his own ancestors proper (who came from the region of Wandu), but to an ancestor from the *"origines pre-mières."*[39]

Throughout central Africa, termite hills are associated with the spirits of the dead, ancestors, nature spirits, and/or the primordial Batwa. Chapter 3 provided an example from the Ngbaka-Ma'bo, who believe that the ancestors of ancient Batwa peoples (i.e., the *mimbo* trapping spirits) sleep in termite hills during the day. Among the Mitsogho, the Boo women's society uses what Gollnhoffer and Sillans refer to as a "sort of earthen cone" as the center of rituals that take place in the forest. The skull of a twin (or a twin's mother) is place underneath because twins are considered to have special links to the nature spirits that initiates seek to meet.[40] Among the Yombe of the Mayombe massive, one of Bittremieux's informants (1920s) indicated that "the dead go to the land of the ancestors (*bimbindi*). No one knows how many years they stay there, but they eventually fall asleep leaning against a *n'senga* tree. They sink into the earth and become termite hills."[41] Nearly 40 years later, Laman's contributors from the same region indicated that the *simbi* (nature spirits) lived in termite hills. "*Simbi*" were described as the "ancestors of long ago" who had undergone a second death in the land of the dead.[42] Termite hills served as rainmaking shrines in the Kingdom of Kongo and numerous Great Lakes dynasties as well. These associations can even be found as far south as Malawi and Zambia, where peoples to the west of the Luangwa River refer to ancient first-comers as both *batwa* and *Utalala mafuso,* "the sleepers in ant hills."[43]

Perhaps more than any other trait, the widespread nature of these associations between termite hills, nature spirits, and the idea of the primordial Batwa suggests that we are dealing with an ancestral religious tradition, one that was carried with Bantu peoples as they moved out of the forest and into savanna grasslands. The examples cited here are but a few; however, they provide an excellent example of how a core cosmological belief can be augmented and adjusted to fit the religious and political needs of both centralized and noncentralized societies across vast expanses of land.

The Bolia

The Bolia Kingdom is located in the southwestern region of the Middle Congo basin. Their language, political system, and religious beliefs greatly resemble those of their noncentralized neighbors (i.e., the Ekonda, Jia, Ntomba, etc). As a linguistic and cultural unit, all of these societies are referred to as the southern Mongo group. Most of these communities live in very close contact with forest specialists they refer to as Batwa. Although the interactions between the two groups are some of the most intimate to be found in the central African forest, Batwa peoples are generally treated with an air of disdain. They are seen as perennial servants, clients in a system of patronage that is extremely hierarchical in nature. Despite this reality, the agriculturalists of this region still acknowledge their status as original owners of the land. As a result, Batwa peoples play an important role in rituals associated with chiefship, kingship, and the production of iron.

The Bolia genesis account parallels those of the Mitsogho and Yaka in a number of ways. The Supreme Creator is associated with water and referred to as Mbomb' Iloko, the "lord from whom the world derives its sustenance."[44] According to the Bolia, humans appeared on the earth because Mbomb'Iloko caused a woman named Ambawanga (mother of twins) to emerge from a termite hill.[45] She, in turn, gave birth to a series of twins, these being the ancestors of the various ethnic groups that now inhabit the region.[46] As is the case with the Mitsogho and Yaka, the Bolia recount that the Batwa were the first humans to be born.[47]

In the beginning, all of these different peoples lived together in an "Eden" that was located next to a large river and the primordial termite hill. Some versions of this myth indicate that each of the groups had its own specialization: the Bolia were warriors, the Ntomba fishing peoples, and the Jia rich in currency.[48] The Bolia were able to establish supremacy because of their formidable fighting skills, and because their leader/founder (Mputu) was aided by a Batwa.[49] This aid is likely perceived as supernatural in origin, for the Bolia consider Batwa peoples to be composed of the same supernatural essence as territorial chiefs and the *nkumu* king. Because of this belief, Batwa individuals serve as assistants to the Bolia king as well. They live closest to him in the royal compound, maintain his sacred "fire of life," and serve as messengers and intermediaries between him and his more "profane" subjects.[50]

The source of this supernatural power is nature spirits (*belima*), described as "neither men nor shades."[51] It is these spirits who choose territorial chiefs and nkumu kings; through their ability to perform miracles, the latter show that they have been approved by the spirits of the land. As was the case among the Mitsogho and the Yaka, these spirits are said to pass through the intermediary of ancestors before they are made available to the living. There are five principle *belima* among southern Mongo speakers, each associated with a different lake. The most senior of these is none other than Mbomb'Iloko, whose shrine is located at the shore of the largest regional body of water, Lake Mai Ndombe. The associations between these *belima,* Ambawamba (the female progenitor of humankind), and the primordial Batwa suggest that the Bolia also work from a fused notion of ancestral/nature spirits—one that links the Supreme creative powers to territorial spirits and the deceased ancestors of first-comers on the land.

The Bakongo

The Bakongo appear in some ways peripheral to this analysis because their religious system reflects discrete references to the primordial Batwa. Although it is possible to identify elements of the more widespread ideology, many have been greatly modified and changed, adding another historical layer to the Ideology of the Primordial Batwa. Because their religious beliefs had such a powerful impact on the societies that surrounded them, it is essential to understand the way the Bakongo used and transformed politico-religious beliefs about mythical first-comers on the land.

In Kongolese thought, we see the same associations between humidity, air/wind, and creation that are present in other west-central African societies. MacGaffey has noted that because the Bakongo see the universe as a reciprocating entity, few genesis stories are told.[52] But Fu Kiau's work shows that if there is not a specific Kongolese genesis myth, there is a cosmology of origins: "In the thought of the Mukongo, all is life. The origin of all things is water, which is also life. As all comes from water, all will live in water." Fu Kiau further explains that rain comes from *mbu*—"the suspended ocean above our heads," and that the cry of the toad (i.e., wind/air) in the pond evokes the universal song of coupling because it is in water that the mystery of reproduction operates.[53]

Unlike Mitsogho, Yaka, and Bolia genesis stories, this passage makes no reference to autochthons as the original human beings. We must therefore rely upon descriptions of nature spirits and mythical autochthons in order to identify the Bakongo vision of the primordial Batwa. Each of these sources makes clear that the Bakongo have melded their image of autochthons with those of nature spirits. This can be seen in the similarity of physical descriptions, which among the Bakongo take on a particularly fanciful bent.

For example, the founding myth of the Kongo Kingdom states that when the legendary founder Ntinu Lukene (or Wene) crossed the Nzadi (Congo) River from the north, he found an aboriginal population of red-skinned, large-headed dwarfs who walked with a waddling gait. These autochthons are referred to in a number of ways: Bambaka-mbaka, Mbwidi-Mbodila, Mbekele, and Bafula Mengo.[54] The first of these ethnonyms cannot be traced etymologically. It is interesting, however, in that it resembles the name "Baka" of Ubangian-speaking forest specialists of southern Cameroon. Mbwidi-Mbodila is derived from a larger composite, *Bambwuudi-Mbodila,* which translates as "I have fallen; I have rotted" and is also the source of the Yaka ethnanym for first-comers, Bambwíiti. This ethnonym references a widespread notion that the autochthons' heads were so large that if they fell down they could not get up unaided. According to Van Wing, *Mbekele* is derived from the verb *bekila* or *bekitila* in Kikongo, which describes a walking style characterized by a waddling or a swaying of the hips.[55] Finally,

Bafula Mengo makes allusions to the notion that these first-comers were experts in the production of iron. As MacGaffey has pointed out, the verb *fula* refers to the use of the bellows in iron production, and in its broader sense means "to breathe on, or "to animate." Perhaps owing to the notion that the "breath" of the bellows is the key element of the reduction process, the verb *fula* eventually took on the meaning "to forge." *Mengo,* on the other hand, refers to the forge itself; it is derived from the term *menga,* "to heat red in the fire."

Physical descriptions of *basimbi* and *bankita* nature spirits parallel those of the autochthons, although they are sometimes reported as being white or pied in color, with long hair. As was the case with the Mitsogho, these colors are symbolic: white is associated with the dead and red is considered a color of transition. Objects or persons who exhibit both of these colors (with a pied or stippling effect) are perceived of as beings of both worlds; they exist in a liminal state, able to pass easily from the world of the living to that of the dead.[56]

These fanciful and symbolically laden descriptions make clear that Bakongo accounts of autochthons refer to a mythical population. As Mac-Gaffey notes, there is no evidence that short-statured Batwa populations ever inhabited the regions that comprised the Kingdom of Kongo, although it is possible that they once did.[57] The fantastic descriptions also make clear that the Bakongo eventually came to envision mythical autochthons and nature spirits with the physical traits of human dwarfs. The reference to large heads is an exaggerated description of the physiognomy of peoples affected by achondroplasia, for this condition results in the development of a disproportionately large cranium. Likewise, the description of a waddling gait or swaying of the hips can be attributed to the conditions of either achondroplasia or hypochondroplasia; individuals affected by this disorder have shortened limbs, bowed legs, or a severe pelvic tilt—all of which can cause an altered gait.[58]

Because of this association, Bakongo peoples consider human dwarfs to be manifestations of the nature spirits on earth. Like the mythical autochthons, they are referred to as Mbaka-mbaka and Mbwidi-mbodila.[59] As among the Yaka, their bodies are seen as *minkisi,* that is, receptacles of the transformative powers derived from the supernatural world.[60] As such, dwarfs played an integral role as officiants in a number of Kongolese religious societies (Kimpasi, Ndembo, Kongo Dieto) until recent times. In a parallel fashion, individuals born with the condition of albinism are seen as embodiments of the *bankita* (aquatic) spirits on earth. Their whiteness is associated with the primordial waters of Kalunga and the land of the dead.[61]

Thus, the Bakongo developed a cosmology rooted in two separate but complementary conceptual systems; one was the Ideology of the Primordial Batwa, and the other was rooted in the notion that physical abnormality is an indicator of spiritual status. It is likely that associations between human dwarfs and water spirits go back to pre-Kongo times. This history can be deduced from the fact that associations between nature spirits and mythical or human dwarfs are found in a number of speech communities that trace their origins to the regions around the confluence of the Congo and Kwa Rivers.[62] Among these communities are the Kongo, Kuba, Chewa, Nyanja, Tonga, and Venda, all of whom recount traditions about mythical large-headed dwarfs.[63] Among the Xhosa of South Africa, water spirits are also considered to manifest in the person of human dwarfs.[64] The notion that this ideology developed in the Congo basin is supported by the fact that the term "Batwa" first appeared among the languages of this region as well.[65]

Considering physical abnormality an indicator of special spiritual status is not unique to the Kongolese either. Chapter 1 provided ample evidence of this ideology at work among the Egyptians, Romans, and Medieval Christians. The Bakongo, however, built upon this ideology in elaborate and inventive ways. Luc De Heusch refers to this phenomenon as the "mythology of the body."[66] In Kongolese belief, any individual born with an unusual body trait (i.e., clubfoot, lacking limbs, paralysis) was associated with nature spirits, although dwarfs and albinos were considered the most powerful *minkisi* of all. The ideology was also extended to include individuals whose birth or infancy were surrounded by unusual circumstances: twins, individuals who were born breech or with the umbilical cord around the neck, those whose incisors appeared on the top of the mouth first. Thus, even people of normal physical appearance could be considered receptacles of supernatural power, an ideology that was integral to the politico-religious legitimization of chiefs and kings.

Because of their extraordinary spiritual status, human beings considered to be *minkisi* cannot be buried in the normal way. As MacGaffey notes, "All 'abnormal' bodies, especially twins and albinos, should not be buried in the clan cemetery but at a crossroads or in water . . . since twins 'are' *bisimbi,* it is not surprising to find that their graves become *simbi* cult objects equivalent to termite hills and grottoes, the same rituals being performed at all these places to influence both fertility and the weather."[67]

We see in this passage an illustration of how the Bakongo have managed to transfer first-comer status to members of their own clans.[68] At the root of this belief system, however, are the same things that are associated with the Ideology of the Primordial Batwa: termite hills, bodies of water or humid locations, the forest, and caves. Discrete references to this more ancient ideology can be discerned from the rather enigmatic descriptions of *bisimbi* spirits collected over the past one hundred years. For example, Kongolese informants often refer to *bisimbi* as "the original ancestors" and have a difficult time when asked to categorize them as nature or ancestral spirits.[69] As a result, there has been a general sense of confusion among Western scholars as to how the *bisimbi* should be classified.[70]

Building on the work of Wyatt MacGaffey, Luc de Heusch has brought a certain degree of order to this confusion.[71] Working from a wide body of ethnographic data, de Heusch argues that the Bakongo and their neighbors (i.e., the Vili, Yombe, Yaka) make clear distinctions between the spirits of their geneological predecessors (*bakulu*) and those associated with nature (*simbi/bankita*). The *bakulu,* for example, are seen as redoubtable figures— spirits that can affect human lives in primarily negative ways. Their powers lie in *preventing* individuals from enjoying prosperity and success, especially in regard to fertility and the hunt. The *bakulu* are also considered to live in underground villages, rarely entering into the lives of people living in the world. Furthermore, it is lineage elders who head the rituals dedicated to *bakulu* spirits, and these rituals most commonly involve the sacrifice of domestic animals, the presentation of palm wine, and prayers near the graves of the dead.

The *bisimbi* or *bankita,* on the other hand, live in nearby forest locations, and are always associated with features of the earth (rivers, caves, rocks). They are considered to be benevolent in nature, entering into the lives of villagers to help them achieve success in agriculture, childbirth, and the hunt. Rituals dedicated to the *bisimbi/bankita* spirits are not headed by lineage elders, but rather by clan or supra-clan chiefs. The rituals involve various types of *minkisi,* objects considered to be receptacles of transformative powers that originate in the supernatural world. Such *minkisi* are never used in rituals dedicated to the *bakulu.* Finally, de Heusch argues that the *bisimbi* and/or *bankita* are conceived of not simply as the spirits of the dead, but rather, "the mysterious ancestors from the beginning of history," or the spirits of those who died a violent death.

Having already elucidated the cosmology of the primordial Batwa, we are now able to make sense of references to "ancestors from the beginning of time." But we must also explain why the spirits of people who die a violent death might be included in this category. Among the Bakongo, as well as many other peoples of the Niger-Congo world, death by unusual or tragic means (i.e., hanging, suicide, drowning, poisoning) is considered so unnatural that the body cannot be buried in a normal way. The deceased are not buried in the local lineage cemetery, but rather, alone in the forest or the bush. In Kongolese religious thought, the spirits of peoples buried in this manner can never join their kin in the underground villages of the dead. Thus, they are associated with the spirits of the bush, as are those of the original outsiders— the primordial Batwa. It is through this shared aspect of being outside the lineage—and therefore more present in the lives of people who remain on the earth—that the spirits of mythical first-comers and individuals who die a tragic death are classified in the same category of supernatural beings.

All of this evidence indicates that, although the Bakongo clearly draw from a number of the same themes as other west-central Africans regarding the idea of the primordial Batwa, they have developed a very elaborate set of methods for transferring first-comer status to members of their own clans.

Dwarfs, albinos, chiefs, deformed individuals, twins, people who died a violent death—all are seen as expert intermediaries to the spirits of the land. Unlike Bwiti adepts who convene with the ancestral/nature spirits only after entering into a drug-induced trance, these individuals are considered permanent receptacles of supernatural force. Thus, human *minkisi* do not simply assume the supernatural powers of first-comers; instead they *replace* them, rendering the Bakongo masters of both the spiritual and physical world.

The aim of this wide-ranging survey was to point out commonalities among west-central African cosmologies and beliefs about the primordial Batwa. The usages and interpretations of this ideology are not identical in each society, but the similarities are so great that they suggest a common ancestral source. In the following section we move on to consider how and when this ancestral source might have come to exist. In this way, we build a history of this ideology and also seek insight into the changing nature of relations between first-comers and late-comers during the Early Iron Age.

HISTORICAL HYPOTHESES: POWER, POLITICS, AND THE IDEA OF THE PRIMORDIAL BATWA

Chapters 2 and 3 argued that rainforest Bantu populations lived lifestyles very similar to their autochthonous neighbors before the introduction of bananas and iron. Because they were reliant on first-comers as mediators to both the ancestral and the territorial spirits of their new lands, Bantu societies also developed a particular set of ideas about power, leadership, and the qualities an individual must possess to rule. I argue that these particular notions were originally rooted in a tripartite conceptualization of power—one that linked nature spirits to autochthons, and autochthons to Bantu founders or lineage heads. As the ethnographic data presented in this chapter have begun to show, references to this original concatenation of power can be found in the religious and political systems of nearly all west-central African societies. In most cases, however, Bantu societies have developed ideologies that allow them to locate members of their own communities in the intermediary first-comer role. This section outlines a history for the development of this phenomenon, arguing that it was an essential prerequisite for the rise of chiefdoms within the equatorial world.

The preceding chapter provided a wide array of archaeological and linguistic evidence to attest the dramatic changes that Bantu societies underwent after the introduction of bananas and iron. Overall, they became healthier, wealthier, and better connected, allowing for social and economic contacts with peoples far beyond the village sphere. These economic changes provoked major transformations in political systems as well.

For an understanding of these developments, I refer to Vansina's history of political growth in central Africa, although presented in a slightly altered form. In contrast to his vision of the "big man," as a leader of bilateral (non-lineage or clan-based) societies and whose authority was rooted in an unusual accumulation of personal wealth, this chapter provides evidence that Bantu communities were organized around lineages from early on, and that leaders gained authority by proving their abilities as intercessors between the spirits and the clan. Because of this difference, I refer to Bantu leaders as "lineage heads" rather than "big men."

Vansina indicates that it was after the introduction of bananas and iron that the institution of the "House" began to appear.[72] Located within villages, Houses became the basic socioeconomic unit of rainforest societies. Most commonly headed by an original founder or his descendants, Houses could comprise 10 to 40 members. All of these individuals were linked to the lineage head through relations of kinship, friendship, clientship, or dependency. Because Houses competed with each other for members and alliances, those that were older and better established might eventually comprise hundreds of people. As was the case with frontier settlements, the internal relations of the House were cast in terms of the corporate kin group, with the founder serving as father to various members of the House. Following the "wealth in people" model, Vansina suggests that the leaders of Houses were admired for their talents as "magnets and managers." This was undoubtedly the case, but as was discussed in chapter 3, status was gained not only through the accumulation of followers and material wealth, but also by composing communities of knowledgeable people. As such, an important element of a leader's success was his ability to establish alliances with first-comers, who were considered experts in the religious sphere.

As the centuries passed, populations grew and trade increased. Accordingly, certain houses began to dominate at the local level. Vansina suggests that this phenomenon first took place along rivers or in marshy lands, where land was scarce and choice of membership in Houses was limited. It may have also appeared in regions where major commercial routes met. In either case, villagers began to identify more closely with the founding or dominant House in the village, and relations between villages began to be conceived in terms of kin relations between founding Houses. The growth of population and trade led to increased contacts and alliances between villages, creating a greater sense of cohesion across districts (regional groupings of villages) and the extended trade networks made apparent in archaeological evidence from the time. As a result of these changes, the model of the corporate kin group was expanded to the district level. Older and more established villages were seen as the elder brothers in a family of village siblings, and the village head of the most senior House (i.e., the earliest established in the region) was considered to be the father of them all. Tribute was no longer simply passed from the common people to the founder, but through an elaborate hierarchy of elder villages up to the district head.[73]

Through this process of political and economic centralization, the institution of territorial chiefship began to take form. Like the rise of dominant houses, this institution occurred in areas where the exploitation of resources and trade networks were most advanced. One such region was the southwest, where rainforests met savanna environments and resource diversity was rich. Vansina has argued that the region first enjoyed a long period of sociopolitical stability with a single House heading entire villages. During this period, neither houses, nor villages, nor districts were able to dominate in the economic or political sphere. By the middle of the first millennium C.E., however, the first traces of increased centralization appeared, with the emergence of the political title *nkani* or "judge."[74] Derived from the same ancient verb that produced the Kikongo words *kanu*, "to decide, judge, settle," and *mukanu*, "judgment,"[75] the appearance of *nkani* attests the increased role of arbitration for Bantu leaders of this era. It is found in the regions that later comprised the Kongo, Loango, and Tio Kingdoms, as well as among the chiefdoms of the Upper Ogooué (southeastern Gabon) and Alima-Likouala valleys (Congo Republic). Another title that was associated with the rise of chiefship was that of master or owner of the land. This title can be understood in both political and religious ways; although it refers to a chief's domination over a geographical expanse, it is also rooted in the belief that chiefs had extraordinary supernatural powers over the land. As Vansina has indicated, the chiefs of this region were seen as a special kind of wizard who held knowledge of or pacts with nature spirits.

Under the new political system, the chief's village became the regional capital, and a plethora of institutions were developed to legitimize and sanctify his rule. Among those that Vansina describes are new types of titled heads within the chiefs' House, new courts of justice, new systems of tribute, and the creation of emblems and objects associated specifically with chiefly rule. None of these were invented at one place or one time, but "were probably perfected in a competitive dialogue between districts over a large area." As leaders began to emulate neighbors who had taken up the new institutions, a common set of politico-cultural traits began to appear throughout the equatorial region. The impact of these changes was profound; as Vansina states, "the creation of chieftancy acted as a catalyst which transformed the basic institutions over a vast area."[76]

I argue that one of the basic institutions to be most transformed was the first-comer politico-religious model that had previously guided relations between Bantu and Batwa. Just as the rise of chiefship necessitated the creation of institutions for regulating succession struggles and relations between founders, a new model was required to deal with the reality of peoples deemed first-comers who were the true owners of the land. As was the case with the institutions of chiefship, this model was likely developed through what Vansina terms a "competitive dialogue" that involved thousands of communities and hundreds of years.[77] The result, I argue, was a common set of Bantu myths, rituals, and political tactics, all designed to honor Batwa first-comer status while simultaneously legitimizing the new system of chiefly rule. Thus, this chapter continues the task begun in chapter 4; it lays out the various components of this ancient political charter, one that would guide relations between Bantu and Batwa for centuries to come. At the same time, the chapter illustrates how each of these components was designed to legitimize not simply late-comer political institutions, but also, more specifically, the political and religious power of territorial chiefs. To do this, we must once again reference Kopytoff's model of political relations on the "internal African frontier" to show that the rise of chiefdoms was accomplished through the same type of accommodationist tactics that have been identified across the Niger-Congo world.

Perhaps the most obvious indication that a new type of relationship with first-comers developed with the rise of chiefship is the appropriation of the title "owner of the land." In Niger-Congo terms, this title can only belong to autochthons, which the Bantu were not. However, its use in reference to territorial chiefs suggests that Bantu societies had undergone a cognitive shift in their understanding of who best served their interests as intercessor to ancestral/nature spirits. Whereas Batwa individuals and even village founders may have played this role in earlier eras, the new political system demanded that they relinquish their role to a more powerful leader—the supra-clan chief. The rise of a new chiefdom was a centralization of religious and political powers; both Bantu and Batwa first-comers were thereby subordinated under the new system of political rule. Through the appropriation of this title, we see what Kopytoff has described as essential to the rise of a new polity—"the redefinition, in culturally acceptable terms, of the concrete meaning of primacy of occupation."[78]

How was it, however, that this appropriation of power was made culturally acceptable? Here we assess a number of techniques. As we noted in chapter 3, the late-comer usurpation of power had to be carried out in very circumspect ways because in Niger-Congo thought, the ritual status of first-comers can never be entirely eliminated.[79] Likewise, political leaders (both Bantu and Batwa) who had formerly enjoyed "brother" status might be disgruntled by their loss of status. To avoid the loss of adherents and potential conflict, the ideology of the corporate kin group was retained and extended, albeit through notions of fictive rather than literal family ties. Vansina's explanation of the rise of chiefdoms shows this process at work among Bantu societies, for he documents the use of lineage ideologies to regulate relations between villages on the district level. Likewise, de Heusch's assertion that it is supra-clan chiefs—not lineage elders—who supplicate territorial spirits suggests that in the southwestern region, territorial chiefs may have striven to differentiate and limit the religious duties of lineage heads by assigning them the task of supplicating genealogical predecessors alone.

But what kind of evidence do we have to indicate that these same dynamics were employed with regard to the Batwa? I argue that the answer lies in the agriculturalist political tactic of asserting descendance from the primordial Batwa. Although such assertions may have been common and even based on fact in earlier eras, it was during this period that they came to be institutionalized as a fundamental element of chiefship in the central African sphere. Claiming Batwa ancestry was a particularly effective political tactic. It legitimized the chief's role as religious expert, honored the ritual expertise of first-comers, and most important, released the new leader from the responsibility of paying homage to those Batwa who might live in his lands, because it focused attention on their *ancestors,* not on the contemporary Batwa. Likewise, by asserting fictive ties to first-comer populations, Bantu leaders were able to insert their own ancestors into the category of spirits that must be supplicated to ensure the well-being of their people and lands.

There is no direct evidence to suggest when Bantu societies of the region began to develop genesis accounts that posed Batwa as the first-comers to the world. Although this phenomenon is common in the west-central African societies, there is not enough evidence to confirm that it was part of a more widespread equatorial tradition. However, when viewed in political terms, this phenomenon can be seen as an especially effective legitimizing tactic. It extends fictional ties with the Batwa to their ultimate limits, allowing all human beings the ability to consider themselves descendants of the primordial Batwa. This was politically expedient for territorial chiefs seeking to direct religious societies that could incorporate all sorts of individuals; "religious experts" could be created by drawing participants from any or all of the lineages that lived in their lands.

Another way the chiefly usurpation of power was made acceptable was by emphasizing interdependence between the rulers and the newly ruled. Again, this is a tactic identified by Kopytoff as common to late-comer polities across sub-Saharan Africa. I argue that this is the source of the Batwa civilizing myths found throughout the equatorial region. As we have seen earlier in this chapter and in chapter 3, these myths pose the Batwa as saviors to agriculturalist societies in a number of ways: as the guides and teachers of migrating Bantu, as the source of specialist religious knowledge, and even as the instigators of the original nature/culture divide. As the chapter 6 illustrates, the origin myths of most central African kingdoms attribute this role to the Batwa as well, although they are most commonly portrayed as magical assistants to founding heroes or kings who carry out their own civilizing or miraculous acts.

Whether these myths focus on the Bantu or Batwa, they reference the notion that heroes are the possessors of extraordinary transformative powers. It is these powers that helped their communities to move from animal to human status, that is, mere survival to economic and religious well-being.

Thus can be explained the seemingly exaggerated contributions of Batwa populations—the prohibition of incest, the cooking of food, the domestication of plants, and the forging of iron. To Bantu settlers of the pre- and Early Iron Age eras, these practices and skills were those that distinguished humans from the animal world. Although attributing the origins of these practices to the Batwa did honor the role of the Batwa in early Bantu history, such practices probably had less import in a world of expanding and competing political institutions. Thus, by the time the civilizing myths were created, agriculturalists of the region are likely to have developed different notions of heroism and power; these notions were based on the much more complex characteristics of integrative sociopolitical institutions, as well as the ability to establish and maintain hegemony over large quantities of people, land, and wealth.

In this context, posing the primordial Batwa as guides, civilizers, or saviors was a politically expedient act. Not only did it appease Batwa communities by honoring their ancestors, but it also provided Bantu rulers with a religiously sanctioned narrative of their own society's origins. The earliest eras of interaction could be thus be portrayed as the first step along an inevitable path to Bantu political and economic hegemony. By posing the Batwa as willing helpers, this historical trajectory is presented as one that had all along been approved of by the original owners of the land.

As MacGaffey has noted, myth is the verbal component of ritual; both express the relationship of particular actions and institutions to the assumed cosmos, locating and interpreting them for the people involved.[80] Accordingly, myths of the civilizing Batwa also have their ritual counterparts. They can be seen in the plethora of central African institutions that integrate Batwa figures (either real, mythical, or metonymical) into rituals of power. The ethnographic data presented in this chapter have illustrated this phenomenon in primarily symbolic ways: the hallucinogen *iboga,* termite hills, and dwarfs have all been used as metonyms for the Batwa in ancestral and fertility cults. In the following chapter, we see that the installations of central African chiefs and kings are simply enhanced versions of initiations into ancestral or fertility cults; accordingly, Batwa figures (real or metonymical) are a required presence in many of their associated rituals. In both instances, it is the territorial chief that serves as expert intercessor to the spirits of the land. Because of the widespread nature of this phenomenon, I argue that it comprises an integral element of the ancestral political charter that was created with the rise of territorial chiefship.[81]

Another political tactic that late-comers commonly use to legitimize their new authority is what Kopytoff has described as the "re-definition of territory." This can be done in literal, conceptual, or ritual ways. As was discussed in chapter 3, this phenomenon is made apparent in Bantu/Batwa relations by the widespread notion of a village/forest divide. Across central Africa, agriculturalist societies insist that they are "people of the village"—despite the fact that their villages are located within the rainforest proper. In modern-day versions of this paradigm, villages are seen as a distinctly human space, superior in all ways. The forest, on the other hand, is considered a mystical domain. Its inhabitants are attributed with extraordinary supernatural powers, be they Batwa, animals, or the spirits of the dead. Although this dichotomization is in modern times cast in terms of a civilized/savage divide, I argued in chapter 3 that it was originally developed as a political tactic that was accommodationist in intent. By dividing the world in this manner, Bantu societies were able to establish hegemony over a large geographical area while at the same time maintaining the notion that the Batwa were somehow masters of the land.

A question remains, however, as to whether the origins of this dichotomization can be associated with the era that saw the rise of Bantu chiefs. Here we must turn once again to the oral traditions that attribute the original division between Bantu and Batwa to the Bantu possession of iron. This theme was identified in the myths of the Aka and Monzombo of southern Central African Republic, it resurfaces in the Mitsogho Bokudu narrative discussed earlier (central Gabon), and it can be found among the Tio as well.[82] If we recognize that the rise of chiefdoms was rooted in the new types of wealth made available through bananas and iron, we might consider that these oral traditions contain a kernel of historical truth. What they "remember" is the role of iron in differentiating Bantu and Batwa societies economically. Chapter 4 provided evidence to support this notion, as archaeological data attest the rise of economic specializations as a result of the introduction of iron. Likewise, linguistic data indicated that ancestors of modern-day forest specialists in both northern Congo Republic (Aka, Bambenjele, and Bambenga) and central Gabon (the Ebongo) began to lessen their ties to Bantu agriculturalists after the introduction of iron.

We thus have a convergence of data from three different sources and two different regions, all suggesting that the Batwa came to be defined as forest specialists after the introduction of iron. When viewed in this context, the village/forest dichotomy can be seen as the political manifestation of a socioeconomic reality that had recently come into place. This, along with the fact that this dichotomy serves as the most basic marker of ethnic distinction between Bantu and Batwa in central Africa,[83] leads me to propose that it was an integral element of the political charter that was developed with the rise of territorial chiefs.

If we accept that traditions chronicling the rupture between Bantu and Batwa societies contain a kernel of historical truth, we might also consider the possibility that first-comers actually played a role in the early production of iron. To do this, we must envision the technique as central Africans do—as a transformative process that calls into play the cosmological forces of the universe. Viewed in its most simplistic terms, the manufacture of iron requires that stones (iron-ore) be dug from the ground and transformed through processes of manipulating air and heat (bellows and forge) to produce a material that can dramatically alter the prosperity of a community within a short period of time. Likewise, early iron producers were likely to have assimilated technical elements of the smelt with those of the primordial creation, for as we saw earlier, heat and air are commonly considered the life-giving forces that caused the appearance of the primordial ancestors, human conception, and birth.

We might also consider the possibility that symbolic associations were made between termite hills and the types of shaft furnaces used in central Africa. Both were conical structures made of earth, not very tall in height. As was shown earlier, termite hills are considered to contain the spirits of both ancestors and nature spirits, these being intermingled with the idea of the primordial Batwa. As is the case with initiation rituals that involve the transformation of human beings, numerous central African societies place pots of supernaturally charged objects under the basin of the furnace. This ritual technique was in use by as early as the seventh century C.E., as De Maret's excavations in Congo have shown.[84] Also, numerous societies of west-Central Africa use the soil from termite hills to construct both the shaft of the furnace and tuyères. Although this practice has generally been considered a technological choice (termite hill soil is of high silica content and can thus withstand the high temperatures of the smelt), it is likely that central Africans practice it with a more symbolic meaning in mind.

Finally, chapter 4 illustrated that the introduction of iron across central Africa was a slow but steady process. In the earliest stage of its appearance—the Late Stone to Metal Age (c. 1500–500 B.C.E.)—only a few regional centers of production developed; it was not until the end of this era that ironworking became widespread. Given the associations mentioned earlier, I see no reason to exclude the possibility that first-comers were the individuals who originally served as religious experts at the site of the smelt. Because the earliest eras of iron production predated the rise of territorial chiefs, the original concatenation of power still prevailed. Thus, Batwa individuals were seen as the most able intercessors to the spirits of the land and would have been called upon to perform rituals to ensure the success of the smelt. Seen in this light, myths about Batwa teaching the Bantu to produce iron begin to make sense; central African societies are referring to the magical elements of the smelting process, not the technological processes themselves. We can see allusions to this notion in Mvele myths about Batwa peoples who taught them the ingredients necessary for the smelt.[85] Likewise, we might interpret "Bafula Mengo"—one of the four Bakongo ethnonyms for autochthonous primordial dwarfs—as "those who blow on the forge." This sobriquet would refer to their role as animators of the transformative process that occurs during the smelt. Drawing on cosmological beliefs that are found throughout central Africa, it represents air/wind as the ultimate source of creation.

Although there is no historical documentation to confirm that Batwa peoples served as ritual specialists in the earliest eras of iron production, we can draw inferences of how this might have worked from George Celis's ethnographic work among the modern-day Ekonda of the Democratic Republic of Congo.[86] The Ekonda are located in the southwestern region of the middle Congo basin; like their neighbors the Bolia, they incorporate Batwa individuals into the public ceremonies and rituals, especially those that call on territorial spirits for aid in the smelting of iron. Because the Batwa are considered masters of both the forest and the fire, they are called upon to produce charcoal, choose the location of the forge, and light the initial fire. Before the reduction process can begin, both the "master of the earth" (the eldest son of the oldest Ekonda lineage) and his Batwa counterpart (the eldest of the "client" Batwa lineage) carry out rituals to ensure a successful smelt. These rituals are dedicated to the ancestors or "invisible masters of the earth." The same Batwa elder also presides over rituals to install a new smith. He is required to hand the tools of the forge to the initiate, symbolizing the transfer of supernatural powers. The initiate, in turn, is required to pass under the leg of the officiating Batwa. This act is likely a reference to ritual "rebirth," as it signifies such among the Bakongo.[87] Van Roy suggests that it is also an act of submission, for among the Yaka (Democratic Republic of Congo) a person of inferior rank may never "step over" a person of superior rank. This notion is reinforced by the Yaka proverb *mbuudi kadiimbuki Nduundu, Nduundu kadiimbuki Mbuudi* ("the Pygmy/dwarf steps over the albino, the albino steps over the Pygmy/dwarf"), which highlights the superior (and unequaled) ritual status of dwarfs and albinos.[88]

The Ekonda example also provides an intimation of how central African blacksmiths came to be considered expert intercessors to the nature spirits and fertility priests. The original concatenation of power (nature spirits/autochthons/lineage heads) was altered, so that blacksmiths could take the place of the Batwa (i.e., nature spirits/smiths/lineage heads). Thus, in regions where first-comers had ceased to exist, it is easy to see how the religious duties of blacksmiths could extend far beyond ensuring the success of the smelt. Chapter 6 shows how this was the case among the Bakongo, who came to rely on blacksmiths as religious experts who were required to install chiefs and kings.

SUMMING UP

This chapter has argued three main points. The first is that the peoples of west-central African have developed their own notion of the primordial Batwa, and that this development took place long before any kind of contact with the West. This ideology surfaces in a number of ways. Some societies see first-comers on the land as first-comers to the world, casting them as central actors in genesis accounts that describe the original populating of the earth. Others consider them to be the originators of Bantu ancestral/fertility cults; this references the notion that, as first-comers, they are closest to the ancestral and territorial spirits that influence the fertility and fecundity of people and land. Finally, although we have seen only few examples so far, Bantu societies place the figure of the primordial Batwa at the origins of their own lineages and clans. Although all of these techniques can be manipulated for political ends, the latter is the most widely employed. In the next chapter, we see how it has been used to legitimize the political and religious powers of not only territorial chiefs, but also of central African kings.

Second, I argue that most west-central African societies have conceptually melded the notion of nature spirits with the spirits of deceased first-comers, thereby creating a category of supernatural beings that are both territorial and ancestral at the same time. These fused spirits were likely the original objects of ancestral/fertility cults, although as we have seen in this chapter, Bantu societies developed elaborate cosmological beliefs that allowed them to insert their own ancestors into this pantheon. In doing so, Bantu peoples have sought to replace the central Batwa figure of the original concatenation of power (nature spirits/autochthons/lineage heads) with members of their own societies. This allowed them to assume control over rituals that ensured the well-being of their own lineages and clans.

Third, I argue that the rise of territorial chiefship amounted to a usurpation of first-comer politico-religious power. This can be seen in territorial chiefs' appropriation of the title "owner of the land," as well as the development of a new political charter designed to recast relations between Bantu and Batwa. Although it is impossible to reconstruct this charter in its entirety, I argue that its remnants can be seen in the common myths, rituals, and traditions that continue to define and guide relations between Bantu and Batwa. Among these are oral traditions that pose Batwa peoples as the original civilizers or instigators of the nature/culture divide; the incorporation of Batwa individuals or their symbolic equivalents into agriculturalists rituals of power (i.e., healing, ironworking, initiation of chiefs and kings); the tendency of territorial chiefs to assert Batwa ancestry to legitimize their authority as owners of the land; and the dichotomization of the environment into two distinct religious and socioeconomic spheres, that is, the village/forest divide.

Although it is difficult to determine if these transformations in Bantu/ Batwa relations were the cause or result of the linguistic and economic distancing phenomenon documented in chapter 4, both most be considered key events in the history of the Batwa. This is an important fact to recognize, for if Batwa communities exist as distinct socioeconomic units within the rainforest today, it is only because their ancestors chose not to assimilate into agriculturalist communities in the past. Unlike millions of hunter-gatherers around the globe, those of central Africa had a viable economic option—to choose to become forest specialists and contribute to regional, long-distance, and eventually global systems of trade.

NOTES

1. As James Fernandez has stated, "the exchange of various cults, like the widespread exchange of dances, is a very old process in Equatorial Africa." He cites Bowdich's account of an albino harp player who sang songs to a "mother figure" in Libreville as evidence that *bwiti* was practiced during much earlier times; its appearance among the Fang is attributed to the early twentieth century. See J. W. Fernandez, *Bwiti: An Ethnography of the Religious Imagination in Africa* (Princeton: Princeton University Press, 1982), 345–48.

2. O. Gollnhofer and R. Sillans, *La mémoire d'un peuple: Ethnohistoire des Mitsogho, ethnie du Gabon Central* (Paris: Présence Africaine, 1997), 23. The elements of the Bokudu narrative presented here are drawn from a compilation of versions they collected during field excursions (1960s–1990s). See pp. 107–148 for the full account.

3. Ibid., 111. The Supreme Being is also referred to as *Ngimbi, Ngembi,* or *Nzimbi.* According to Gollnhofer and Sillans, the name *Ngimbi/Ngembe/Nzimbi* was likely introduced through missionary efforts, for it is a local variant of the more widespread *Nzambi,* which Westerners incorporated into their liturgy as a reference to God.

4. Ibid., 120–121. In some versions, the ancestral turtle (*kudu*) takes this task on by himself; in others, it is *Ngadi* (the thunder) that divides the earth, or *Kombe* (the sun).

5. Ibid., 115. This passage, as well as the quotes in the paragraph that follows, are attributed to the *ghevovi* Nzondo-a-Mighino.

6. Ibid.

7. Ibid., 116.

8. Ibid., 81.

9. Ibid., 117.

10. Jan Vansina, *The Children of Woot: A History of the Kuba Peoples* (Madison, Wisconsin: University of Wisconsin Press, 1978), 30–31.

11. Luc de Heusch, *Le roi Ivre ou l'origine de l'état* (Paris: Éditions Gallimard, 1972), 47–53.

12. D. P. Collet, "Metaphors and Representations Associated With Pre-colonial Iron-Smelting in Eastern and Southern Africa," in *The Archaeology of Africa: Food, Metals, Towns,* ed. Thurstan Shaw, et al. (London: Routledge, 1993), 505.

13. Herman Baumann, *Schöpfung unde Urzeit des Menschen in Mythus der africanischen Völker* (Berlin: Deitrich Reimer/Andrews & Steiner, 1936), 78, 209; cited in Vansina, *Children of Woot,* 323, footnote 10.

14. Vansina, *Children of Woot,* 30.

15. Gollnhoffer and Sillans, *La mémoire,* 122.

16. Ibid., 142.

17. See, for example, Jan Vansina, *Paths in the Rainforest: Towards a History of Political Tradition in Equatorial Africa* (Madison: University of Wisconsin Press, 1990), 56; this notion is reiterated in Eugenia Herbert, *Iron, Gender and Power: Rituals of Transformation in African Societies* (Bloomington, Indiana: Indiana University Press, 1993), 137.

18. Collet, "Metaphors," 505.

19. Monica Wilson, *Communal Rituals of the Nyakusa* (London: Oxford University Press, 1959); de Heusch, *Le roi Ivre.*

20. Collet, "Metaphors," 505.

21. Gollnhofer and Sillans, *La mémoire,* 143.

22. Ibid., 146.

23. Another version of this episode states that *Muanga* decided to balance this situation, however, by sending Blacks their own brand of secret knowledge—the knowledge of *iboga.* Since then, "Blacks and Whites have been following each other, attempting to discover the secret knowledge of each" ("all the secrets are on the paper and also in the *iboga*"). Ibid., 148.

24. For a discussion of these various initiation societies, see Gollnhofer and Sillans, *La mémoire,* 83–99.

25. James W. Fernandez, "Tabernanthe Iboga: Narcotic Ecstasis and the Work of the Ancestors," in *Flesh of the Gods: The Ritual Use of Hallucinogens,* ed. P. T. Furst (New York: Praeger, 1972), 245.

26. Ibid., 256.

27. Gollnhofer and Sillans, *La mémoire,* 124.

28. Fernandez, "Tabernanthe Iboga," 256, fig. 37.

29. Ibid., 247.

30. Ibid.

31. Ibid., 245.

32. P. Laburthe-Tolra, *Les seigneurs de la forêt: Essai sur la passé historique, l'organisation social et les norms éthiques des anciens Beti du Cameroun* (Paris: Publications de la Sorbonne, 1981), 156; cited in S. Bahuchet, *La rencontre des agriculteurs: Les Pygmées parmi les peuples d'Afrique Centrale* (Paris: SELAF, 1993), 61.

33. Bahuchet, *La rencontre,* 63.

34. Hubert Van Roy, "Les Bambwíiti, peuplade préhistorique du Kwango," *Anthropos* 68 (1973): 818.

35. Ibid.

36. L. de Beir, *Les Bayaka de M'Nene N'Tombo Lenge-Lenge* (St. Augustin: Anthropos-Institut, 1975), 182–183. This account makes reference to numerous elements common to the broader Kongolese cultural sphere. As was the case with *Bambwiiti,* the term *Bambaka* is used throughout the Kongolese cultural sphere; an explanation of its semantic extension to include human dwarfs is presented following. Aquatic nature spirits are referred to as *basimbi* among most Kongolese, and the notion that the first humans were somehow incomplete is widespread as well.

37. Testimony of the *bakaalamba* Kasongo Luunda, as cited in Van Roy, "Les Bambwíiti," 841.

38. Wyatt MacGaffey, *Religion and Society in Central Africa: The BaKongo of Lower Zaire* (Chicago: Chicago University Press, 1986) 132–33.

39. Van Roy, "Les Bambwíiti," 847.

40. Gollnhofer and Sillans, *La mémoire,* 96.

41. J. Bittremieux, *Mayombische namen* (Leuven: Drukkerij der HH Harten, 1934); cited in MacGaffey, *Religion and Society,* 74.

42. K. E. Laman, *The Kongo III, Studia Ethnographica Upsaliensis* (Uppsala: Almqvist and Wilsells, 1962) 32; cited in Luc de Heusch, *Le roi de Kongo et les monstres sacrés* (Paris: Éditions Gallimard, 2000), 164.

43. Benjamin Smith, "Rock Art in South Central Africa" (Ph.D. thesis. Cambridge University, 1995), 59.

44. Vansina, *Children of Woot,* 39.
45. MacGaffey, *Religion and Society,* 182.
46. Vansina, *Paths,* 120.
47. E. Sulzmann, "Batwa und Baoto: Die Symbiose von Wildbeutern und Pflanzern bei den Ekonda und Bolia (Zaire)," *SUGIA* 7, no. 1 (1987): 370; translated into French as "Batwa et Baoto: Symbiose chasseurs-ceuillers et planteurs chez les Ekonda et les Bolia (Zaire, region de l'Equateur et de Bandundu)," *Revue d'Ethnolinguistique (cahiers du LACITO)* 4 (1989), 39–57; cited in Bahuchet, *La rencontre,* 63.
48. Vansina, *Paths,* 120.
49. MacGaffey, *Religion and Society,* 182.
50. Sulzmann, "Batwa et Baoto," 54.
51. MacGaffey, *Religion and Society,* 182.
52. Ibid., 57.
53. A. Fu Kiau, *Le Mukongo et le monde que l'entourait* (Kinshasa: Office National de la Recherché et du Développement, 1969), 118, 125; cited in de Heusch, *Le roi de Kongo,* 173.
54. These descriptions and the associated ethnoyms are found in MacGaffey, *Religion and Society,* 193–94, and J. Van Wing. See *Études Bakongo: Sociologie, religion, et magie,* 2nd ed., (Brussels: Desclée- De Brouwer, 1959), 46; cited in Van Roy, "Les Bambwíiti."
55. This description is derived from J. Van Wing's use of the term "*déhanchée.*" He states, "le nom Mbekele vient de bekila, avoir la marche déhanchée comme un pygmée." See Etudes Bakongo, 46, cited in Van Roy "Les Bambwíiti," 821 The same imagery is found among the Vili (C. Tastevin, "Les Pygmées," *Missi* 14, no. 3 [1949]) and the Yaka (Van Roy, "Les Bambwíiti," 822).
56. MacGaffey, *Religion and Society,* 73.
57. W. MacGaffey, "The Dwarf Soldiers of Simon Kimbangu: Explorations in Kongo Cosmology" (unpublished article), 6.
58. As was mentioned in chapter 1, both of these traits are associated with what is termed "pathological" forms of dwarfism, because they are caused by disturbances in endocrine glands (pituitary, thyroid) or congenital diseases affecting the development of bones (V. Dassen, "Dwarfism in Egypt and Classical Antiquity: Iconography and Medical History," *Medical History* 24, no. 2 [1988]: 253–276, 258). Short-statured forest specialists of central Africa do not exhibit these traits; their "dwarfism" is termed "hereditary" or "constitutional," and considered to be a result of genetic adaptation to the rainforest environment. Their bodies are entirely proportionate, with no distortions of the head, face, or limbs.
59. MacGaffey, *Religion and Society,* 194.
60. Van Roy, "Les Bambwíiti," 877.
61. The earliest mention of dwarfs and albinos in religious ceremonies comes from Cavazzi's description of *kimpasi* (1690). He noted that dwarfs (*mbaka*) played the primary role in *kimpasi* ceremonies, whereas cripples (box-footed individuals) and albinos were accorded a "secondary rank" (G. Cavazzi, *Istorica Descrizione dei tre Regni Congo, Matamba, et Angola* (Milan, 1690); cited in de Heusch, *Le roi de Kongo,* 156). In the 1920s, Van Wing noted the presence of dwarfs and albinos (Van Wing, *Études Bakongo*); in the 1950s, Mankenda documented the participation of dwarfs, albinos, and twins (A. Mankenda, *L'initiation au Kimpasi et les rites Nkita chez les Kongo* [Mémoire de Licencié, Université Libre de Bruxelles, Belgium, 1971]).
62. This assertion derives from an understanding of Bantu expansion that does not propose an initial east/west split. See discussion of "Savanna Branch" of Bantu languages,

formed in around the regions of the confluence of the Congo and Kwa Rivers, chapter 2. For a fuller explanation, see C. Ehret, "Bantu Expansion: Re-Envisioning a Central Problem of Early African History." *The International Journal of African Historical Studies,* 34, no. 1 (2001): 5–41.

63. See Vansina, *Children of Woot* (51) for Kuba founding myths in which the Cwa (Batwa) play a central role. The Bakuba also created a special large-headed mask (Bwoom or Mbwoom) to embody the ideology of the primordial Batwa (see front cover photo). References to Chewa, Nyanja, Tonga, and Venda imagery regarding the primordial Batwa can be found in Benjamin Smith, "Rock Art," 59–61. In all of these cases the large head/forehead is likely a reference to superior religious and supernatural skills. This is the case among the Bakongo, for as discussed in chapter 4, the Bakongo consider the forehead the repository of the soul (MacGaffey, Religion and Society, 124).

64. Robert Slenes, "The Great Porpoise-Skull Strike: Central African Water Spirits and Slave Identity in Early-Nineteenth-Century Rio de Janeiro," in *Central Africans and Cultural Transformations in the American Diaspora,* ed. Linda Heywood (Cambridge: Cambridge University Press, 2002), 183–208. The original reference to the Xhosa case comes from W. C. Willoughby, *Nature Worship and Taboo* (Hartford: The Hartford Seminary Press, 1932), 2.

65. Based on an analysis of the distribution of the term Batwa, Thilo Schadeberg has noted, "we cannot be sure that the word goes back to the times when proto-Bantu was spoken in the Cameroon area. Rather, we should assume that the word came into the ancestral language when the Bantu languages reached the Congo basin." See "Batwa, the Bantu Name for the invisible People," in *Challenging Elusiveness: Central African Hunter-Gatherers in a Multidisciplinary Perspective* (Leiden: CNWS, 1999), 23.

66. de Heusch, *Le roi de Kongo,* chap. 8.

67. MacGaffey, *Religion and Society,* 87.

68. The Mitsogho have a similar system of beliefs. According to them, the spirits of all deceased people go to live with *Kombe* (the sun) in the village of the dead. However, those who were initiated into *bwiti* or other secret societies also have the possibility of becoming "*bwiti*" or the objects of lineage ancestral cults. To do this, they must first undergo what Gollnhofer and Sillans have described as a "process of socialization" in the other world. After this, they can transmigrate through water and become *mighesi* water spirits. These are found in each lineages' own particular waterfall or marshland, along with the spirits of the female creative force/spirit, *ya mwei* (Gollnhofer and Sillans, *La mémoire,* 81–82).

69. When asked to categorize *bisimbi* spirits in this way, Kongolese informants have been ambiguous. For example, Van Wing noted in 1959, "Some say that they [the *basimbi*] were never men, others claim that they are men of the water as we are men of the earth" (*Études Bakongo,* 290; cited in MacGaffey, *Religion and Society,* 76.) Likewise, one of Laman's contributors of the 1920s stated: "Perhaps they came from the human race, because some *bisimbi* are *min'kisi* and some are living people and others are the dead who were formerly people. Nzambi alone knows how to explain this situation. We men do not really understand it." (K. Laman, *The Kongo III*; cited in MacGaffey, *Religion and Society,* 82).

70. As MacGaffey states, "ancestors, ghosts, and *simbi* spirits have many attributes in common, and it is often neither possible nor necessary to ask which class is meant" (MacGaffey, *Religion and Society,* 72).

71. The discussion presented here is drawn from de Heusch, *Le roi de Kongo,* chap. 10. See also MacGaffey, *Religion and Society,* 67–68.

72. The discussion of political centralization presented here is drawn in its entirety from Vansina, *Paths,* 105–11, and 146–149.

73. Ibid., 107.

74. Ibid., 147.

75. Ibid.

76. Ibid., 148.

77. Ibid.

78. Kopytoff, "The Internal African Frontier: The Making of African Political Culture," in *The African Frontier: The Reproduction of Traditional African Societies,* ed. I. Kopytoff (Bloomington and Indianapolis: Indiana University Press), 54.

79. Although it is possible that actual populations of first-comers could be eliminated, the earliest-arrived late-comers were inevitably assigned their place; this illustrates the fundamental importance of the "principle of precedence" in the Niger-Congo world. This phenomenon has been noted by other scholars such as Tal Tamari, "The Development of Caste Systems in West Africa," *Journal of African History* 32, no. 2 (1991): 235–241. She discusses it in terms of the Sundiata Epic. According to her, the bards and blacksmiths who had formed an alliance with Sumanguru could not be entirely divested of their powers after his defeat. Their role was thus reinterpreted to be one of craft specialization, so that their supernatural skills would not threaten Mande power. Tamari argues that this dynamic engendered the caste system of the Malian Empire. This example is drawn from Herbert's discussion of Tamari's work (*Iron, Gender and Power,* 151–52); as Herbert further notes, this phenomenon is also apparent in Kongo traditions, where "even when groups are conquered politically, they are considered to retain certain rights and powers. Earth priests are a common example of this in West Africa. Tamari argues that the bards and blacksmiths are another . . . " (152).

80. MacGaffey, *Religion and Society,* 42.

81. Again, Kopytoff has identified this phenomenon as common to the rise of late-comer polities. At one point, he associates it with Bantu/Batwa relations, stating that the former "structurally tamed" the latter, thereby keeping them at a "social and political distance, but incorporate them into ritual order by assigning them a particular ritual role based on their special relationship to the land" ("The Internal African Frontier," 55). Likewise, he notes that "as the polity matured, the ruler-subject division and inter-dependence were incorporated into the integrative symbolism of royal ritual" (Ibid., 17). We see examples of this in the discussion of kingdoms in chapter 6.

82. As is the case with most west-central African societies, the Tio report that the Pygmies were the smiths of ancient times, but in teaching the skill to Bantu, they lost control of it and dedicated themselves to collecting honey in the forest. See Georges Balandier, *Afrique Ambiguë* (Paris: Plon, 1957); cited in M. C. Dupré and B. Pinçon, *Metallurgie et politique en Afrique Centrale: Deux mille ans de vestiges sur les Plateaux Batéké Gabon, Congo, Zaire* (Paris: Karthala Press, 1997), 130. Dupré and Pinçon also cite numerous societies who tell myths of Pygmies who introduced iron, for example, among the Burundi, where Batwa individuals actually do produce iron (G. Celis and E. Nzikobanyanka, *La Métallurgie traditionnelle au Burundi: Techniques et croyances* [Tervuren: Musée royale de l'Afrique Centrale, Archives d'anthropologie 25, 1976); the Teke-Tsayi (M. C. Dupré, "Naissances et renaissances du masque Kidumu: Art, politique et histoire chez les "Téké-tsaayi, Republique Populaire du Congo" [Thèse d'État, Paris V, 1984]); the Nzebi (G. Dupré, *Un order et sa destruction: Économie, politique, et histoire chez les Nzabi de la République Poulaire du Congo* [Paris: ORSTOM, 1982]); and the

!Kung of Okavangu (A. G. Mesquitela Lima, "Le Fer en Angola," *Cahiers d'Études Africaines* 66–67, no. 27 [1977]: 345–351).

83. R. R. Grinker, *Houses in the Rainforest: Ethnicity and Inequality among Farmers and Foragers in Central Africa* (Berkeley: University of California Press, 1994), 77.

84. Comments, African Studies Association Meeting, Madison, Wisconsin, 1988; as cited in Herbert, *Iron, Gender and Power*, 70.

85. J. Guyer, "Indigenous Currencies and the History of Marriage Payments; a case study from Cameroon," *Cahier des Études Africaines*, 36 (1986): 577–610.

86. G. Celis, "Fondeurs et Forgerons Ekonda (Equateur, Zaire)" *Anthropos* 82 (1987): 109–34.

87. Wyatt MacGaffey, personal communication, July 31, 2003. Celis's interpretation of this act is that this symbolically poses the smith as the Batwa officiant's "woman."

88. Van Roy, "Les Bambwíiti," 844.

6

ALTERED ASSOCIATIONS: BANTU AND BATWA, C. 1000–1900 C.E.

Vastly new and different historical developments took place in west-central Africa between 1000 and 1900 C.E. By the thirteenth century, numerous societies had developed very complex and hierarchical systems of political rule (e.g., the Kingdoms of Kongo, Loango, Tio), and by the fifteenth century, central Africans began to be integrated into global economies through contacts along the Atlantic coast. What followed was a period of social, economic, and political upheaval unprecedented in central African history, for the Atlantic slave trade continued unabated in these regions for nearly four hundred years. By the latter parts of the nineteenth century, the situation was no better, for central Africans saw their land being occupied by Europeans who imposed brutal systems of forced labor to gain access to raw materials that could fuel the industrial revolution of the North.

Attempting to cover this entire period in one chapter may appear an inordinate task because the magnitude of changes might seem to warrant a periodization based on particular centuries or even decades. But the story of Bantu and Batwa relations dictate longer-range periodizations, and the evidence best reveals the nature of their interactions over different extended periods of this past. Linguistic evidence is especially useful, for it allows us to reconstruct and compare broad histories of societies living in distant locations during these watershed times. As we move into the later stages of this period (i.e., the Atlantic Age), we are able also to employ evidence found in historical documentation, such as travelers' accounts, ethnographic surveys, and oral traditions—all of which help to give detail to histories reconstructed at a more local level.

Accordingly, it is not the goal of this chapter to explore in detail the histories of either centralized kingdoms or the Atlantic era of trade; numerous scholars have already produced such histories, and I will draw from many of them here.[1] Instead, this chapter illustrates the manner in which these historical transformations reshaped the lives and economies of Batwa communities. By focusing on the ancestors of Batwa peoples in three regions, the northern Congo Republic, central Gabon, and southern Congo Republic/Gabon, we discover that the overarching political and economic changes of each region played out in differing manners. In the more northern forest regions, Batwa communities remained significant as autonomous contributors to regional trade networks until very late in the Atlantic Age. In the southwestern regions, in contrast, the development of more centralized economies and larger states, followed by the penetration of Atlantic era trade, began to undermine Batwa economic roles early on. Seen in this light, the extreme denigration and exclusion of Batwa societies is a relatively recent phenomenon; its development was not natural or inevitable, but the result of specific developments that occurred over the past one to five hundred years.

The chapter begins with a brief overview of west-central African history over the past thousand years. Next, we look at what the geographical spread of Atlantic Age loanwords can tell us about the patterns of socioeconomic contacts among Bantu and Batwa over the last five to seven hundred years. Finally, a combination of historical sources helps us to chronicle the changing nature of Bantu and Batwa relations in the three regions.

OVERVIEW OF HISTORICAL DEVELOPMENTS, c. 1000–1900 c.e.

By 1000 c.e. the societies of west-central Africa had already faced a major shift in the structures of both politics and economy. New forms of wealth made possible by long-distance trade led to the formation of more centralized political systems. Territorial or supra-clan chiefs were now common, and between the tenth and fourteenth centuries, principalities and kingdoms began to emerge in the southwest. As polities expanded and their associated institutions spread, both Bantu and Batwa first-comers were subordinated under new types of political rule. At the same time, economic opportunities grew because newly developed political entities drew from increasingly expanded networks of alliance and trade.

There are both linguistic and archeological indications that the transition to these new types of political formation took place between 500 and 1000 c.e. in central Africa. In archeology the spread of important regalia of chiefly rule, flange-welded single and then double bells, appears to confirm this shift. These bells appear to have spread first from the northwest, diffusing both up the Congo and Lualuba Rivers into the southern Congo basin and down the

Table 6.1 The Formation of New Speech Communities, c. 700–1000 C.E.

Proto-Speech Community:	# of com. formed:	Lexical cognation	Newly-formed speech communities:
Proto-*Bambenjele-*Bambenga (C-10's)	2	70%	*Bambenjele, *Bambenga, *Aka
Proto-Nzem-Bomwali (A-80's)	4	69-78%	Nzem, Bekwil, Yambe, Bomwali
Proto-Ebongo-Itsogo (B-30's)	2	72%	*Ebongo-Itsogho, Itsogho
Proto-Ipunu-*Irimba (B-40's)	2	71%	Ipunu, *Irimba
Proto-*Igama-Vili (B-40's, H-10's)	3	60-69%	Proto-*Igama-Lumbu, Vili
Proto-Nzebi-Ibeembe (B-50's)	2	68%	Proto -Nzebi, Gibongo- Ibeembe
Proto-Gibongo- Ibeembe (B-70's, H-10's)	2	68-74%	Gibongo-Ilaali, Ibeembe
Proto-Gibongo-Ilaali (B-70's)	2	74-76%	Ilaali, *Gibongo-Iyaa

* = forest-specialist languages

Congo into west-central Africa.[2] The fact that such regalia were adopted so widely and over a relatively few centuries is evidence itself for the widespread existence of a new kind of chiefly power, one that relied on new institutions to legitimize its rule and that would have been a ready acceptor of new kinds of regalia expressive of chiefly authority.

This combination of economic and political change seems reflected as well in a clustering of new language divergences around 700–1000 C.E. As Table 6.1 points out, at least 19 new speech communities were formed in west-central Africa during this time.[3] All of these divergences took place locally, either through social differentiation within a single speech community or through new settlement into lands nearby. Expansion across vast areas of land or riverine routes did not occur during this era, suggesting that new communities arose through the identification and tapping of resources closer to home. Accordingly, Bantu expansion after c. 700 C.E. was a period of settling in. The only notable exception to this pattern was the proto-Njem-Bomwali (A-80) speech community. Near the turn of the millennium this society underwent a wider divergence to form the Njem, Bekwil, Yambe, and Bomwali, a development likely brought about by geographical expansions of proto-Njem-Bomwali speakers within southeastern Cameroon and the northern regions of Congo and Gabon.

The more general settling-in pattern is evident in linguistic data related to both Bantu and Batwa societies. In the northern Congo panhandle, for example, we see the divergence of proto-Babinga, spoken by peoples linguistically ancestral to modern-day forest-specialist communities: the Bambenjele, Aka, and Bambenga. Because these speech communities are today located in the western, northern, and eastern reaches of northern Congo, respectively, it is likely that they were earlier centered in areas to the northeast of the Sangha River.

In the central regions of Gabon, proto-Ebongwe speakers, linguistically ancestral to the Ebongo peoples living in the du Chaillu massif today, began to lessen the closeness of their ties to the proto-Itsogho language community. These two communities had been living in close contact south of the Ogooué River for at least five hundred years. After their divergence, probably toward the close of the first millennium C.E., each began to develop sound changes unique to them alone.[4] As we will see, Ebongwe speakers played a central role in trade networks that stretched along an Ogooué-Ivindo route.

Similar dynamics characterized the southwestern regions. Proto-Lumba speakers diverged from the proto-Vili, the latter occupying the coastal regions of southern Gabon and Congo by 700–1000 C.E. Sometime after this divergence, proto-Lumbu speakers came into contact with the linguistic ancestors of modern-day Bagama forest specialists. These two communities shared the same language for a time, eventually to diverge after c. 1500 C.E. Farther inland, the linguistic ancestors of modern-day Barimba forest specialists (now living southeast of Moabi) began to lessen their contacts with Bapunu agriculturalists and form their own Irimba language. To the east, a series of divergences began with the split between proto-Nzebi and proto-Iyaa-Ibeembe; the latter was ancestral to modern-day Iyaa, Ilaali, and Ibeembe languages. By the turn of the millennium, all three of these existed as distinct speech communities, although our evidence suggests that Iyaa speakers carried out close relationships with the linguistic ancestors of three groups of forest specialists that live in the regions around Sibiti today. These are referred to as the proto-Ibongo-Iyaa speakers; we return to their history following.

Vansina has argued that principalities began to be formed in these southern regions by 1200 C.E.[5] They arose as chiefdoms, grew in power and were able to conquer or subordinate neighboring chiefdoms. As was the case with chiefship, the institutions and rituals associated with this new type of territorial power were built on ancient ideas of power and legitimacy. The new princes or paramount chiefs were referred to as "masters of" or "owners of " the principality over which they ruled, and rituals of enthronement were designed to ensure their access to or control over the spirits of the land. As head of a principality, the prince ruled over all other territorial chiefs; he was the judge "in the last instance" and reserved the right to condemn to death. His revenues were obtained through fees for judgments, tribute, and loot; military forces, however, were likely limited to a few hundred men.

With the rise of principalities, new distinctions in social status began to arise: aside from an aristocratic class, there were also pawns, clients, dependents, persons paid to atone for the death of others, and prisoners of war. The latter category approximated the status of slave. As Vansina notes, however, there was no term to designate a bought slave during this time.[6]

By the fourteenth century, a number of principalities had fused, allowing for the development of full-fledged kingdoms in the coastal regions north of the Congo River (Loango), around the mouth of the Congo River (Kongo), and farther to the northeast near Malebo pool (Tio; see Map 6.1). These polit-

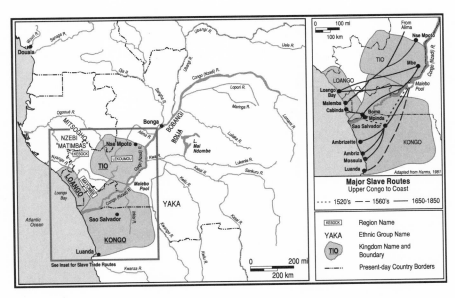

Map 6.1. West-Central Africa during the Atlantic era, 1500–1900 C.E.

ical units encompassed tens of thousands of inhabitants; once again, older institutions and ideologies were adapted to fit new political and economic realities. All of these kingdoms recognized two distinct bodies of titleholders—those associated with the royal court, and those who derived power from being owners of the land (i.e., territorial chiefs). As we see following, the Ideology of the Primordial Batwa played an integral role in legitimizing the powers of both territorial chiefs and kings. This phenomenon is apparent in all of the major kingdoms of west-central Africa (Kongo, Loango, Tio, Bolia, Kuba) and continued to hold importance throughout the Atlantic Age.

The Kingdom of Kongo had been in existence for about a century and a half when Portuguese traders arrived along the coast (1483). During the first few decades of contact, the Portuguese established the same type of economic, religious, and political alliances as they did with other sovereign nations. The Kongolese aristocracy accepted Christianity, making it the official religion of the state. In return, the Portuguese sent priests, craftsmen, traders, and luxury goods. These transformations had a profound impact on the Kongolese state; in the early stages the aristocracy monopolized the new resources, and power became more centralized in the figure of the king. It was the slave trade, however, that eventually undermined the kingdom's unity, although not till 180 years after the initial contacts with Europeans.

The royalty began supplying war captives to Portuguese stationed at Sao Tomé in the late fifteenth century. By 1510 the Portuguese were buying captives and selling at them at various points along the west African coast (Gold Coast, Madeira, Cape Verde). The impact was felt from early on; in 1526 the Kongolese King Alfonso I complained to King John of Portugal that these activities were ruining his kingdom. He undertook several measures to lessen the impact of the slave trade, but to little avail. By this time, the Portuguese had made contact with interior traders and the Malebo Pool and the supply of slaves continued unabated.[7] It was with the discovery of Brazil, however, that the demand for African labor rose to unprecedented heights. Raiding and kidnapping became as important as war for the procuring of captives, and the Portuguese encouraged local conflict as a way of ensuring supply. Thus, the Atlantic slave trade continued to expand, taking its victims from areas farther and farther inland.

Historians commonly divide the era of the Atlantic slave trade in central Africa into three periods or phases.[8] The first is the period of contacts outlined earlier, when the Portuguese began trading slaves and focused on captives from regions around Kongo and Malebo pool. By 1560 these activities had caused so much warfare and disorder around the peripheries of the Kongo Kingdom that the trade from Malebo pool began to decline. The Portuguese then shifted their focus to Luanda in the south, where captives from the interior regions of Angola (Matamba and Kasanje Kingdoms) were sold. Meanwhile, Dutch traders established trade relations with the Vili of the Loango Kingdom in the early seventeenth century. Ivory was the main trade item at this point, for it was in great demand in both the Netherlands and Germany.[9] The amplitude of this trade can be seen in the weight of ivory cargoes that the Dutch trader Pieter van den Broecke carried away on his three journeys to Loango between 1608 and 1612: 37,213 pounds, 65,000 pounds, and 96,000 pounds, respectively.[10] However, the Dutch capture of Curaçao Island and the northeastern parts of Brazil in the 1630s led them to enter into the slave trade as well. What had been a relatively small trade in slaves during the 1630s, of perhaps 300 per year, expanded to as many as 3,000 a year by 1670.[11]

Thus was ushered in the second phase of the Atlantic slave trade, dated roughly 1650–1850. This period saw the expansion of slave trading to its farthest extent, for it was during the seventeenth century that the demand for slaves in the Americas reached its height. Higher prices were paid than ever before, providing incentive for peoples as far as the central Congo basin to enter into the trade. During this period, the Bobangi traders rose to prominence as carriers of both slaves and ivory along the middle reaches of the Congo River. They began by bringing captives from the Ubangi region down the Congo and selling them to traders along the Alima. Later they obtained captives from numerous tributaries of the middle Congo River, selling them to Tio merchants at Nse Mpoto and Malebo Pool.[12]

During this phase of the Atlantic era, slaves were sold from ports all along the Gabonese, Congolese, and Angolan coasts. Four different overland routes carried captives to Loango Bay: one went from Malebo pool to the coast, another from the Tio capital of Mbe to the coast, another from the Tio market at Nse Mpoto (near Bolobo), and another followed footpaths from the Upper Alima to the coast.[13] Through these connections, Loango supplied 4,000–6,000 captives per year through much of the eighteenth century. By the 1780s however, European demand reached an all-time high. It is estimated that, during this decade, Loango sold as many as 15,000 captives per year. The increased demand also led to the reopening of trade in the Congo River Estuary after 1760, with ships stopping at Boma on the north shore. To the south, new ports were also opened up at Ambrizette, Ambriz, and Mossula. Established in the 1770s, they offered access to captives through the reopening of a trade route from Malebo Pool to Sao Salvador, the old Kongo capital, to the coast. By supplying captives at lower prices than their northern neighbors, the traders at Ambriz managed to export 5,000–6,000 captives per year. This trade lasted well into the nineteenth century, with 30,000 individuals being sold abroad during the 1820s.[14]

The third phase of the Atlantic trade era dates from the mid-nineteenth century onward and corresponds to the rise of the industrialism in Europe and the United States. It was characterized by a decrease in the international demand for slaves. At the same time, however, Africa came to be seen as a source for raw materials such as palm oil, and later rubber, needed to fuel industrialism in the West. As Africans shifted their economies to meet these new demands, ivory once again became the focus of international trade. Prices at Luanda rose more than 300 percent after 1836, and exports grew from a ton and a half in 1832 to more than 80 tons in 1859.[15] Meanwhile, slave trading continued within the continent of Africa, for as Harms explains, "the political and social processes that had fed the slave trade could not be easily halted."[16] Along the middle reaches of the Congo River, the economies of ivory and slavery were intimately tied. Bobangi merchants reaped enormous profits by buying ivory from inland regions such as the Sangha River valley and Moringa-Lopori basin, where local communities were not aware of the market value of ivory at the coast. The Bobangi then used these profits to buy slaves and expand their own settlements, all of which added to their commercial influence and power. Slaves were still being sold in this region as late as the 1880s, when the first European intruders arrived. Meanwhile, clandestine slave trading continued at the coast into the 1860s, with Americans buying slaves to take to Cuba.[17]

The devastation and tragedy wrought on central Africans by the Atlantic slave trade was immense. Because this region served as a source of captives throughout the entirety of the Atlantic slave trade era, the demographic losses were exceedingly high. Current estimates indicate that nearly 45%, roughly five million of the total eleven million Africans imported to the Americas between 1519 and 1867, were embarked from central African shores.[18] Yet it was not simply the loss of loved ones or neighbors these peoples had to cope with; warfare, dislocation, famine, and the introduction of new diseases led to an unprecedented loss of life among those who remained on the continent. These tragedies were accompanied by the transformation and/or destruction of the political, economic, and religious systems that had sustained central African societies for centuries.

Perhaps the most significant transformation for west-central Africans was the development of thoroughgoing forms of social, political, and economic stratification at the local level. This phenomenon was brought about by economic transformations set in motion by the introduction of large quantities of European imports and Africans' willingness to enter into new systems of merchant capital and trade. Most important among the imports were textiles, alcohol, and firearms; these were the products Africans primarily sought in exchange for slaves, comprising nearly 75% of the European value of imported goods.[19] Accompanying these were various and sundry European-produced items, such as knives, glassware, pots, beads, hats, and the like. They were included in the bundles of goods that Europeans offered in exchange for slaves at the coast.

Beyond the coercive powers that firearms provided, the introduction of these imports was not deleterious to west-central African economies in direct ways.[20] Indeed, as Joe Miller has pointed out, the great volume of imports led to an increase in trade, thereby stimulating and intensifying local production until as late as the 1830s.[21] What was damaging, however, was the "crucial gains they gave their possessors in converting material goods into the fundamental values of the African political economy, into dependents and dependency."[22] Because imported goods had advantages over local products in securing the right to dependents, "more goods supported more exchanges involving more people over greater geographical ranges and thus, increased dependency in both senses relevant to Africa: assembling more people and working them more intensely."[23] This phenomenon engendered a transformation in west-central African sociopolitical systems, for the buying of slaves became the preferred method for expanding one's following. As we see in this chapter, it also had a profound impact on Bantu relations with Batwa, for as Atlantic economies penetrated the region, the demand for forest products, especially ivory, also increased.

When assessing historical records of the Atlantic Age, it is important to acknowledge that virtually all observations of Bantu/Batwa relations in equatorial Africa were made during a period of social and economic disruption unlike any that had come before. This is especially important to recognize for the more northern, interior regions of the rainforest, where the greatest number of Batwa societies are found. The full effects of the slave trade did not reach these regions until the second half of the nineteenth century—precisely the period when the first Europeans began to arrive. Because of their own ideas about progress and social evolution, European observers tended to view the subjugation of Batwa communities as natural or inevitable. At the same time, by associating Batwa societies with the legendary Pygmies of Herodotus, they extrapolated the dynamics of nineteenth-century patron-client relations far into the past. In this chapter, we try to go beyond the limits that the patron-client model imposes; by working from multiple sources of data and assessing them from the perspective of the first-comer paradigm, we can tell more nuanced and regionally focused histories.

TRADE ROUTES AND ASSOCIATED LEXICON, c. 1200–1900 C.E.

One avenue into Batwa history during the Atlantic Age is to identify how specific communities contributed to long-distance systems of trade. The mapping of loanwords associated with newly introduced products, crops, or ideas is an especially useful tool in this endeavor. During the Atlantic era, a great many new products and crops were introduced along the coast. In some cases, these items received African names through a process of semantic extension or shift; in others, coastal peoples adopted the names that Europeans provided. In both scenarios, the terms eventually spread to neighboring peoples along with the new product. Because most societies adopted the product along with its associated word, it is often possible to map a trail of borrowed terms across the central African landscape. These trails generally form contiguous distributions across language groups and geographical space; they therefore provide evidence not only for the presence and direction of ancient trade routes, but also for contacts between societies.

The trade routes identified through this analysis do not provide new information, per se, because numerous scholars have documented their existence in previous studies of Atlantic era trade. What is innovative, however, is the identification of lexicon that accompanied the products and crops that traveled these routes, such as the words for "gun," "maize," "peanut"(*Arachis hypogaea*), "manioc," and "European cloth. We can also trace the distribution of terms for locally produced prestige objects such as ivory and raphia cloth because these items also passed by trade across large areas. Although the history discerned through this analysis can be considered reflective of only the Atlantic Age, most scholars agree that the trade systems of this era simply tapped into and built upon long-distance commercial networks that were already in place. For this reason, I consider the evidence viable for earlier eras, such as the period 1000–1400 when the kingdoms of the southwest began to be formed. Finally, we also trace lexicon that provides insight into altered perceptions of status, power, and wealth such as "slave," "slave-owner," "chief," "rich person," and "master-hunter."[24] Although the societies of west-central Africa often had terms referring to these concepts in periods before the Atlantic era, it is possible to trace altered meanings and the replacement of older terms as the slave trade came to expand.

Not surprisingly, the data indicate that new trade items and crops were introduced into west-central Africa along riverine routes. Three main areas of entry can be identified: the Douala Estuary/Sanaga River region, the Gabon Estuary and Ogooué River, and the Congo River. The one exception to this rule is the term *ndoki,* "gun," which is derived from the Arabic word for *bunduq* (also "gun"). There are numerous attestations of this term in the Great Lakes region to the east and along the Swahili coast; its distribution pattern suggests movement westward along the Congo and Ubangi Rivers. Within the far western reaches of the rainforest it is found only in the Congo panhandle and at few locations around the Congo/Ubangi confluence. Because we know that guns were not introduced into the northeastern regions of the equatorial rainforest until after the Egyptian conquest of Sudan in 1821, it is likely that the peoples of this region did not gain access to firearms from the east until after the mid-nineteenth century.

The term *-jàli* (or *-gàli*) came to refer to guns in the northwestern regions of the rainforest. This term is a semantic extension from the proto-Bantu term for "lightning" (**-jàdɨ*), referring to the flash of light produced when gunpowder explodes.[25] It occurs along both the Duala/Sanaga and the Gabon Estuary/Ogooué River routes, with both distributions converging in the regions around Ouesso (where the Ngoko and Sangha Rivers meet). Along the lower reaches of the Congo River, words derived from the proto-Bantu term **-tá,* "projectile, bow and arrow," prevail. This word reflects a spread of guns from the mouth of the Congo River into central Gabon, up the Congo River to its confluence with the Ubangi, and southwestward into Angola and the southwestern regions of today's Democratic Republic of Congo.

Arachis hypogaea, the New World peanut, entered into the continent through movement along all three of the riverine routes. In the far north, the term *-wɔndɔ* shows a clear distribution up the Sanaga River and south toward the Ouesso region, most likely passing along the Nyong and Dja Rivers. In the Gabon Estuary, an Amerindian word, *-pinda,* was adopted; it then passed into the middle reaches of the Ogooué River and southward into the southern regions of Gabon and Congo. Finally, the term *-nguba* was applied to the new crop by peoples living near the mouth of the Congo River. It traveled up the river and onto the lower reaches of Ubangi, entering into the Congo panhandle region as well. Aside from one attestation of the term *-pinda* in the Kanyok language of the Luba group, *-pinda -nguba,* and *-wɔndɔ,* cannot be found beyond the trade networks of these three riverine routes. Peoples living to the east and south simply applied the term **-jùgú* (C.S. 961) to the new crop. This is the proto-Bantu word for *Voandzeia subterranean,* that is, the indigenous African groundnut. The widespread attestations of this term to the east and the south of the Congo River may suggest that peoples living in these regions received the new crop through trade routes stretching from the East African coast to the interior of the continent.

Chapter 4 provided an intimation of trade connections going back to the first millennium B.C.E. along an Ogooué-Ivindo route, one of the key indicators being a common word *-goba,* "ax" in the Himba language (central Gabon) and the Baka, Bangombe, Bomassa, and Bobangi languages of the Congo panhandle. This pattern of distribution suggests a loanword spread because the term is found at both ends of a riverine route and in languages from entirely different branches of the Niger-Congo language family. We see this pattern more clearly for the Atlantic-era term *-seba,* "ivory." To the far northeast (in the Congo panhandle), *-seba* is found in Bambenjele, Aka, and Lingala as a generic word for "horn." It is additionally attested in Bomwali, where it refers to both "horn" and "ivory tusk." Farther to the south it is found in a great many languages of central and coastal Gabon (Okande, Ebongwe, Himba, Kele, Ungom, Galwa, Seke, and Nkomi), where it refers specifically to "ivory tusk." The distribution of this term along the Ogooué and Ivindo Rivers, as well as the evidence of semantic narrowing as it was passed from east to west, suggest that is was originally a loanword that had origins among peoples of the Congo panhandle. *-seba* is also the source of the ethnonym Ossyeba, which the Okande gave to the Fang-Maké as they moved into central Gabon during the nineteenth century.[26] Literally meaning "the people of ivory tusks," this sobriquet documents the important role that the Maké played as middlemen traders at the confluence of the Ivindo and Ogooué Rivers.[27]

Further evidence of the importance of the Ogooué-Ivindo trade route can be seen with the term *-ganda,* which in the regions near Ouesso refers exclusively to European cloth. The lack of similar attestations for this term on or around the Congo River, and its limited yet continuous spread from the Gabon Estuary toward the northeast under this meaning, suggests that the product was introduced from the west. This trade is likely to have begun in the seventeenth century, when the Dutch traded both raphia and European cloth in the Estuary region of Gabon.[28] Currencies in raphia cloth may have been introduced into the regions around Ouesso along this same route; Njem speakers say that their ancestors used this cloth for marriage payments and obtained it from Bekwil speakers living to the southwest (near Souanké).

The Bekwil must have played an important role as middlemen traders in former times, for it is they who introduced sugarcane (*Saccharum oficinarum*) into the panhandle region as well. Indonesians probably first brought this crop to the East African coast early in the first millennium C.E., but as Guthrie has noted, the exclusively western attestations of forms derived from **-kùùgú* (C.S. 1201) seem to indicate a separate western introduction.[29] Various versions of this word are found across the northwestern regions of the equatorial rainforest, suggesting an introduction by the Portuguese in the

Duala or Gabon Estuaries and a subsequent spread along riverine routes. Within the Congo panhandle, the same word appears in a skewed shape, *mungaku,* in the Mikaya, Bongili, Bambenjele, and Bambenga languages. The source of this word is the Bekwil language; regular processes of sound shift unique to this language alone produced the intermediate shape, *-gwak* from the original **-kùùgú* form,[30] thus giving rise to the further borrowed shape *mungaku.*

Another indication that the Bekwil were involved in long-distance trade along the Ogooué-Ivindo route can be seen in the distribution of terms for *Manihot utilissima,* manioc. This crop was introduced at numerous seaports along the west-African coast after 1500. Terms referring to it and its various varieties are numerous within each language community and diverse across language families. In most cases, processes of semantic shift took place, whereby older terms for more familiar root crops were applied to the new product. However, a possible route of initial introduction of the crop is discernible in the west, where the generic term *-piti* appears in languages along the Ogooué and Ivindo Rivers, reaching eventually to the Ouesso region, where it appears in the Bekwil language alone. A more southern introduction of manioc can be seen in the distribution of the term *-bala,* a generic referent to manioc in Kikongo and in numerous speech communities up the Congo River. Interestingly, both *-piti* and *-bala* are attested in Nzebi and Ibongo-Nzebi of the du Chaillu massif. These double attestations suggest that the Nzebi and their Batwa neighbors participated in trade networks to both the north and the south. They also provide an indication as to how far the Ogooué and Congo River commercial spheres extended. As was the case with words related to iron, the du Chaillu massif appears to be the region where these two commercial spheres met.

Further indications of the extent of the Congo River commercial sphere comes from the distribution of the term *putu,* "maize." In the Kongo and Loango kingdoms, maize was called *masa ma mputu,* or "grain of the Portuguese." In the shortened version, *putu,* it was introduced to the peoples of southern and central Gabon: the Nzebi, Ibongo-Nzebi, Mitsogho, Ebongo, Himba, Punu, and Ndumu. This distribution pattern parallels that of *-bongo* for the raphia cloth currencies produced by the Vili and Kakongo for long-distance trade; the term appears as well in the Nzebi, Ibongo-Nzebi, Ebongwe, and Himba languages of Gabon. An alternative word for maize (*cangu*) is found in societies located on and around the Congo River north of the Pool. Originally the term for sorghum in the western parts of the southern savanna zone, *cangu* was reapplied to maize along the lower Congo. With this new meaning, the word subsequently spread up the Sankuru and Kasai Rivers. As is the case with many of the terms for introduced crops, the various attestations of this term show few sound shifts. This feature, combined with its distribution over vast areas of land, suggests that maize diffused relatively rapidly.

Although ivory was an important trade item before the Atlantic era, the European presence amplified the demand for this product from the sixteenth century on. Three distinct words for "ivory" are used along the Congo River; the distribution of each roughly parallels the known spheres of commercial influence that existed during the Atlantic era. One of these terms, *pungi,* predominates in languages from the mouth of the Congo River east to its confluence with the Kwa and in regions both to the north and the south of this riverine stretch. Its attestation as far north as the Ogooué River and Gabon Estuary, as well as its continuous distribution across diverse language groups, provides evidence of a loanword spread. This pattern of distribution also parallels that identified for *bongo,* "raphia cloth currency," and *-putu,* "maize": all three illustrate the impact that the economies of Kongo and Loango had on peoples of southern and central Gabon. The Okande, expert traders of the middle Ogooué during the nineteenth century, use both *-pungi* and *-seba* for ivory. This suggests that they drew their ivory from both the central Gabonese rainforests and the Congo panhandle (Ogooué-Ivindo trade route) to supply the Gabon Estuary, where ivory was traded from 1650 onward.[31]

Beyond the confluence of the Congo and Kwa Rivers, the term *-pungi* disappears and is replaced by *-onjo.* This term is found in the languages of the Bobangi, Kela, and Soko, as well as numerous Mongo dialects spoken within a limited eastern reach of the middle Congo River. It is also found in the Bambomba languages spoken farther north along the western banks of the Ubangi River, and in a possible skewed form (*munja/minja*) among the Inyele and Bambenga (C-10) speakers who live near Dongo. These stretches of the middle Congo and Ubangi Rivers were formerly the commercial domain of Bobangi middlemen traders, prominent suppliers of interior ivory and slaves during the Atlantic era. The predominance of *-onjo* in languages of the middle Congo regions is to be expected because they all belong to the C-30 group of languages. However, its presence in the Mongo languages to the east, as well as the skewed form in Inyele and Bambenga, suggest that *-onjo* came to prevail as the regional term for "ivory" under the influence of Bobangi traders.

Despite its use among riverine peoples of the Congo panhandle, *-onjo,* "ivory," does not appear in any of the C-10 languages of the more interior regions. Instead, they use their own word, *longo,* as the generic term for "horn" as well as "ivory" or "elephant tusk." It is attested in the Bongili, Kabunga, Mikaya, Bambengangale, and Baluma languages, the latter three being languages of forest specialists. Bambenjele forest specialists and the Bomassa, an Ubangian fishing people, use this term as well, but only as "ivory tusk." The Bambenjele actually use two forms of this word, *mongo/miongo* and *mulongo/milongi.* Because the loss of [l] is fairly regular in this language, the Bambenjele use of the longer form might be considered a loanword reflecting contacts and trade with their neighbors.[32] The Bomassa use of *-longo* is clearly due to trade influences, for they have dropped the

Ubangian term *te-ja,* "tooth," which is still used by their Baka and Bangombe forest-specialist neighbors.

All of these data suggest that *-longo* was present in the ancestral proto-Sangha language (formed c. 2000–1500 B.C.E.[33]) as the word for "horn," and that during the Atlantic era, it became associated with ivory tusks. This is an important historical datum, for it suggests that the region enjoyed a certain sense of linguistic and cultural continuity despite the drastic transformations that occurred in the region during the Atlantic Age. This phenomenon cannot be attributed to geographic or economic isolation, for, as Harms has noted, the Sangha River valley was one of the major suppliers of ivory for the central Congo basin.[34] However, as the primary producers and exporters of this resource, the peoples of this region, both Bantu and Batwa, never came to adopt the terms for ivory that prevailed upon the Ogooué-Ivindo or Congo River routes (*-seba* and *-onjo,* respectively). A similar phenomenon can be seen with their word for raphia cloth, *mundimba/mindimba,* which also refers to the tree species from which the cloth is made. Because the term for cloth is semantically linked to its original source of production, it is likely that the peoples of this region continued to manufacture their own cloth, rather than relying on the supplies of raphia currencies that fed into the Ouesso region from southwestern commercial spheres (see *ganda,* earlier).[35]

To explain this phenomenon, we must look at the system of commerce that prevailed in the central Congo basin after the rise of the Atlantic slave trade. As Harms has noted, by the nineteenth century, trade along the various confluents of the Congo River was controlled by a series of blockade villages. One of the most important of these was Bonga, located at the confluence of the Sangha and the Congo Rivers. Nineteenth-century travelers' accounts indicate that merchants from upriver were required to sell their products to the merchants at Bonga, who in turn sold them to the Bobangi.[36] The merchants at Bonga also served as the source of local currencies. As late as 1898, the explorer A. Fournier remarked that the only currency peoples of the upper Sangha would accept were *mondjocous,* spiral-shaped copper currencies that had to be bought directly from the "Bonghas."[37] In this type of system, both Bantu and Batwa societies of the panhandle region suffered a serious disadvantage in the terms of trade. This can be seen by the fact that during the nineteenth century European goods sold along the Sangha River for twice the price they obtained on the Alima River, only one hundred kilometers to the south.[38]

The unusual economic circumstances of the Congo panhandle lead us to an important point. When attempting to reconstruct the history of relations between Bantu and Batwa, it is important to understand the nature of local economies in different eras of time. As we see following, economic factors played an important role in determining how dependent or autonomous Batwa societies could be. Having laid out the broad patterns of trade routes and associated terminologies, we will now turn to the task of reconstructing the more detailed histories for three different regions: the Congo panhandle, central Gabon, and the southwestern regions of Congo Republic and Gabon.

NORTHERN CONGO

By c. 1000 C.E. proto-Bambenjele, proto-Aka, and proto-Bambenga existed as distinct speech communities within the central regions of far northern Congo Republic. As the analysis of proto-Babinga vocabulary showed (chapter 4), it is likely that these communities continued to refine their skills as expert procurers of forest products, for each developed their own words for forest dwellings and digging tools after this time. Lexical data indicate that the Batwa societies of this region remained in close contact during the period when New World crops were introduced, and that they did not engage in exclusive social or economic relations with any specific Bantu- or Ubangian-speaking group. For example, all of the forest specialists of the region use the same terms for "peanut" (*-nguba*) and "sugar cane" (*-gaku*) as their Bantu-speaking neighbors; these terms entered the region from the Ogooué-Ivindo and Congo River trade routes, respectively. However, Aka and Bambenjele forest specialists use terms of Ubangian origin in reference to "maize" (*mbombo*) and "manioc" (*boma*). These words were likely adopted through contacts with the linguistic ancestors of modern-day Ubangian-speaking ancestors such as the Bomassa (a fishing people) and the Baka and Bangombe (forest specialists).

Especially informative is the fact that Bambenga speakers—who today live far to the east along the Ubangi River—also attest *boma*, "manioc," and *mbombo*, "maize." Aside from these two terms, all of their words for crops are the same as those used by the Inyele, their modern-day "patrons." This suggests that Bambenga speakers were introduced to these crops before they entered into association with the Inyele, and that they formerly held much closer contacts with the other forest specialists of the region. Because manioc and maize probably did not reach this far inland until the seventeenth or eighteenth century, these data suggest that the ancestors of modern-day Aka, Bambenjele, and Bambenga speakers maintained a considerable degree of social and economic distance from their Bantu-speaking neighbors until that time.

Guns were not imported into west-central Africa in large quantities until the eighteenth century.[39] Because exclusive ownership was strategic to gaining power over neighboring peoples, arms moved very slowly toward the interior regions. As we have noted, the peoples of the Congo panhandle region obtained guns from the east, a development that probably did not occur until at least the mid-nineteenth century. A similar scenario seems to have prevailed in regions to the west of the panhandle as well. In 1861, du Chaillu encountered numerous Fang traders who were moving toward the coast and noted that they had very few guns. By 1874, however, Marche reported that the Ossyeba communities living at the confluence of the Ogooué and Ivindo Rivers were well armed.[40] Likewise, Bruel noted in 1911 that Bobangi traders brought guns into the regions near Ouesso, where they exchanged them for slaves and ivory supplied by the Njem and Bomwali peoples.[41] Thus, we are dealing with a relatively late period for the arrival of guns, as well as the violence and socioeconomic disruption that accompanied their introduction.

The acquisition of arms had a devastating impact on peoples of the southern Cameroon and northern Congo Republic/Gabon. Siroto documents this history among the Bekwel, who were living around the headwaters of the Ivindo River when guns came to the Bulu (a Fang-speaking population that lived to their north and west.)[42] The Bulu used the guns to attack Njem communities to the west of the Bekwel. Because the Bulu stole numerous women and children, the Njem used guns to recoup their losses among the Bekwel. Bekwel communities were decimated and began to move south and east. In the process, they pushed Bakola and Bakele people even farther south. The Bekwel were eventually able to gain access to guns in one of two ways; they either entered into affinal or client relations with the conquering Njem, or they obtained arms through trade with peoples to the east (i.e., the Congo panhandle). Once in possession of guns, they continued to move southward, chasing Mahongwe, Bakota, and Bangom peoples out of their way. Thus, the introduction of arms set off a chain reaction of conflict and migration, with entire communities being removed from their lands. These dynamics probably began in the regions to the north of the Cameroon/Congo/Gabon borderlands during the early decades of the nineteenth century; as Siroto notes, they carried on until the advent of European military power.[43]

In the regions to the east of the Congo panhandle, a different kind of transition was under way. As we have noted, the eighteenth century saw the rise of Bobangi traders, major suppliers of slaves and ivory throughout the latter half of the Atlantic Age. At their height of power, they dominated a five-hundred-kilometer stretch of the middle Congo River, reaching from the confluence with the Kwa to the regions of the equator. Originally a fishing people living in autonomous riverine villages, the Bobangi developed an elaborate system of political and economic alliances to monopolize access to ivory and slaves. This was achieved through the institution of *bondeko* or "blood brotherhood." As Harms notes, this was a covenanted relationship, for *bondeko* was used in reference to both fiancées and blood brothers. In the trading context, it established a set of mutual obligations. A partner was required to house and feed the alien trader when he arrived in his village, help him pay debts, attend the funeral ceremonies of family members, exchange gifts, and aid him in the case of war. *Bondeko* relations were carried out across ethnic and regional boundaries as well; as Harms notes, traders living near the geographical fringes of an area generally operated in both.[44]

The dramatic increases in prices paid for ivory led to an unprecedented period of expansion for the Bobangi during the last decades of the nineteenth century. By obtaining ivory from interior regions at very low prices, Bobangi traders were able to reap great profits. They used these profits to buy their own slaves, settling them in villages along the river's edge. By the end of the nineteenth century, the number of slaves in Bobangi villages and settlement far outnumbered free persons. Although the Bobangi made distinctions between as many as eight different categories of slaves, the most fundamental was between *montamba,* an individual who had been sold by his kin group, and *montonge,* an individual who had been captured through warfare, raiding, or kidnapping.[45] Because the former were unable to return to their own communities, they often became trusted servants and successful subagents in Bobangi society and systems of trade. The latter, however, were quickly sold down river to avoid any chance of escape and return to the homeland.

Because of their full-time participation in long-distance trade, what were formerly autonomous Bobangi fishing villages developed into full-fledged trading firms. Each had its own leader, alliances, and commercial network. As in other regions of the continent, new political institutions developed reflecting social and economic change. The most important was the title of *mokonzi,* head of a village-cum-trading firm. Harms suggests that this title developed along with the rise of long-distance trade, because the Bobangi language attests a verb, *-konza,* "to amass wealth," and the noun, *nkonza,* "something of value." Given these semantics, *mokonzi* literally refers to "one who has amassed wealth."[46] Although the position encompassed many of the tenets associated with territorial chiefs, it was not inherited. Instead, a candidate had to prove his status as *mokonzi* by hosting an extravagant 30-day feast/dance, to which all neighboring and allied chiefs were invited.

There also appears to have been an even more esteemed title accorded successful traders, referred to as *botoke.*[47] Although there were no *botoke* title holders left in the region when Europeans arrived, oral traditions associate it with the mythical origins of Bobangi wealth at Bobangi Esanga, " the island of the Bobangi," on the Congo/Ubangi River peninsula. These traditions indicate that a resident first suggested the title, but was told it was too grand for him. He went on to produce the arms, however, that allowed the earliest Bobangi to move up the river and begin capturing slaves. The title was sometimes personified in the figure of a "founder-hero," and eventually became the central symbol of the greater Bobangi alliance. During the nineteenth century, canoes arriving at a Bobangi village were required to sing "Every country has its lord; The lord of the river is *botoke.*"[48]

Harms has masterfully explained how central Africans see the acquisition of wealth as a "zero-sum game."[49] Because they believe that there is a limited amount of wealth in the world to be gained, the gain of one individual is seen as a loss for another. Accordingly, the extreme amounts of wealth accumulated by traders during this period came to be explained in terms of the super-natural, that is, the possession of superior transformative powers. Thus, the holders of *mokonzi* and *botoke* titles were viewed in much the same light as territorial chiefs. They were said to have "eyes in the night" (i.e., the ability to convene with spirits after dark) and "strength," the power to work miracles and control the spirit world. Such power was obtained either through having a special growth on one's intestine (*likundu*)—the source of transformative powers—or through the help of a *nganga* (religious and medical specialist).[50]

The Bobangi also associated the transformative powers of these chiefs with water. Botoke chiefs were buried only in the river because it was believed that they had a home underwater where they returned after death. There was also a great fear of whirlpools, for the Bobangi believed them to be owned by powerful *nganga* (most likely the spirits of deceased *botoke* chiefs). To pass through whirlpools, one had to "pay" the water spirits, often through the sac-rifice of a family member. Thus, the Bobangi believed that wealthy traders designated a family member to pass through whirlpools and within a period of days that individual would fall ill and die. These beliefs illustrate the man-ner in which Bobangi peoples attempted to conceptualize the great economic inequality that developed as a result of the slave and ivory trade. Seen as pow-erful sorcerers or witches, rich traders and *mokonzi* chiefs came to be associ-ated with the supernatural powers that cause evil, suffering, and death in the world.

Bobangi political institutions, economic practices, and religious beliefs appear to have had wide influence among peoples of the Congo panhandle, both Bantu and Batwa alike. The title of *mukonzi,* which may have originated among the Bobangi, continues to be used among the majority of C-10 lan-guage speakers of the region. Among the agriculturalist and fishing peoples of the region, the *mukonzi* is the quintessential territorial chief, a person who "claims authority over a group of people and an area of land or river" and is responsible for assuring their "physical, mystical, and spiritual welfare."[51]

The Bambenjele recognize *mukonzi* status among agriculturalist/fishing populations, but use a slightly different noun, *-konza* (derived from the same underlying verb, *-konz-*) to refer to leaders of their own communities. Because their societies are guided by a culture of sharing, notions of owner-ship—especially over physical objects, land, or people, are not absolute. As Lewis states, "the closest [Bambenjele] people get to accepting similar notions of ownership similar to those of *Bilo* or capitalists is in relation to certain ritual and mystical knowledge (intellectual property) that will be denied ineligible people."[52] Thus, although the Bambenjele term *konʒa* refers to "possessor" or "guardian" in its most general sense, it is also applied to the individual most skilled in accessing the spirits of the forest—the *konʒa ya mokondi*. The Mikaya use the same term (*kondʒa/bakondʒa*) to mean "master of the hunt," again referring to a possessor of special skills.

The Bambenjele also ascribe to many of the same notions as the Bobangi regarding sources of supernatural powers and material wealth. They refer to an intestinal growth as the source of magical powers (*-gundu* rather than *-kundu*) and assume that individuals become exceedingly rich and powerful through malevolent means. The latter remains a source of great anxiety and conflict today, for as Lewis has noted, villagers regularly use curses and threats of witchcraft to compel Batwa populations to comply with their demands. Such threats are taken seriously by the Bambenjele, as is made evident in the comments of one of Lewis's elder informants:

> Some people are with nothing. People of peace, without bad eating habits. But peaceful people are without strength. They just like eating food together. . . . Others, they eat people. Sorcerers have strength, they eat people. Sorcerers get rich eating other people. Look at the Bilo, they are all rich.[53]

This passage illustrates that Batwa people of the Congo panhandle not only work from the same conceptualizations of wealth and power as the Bobangi, but they use the same metaphors to describe supernatural powers as well (i.e., "strength"). The passage also makes evident that we must locate Batwa societies within the same cultural and historical contexts as their agriculturalist neighbors if we are to understand their past. Given this logic, it seems likely that the hierarchical and oppressive patron-client relations that define Bantu and Batwa relations in this region today are the result of socioeconomic transformations that took place in the recent past. What follows is an argument for how and when such relations came to exist.

The incipient stages of this transformation are likely to have developed as Atlantic systems of slave raiding penetrated the region from the middle reaches of the Congo River. The fact that inhabitants of northern Congo borrowed their term for slave from peoples to the east is one of the key indicators of this relation, for the Bobangi term *montamba* came to refer to an individual whose kin group had sold them into slavery. Its original meaning was probably much closer to that described by Whitehead, "a person discarded to some menial work on account of some personal defect."[54] This term appears as *mutamba* among the Bambenjele, Mikaya, Bambenga, Bongili, and Inyele of the Congo panhandle region. Although broadly translated as "slave," closer questioning reveals that it refers to "war captive" or "hostage" as well.[55] This type of semantic narrowing is often an indicator of loanwords, and its association with violence fits with its having come into use in the region during the Atlantic Age. Likewise, when this term was elicited from the various speech communities of the region, language consultants showed a consistent inability to concur on a "correct" class prefixation schema. Among the Mikaya, Bambenjele, Bambenga, and Bongili peoples, both class 1/2 (human) prefixes and class 3/4 (nonhuman) were applied. Such confusion suggests that the term is of relatively recent introduction; accordingly, so is the institution of slavery itself.

A number of oral traditions imply that it was only during the Atlantic Age, and probably late in that period, that exclusive relationships between agriculturalist and forest-specialist communities began to be made. One of Lewis's Bambenjele consultants remarked, "At first we were all alone in the forest. No one else was here. Then we stayed in *zimo* [abandoned *Bilo* plantations]. Sometimes we would visit the *Bilo* to get tobacco and *minjoko*. Then we made friends and would even stay near their villages."[56] Although this might be considered a time-collapsing history of Batwa occupation of the forest, I argue that it is more likely a literal remembrance of the Bambenjele's historical experience over the past few hundred years. It was the introduction of a new economic system, one based on currencies that were very closely regulated along the Sangha River (i.e., *minjoko*), that led this informant's ancestors to seek closer relations with a particular agriculturalist group. The association with tobacco, an introduced American crop, reinforces placing these developments in the Atlantic Age.

Another oral tradition, this one collected by Demesse in 1958, explains how the agriculturalists of Bagbali established relations with their Bambenjele neighbors near the turn of the century. The Pomo raided a village and captured a Bambenjele man; they then took him to their village and explained that they did not intend to kill his brethren, but instead offered him bananas and manioc. In return, they demanded that his community supply meat from the hunt. The Bambenjele community then moved to the Pomo village. After a long period of negotiations, the head of the Pomo village carried out an "exchange of blood" with a Bambenjele notable named Molumba. This individual thereafter served as a spokesman for the Bambenjele group.[57]

These traditions show that in the era of Atlantic Age economies, the agriculturalists of the region clearly gained an upper hand; it was they who controlled the distribution of regional currencies, and it was they who had access to guns. Yet even during this era of slave raiding and violence, associations with Batwa communities could not be established solely through outright force. This was likely because the products that Batwa communities supplied were in such high demand; to ensure continued access to ivory and meat, the agriculturalist societies of this region were required to allow Batwa communities the freedom to carry out their economic pursuits as they formerly had. Furthermore, if forest specialists were not satisfied with the terms of the arrangement, they might easily rupture relations and seek more beneficial associations with other agriculturalists.

The mention of a "blood-exchange" in the 1958 traditions also provides an important piece of historical information, for it suggests that bonds of blood brotherhood were earlier used to establish partnerships between Bantu and Batwa.[58] Given the fact that a number of Bobangi institutions penetrated the

Congo panhandle region during the era of Atlantic trade, it is likely that Bobangi notions of blood brotherhood were used to regulate relations between Bantu and Batwa communities as well. Indeed, much of the information that Lewis's consultants have provided suggests that this was the case. The Bambenjele assert that, for them, the ideal relationship with villagers (*bilo*) should be "based on friendship, sharing, mutual aid and support, and on equality and respect for one another." In their thinking, generosity is linked to status. "Thus, if a Bilo claims to be superior to a Mbenjele, he has to prove it by giving more than the Mbenjele could ever reciprocate."[59]

Although one might attribute such values to the egalitarian ethics of hunting and gathering societies, they can also be seen as a direct reflection of the mutual obligations entailed in relations of *bondeko* blood brotherhood. Among the Bobangi, a *mukonzi* was defined, indeed, came to exist, through similar acts of generosity: organizing feasts, paying debts, giving shelter, supplying imported goods. When cast in this light, the various types of aid that villagers are currently supposed to provide for their Batwa clients can be seen as an extension of blood-brother obligations: paying bridewealth; providing funds for and attending the funerals of important Batwa individuals; trading iron, tobacco, or imported goods for meat. Because ivory underwrote the economies of the late nineteenth century, it would have been the most valued gift Batwa communities could have offered in reciprocation. With the decline in both the supply and demand for this product, Batwa populations began to lose the bargaining power they formerly held.

Despite this reality, remnants of what were probably much more egalitarian relations linger on. Like the Bobangi, the villagers and forest specialists of this region refer to their relationship through the idiom of marital ties; they refer to each other as "in-laws," but only when friendly relations prevail. To outsiders and in times of conflict, the villagers assert that they are the "owners" or "parents" of the Batwa.[60] The Bambenjele seem to see this as an absurd skewing of the manner in which relations are supposed to proceed. As an elder explained to Lewis, "*konʒa* really means 'friend.' Our fathers found them and gave them to us. If we need food he gives it to us. We give him things too. But it's a friend, not an owner . . . if your *Bilo* surpasses himself in wickedness, you must find another friend." Likewise, another elder continued, "We say, '*Milo wamu*' ('my *Bilo*') but all it means is friend. It's the *Bilo* who don't understand. They think they are all chiefs."[61] These comments suggest that modern-day social dynamics are seen as a distortion of what prevailed in the past. Bambenjele frustrations express the fact that everyday villagers have gained authority over their communities, asserting a type of social and economic domination that was formerly associated with *mukonʒi* chiefs alone.

The developments of the late nineteenth and twentieth century consolidated this phenomenon. By the early twentieth century, chiefs and middlemen traders had gained enormous profits from the central African ivory rush and could impose very disadvantageous terms in their transactions with the northern Batwa. In 1914 when a Pygmy of the Sangha River region killed an elephant, he brought the ivory and half the meat to his local patron, or chief. For this he received iron products worth about 20 francs. The chief then sold the ivory for 500–600 francs and ate the meat.[62]

Such exploitation undoubtedly led to severe social and economic inequalities between forest specialists and agriculturalists. Nonetheless, restrictive forms of slavery were never successfully inflicted on Batwa populations of these northern regions. Regnault notes as much in 1911; he described the Batwa communities he encountered as "voluntary tributaries," despite the efforts of local agriculturalists to portray them as servants or slaves.[63] Likewise, during the earliest eras of European occupation, the greatest cause of "palavers" and complaints to European authorities were agriculturalist/fishing people's complaints that their "Babongo" had abandoned them.[64] The frustration of agriculturalists who tried to "enslave" local Batwa populations is apparent in the comments of a Bongili *konʒa* interviewed by Lewis. As he states, "It was a clever trick! . . . The Mbenjele agreed to all that was said to them about being *motamba* (captive), and that the Bilo was *owner* but did not understand the implications. They had eyes only for the iron being offered them."[65]

All of this evidence indicates that the Batwa population of the northern Congo maintained autonomy as forest specialists until late in the Atlantic Age. They do not appear to have carried out relations with a single agriculturalist group until the very recent past, for linguistic evidence attests a history of contact and trade with multiple communities, both Bantu and Ubangian, throughout most of the Atlantic era. This history is further confirmed by the fact that relations of blood brotherhood began to be established between Bantu and Batwa during this time. As Joseph Miller has pointed out, these arose in west-central Africa with the rise of commercialism, and were designed to facilitate trading opportunities between "unrelated parties with goods to exchange or producers with market opportunities among distant populations with whom they shared no prior connections."[66] Although such institutions were originally rooted in notions of mutual reciprocity and respect, agriculturalist chiefs gained an advantage from their contacts in wider trading spheres. During the late nineteenth century, they were thus able to reap great profits on ivory supplied principally by the Batwa. As primary producers with no control over the terms of the trade, Batwa communities eventually came to occupy the lowest levels of the socioeconomic systems that prevailed during the Late Atlantic Age.

This situation was exacerbated as concessionary companies entered into the region, for they imposed systems of forced labor on agriculturalists to gain access to forest products such as rubber, ivory, and copal. Agriculturalists, in turn, became increasingly oppressive toward their partner Batwa, using violence and intimidation to force them to collect these products in their stead.[67] A number of scholars have argued that it was during the colonial period that extreme forms of social exclusion and discrimination toward the Batwa of northern Congo developed.[68] This history is intimated by recent transformations of Batwa-related oral traditions as well. Those collected in the 1940s and 1970s portrayed the Batwa as civilizers, teachers, and first-comers on the land. However, oral traditions told today, and embraced by agriculturalist populations alone, cast the Batwa as uncivilized in a markedly social-evolutionist mode. They recount that it was only after they had been captured and brought to agriculturalist villages that the Batwa gained knowledge of fire, iron, agricultural products, and clothes.[69]

CENTRAL GABON

Similar histories of Batwa relations with Bantu can be traced in the forested regions of central Gabon. A notable example is that of the Mitsogho, Himba, and Ebongo populations, all of whom live in the du Chaillu massif south of the Ogooué River. The Ebongo are forest specialists who speak a version of the Itsogho language referred to as "Ebongwe."[70] Today, the Ebongo live approximately 30 km to the north of Massima in a village called Okondja (Ngounié Province). Although they live alone in this village and spend a great deal of time in forest camps, the Ebongo are tied to the Mit-sogho of Massima in a number of ways. The Mitsogho supply them with the guns and cartridges used for killing larger game, usually as a form of employment, whereby the Ebongo are allowed to keep part of the prey.[71] Mitsogho chiefs also serve as their representatives in local and national political affairs, despite the fact that the Ebongo have their own government-appointed chiefs. Although relations between the two groups are hierarchical and the Mitsogho refer to the Ebongo as their former slaves, it would be inaccurate to portray their relations as the typical patron/client arrangement; the Ebongo are more autonomous than this paradigm generally implies. They are, however, the least empowered peoples of the region and generally treated as an underclass.

In chapter 4, we began to tease out elements of Ebongo history by looking at terms related to iron and iron production; here we focus on the eras after c. 1000 C.E., when proto-Ebongwe speakers had lessened their ties to Itsogho-speaking agriculturalists. As was the case with the Batwa communities of the Congo panhandle, the Ebongo of central Gabon use a number of terms that appear to be unique to them alone. Nearly all of these relate to forest products and the techniques used to extract them. Table 6.2 provides a list of these terms; so far only a few are traceable to proto-Bantu or found in the wider Bantu-speaking world. Because these are not reconstructed forms, it is impossible to discern whether the Ebongo used these terms before, during, or after their periods of intense contact with proto-Itsogho speakers. Their unique

Table 6.2 Ebongwe Lexicon

Terms found in Ebongwe language alone:
(vs. Itsogho and Himba)

- *tʃogo* "swarm of bees"   - *tumbelumbe* "flying termite sp." -*ŋgindiŋgi* "cola nut sp."
- *kata* "beehive"   - *ndambo* "chique"   -*nʒua* "rainy season" (P.B.)
- *binza* "honey fly"   - *sun-* "to shoot an arrow"   -*ŋgando* "water spirit"
- *toe* "bird-guide" (for honey)   - *solo* "quiver"   -*lombe* "forest spirit"
- *boholo* "queen bee"   - *baga* "dagger" (P.B.)   -*βoto* "clearing in forest"
- *ŋgondo* "honey container"   - *pɛm-* "to capture"
- *mbuaŋga* "sitatunga"   - *duku* "pit trap"
- *ndʒotʃi* "housecat"   - *βamba* "digging stick"
- *zome* "Cephalophe of Gabon"   - *boto* "packet of tobacco"

Terms shared with Himba language:

- *bema* "black dye/tree sp."   - *dʲobo ~ jobo* "civet" (W. B.)
- *kata* "packet of tobacco"   - *kope* "women's cache-sexe" (made of raphia cloth
- *moŋgo* "ancestors"   - *kaka* "secondary forest"
- *binza* "honeycomb"   - *wɛŋgu* "ankle shakers" (for dance)
  (-*binʒe*, Himba)   - *tʃɛba* "ivory"

Atlantic Era Terms /Associated Trade Routes
(vs. Itsogho and Himba)

	Ebongwe	Itsogho	Himba
Manioc	-*piti* (Ogooué-Ivindo)	-*begu* (local?)	-*piti* (Ogooué-Ivindo)
Maize	-*putu* (lower Congo River)	-*putu* (lower Congo River)	-*putu* (lower Congo River)
Raphia cloth currencies	-*bongo* (lower Congo River)	-*bongo* (lower Congo River)	-*bongo* (lower Congo River)
gun	-*ta* (lower Congo River)	-*ta* (lower Congo River)	-*gali/jali* (Douala/Gabon Estuary)
European cloth	-*ganda* (Ogooué-Ivindo)	-*tʃanda* (lower Congo River)	-*ganda* (Ogooué-Ivindo)

presence in the Ebongwe language, however, does attest an ongoing sense of cultural and economic autonomy despite close associations with Itsogho- and Himba-speaking communities.

This history is further substantiated by lexicon related to the Atlantic era and by terms that the Ebongo share with Himba speakers alone. For example, both Himba and Ebongwe attest *-tʃɛba,* "ivory"; *-piti,* "manioc"; *-kope,* "women's cache sex" (made of *-bongo* raphia cloth); *-jobo,* "civet"; *-bema,* "black dye"; *-binza,* "honeycomb"; and *-kata,* "packet of tobacco." Not surprisingly, each of these are sought-after items of regional trade. As we learned earlier, *-tʃɛba,* "ivory," and *-piti* are lexicon especially associated with the Ogooué-Ivindo route. These data suggest that, despite the close associations Ebongwe speakers have held with Mitsogho communities in both the past and present, they participated in trade networks outside the Mitsogho cultural sphere. The Mitsogho appear to have traded their ivory to the south, for they use the term *-pungi,* associated with the lower Congo River trade route. Also introduced from the south were maize (*-putu*) and raphia cloth currencies (*-bongo*); all three of the languages use these terms. In contrast, the Himba appear to have encountered arms through trade contacts to the north. They attest the Douala/Gabon Estuary term for "gun," *-jàli* (or *-gàli*). The Mitsogho and Ebongo, on the other hand, both use words derived from **-ta,* associated with the lower Congo River route.

The picture that emerges from these data is that the ancestors of the modern-day Ebongwe speakers of Okondja became increasingly involved in northern trade networks after their divergence from Itsogho speakers between 500 and 1000 C.E. The processes leading to this divergence may have begun during the Early Iron Age, for, as was noted earlier, the Ebongwe language adopted the term *baga* (dagger), a term that entered the region with the initial introduction of iron from the north. The evidence of later trade contacts to the north, as well as the development of sound changes unique to the Ebongwe language alone, suggests that their divergence from proto-Itsogho speakers was due to geographical movement rather than in situ processes of social differentiation. Likewise, the large number of unique Ebongwe terms for forest resources and extraction techniques attests that the Ebongwe played a role as procurers of forest products for regional systems of trade. As was the case in the northern Congo panhandle, this economic specialization would have led to increased geographical mobility, contacts with multiple agriculturalist communities, and a greater sense of social and economic autonomy among the forest specialists themselves.

With the rise of kingdoms to the west and the south, it is likely that these same processes occurred among other hunting and gathering societies of the central Gabonese rainforests. Indeed, a similar scenario can be discerned to the west, through a close reading of Andrew Battel's traveler accounts combined with linguistic evidence. Andrew Battel was an Englishman who lived in the Loango Kingdom between 1608 and 1610. During his sojourn, he traveled to a number of interior provinces. One of these was Kesock, an eight-day walk east of the Mayombe region. Regarding forest specialists, he writes:

> To the north-east of the Mani Kesock (king of Kesock) are a kind of little people called Matimbas, which are no bigger than boys of twelve years old,

but are very thick, and live upon only flesh, which they kill in the woods with their bows and darts. They pay tribute to Mani Kesock, and bring all their elephants teeth and tails to him. They will not enter into any of the Marombos (i.e., *Mayumbas'*[72]) houses, nor will suffer any to come where they dwell; and if by chance any Marombo or people of Longo [Loango] pass where they dwell, they will forsake that place and go to another.[73]

It is possible to identify the geographical location of Kesock province by comparing the length of time required to arrive there with the three months required to journey to and from Bukkameale, the most interior province of the region, according to seventeenth-century Dutch geographer Dapper. Dapper's map locates Bukkameale two to three hundred miles inland from the coast.[74] Calculating from a ratio of 45 days for two to three hundred miles of foot travel, we can deduce that eight days of walking would take an individual between 35 and 54 miles into the interior (56–84 km). Taking a due east direction from the Mayombe regions of Gabon, this locates the Kesock province in the southern parts of the present-day Nyanga province, where Ipunu-speaking peoples have resided since the first-millennium B.C.E. (chapter 4).

The capital of Kesock was likely located on the upper reaches of the Nyanga River, for members of the German expedition to Loango (1873–1876) met a certain "Mani Kasoche" on the "Upper Ngonga."[75] This location is further substantiated by Battel's mention that the "matimba" populations were from the northeast. This is a version of the name of the modern-day Barimba forest specialists, who still inhabit regions to the north of the upper Nyanga; they are currently found in a triangular expanse of forest stretching between Moabi, Ndenguilila, and Ndende.[76] The variations in pronunciation (Matimba vs. Barimba) can be explained by Dapper's probable conflation of single and plural prefixes (*mu-* singular; *ba-* plural) and a regular sound shift that later occurred in the Ipunu language, by which *t > r when located between vowels.[77]

Although Battel's description of the Matimba tends to be read as evidence of the timidity and/or subjugation of Batwa peoples, it can just as easily be seen as evidence of a very independent people trying to maintain their status as such. Linguistic dating better supports this latter view, for it indicates that proto-Irimba speakers diverged from the ancestral Bapunu communities during the century or two before 1000 C.E. Given their location just north of where the Loango Kingdom took shape in subsequent centuries, it seems likely that they, too, took up the role of specialist procurers of forest products to enter into expanding systems of trade. It is also important to note that in the early seventeenth century the Matimba were delivering tribute to the Mani Kesock directly. This relationship confirms that they remained an autonomous community into the early Atlantic period, and that they did not serve as clients, or serfs, to regional chiefs. Their restriction of access to their lands may have been due to a desire to protect their market; likewise, it may also be attributed to the effects of slave trading and raiding, which had been going on in these coastal regions for nearly a century by 1608. The presence of slave trading in these regions is attested by Battell, who commented that within a month he was able to buy twenty thousand elephant hairs for 30 slaves.[78]

Returning to the case of the Mitsogho and Ebongo, an analysis of Mitsogho religious myths and rituals suggests that the forest specialists of central Gabon retained social and economic autonomy until relatively recent dates. Unlike peoples to their south, the Mitsogho do not incorporate Batwa individuals or their symbolic equivalents (human dwarfs) into rituals of power. Although Ebongo forest specialists currently participate in religious societies such as *bwiti* and *boo,* they do so in the same manner as Mitsogho initiates, undergoing rituals that allow them to gain access to the spirits of the land. Although this can be seen as a Mitsogho attempt to co-opt first-comers into their own religious societies, this act is carried out in very egalitarian ways. As we saw in the last chapter, the Mitsogho rely on words, objects, and plants as metonyms for the primordial Batwa, rather than actual Batwa populations themselves: the original branch of *bwiti* is referred to as *bwiti-Disoumba,* wooden poles serve as symbols for Motsoi's original descent to earth (i.e., the original creation), and *iboga* is associated with the flesh and spirit of Bitumu, a deceased Batwa. Likewise, the image of the primordial Batwa is one of an esteemed religious expert, not one of a sacred helper or assistant, as is seen in regions farther to the south.

As MacGaffey has noted, "rituals serve to remind the congregation just where each member stands in relation to every other and in relation to a larger system."[79] Given this reality, we must conclude that the Mitsogho were until recently unable to, or more likely, uninterested in, subordinating local Batwa populations to their political or religious rule. The fact that the Mitsogho have retained highly decentralized political systems may be the most important reason for this phenomenon. Chiefly power does not extend beyond the village sphere; their *kumu* is the "owner of the village" (*kumu-a-mboka*) rather than the "owner of the land." The Mitsogho, it seems, provide us with a vision of the type of local political systems that characterized the early Bantu before the rise of territorial chiefships and long before the rise of kingdoms. *Kumu* serve as judges *(evovi),* historians, and religious experts on behalf of their lineage, while at the same time organizing religious societies that bring together individuals from neighboring clans. In this system, the original concatenation of power remains intact—nature spirits are considered to pass transformative powers to autochthons, and autochthons in turn, to lineage heads (who serve as the ritual experts for the Bwiti cult). It is for this reason that the elements of the Ideology of the Primordial Batwa are unusually clear among the Mitsogho.

Economics undoubtedly played an important role in the autonomy of the ancestral Ebongwe-speaking society as well. In these forested regions that lie on the peripheries of two different trade routes (i.e., Ogooué-Ivindo and Lower Congo River), agriculturalists are likely to have relied on forest specialists as key producers for interregional trade. In this context, it would have been more beneficial to leave such communities to their own devices; it was, after all, Batwa societies who provided access to products most valuable in local, long-distance, and eventually global trade.

As was the case in the northern region of Congo Republic, the violence associated with Atlantic trade did not arrive in this region until relatively late. Chamberlain has documented a near simultaneous invasion of European trade companies and Fang speakers along the middle Ogooué during the 1860s.[80] This provoked a great deal of conflict between Fang producers and African subagents in the employ of European companies.[81] Characterized by periods of intense violence and bloodshed, this conflict carried on throughout the 1870s and did not stop until the end of the century. At the same time, prices for ivory rose sky high; between 1840 and 1880, ivory was, on a per pound basis, over five times more valuable than its nearest competitor, an adult slave valued at 250 francs.[82] As Chamberlain notes, a large tusk "was worth a near fortune in central Gabon." As we see following, the great profits to be gained in the ivory trade also caused the Nzebi to enter into a period of intense conflict with peoples living in the southern Gabonese rainforest. This phase of violence began in 1880 and in some cases did not stop until as late as the 1930s.[83]

Thus, Mitsogho and Ebongo societies entered into a new era of history from the 1860s on, one that was characterized by intense competition for forest resources and violence on a scale that had never been seen before. Mitsogho elders from the villages of both Eteke and Massima report that they attempted to make slaves of neighboring Ebongo populations. According to them, raids were carried out on Ebongo villages while the men were out on the hunt, so that women and children became the most common prisoners. These captives were thereafter referred to as *mobea,* a word derived through regular sound changes from **-pika,* "slave," a term associated with the lower Congo River trade route and found throughout southern Congo and Gabon. The Mitsogho may have carried out such raids to augment population numbers in their clans, for if such slaves were indeed taken, they have been fully integrated into Mitsogho society today.[84] It is also possible that such slaves were held hostage by the Mitsogho to compel Ebongo men to supply ivory and meat. Such would explain the fact that the Ebongo continue to carry on relatively autonomous lifestyles today.

The entirety of these data imply a history similar to that of the panhandle region of Northern Congo. Hunter-gatherers appear to have taken up an economic specialization as procurers of forest products after living in close contact with the Bantu societies with whom they shared languages. This phenomenon emerged in periods when regional systems of trade underwent periods of great expansion (i.e., 1000–500 B.C.E., 700–1200 C.E.). Thereafter these Batwa societies remained autonomous—but not isolated—contributors to regional systems of trade. This new state of affairs lasted until the latest stages of Atlantic trade, when the demand for ivory drastically increased. In an attempt to profit from the ivory rush of the late nineteenth century, agriculturalist populations of central Gabon sought to control Batwa labor by violent means. The aim of such actions was to ensure continued access to ivory—the resource that underwrote local economies and slave trading into the first decades of the twentieth century.

THE SOUTHWEST

For the southwestern regions, we have a considerably different history to tell, for it is here that centralized polities came to exist and Batwa societies much earlier experienced subordination to neighboring agriculturalist populations. Vansina has argued that "the royal ideologies of equatorial Africa seem to have developed out of less elaborate variants linked to local leaders." Thus, institutions of "sacred kingship," in his view, can be seen as "enriched variants of what was originally an ideological complex justifying and legitimizing the authority of 'big men.'"[85] As made clear in chapter 3, this book works from a distinct premise, required by the linguistically reconstructed meanings of lineage/clan and chiefly words in earliest Bantu—namely, that the institutions of "sacred kingship" are enriched variants of an ideological complex that originally developed to legitimize the authority of Bantu lineage heads. This ideological complex was rooted in the tripartite concatenation of power, which envisioned transformative powers as passing from nature spirits to autochthons to Bantu lineage heads.

I have also argued that for the larger part of history, these Bantu leaders were held in awe for their ability to interact with the spirits on behalf of their lineage or clan. In the last chapter we documented the changes that then occurred in these ideas as institutions of territorial chiefship arose in the first millennium C.E. Key to this development was the symbolic usurpation of ritual powers normally accorded to Bantu leaders deemed autochthons or to the Batwa. As territorial chiefs assumed the title "owner of the land," the peoples of these southern regions came to see them as the most capable intercessors to territorial/ancestral spirits that influenced prosperity of their own groups. The continued importance of these two ideologies is made apparent in the politico-religious systems of a number of southwestern centralized states; as the brief survey that follows shows, each relied on mythical Batwa figures or their symbolic equivalents in stories and rituals that legitimized the powers of territorial chiefs and kings.

West-Central African Kingdoms and the Politics of the Primordial Batwa

The Kongo Kingdom

In the fifteenth and early sixteenth centuries, the Kongolese political system rested on dual underpinnings: the Mwissikongo dynasty as political rulers, and certain Bantu first-comers as religious experts to the king. The latter were members of the Nsaku Lau clan, whose ancestors were said to have been present on the right bank of the Congo River when the conquering king Ntinu Wene arrived.[86] Like the primordial Batwa, the Nsaku Lau were reputed to be expert ironworkers and healers, that is, owners of the transformative powers associated with first-comers on the land. Some versions of the founding myth recount that the leader of the Nsaku Lau gave his daughter in marriage to Ntinu Wene.[87] This history was reenacted each time a Kongo king was enthroned, for it was an inviolable rule that candidates to the kingship must marry a Nsaku Lau girl. This legitimized the king's power in the eyes of his subjects, for as conquering late-comers, the Mwissikongo dynasty could not technically claim ritual primacy over the land.

This dual system of leadership was based on a model used in local chiefdoms and principalities. The Nsaku Lau clan, for example, had both a political and a religious head. In the sixteenth century, both of these individuals played an integral role in the politics of the wider Kongo Kingdom. The political head was referred to as the "Duke" of Mbata, (the province where the Nsaku Lau lived). As the "eldest" and most powerful territorial chief, only he could eat at the table of the king.[88] The religious head was referred to as the Mani Vunda, and it was he who directed the rituals required to enthrone a king.[89] As a religious expert serving the entire kingdom, the Mani Vunda was considered both a rainmaker and fertility priest. It was with his permission that crops were planted and harvested; he also performed rituals to cure mental illnesses and ensure successful hunts. The political power of both of these individuals is made apparent by the fact that it was they, along with the governor of the Soyo province, who chose the successor to the Kongolese throne.

Ethnographic accounts collected in the 1930s indicate that the Nsaku Lau traced their ancestry to autochthonous *mbakambaka* dwarfs. One of Cuvelier's informants (a member of the Nsaku Lau clan) reported that the original Mani Vunda was descended from a *mbakambaka* healer that had cured Ntinu Wene of convulsive fits.[90] Likewise, the Nsaku Lau expertise in ironworking is attributed to *mbakambaka* ancestry, for as we saw in the last chapter, these mythical dwarfs were considered masters of the forge. Although this myth was recounted in the twentieth century, there is evidence to suggest that the Ideology of the Primordial Batwa informed religious views as far back as the seventeenth century During that period, missionaries noted that dwarfs served as assistants in Kimpassi rituals that were designed to initiate candidates as ritual experts to nature spirits.[91] It is therefore possible that the Nsaku Lau asserted links to the mythical autochthons of Mbata province in earlier centuries as well.

As is evident, the Kongolese political model is rooted in the same tripartite concatenation of power that prevails among Bantu peoples living in the rainforest to the north. In this case, however, the Batwa have become background figures in oral traditions that commemorate the founding state, whereas the lineage head of Bantu first-comers took on the role of expert intercessor to nature spirits in the service of the king.

Kongolese political rituals also recognized the importance of first-comers as ritual experts who could ensure the successful production of iron. This can be seen in the role that the Duke of Mbata played during enthronement ceremonies. Cast as the master-blacksmith of the entire kingdom, only he could touch the iron hammers (*nzundu*) that served as the royal emblems of the state.[92] He handed these hammers to the king as part of the installation rituals, just before he was seated on his throne. By doing so, the Duke of Mbata symbolically transmitted the supernatural powers associated with ironworkers and autochthons to the Kongolese head of state.

The importance of blacksmiths as intercessors with nature spirits remained current in the Mbata province well into the twentieth century, when they served as fertility priests and investors of local chiefs (*chefs couronées*). As MacGaffey has noted, blacksmiths are directly associated with *bisimbi* water spirits through their initiation process, which requires that they dive into the river and extract a large stone. This stone serves as the anvil in their workshop, and is considered to be a manifestation of the *bisimbi* spirits who aid in the successful production of iron tools. The association between *bisimbi* spirits and particular locales is made evident by the fact that when a blacksmith sought to change the location of his workshop, he was required to dive into a river at the new location and extract a new stone.[93]

The ethnographic record for Kongolese political and religious beliefs is longer than any other available; however, here I have presented just a few examples of the way the Ideology of the Primordial Batwa was transformed. Although there is no evidence that autochthonous hunter-gatherers were still present in the region when the kingdom was formed, the ideology played an integral role in legitimizing the power of territorial chiefs, blacksmiths, and kings. This is most evident in sixteenth-century political institutions, in which transformative powers were considered to pass from the nature spirits to the Nsaku Lau autochthons to the King. By the twentieth century, when the Kongo Kingdom had long been in decline, the role of the first-comer fell to local blacksmiths and chiefs, the former installing the latter to serve as religious experts in times of severe crisis, epidemic, or drought. Although the political figure of the primordial Batwa has been lost through the various processes of first-comer replacement, its religious aspects remain present in beliefs and rituals involving *bisimbi* water spirits, dwarfs, and ancestors who had served as *minkisi* while alive (see chapter 6).

The Yaka

The Yaka, who lived east of the Bakongo, never came to form a large kingdom; during the seventeenth century, however, they were incorporated into the Lunda kingdom that rose to the east. Because local political and religious systems were left intact under Lunda rule, Yaka ethnographies provide a great many of references to the Ideology of the Primordial Batwa. For example, the Yaka tell stories of ancient *bambwiiti* smiths who dove underwater and painfully removed boulders to be used at the forge.[94] Likewise, Yaka *bakaalamba* (territorial chiefs) claim descent from *mbakambaka* or *bambwiiti* to legitimize their rule.[95]

Also common are traditions of ancient *mbaka* chiefs who founded their own villages. This memory endures in the place names of two different villages, Imbaka Zumbu on the upper Yuku River and Kimbaka, southeast of Pelende.[96] Tradition, perhaps influenced by the Bakongo examples, recount that the founders of these villages were dwarfs. The chief of Kimbaka during the 1960s proudly claimed his own role in this heritage, stating, " I am *mbaka*, who has been initiated by the spirit of *khita;* a prescription that came from *Ndzaambya Phuungu* (the Great Creator). The *minkissi* are from Koola." This statement makes referents to key elements of the Ideology of the Primordial Batwa; not only does the chief claim Batwa ancestry, he also asserts that his powers derive from water spirits and ultimately, God. The dwarf founders of Kimbaka and Imbaka were also said to be from Koola, which was the homeland of the conquering Lunda chiefs. As autochthons from these regions, they were associated with the most powerful politico-religious powers known to the Yaka at that time.[97]

The Loango Kingdom

Like the Kongolese, the Vili of the Loango Kingdom developed political institutions around a system of local territorial chiefs (*nthomi*) considered owners of the land. Twentieth-century accounts attest the importance of the *nthomi* in the training and installation of kings. Claimants to the throne were required to spend a year in training with each of the seven original *nthomi*, who would teach him how to convene with the spirits of the land. The *nthomi* also served as representatives to the Great *Bunzi* Priest, whose shrine was located in Ngoyo, north of the mouth of the Congo River. *Bunzi* was the supreme nature spirit, described variously as the giver of life and fertility, the source of all good, the bringer of rain, and the "mother" of all *simbi* (nature spirits).[98] The Bunzi priest was charged with the task of installing new kings, and kings had to provide tribute to him throughout their reign. In turn, the Bunzi provided the king with kaolin (white clay) and other ritual materials.

These were distributed to the local populations to ensure the fertility and fecundity of people and lands.[99]

Vili visions of the primordial Batwa paralleled those of the Bakongo as well. Travelers to the kingdom remarked that both dwarfs and albinos were held in great esteem at the royal court. These observations were passed down to us by Olfert Dapper, a seventeenth-century Dutch geographer, who described the region.[100] Although Western scholars generally assume that early travelers observed Pygmies at the royal court, it is more likely that they were referring to dwarfs alone. This can be read from two elements of Dapper's discussion. First, he mentioned that the "dwarfs" had "extraordinarily large heads," a comment that would not have been likely if the travelers had actually observed Batwa individuals. Second, Dapper did not go into a detailed description of these individuals' physical traits. This suggests the travelers (from whose accounts Dapper drew) were already familiar with the condition of human dwarfism and did not find it to be particularly noteworthy or unusual. This can be contrasted with Dapper's discussion of the African albinos, which the travelers appear to have never encountered before. Drawing on their accounts, Dapper went into a very detailed discussion of their bodily characteristics and ritual roles, proposing theories as to the most probable cause of their "whiteness."[101]

Dapper's discussion of the dwarfs does, however, provide us with insight into the way that coastal Africans had assimilated the Ideology of the Primordial Batwa with their image of forest specialists who lived farther inland. "The Blacks," he states, "insist that there is a province full of forests, where one finds nothing but these dwarfs, and that it is them who kill the most elephants. These small men are called the *Bakke-Bakke* and *Mimos*."[102] "Bakke-Bakke" is surely the same term as *mbakambaka,* which is used widely throughout the Kongolese cultural sphere.

The Ideology of the Primordial Batwa is also evident in myths regarding the origin of the Loango state. Although oral histories ascribe the founding of the Loango Kingdom to Nkungu, a civilizing magician-smith from Ngoyo,[103] those that detail the origins of the second dynasty are more intimately linked to nature spirits and the Ideology of the Primordial Batwa. According to a version collected by Hagenbocher-Sacripanti (1973), the original dynasty fell out of power because its princes had committed a series of abuses. Because the throne was empty, the autochthonous *nthomi* went to the *Bunzi* priest to ask for advice. He instructed them to bring him a person who was particularly sacred. After reflecting upon this, they went to the forest and brought back a young Pygmy girl. The *Bunzi* priest deflowered her and made her pregnant, and she eventually gave birth to twins—a boy and a girl.[104] The boy was named Mwe Pwati, and he was the founder of the second dynasty. This dynasty differed from the original in that power was passed through matrilineal lines.

In creating this myth, the founders of the second dynasty rejected the common charter of dynastic origins, which in Bantu Africa tend to refer to an outsider magician/smith who found the new state. Instead, they revert back to the common genesis myth, which places nature spirits, twins, and Batwa figures at the origins of all creation. Reference to the genesis can also be seen in accounts of the journey that the Pygmy girl took after having been deflowered by the Bunzi priest. She is said to have traveled by ocean to Loango, "carefully evading certain currents of water that were inhabited by dangerous forces."[105] Upon arrival she was married, and it was then that she gave birth to the leaders of the second dynasty.

Given the emphasis on ocean travel, I argue that this myth was probably created after the advent of Atlantic trade. The great wealth and power that merchants gained by participating in the slave trade would have led coastland societies to view the ocean as a more powerful source of nature spirits and prosperity than local rivers and lakes. Likewise, by asserting direct descent from nature spirits and the primordial Batwa, members of the second dynasty may have been attempting to reassert the importance of religious expertise in a world where merchants were beginning to infringe on their political and economic powers.

This same motive has been identified as the source of prohibitions (*xima*) that were placed on traditional authorities as the involvement with Atlantic trade increased.[106] In the nineteenth century, the Maloango (King of Loango) and territorial chiefs were restricted from touching objects made in Europe, entering into the houses of Europeans, crossing the boundary rivers of the kingdom, or even looking at the sea. As Phyllis Martin has noted, these restrictions were most likely put in place by the conservative elements of the kingdom (i.e., religious authorities), individuals who understood that traditional systems of authority were being destroyed. At the same time, such prohibitions were "doubtless welcomed by the *nouveaux riches* that were also concerned with curtailing the actions of the Maloango and the class of nobles for their own ends."[107]

John Thornton has documented a similar shift in Kongolese founding traditions during the height of the Atlantic trade. In the early eighteenth century, the missionary Francesco de Pavia noted a new oral tradition of Kongo's origin, one that "replaced the conquering army of the original founder Nimi a Lukeni (or Ntinu Wene) with a very skillful blacksmith who had founded the country by uniting warring factions."[108] As Thornton has argued, the creation of this new myth was a reflection of political transformations that had already occurred. Because of the effects of 60 years of civil war, Kongo was no longer a centralized, hierarchical polity run by a powerful king and his military, but a loose confederation of provinces whose power rested on conciliation.[109]

On a cosmological level, however, the creation of this myth can be seen in the same light as the myth that the founders of the second dynasty at Loango created. Posing the founding king as a blacksmith highlighted his importance as expert intercessor to the spirits of the land. This, in turn, harked back to the original concatenation of power, in which nature spirits served as the ultimate source of political legitimization and rule. The transformation of the Kongolese founding myth can thus be seen as an attempt by nobles to reassert traditional notions of authority, especially during a period when authority was becoming much more local in nature, and their positions were being threatened by the rise of merchants and slave traders linked to the coast.

The wealth and power accumulated by these traders eventually led to the demise of both the Loango and Kongo dynasties. Although merchants sought to associate themselves with the aristocracy by buying titles, setting up large households, and imitating the noble manner of dress, such tactics inevitably led to a loss of respect for traditional rule. By the late nineteenth century, the Maloango had essentially become prisoner to his own title, for he was barred from ever leaving the royal compound.

A case documented by Laman suggests that a similar phenomenon occurred in Kongo.[110] At the turn of the century, the successor to the title of *ntinu* (duke) in the Nsundi province was purportedly captured as a young child and forced to endure a lifetime of humiliating acts. The boy was forced to watch his captives eat while he starved, and every day was taken to nearby crossroads where his face was rubbed in the dirt. Upon reaching adulthood, he was castrated; it was only then that he was accorded the title of *mpu,* local religious expert and chief. MacGaffey and Doutreloux also heard stories, between the Mboma and Manteke, respectively, of chiefs being required to undergo castration.[111]

Although these accounts may not reflect actual historical events, they do make clear that a shift in attitude toward traditional forms of authority had occurred.[112] The installation ceremonies for chiefs and kings had often required symbolic acts of submission (especially to religious leaders) in former times; these stories, however, suggest that such institutions, and the individuals they honored, had become the object of parody by the late Atlantic age. Underlying such narratives is an attitude of rancor toward the individuals and institutions that had guided west-central African societies for centuries on end.

In this climate, it is easy to imagine that the attitude toward Batwa peoples and their symbolic equivalents underwent a transformation as well. In an age where political leaders lost full regard for human life and traditional authorities were abused for purely political ends, we also see a shift in the way these southwestern societies employed the Ideology of the Primordial Batwa. This transformation is intimated in accounts of the last investiture of a Vili king (late nineteenth century), in which the supreme Bunzi priest demanded that he be given a Pygmy child before he would authorize the enthronement of the candidate chosen by territorial chiefs. As one of the many goods the local chiefs were required to provide, this demand suggests that Batwa and/or dwarf individuals were by then being captured and treated as property much like other peoples of the interior regions. Likewise, Yaka chiefs recount stories of former *bakaalamba* who captured *Bambwíiti* individuals and subjected them to ritual killings to enhance their own status. As the chief of the Swa Ibaanda *groupement* in Kingunda stated:

"If the *kalamba* (territorial chief) stood up from his chair, he took in his hands the horns of two antelopes (medicinal containers) and he had to have two *Bambúúdi* (i.e., Bambwíiti or dwarfs) by his side—one on the left and one on the right. They held the corners of his *pagne* (cloth wrap) in their hands and the chief forced the points of the horns under their ribs. After their death others replaced them."[113] A similar tradition is told in the region of Mulopo Mayombo, although in this scenario, the chief held two arrows in his hands, and he is said to have "nailed the two dwarfs to the ground in rising up from his seat."[114] When asked why a chief would commit such a heinous act, the informant responded, "The chief Mayombo executed them so that they would leave the country, to take charge of their territories and assure his own power, in order to reign on his own."

Van Roy, who collected these traditions, considers them to be remembrances of the last phase of Yaka/Batwa contact, and through association with names of Lunda rulers, places them in the last half of the seventeenth century. However, widespread occurrence and variability of this story suggest to me that they are a form of local folklore that attempted to explain the growing power of territorial chiefs. They represent a marked departure from the majority of traditions about the Bambwíiti, which tend to focus on associations with nature spirits, descriptions of the hunter-gatherer lifestyle, and accounts of intermarriage with Yaka chiefs. For this reason, I propose that they were most likely developed in the later stages of the Atlantic Age (i.e., eighteenth to nineteenth centuries), when the social and economic disparities between slave-trading chiefs and their more common followers were growing alarmingly large.

Our discussion of the southwestern rainforest/savanna region has so far focused on the ritual and political manifestations of the Ideology of the Primordial Batwa. If rituals do remind members of a society where they stand in relation to one another and the larger system, the southwestern cases provide clear evidence of Batwa societies being subordinated to Bantu agriculturalist rule. In both political and ritual contexts, Batwa individuals or dwarfs are seen only as ritual assistants or helpers, pawns to be used in legitimizing chiefly or kingly rule.

Amazing, however, is the endurance of the Ideology of the Primordial Batwa. Through a period of at least fifteen hundred years, one that saw increasing political changes and the rise of territorial chiefs and then princes, and kings—the image of the autochthon as religious expert was never lost. It endured even—or perhaps especially—in regions where autochthonous populations were no longer found. Such was the case with the Bakongo, who embellished the ideology by equating mythical autochthons with human dwarfs. As we discussed in chapter 5, it is likely that this particular vision of the ancestral Batwa was present in west-central Africa before the kingdom of Kongo arose, for it can be seen among other Bantu-speaking groups located in central Africa and southern Africa alike.[115] But what does this information tell us about forest specialists that actually lived in the southwestern region at this time? Linguistic data collected among a number of forest-specialist communities of southern Congo Republic and Gabon reflect similar processes of social and economic exclusion; accordingly, we turn to an analysis of such evidence now.

Linguistic Evidence: Forest Specialists of the Southwestern Regions, c. 1000–1900 C.E.

Although the Ideology of the Primordial Batwa might still have underpinned legitimacy in chiefdoms and kingdoms during the Atlantic Age, the actual Batwa peoples of the southwestern fringes of the rainforest faced earlier, more severe challenges than Batwa communities farther north. The linguistic evidence of this history looks different as well. The most striking characteristic of the linguistic data for the southwestern regions is the high rate of genetic relatedness between the languages of modern-day forest specialists and those of the agriculturalists with which they associate (80–94 percent, see Table 6.3). Except for the Barimba, all of the Batwa speak dialects of or the same languages as the agriculturalists with whom they associate. Although we cannot know when the original contacts between these communities were made, or if the Batwa communities spoke different Bantu languages in the past, the high rates of cognation do indicate a history of very close contacts in the recent past. Furthermore, in nearly all instances, these Batwa communities use the same terms for Atlantic trade items as their agriculturalist neighbors; this suggests that associations have been in place for at least the past four to five hundred years.

These data differ from those associated with Batwa communities in the north, who maintained enough autonomy to develop their own languages out of those that they once shared with neighboring agriculturalists. The evidence from these southwestern communities thus appears to confirm the scenario suggested through analysis of political and ritual practices—that Batwa societies of the southwest were politically and/or economically subordinated by their agriculturalist neighbors. However, we must also consider the economic systems that prevailed in these southwestern regions. As we saw in chapter 6, the rise of centralized polities was founded on the expansion of economic spheres. As new regions were integrated into expanding principalities and kingdoms, all types of communities began to lose local economic autonomy.

Table 6.3 Forest-Specialist Languages of Southern Congo Republic and Gabon

Language/Ethnonym Location	Dialect most closely related (w/cognation %)
Irimba/Barimba 24 km S.E. of Moabi, Nyanga Province, Gabon	w/Ipunu (71%)
Igama/Bagama 5 km E. of Mambi, Mayumba Province, Gabon	w/Lumbu (81%)
Iboongo-Nzebi/Babongo Fungi village, 5km S.W. of Nzenzele, Ngounié Province, Gabon	w/Nzebi (91%)
Iboongo-Iyaa/Babongo Indo village, 5km from Sibiti, Lekoumou Region, Congo Republic	w/Ibongo-Beembe (94%) w/Ibongo-Ilaali (92%) w/Iyaa (86%)
Iboongo-Ilaali/Babongo Boudouhou village, 19km from Sibiti, Lekoumou Region, Congo Republic	w/Ibongo-Beembe (94%) w/Ibongo-Iyaa (92%) w/Iyaa (88%)
Ibongo-Ibeembe/Babongo Kolo village, 14 km from Sibiti Lekoumou Region, Congo Republic	Ibongo-Ilaali (94%) Ibongo-Iyaa (94%) Iyaa (83%)

More integrated markets, increases in regional specialization, and hierarchical systems of trade prevailed, with the peoples near the center (i.e., royal capitals) realizing the greatest benefit. In such a system, forest specialists, like all peoples around them, would have had fewer options regarding whom they traded with in both medium- and long-distance networks. This in turn, could have led to much closer associations between specific Batwa and Bantu groups than those that characterize Bantu/Batwa relations in the north. Thus, although the high cognation percentages between Bantu and Batwa languages of these southwestern regions indicate a different historical experience, they cannot be seen alone as evidence for the subordination of the Batwa.

To better illuminate this history, we can identify and interpret the historical significance of phonological differences that exist between Bantu and Batwa versions of the same language. This type of analysis documents the process of language change at work, for the development of different pronunciation can be the first step toward the creation of new dialects and languages. As we see following, comparative analysis of the phonological systems of Iyaa and Nzebi-speaking forest specialists and their agriculturalist neighbors provides us with evidence of in situ social differentiation over the last four hundred years, a differentiation that appears to be rooted in practices of social exclusion and violence rather than the types of geographical distancing that prevailed in the north.

As we saw, linguistic data were collected among three different forest specialists living in the regions around Sibiti (Lekoumou Region, Republic of Congo). Although all are simply referred to as "Babongo" populations, they live in association with three different agriculturalist groups: the Iyaa, the Ibeembe, and the Ilaali. The lexicostatistical classification indicates that these three Ibongo groups originally formed a single speech community, and that they adopted their language from peoples linguistically ancestral to all three agriculturalist groups (termed here the proto-Iyaa-Ilaali) sometime prior to c. 1000 C.E. After this date, the agriculturalist group diverged, forming the proto-Iyaa, proto-Ilaali, and proto-Ibeembe. Peoples linguistically ancestral to the modern-day Babongo populations continued to interact primarily with the proto-Iyaa; this is evidenced by high cognation rates between Iyaa and all three of the Ibongo speech communities, as well as shared vocabularies for Atlantic trade items.

During the period when the proto-Ibongo and proto-Iyaa communities were interacting, major new sound shifts were appearing in the agriculturalist languages of the region. Notably, these shifts shortened words by dropping the second syllable and lengthening the final vowel. Vansina has cogently argued that these widely diffusing sound shifts originated in the language of the Tio Kingdom, and diffused with the spread of Tio (Teke) cultural hegemony in regions to the west and the southwest of that kingdom in the fifteenth and sixteenth centuries.[116] Interestingly, however, the languages of the Babongo forest specialists did not undergo these same sound changes. Instead, Babongo communities in the regions around Sibiti retained the earlier forms of pronunciation, attested today by the more conservative phonologies of all three Babongo languages. In sociolinguistic terms, this kind of resistance to language change—rejecting prestige-driven fashion in pronunciation—amounts to an assertion (often consciously made) by a people that they are distinct, and that no matter how they are treated, they are choosing their own cultural paths to follow. By the seventeenth or eighteenth centuries, as the glottochronological estimates suggest, this assertion of cultural autonomy included the retention of older vocabulary and the adoption of new words of their own in the basic vocabularies of the proto-Ibongo community as well.

There thus appears to have been a different sociolinguistic context for the lessening of contacts between proto-Ibongo and their agriculturalist neighbors than that which we saw among Batwa societies located to the north. The Barimba of central Gabon, for example, developed their unique version of the formerly shared Bantu language (proto-Ipunu), and had spoken it for roughly over one thousand years by the seventeenth century. Such developments could only have occurred through the long-term maintenance of a significant degree of social and economic autonomy. But the Ibongo dialects emerged from a more hierarchical social context during the seventeenth and early eighteenth centuries, one in which the more rigid separation of closely associated social groups encouraged the development of a distinct way of speaking among a subordinated group.

Comparative analysis of the Nzebi language as spoken by both Bantu and Batwa communities provides further evidence of in situ differentiation between closely associated groups. These data were collected among the Nzebi of Nzenzelé (Ngounié Province, southern Gabon) and a Babongo community that today lives five kilometers to their southwest in a small camp called Fungi. The Nzebi of Nzenzelé guardedly state that the inhabitants of Fungi were formerly their "slaves," and in the present-day context, the latter are treated with a great deal of disdain.[117] Although the rate of cognation between the two communities' languages is exceedingly high, (91%) the Babongo speak a version of Nzebi that is again characterized by a more conservative phonology. As was the case with the Iboongo-Iyaa, this phenomenon can help us to discern a history of contacts in the recent past.

Particularly informative is an analysis of phonological variations with the terms for "gun" and "slave." Both Nzebi and Ibongo-Nzebi use a word derived from the term *-jàli (or -gàli), which was introduced in more northern regions along the Ogooué-Ivindo route: the Nzebi attest nʒɛdi/mandʒɛdi, whereas Ibongo-Nzebi attest a form phonologically closer to the original, nzari/manʒari. Because the vocalic sound shift that produced the Nzebi form is regular to the language *(*a > ɛ/_*i#, *e#)*, we can conclude that this sound shift occurred after the gun was introduced to the Nzebi and Ibongo-Nzebi under the older -nzari form.[118] Another regular vocalic sound shift has rendered -pika (the widespread term for "slave") -peka in the Nzebi language.

Although this sound shift is not regular to the Ibongo-Nzebi language, it too attests -peka, "slave." The presence of this skewed form in Ibongo-Nzebi shows that it was adopted through contact with the Nzebi. Taken together, these data imply that the gun was introduced while the two societies enjoyed close contacts, that a period of separation ensued during which the Nzebi developed a number of sound shifts unique to them alone, and that the Ibongo-Nzebi adopted the skewed form of "slave" after this period of separation had occurred. The development of extensive slaving, in other words, came notably later than the introduction of guns. From these data, as well as modern-day acknowledgments that the Babongo of Fungi were formerly "slaves," we can deduce that the linguistic ancestors of modern-day Ibongo-Nzebi speakers began to suffer at the hands of the Nzebi after the latter had obtained access to guns.[119]

Georges Dupré argues that during the late Atlantic Age, because of pressure from southward-moving Fang populations, the Nzebi begin to undertake their own southward expansion during the late nineteenth century.[120] In the southern regions of the Congo, they settled peacefully among preexisting agriculturalist communities. However, from 1880 on, the Nzebi were increasingly involved in violent conflict with the peoples located in the forested regions to the north. This conflict arose over access to ivory and other forest resources, and did not completely cease until as late as the 1930s.[121] Babongo communities of the Nzenzelé region remember this history, for as one elder recounted, "The Nzebi came from Congo to kill elephants."[122] It is likely that they were supplanted as specialist purveyors of ivory during this period, for they have lost older hunting techniques associated with elephant hunting as well. Although the inhabitants of Fungi report that their relatives living near Mbigou use bows, spears, and elephant traps, they themselves rely solely on the gun to hunt large animals today.

The combination of ritual, mythical, historical, and linguistic data compiled here shows that Batwa peoples of the southwestern rainforest regions were much less autonomous than those of northern Congo and central Gabon. Their history resembles that which Vansina has attributed to all central African Batwa from the Early Iron Age on—one in which Batwa communities were attached to Houses as purveyors of forest goods. But this historical scenario is not applicable to most of the history of forest specialists, and especially not to the Batwa of central Gabon and northern Congo Republic. All of the societies of the wider region, including Batwa, were linked up into social and economic networks along similar lines. As centralized polities expanded, lineages, villages, districts, and even principalities increasingly defined their responsibilities to one another according to the older model of kin-group relations. The establishment of patron-client relations between Bantu and Batwa communities can be seen in this light. In this context, I argue, it is not appropriate to view the Batwa for any but a short part of their history as serfs. Although a number of individuals may have early on served as religious experts and/or servants to powerful chiefs and kings, the majority would have long continued to live as autonomous procurers of forest products for entry into regional systems of trade.

This dynamic is likely to have changed only as the violence and warfare associated with Atlantic trade systems began to prevail. As primary producers in an economic system that was became increasingly exploitive, Batwa communities of these southern regions undoubtedly fell victim to the same historical processes as their neighbors. The focus on trade shifted from royal capitals to coastal entrepots from the seventeenth century on, and new types of social and economic hierarchies developed from the coast inland. Middlemen traders vied for top positions in this commerce, pushing primary producers to the bottom of the social and economic structures. By the late eighteenth centuries, these latter populations became the objects of trade themselves.

The divergences of the proto-Igama language from proto-Lumbu and the proto-Ibongo-Iyaa language from proto-Iyaa suggest certain Batwa groups became more distanced from their agriculturalists neighbors in the last four to five hundred years. Although these cases suggest processes of in situ social differentiation, other Batwa communities may have opted to retreat to the forest as well. Their preservation of conservative features of language fits the sociolinguistic model of the behavior of a people subordinated to another people, but resisting in the one safe way open to them, by asserting their own way of speaking. All told, the forest specialists of this region suffered a much longer, more oppressive, and more destructive experience of the Atlantic era than the other Batwa communities whose histories are chronicled here.

Like many of their agriculturalist neighbors, they are likely to have entered into more exploitative relations of subservience as pawns, clients, and slaves simply to survive. Accordingly, I argue that scholars should not rely on Atlantic or post-Atlantic era observations of Bantu and Batwa interactions as indicators of the socioeconomic relations that prevailed in much earlier times.

SUMMING UP

This chapter makes clear that there is no *one* history of Batwa peoples during the Atlantic Age. As the regional histories have shown, one must take into account local political and economic systems to determine how forest specialists coped with the powerful new and often destructive factors at work in central Africa during this time. Likewise, one cannot understand the nature of modern-day Bantu and Batwa relations without referring to even earlier times, for as this chapter contends, the processes that led to the subordination of Batwa societies in the southwest are likely to have commenced during the period when centralized states began to arise.

This history is reflected by linguistic data as well. In the northern regions of the Congo Republic and Gabon, forest specialists were able to maintain a certain degree of social and economic autonomy until late in the Atlantic Age. As a result, they today speak Bantu languages that are unique to them alone. These languages were developed over the last one thousand years, and show evidence of trade and contact with numerous agriculturalist societies, both Bantu and Ubangian alike. This differs from the situation in the southwest, where Batwa societies generally speak the same languages as their closest agriculturalist neighbors, or alternatively, dialects that began to emerge over the past three to four hundred years. In both cases, the Batwa have retained more archaic phonologies and patterns of pronunciation; I argue that this phenomenon testifies in situ processes of social and economic marginalization that occurred as a result of the Atlantic slave trade. As was the case with agriculturalists who worked as primary producers during this era, Batwa communities were forced to enter into patron-client relations with more powerful neighbors simply to survive.

Despite these dissimilarities, a common historical thread exists to tie all central African societies together during this time, both Bantu and Batwa alike. As Joseph Miller has stated, "the violence attending slaving in central Africa forced political consolidation and sharpened identities . . . converting diffuse differentiated complementarities into cogently collective 'ethnic' defensiveness, even hostility."[123] Thus, although this work has argued that ethnic distinctions between forest specialists and agriculturalists developed as a result of the Early Iron Age transformations, it also contends that such identities were much more fluid before the advent of the Atlantic Age.

It is likely that the politics of ethnic defensiveness and hostility impacted Bantu/Batwa relations in the southwestern regions from the seventeenth century on; such dynamics would not only explain Batwa peoples' desire to retain older forms of pronunciation, but also their general attitude of resignation regarding Bantu hegemony as it affects them today. In the northern regions, however, the socioeconomic upheavals that accompanied Atlantic economies were not felt until the mid to late nineteenth century. Accordingly, Bantu and Batwa continue to present highly contested notions of authority, power, and friendship. The results of this history can be seen in the much more overt types of conflict that characterize Bantu and Batwa relations in these regions today.

Throughout these historical transformations, the Ideology of the Primordial Batwa widely remained a central feature of the political and religious systems of west-central Africa. Although the figure of the ancestral Batwa may have receded to the background myths, rituals, and oral traditions of highly centralized states, its core tenets—especially those referring to the original concatenation of power—were reasserted in periods when leaders needed to legitimize new types of political rule. In this sense, the Ideology of the Primordial Batwa must be considered a uniquely Bantu example of a root metaphor. It has been adjusted to fit major transformations in social, political, and intellectual thought, thereby remaining vital to central African societies for centuries on end.

We have seen numerous modern examples of this metaphor at work. The ethnography of the *mimbo* cult among the Ngbaka-Ma'bo, Mitsogho narratives about the origins of the universe and the Bwiti cult, the rituals of Bolia kingship—all provide evidence that this ideology continued to inform the religious experiences of west-central Africans well into the twentieth century. What we have learned already should encourage future scholars to uncover such histories, for it is only from the fuller reconstruction of Bantu and Batwa peoples' pasts that a clear understanding of central African history will emerge.

NOTES

1. For detailed histories of the impact of the Atlantic Trade in west-central Africa, see (among many others) Joseph Miller, *Way of Death: Merchant Capitalism and the Atlantic Slave Trade, 1730–1830* (Madison: University of Wisconsin Press, 1988); Phyllis Martin, *The External Trade of the Loango Coast, 1576–1870. The Effects of Changing Commercial Relations on the Vili Kingdom of Loango* (Oxford: Oxford University Press, 1972); K. D. Patterson, *The Northern Gabon Coast to 1875* (Oxford: Oxford University Press, 1975); John Thornton, *The Kongolese Saint Anthony: Dona Beatriz Kimpa Vita and the Antonian Movement, 1684–1706* (Cambridge: Cambridge University Press, 1998); Jan Vansina, *Paths in the Rainforest: Towards a History of Political Tradition in Equatorial Africa* (Madison: University of Wisconsin Press, 1990), chap. 7, 8; Christopher Chamberlain, "Competition and Conflict: The Development of the Bulk Export Trade in Central Gabon During the Nineteenth Century" (Ph.D. diss., University of California, Los Angeles, 1977). For a vision of this history from a broader Atlantic Perspective, see John Thornton, *Africans and Africans in the Making of the Atlantic World, 1400–1800* (Cambridge: Cambridge University Press, 1992); Robert Harms, *The Diligent: A Voyage Through the Worlds of the Slave Trade* (New York: Basic Books, 2002); and Linda Heywood, ed., *Central Africans and Cultural Transformations in the American Diaspora* (Cambridge: Cambridge University Press, 2002).

2. Jan Vansina, "The Bells of Kings," *Journal of African History* 10, no. 2 (1969): 187–97.

3. For a detailed analysis of the linguistic data behind these and following linguistic histories, see K. Klieman, "Hunters and Farmers of the Western Equatorial Rainforest, Economy, and Society, 3000 B.C. to A.D. 1880" (Ph.D. diss., University of California, Los Angeles, 1997), chap. 2. The conclusions broadly parallel those of the 1981 Bastin et al. language classification, an interpretation of which appears in Vansina, *Paths,* 47–55.

4. See Klieman, "Hunters and Farmers," chap. 2 and app. 4 for more detail on chronologies and sound changes involved.

5. This and the following information regarding the rise of principalities is found in Vansina, *Paths,* 149–155.

6. Ibid., 152.

7. Robert Harms, *River of Wealth, River of Sorrow: The Central Zaire Basin in the Era of the Slave and Ivory Trade, 1500–1891* (New Haven: Yale University Press, 1981), 2.

8. This description of the Atlantic Slave trade is based on Harms, *River of Wealth,* 24–47 and Vansina, *Paths,* 198–211.

9. Martin, *External Trade,* 47. As she notes, ivory came back into fashion in Europe during the sixteenth century, being used in Amsterdam and Germany for draught-boards, musical instruments, weapons, tankards, as inlays for furniture, and to make religious objects.

10. Ibid.

11. Harms, *River of Wealth,* 27.

12. Ibid., 28.

13. Ibid., 27. Harms has produced information on these four routes and the numbers of captives associated with them through analysis of the following sources: Martin, *External Trade,* 86–87, 124–129; René Tonnoir, *Giribuma,* Vol. 14 (Tervuren: Musée Royale de l'Afrique Centrale, Archives d'Ethnographie, 1970); Jan Vansina, *The Tio Kingdom of the Middle Congo,* 1880–1892 (London: Oxford University Press, 1973), 252–54.

14. Harms, *River of Wealth,* 27.

15. Ibid., 39–40. This jump in price was provoked by the Portuguese government abolishing its monopoly over the trade in ivory.

16. Ibid., 30.

17. Martin, *External Trade,* 148.

18. Linda M. Heywood, ed., introduction to *Central Africans,* 8. The statistics are drawn from Joseph C. Miller's article in the same volume, "Central Africa During the Era of the Slave Trade, c. 1490s–1850s," 21–70.

19. Joseph C. Miller, *Way of Death,* 71.

20. The impact of firearms was somewhat limited early on; they were imported in modest quantities only from the seventeenth century, and not circulated widely. See Miller, *Way of Death,* 79, 90.

21. Ibid., 72.

22. Ibid., 94.

23. Ibid., 101.

24. The lexical data used in this analysis are drawn from a larger corpus of data I collected while in the field, as well as from Malcolm Guthrie, *Comparative Bantu,* 4 vols. (Farnham, England: Gregg Press, 1967–71); H. A. Johnston, *A Comparative Study of the Bantu and Semi-Bantu Languages* (Oxford: Oxford University Press, 1919–1920); and numerous dictionaries for languages of the western equatorial region (see Bibliography). Regular sound correspondences have been established for each of the Bantu languages collected in the field (the A-80, C-10, B-50, B-40, and B-30 groups) allowing for the identification of loanwords (as opposed to inherited vocabulary.). See Klieman, "Hunters and Farmers," chap. 6 and app. 4 for more details.

25. See Guthrie, *Comparative Bantu,* Comparative Series no. 922.

26. The palatalization of *s (*seba>syeba*) is explained by the application of the 11/10 class prefix (*ny) that is applied to long, thin objects. This also explains the variant forms of this ethnonym that are found in archival sources ("Osyeba," "Bichiwa"); this sound shift produces varying degrees of palatalization in different languages of the Okani group.

27. See chapter 2 of Chamberlain, "Competition and Conflict" for an explanation of the various ethnic groups involved in trade along the Ogooué River at this time.

28. Martin, *External Trade,* 62.

29. Guthrie, *Comparative Bantu,* 310.

30. Klieman, "Hunters and Farmers," 323.

31. Patterson, *The Northern Gabon Coast,* 13.

32. See Klieman, "Hunters and Farmers," 350, for evidence of this sound shift. It predominates in Bambenjele, and shows up irregularly in Aka, Bambenga, and Mikaya.

33. Ibid., chap. 2.

34. Harms, *River of Wealth,* 41.

35. Harms substantiates this in his explanation of economic systems along the middle Congo River, for he states that "upstream from the Pool the Bobangi and other river people did not use cloth as a measure of value, and only rarely as an instrument of exchange." *River of Wealth,* 89.

36. A. Courboin, "Les populations de l'Alima, Congo francais," *Bulletin de la Société Royale de Geographie d'Anvers* 28 (1904): 273–275; A. Dolisie, "Notice sur les chefs Bateke avant 1898," *Bulletin de la Recherches Congolaises* 8 (1927): 49. Both cited in Harms, *River of Wealth,* 245 n. 5.

37. AEF 4YI, Mission Fourneau "Ouesso-Gabon" (Dec. 1898–1899), Archives National de l'Outre Mer.

38. Harms, *River of Wealth,* 100.

39. Ibid., 44.

40. A. Marche, *Trois voyages dans l'Afrique Occidentale* (Paris: Hachette, 1882), 221; as cited in Leon Siroto, "Masks and Social Organization among the Bakwele People of Western Equatorial Africa" (Ph.D. diss., Columbia University, 1969), 69.

41. G. Bruel, "Les populations de la Moyenne Sangha: Les Pomo et les Boumwali," *Revue d'Ethnographie et de Sociologie* 1 (1910): 6; cited in Siroto, "Masks," 68.

42. Siroto, "Masks," 67.

43. Ibid., 68.

44. Harms, *River of Wealth,* 90.

45. Ibid., 33.

46. Ibid., 146.

47. For details on the origins of this ideology and chiefly status, see Harms, *River of Wealth,* 122–24, 136–44.

48. Ibid., 134.

49. Ibid., chap. 11.

50. This explanation of *mokonzi* supernatural powers is drawn from Harms, *River of Wealth,* 200–206.

51. Jerome Lewis, "Forest Hunter-Gatherers and Their World: A Study of the Mbenjele Yaka Pygmies of Congo-Brazzaville and Their Secular and Religious Activities and Representations" (Ph.D. thesis, London School of Economics and Political Science, 2002), 221.

52. Ibid., 240. *"Bilo"* is the Mbenjele term for the various groups of agriculturalists they live in association with today.

53. Ibid., 222.

54. J. Whitehead, *Grammar and Dictionary of the Bobangi Language* (London: 1899), 453.

55. K. Klieman, field notes (where it appears as both "hostage" and "captive"); Lewis, Forest Hunter-Gatherers," 221.

56. Lewis, "Forest Hunter-Gatherers," 245. *Minjoko,* as noted previously, were a type of iron and copper currency imported into the region from the trading village of Bonga at the confluence of the Sangha and Congo Rivers. The metal was shaped into a coiled spiral, and could used for the making of tools.

57. L. Demesse, *Changements techno-économiques et sociaux chez les Pygmées Babinga, Nord-Congo et Sud-Centrafrique* (Paris: SELAF, 1978), 136.

58. The practice of establishing blood-brotherhood relations between Bantu and Batwa was noted by M. Regnault as well, a colonial official who visited the far northwestern regions of the Congo panhandle during the first decade of the twentieth century ("Les Babenga: Negrilles de la Sangha," *L'Anthropologie* 22 [1911]: 287). There he came upon a village of Batwa peoples living near the N'Doki River, who had as their head a "veritable chief." Through success as an elephant hunter, this "chief" had accumulated considerable wealth, and it was he who regulated exchanges between Batwa and their neighbors for ivory and meat. In this role it was he who interacted with the neighboring Yassua (A-80 Bantu) chief. Regnault noted that the Batwa chief had entered into a blood-brother relationship with this chief to "cement the alliance between the two populations." He also explained that the Batwa chief served only as a representative of

the families who lived around him, for "in reality, his authority over the people is limited to the domain of common interests; he has no serious influence in the families." This phenomenon was apparently common at the time, for he mentions that numerous Babenga chiefs recognize a common "grand chief," although it was a "purely honorific title." Regnault referred to another such chief at a village named Dalo, in the Pomo-speaking regions around Ouesso.

59. Lewis, "Forest Hunter-Gatherers," 228.

60. Ibid., 227.

61. Ibid.

62. The account and figures cited here are drawn from Harms, *River of Wealth*, 41.

63. Regnault, "Les Babenga," 285.

64. Ibid.

65. Lewis, "Forest Hunter-Gatherers," 221.

66. Joseph C. Miller, *Way of Death*, 57–58.

67. For details on this period, see S. Bahuchet and H. Guillame, eds., "Relations entre chasseurs-collecteurs Pygmées et agriculteurs de la forêt du Nord-Ouest du Bassin Congolais," in *Pygmées de Centrafrique: Etudes ethnologiques, historiques, linguistiques, sur les Pygmées "Ba.Mbenga" [Aka/Baka] du Nord-Ouest du Bassin Congolais*, ed. S. Bahuchet (Paris: SELAF, 1979); J.-M. Delobeau, "Les Pygmées dans la Colonization," *Afrika Zamani-Revue d'Histoire Africaine (Yaoundé)* 14 and 15, (1984): 115–133. C. Robineau, *L'Évolution Économique et Sociale en Afrique Central: L'Exemple de Souanké (République de Congo Brazzaville)* (Paris: ORSTOM, 1966); C. Robineau, "Contribution à l'Histoire du Congo. La Domination Européene et l'Exemple de Souanké (1900-1960)," *Cahiers d'Études Africaines* 7: 26(2) (1967): 300–344. For a more general history see C. Coquery-Vidrovitch, *Le Congo au Temps de Grandes Compagnies Concessionaires, 1898–1930* (Paris and La Haye: Mouton and Co., 1972).

68. For example, see Axel Köhler, "Forest, Hearth and Home: Baka Village Life in Northwestern Congo," (Ph.D. thesis, University of Manchester, 1998), chaps. 6 and 8.

69. Lewis, "Forest Hunter-Gatherers," 221. Such comments were also common among the agriculturalists communities from whom I collected data in regions around Ouesso, Congo Republic.

70. This is the Mitsogho version of the more widespread "Babongo," used to refer to forest specialists throughout central Gabon.

71. Guns are used to kill elephants and antelope; the Ebongo use bows, arrows, and poison to kill monkeys.

72. Ravenstein, who translated Battell's text into French, suggests that "Marombos" is a misprint for "Mayumbas," based on its appearance in other passages of the text. See E. G. Ravenstein, *The Strange Adventures of Andrew Battell of Leigh, in Angola and the Adjoining Regions* (Liechtenstein: Hakluyt Society, 1901), 59.

73. Ibid.

74. The figure of 200–300 miles distance is drawn from Martin, *External Trade*, 17. The calculation is 200 miles /45 days = 35 miles/8 days; 300 miles /45 days = 53 miles/ 8 days. Converted to kilometers, this calculation suggests that after eight days of walking, one would arrive between 56 and 84 km to the east.

75. Ravenstein, *Strange Adventures*, 58. "Ngonga" is probably a misprint or faulty transliteration of "Nyonga" (i.e., Nyanga). See E. Pechuel-Loesche, *Die Loango Expedition* (Leipzig: Verlag Paul Frohlig, 1907).

76. R. Mayer, "Langues des groupes des Pygmées au Gabon: Un état de lieux," *Pholia* 2 (1978): 114. As Table 6.3 indicates, I collected linguistic among Barimba peoples living 24 km southeast of Moabi.

77. Guthrie, *Comparative Bantu,* 35.

78. Ravenstein, *Strange Adventures,* 58.

79. W. MacGaffey, *Religion and Society in Central Africa: The BaKongo of Lower Zaire* (Chicago: Chicago University Press, 1986), 42. The quote itself is derived from E. R. Leach, "Ritual," in *International Encyclopedia of the Social Sciences* (New York, MacMillan Publishing Co., 1968), 524.

80. Chamberlain, "Competition and Conflict," 166.

81. Ibid., viii.

82. Ibid., 160.

83. G. Dupré, *Un ordre et sa destruction: Economie, politique, et histoire chez les Nzabi de la République Populaire du Congo* (Paris: ORSTOM, 1982), 134.

84. There are no distinctly Batwa individuals living among the Mitsogho of Eteke, "Batwa" being defined in both physical and cultural ways. This is in contrast to more southern regions, where Batwa families, reputed to be former slaves, live among agriculturalist communities and are treated as a distinct underclass. Such was the case among the Nzebi of Nzenzele, Gabon, and a number of families living among the Iyaa near Sibiti, Congo Republic.

85. Vansina, *Paths,* 74.

86. This account of Kongo origins draws from *Historia Do Reino de Congo,* written c. 1620 by an anonymous author and edited by A. Felner (Angola: Coïmbre, 1933). Cited in de Heusch, *Le roi de Kongo et les monstres sacres* (Paris: Éditions Gallimard, 2000), 76.

87. This is a common theme in the founding myths of Bantu polities; it suggests outsider founders were accepted by first-comer autochthons from the start.

88. Georges Balandier, *La vie quotidienne au royaume du Kongo du seizième au dix-huitième siècle* (Paris: Hachette, 1965), 70.

89. Descriptions of the religious and political responsibilities are drawn from de Heusch, *Le roi de Kongo,* 77–79. The role of the Duke of Mbata in enthroning kings is documented as early as 1622, when he was accompanied in his task by a Portuguese priest. See L. Jadin, "Apercu de la situation du Congo et rites d'élection des rois en 1775, d'apres le P. Cherubino da Savona, missionaire au Congo de 1759 à 1774, *Bulletin de l'Institut Historique Belge de Rome* 36 (1963): 185–483.

90. J. Cuvelier, "Traditions Congolaises," *Congo* 2 (1931): 199; de Heusch points out that the mention of convulsive fits is likely a reference to spirit possession.

91. Cavazzi mentioned the presence of dwarfs in his 1687 work, *Istorica Descrizione dei tre Regni Congo, Matamba, et Angola;* cited in J. Van Wing, *Études Bakongo,* vol. 2, *Religion et Magie* (Brussels: Colonial Belge Institut Royal, 1938), 229.

92. de Heusch, *Le roi de Kongo,* 108.

93. MacGaffey, *Religion and Society,* 68.

94. Y. Struyf, "Langues et coutumes congolaises," *Missions Belges de la Compagnie de Jesus* (Brussels) 8 (1906): 296; cited in H. Van Roy, "Les Bambwíiti, peuplade prehistorique de Kwango," *Anthropos* 68 (1973): 838.

95. See Van Roy, "Les Bambwíiti," 825, 826, 843, 866.

96. "Imbaka" and "Kimbaka" refer literally to "emplacement of the dwarf" (Van Roy, "Bambwíiti," 825).

97. Janssen and Bruggeman found this account of the founding of this village in the colonial archives: "Kimbaka . . . was founded by a dwarf, Mukishi Mbaka, who carried the raphia sack of Kiamfu and walked under the tipoy of his master. This dwarf was the fetish, *mukishi,* of Muni Putu, who gave him a village. He was replaced at the *musumba* (Lunda

chief's compound) by *thóómbo* (hostages who replace a chief)." Van Roy, "Bambwiiti," 825.

98. See de Heusch, *Le roi de Kongo*, 48–49, 58, for the sources of these descriptions. As was the case in other west-central African societies, manifestations of *Bunzi* were associated with water—especially torrents in rivers or sudden inundations.

99. de Heusch, *Le roi de Kongo*, 47. Information obtained from F. Hagenbucher-Sacripanti, *Les fondemenys spirituals du pouvour au royaume de Loango* (Paris: Orstom, 1973), 72.

100. O. Dapper, *Naukeurige beschrijvinge der Afrika* (Amsterdam, 1668). Translation from Flemish, *Description de l'Afrique* (Amsterdam: Wolfgang, Waesberge, Boom and Van Someren, 1686; reprint, New York: Johnson Reprint, 1970), 332.

101. Ibid. As a possible explanation, he suggested that they were suffering from a form of leprosy that cause their skin to be excessively dry; this is why, according to him, other "Blacks" put so much oil on their skin (to protect against catching this disease).

102. Ibid.

103. A founding myth collected by Pechuel-Loesche in the early twentieth century explains the original founding of the kingdom as the work of Woyo smiths who arrived from the south (Ngoyo Kingdom). Their leader, a "civilizer-hero" named Nkungu, was gifted with magical skills and a mastery of fire. Wherever he went, rainfall was plentiful and fruits ripened. After a series of magical acts that prevented him from drowning on the Chiloango River, the local people were so impressed that they followed him in awe. They saw that wherever he went fire burned and the land became green and verdant. Because of his mystical skills, he became king. Pechuel-Loesche, *Die Loango Expedition*, 157; recounted in de Heusch, *Le roi de Kongo*, 44.

104. Martin, *External Trade*, 8; de Heusch, *Le roi de Kongo*, 46.

105. de Heusch, *Le roi de Kongo*, 46.

106. The period when these prohibitions were instituted is not known; they were in effect when traders such as Battell, Broecke, and Brun visited the kingdom in the early seventeenth century. For a discussion of this issue, see Martin, *External Trade*, 170.

107. Ibid., 171.

108. John Thornton, *The Kingdom of Kongo: Civil War and Transition, 1641–1718* (Madison: University of Wisconsin, 1983), 84.

109. Ibid., 118.

110. This account taken from de Heusch, *Le roi de Kongo*, 101.

111. MacGaffey, *Religion and Society*, 70; A. Doutreloux, *L'ombre des fetiches. Société et culture Yombe* (Louvain et Paris: Nauwelaerts, 1967), 172, as cited in de Heusch, *Le roi de Kongo*, 101.

112. Wyatt MacGaffey considers Laman's account of the *ntinu Nsundi's* ordeals "purely mythical" (personal communication, July 31, 2003). In his most recent work he explains that the legend "provided a kind of template for the investiture of chiefs" during the period c. 1890–1905, "when sleeping sickness was rampant and the indigenous political system was breaking down." See W. MacGaffey, *Kongo Political Culture: The Conceptual Challenge of the Particular* (Bloomington and Indianapolis: Indiana University Press, 2000), 148–150.

113. Van Roy, "Les Bambwíiti," 845.

114. Ibid., 859.

115. See notes 63–65, chap. 5, for a full accounting of the southern examples.

116. Vansina, *Paths*, 151.

117. This was the most extreme case of societal division and discrimination I saw among all Bantu and Batwa groups studied. It was first made evident when my assistant, a 28-year-old Nzebi man who had lived in Nzenzelé all his life, admitted to me he was afraid he would not be able to understand the language of Babongo peoples living in Fungi. He was extremely surprised to find out they spoke the same language he did. The fact that he had spent his entire life in the village and had no knowledge of this fact indicates a real lack of interaction between the two communities. Furthermore, the Babongo inhabitants of Fungi were markedly suffering from poverty, lack of food, and health care. When I asked why they didn't take a dying elder to the health clinic in Nzenzelé, five kilometers away, they responded succinctly that they were treated too badly by the Nzebi.

118. The only other way this difference in pronunciation could be explained is if the Ibongo-Nzebi had borrowed the *nzari* form from a neighboring community. The Himba to the north do attest *enzaji*. However, if the Ibongo-Nzebi had borrowed this term from them, it would likely appear with the /j/ instead of /r/ and would also be seen as a loanword in other languages of the region. There is no evidence of this; thus, I conclude that the gun was introduced among Nzebi and Ibongo-Nzebi speakers as *nzari* and subsequent sound changes rendered it *nʒedi* in the Nzebi language alone.

119. This history is intimated by the comments of a Babongo elder of Fungi; when I asked whether he had obtained guns through the Nzebi, he replied "Guns! We were their slaves, why would they give us guns?!" K. Klieman, field notes, 7–23–94.

120. Dupré, *Un ordre,* 134.

121. Ibid.

122. K. Klieman, field notes, 7–27–94.

123. Miller, "Central Africa," 45.

CONCLUSION

This book has provided historical syntheses and theoretical approaches that begin to answer a number of long-standing queries about the central African past. These syntheses and approaches centered on three broad themes: Bantu settlement within the equatorial rainforest, the history of Bantu and Batwa relations, and the Ideology of the Primordial Batwa. In this brief conclusory section we address the implications of these new hypotheses and theories for the fields of central African and African history, and also suggest possible directions for future research.

The history of Bantu settlement into the west-central African reaches of the rainforest has, till now, been treated in a cursory manner. This book provides the first set of historical hypotheses regarding the direction, nature, and chronologies of Bantu settlement patterns within the modern-day regions of the Congo Republic and Gabon, the very regions where the Bantu expansions first began. Drawing from the increasing amount of archeological research carried out in these regions over the past 10 years, the book identifies parallels in the diffusion of early Bantu speech communities and the archeological remains of the technologies they brought with them, primarily ceramics and polished stone tools. The assertion of such parallels, however, does not presume that Bantu speakers were the only inhabitants of central Africa to use such technologies, nor that they afforded them any type of superiority over their autochthonous neighbors right from the start.

Working from Vansina's notion of a slow revolution in agriculture and the archeological classificatory category of a transitional Stone to Metal Age, I have argued that Bantu speakers lived for periods of between six and sixteen hundred years (depending on the location) in relative economic and technological parity with the autochthons they met. This hypothesis is founded on analysis of both linguistic and archeological data, both of which suggest an earlier date for the first arrival of Bantu speakers than has previously been acknowledged. By taking into account what have generally been considered anomalously early dates for the appearance of ceramics and polished stone tools, and identifying parallels in the linguistic evidence for the formation of early Bantu speech communities, this work argues that an avant-garde of Bantu speakers was present in the rainforest from as early as the fifth millennium B.C. along the coast to the fourth millennia B.C. in the far northwestern rainforest. Accordingly, I have argued that it was during this period that immigrants and autochthons were most intimately interconnected. This dynamic allowed for, at many locations, the sharing of languages, cultures, technologies and genes.

This new understanding of the Bantu expansion into the rainforest provides us with historical hypotheses and chronologies to address a phenomenon that both linguists and geneticists have long acknowledged—that the ancestors of modern-day Bantu and Batwa societies must have, at some point in the past, enjoyed a history of much closer contacts than they do today. It also confirms what Vansina has claimed, that the presence of Bantu agriculturalist communities in west-central African did not provoke a Neolithic Revolution in and of itself. Instead, dramatic transformations in economic and technological practices began to occur only after the introduction of banana farming and iron. Both of these began to spread in the region during the last millennium B.C.E., a period by which, in some regions, Bantu speakers had already been established for hundreds of years.

This work also goes beyond analysis of archeological and linguistic evidence to develop historical hypotheses about the nature of immigrant and autochthon relations during pre-Iron Age times. Working from the proposition that similarities in first-comer and late-comer relations documented across sub-Saharan Africa relate to Niger-Congo religious beliefs, I have developed the first-comer model to serve as an aid in moving beyond evolutionist paradigms to interpret the Batwa past. This model asserts that Bantu agriculturalists felt it essential to honor, emulate, and appropriate the rituals and/or ancestral spirits of peoples they deemed autochthonous to the land. Only in this way could they ensure the prosperity of their own communities, for territorial spirits, which the spirits of deceased first-comers came to be associated with, were believed to influence the fertility and fecundity of both people and land. This understanding provides not only a motive for ongoing relations after the Bantu were established in the rainforest, but also proffers clues as to how Bantu languages came to be spoken across nearly one-third of the continent in later times.

For many years, it was assumed that a certain Bantu prestige or superiority explained this phenomenon. It has never been clear, however, where such prestige might have stemmed from. As Vansina has noted, "the technological differential, especially in early times, was small. Did Bantu speakers have a monopoly on some form of trade? Were they conquerors, or somehow superior in religious matters? There is no evidence so far to support any of these suppositions, for the early dispersals at least."[1] This first-comer model provides an initial answer to this query. Contrary to conventional thinking, however, it asserts that autochthons held a certain degree of social prestige, for the Bantu posed them as religious experts to their own societies during the earliest stages of settlement. It is this phenomenon that might explain why Bantu societies were so successful in spreading their language and culture: their religious beliefs required the use of accommodationist policies toward the autochthons they met.

These policies, in turn, are likely to have encouraged first-comers to establish ongoing socioeconomic relations with or, alternatively, assimilate into, Bantu communities from early on. Both of these dynamics would have allowed the Bantu to establish larger and more prosperous communities, thereby enhancing their ability to move into new lands.

The present-day existence of Batwa communities, however, suggests that not all autochthons chose to assimilate into Bantu populations. Using methods of comparative historical linguistics, this work has traced the history of a number of such communities, located in the Northern Congo Republic, Central Gabon, and southern Congo Republic and Gabon. In doing so, the book addresses long-standing questions as to how and why nonagriculturalist populations have been able to retain a distinct ethnic and economic status within the rainforest region for centuries on end. The answer to this query is found in the social, political, and economic systems that developed after the introduction of bananas and iron. It was during this period (1500–500 B.C.E.) that Bantu communities began to develop a fully agricultural lifestyle. Regional and local economic specializations began to appear, as did longer-distance trade networks and political institutions to link the communities involved in such trade.

Batwa societies were not simply bystanders to these historical events. Both linguistic and oral data suggest that the ancestors of modern-day Batwa communities began to lessen their contacts with the Bantu communities they shared languages with at this time, thereby rejecting assimilation into the agriculturalist communities that increasingly gained hegemony over the land. The Batwa developed an economic specialization of their own, serving as procurers of forest products for entry into regional systems of trade. Because they provided products that remained in high demand in local, regional, and eventually global trade networks, the forest-specialist lifestyle remained viable until late in the Atlantic Age.

An understanding of this history also helps to explain why Batwa communities did not adopt technologies of iron production, and why there are today no Batwa communities that subsist on forest resources alone. The original forest-specialist communities were formed by groups that once had close ties to agriculturalist communities, not peoples who had lived isolated in the rainforest for thousands of years. Because of this, they were already familiar with the benefits of cultivated foods and iron. Thus, from its very inception, the forest-specialist lifestyle included these products. The forest-specialist lifestyle was a rejection of the increasingly sedentary economies developing in the region, not of contacts with agriculturalists themselves.

This historical scenario also suggests an answer to the issue of how Batwa societies lost the autochthonous languages their ancestors might have once spoken. Again, they are the descendants of communities that lived in close contact with agriculturalists before the Iron Age, but then broke away. The Batwa have long been considered anomalous regarding this issue because they are compared with autochthonous peoples of the southern African regions (e.g., the San and Khoi) who have retained non-Bantu languages of their own. This dissimilarity simply highlights the point that the Batwa of central African have had a *very* different past. Given this reality, we must reconsider the applicability of anthropological approaches that identify and theorize commonalities in hunter-gatherer communities in Africa and across the globe. Difference can be used as an analytical tool in and of itself; by locating such communities in local and regional histories, we are provided with a better understanding of how they came to live the lives they do today.

Although this book asserts that forest specialists have occupied a unique and viable socioeconomic niche within the equatorial regions for as many as three thousand years, it cannot be said that their relationships with agriculturalists remained unchanged. Two distinct periods of interrelational transformation have been identified, the first associated with the rise of territorial chiefs (c. 500–1000 C.E.) and the second with the upheavals of the Atlantic Age (c. 1500–1900 C.E.).

In the first period, the politico-religious status of Batwa communities was usurped, for territorial chiefs came to be seen by agriculturalists as the new owners of the land. Accompanying this transformation was the creation of a new political charter designed to recast relationships with autochthons, reducing their politico-religious powers as expert intercessors to the spirits of the land. The remnants of this charter can be identified in the commonalities of central African myths, rituals, and traditions that honor the civilizing role of the ancestral Batwa. I have argued that these myths were part of the broader set of chiefly legitimizing institutions that spread widely in central African during the first millennium C.E. As political systems became increasingly centralized, especially in the societies of the southwest, Batwa individuals were incorporated into rituals and ceremonies designed to legitimize Bantu chiefs and kings. By encouraging traditions that posed the Batwa as teachers and civilizers to their own societies, as well as claiming ancestry from or intimate interactions with ancestral Batwa, Bantu leaders sought to legitimize their own rise to power. At the same time, however, the new political charter allowed them to restrict neighboring Batwa peoples' participation in politico-religious institutions to a largely symbolic role.

These political tactics were likely to have been enhanced versions of those used by lineage heads in earlier times, for as stated earlier, such leaders would have been eager to appropriate the ritual knowledge that allowed them to influence the spirits of the land. Likewise, myths and oral traditions that posed the ancient Batwa as civilizers to the Bantu world were likely derived from a more ancient set of cosmological beliefs that posed the Batwa as first-comers to the world. This book has provided numerous examples of Bantu genesis accounts that focus on the figure of the Batwa as the earliest creations of the Demiurge; in nearly all cases, these beings are associated with the pri-mordial waters of the original creation, thereby rendering bodies of water the primary location where west-central Africans sought to make contact with the spirits of the land. Equally widespread was the belief that such spirits dwelt in termite hills; as a result, they were incorporated into religious rituals as emblems of the ancestral first-comers and transformative powers that emanated from the supernatural world.

As time passed and ethnic identities became more distinct, these cosmolog-ical beliefs were expanded upon by various communities in unique ways. This occurred in both centralized and noncentralized societies; the core ele-ments of the cosmology are still identifiable in each. Perhaps most fascinating are the metaphorical associations that surfaced in the Kongolese cultural sphere, where human dwarfs came to be symbolic replacements for the figure of the primordial Batwa. This ideology probably developed among more ancient Bantu speech communities originally located along the middle Congo River, for associations between mythical or human dwarfs and nature spirits are found in a number of speech communities that trace their ancestry to back to this region, where actual Batwa can be found. Among these are the Bakongo, Bayaka, and Bakuba in central Africa, and the Chewa, Nyanja, Venda, and Xhosa of southeastern Africa (Zambia, Malawi, South Africa). The enduring nature of these beliefs, as well as their ability to be adjusted to different political contexts and eras of time, suggests that we are dealing with a root metaphor of the Bantu-speaking world. In its antiquity and ability for adjustment it parallels the Idea of the Pygmy, a Western root metaphor that continues to influence our own perceptions of modern-day Batwa.

It is intriguing to note that the cosmological beliefs of both Egyptian and Bantu societies posed human dwarfs as religious experts to the supernatural world and associated them with the original act of creation. Could this ideol-ogy have roots in an ancient African antecedent, or is it simply the result of coincidence? It seems possible that both societies linked dwarfs to creation through association with the act of childbirth, because newborn infants—like human dwarfs—are endowed with disproportionately large heads. Although these types of associations may seem odd to the Western mind, it must be remembered that Euro-American visions of the Batwa as primordial remnants have their ultimate roots in an equally chimerical metaphor, the Great Chain

of Being. All of these cosmological models—Egyptian, Bantu, and Western—were developed to answer the same eternal human question: who are
we, and from whence did we come?

By outlining the key elements of the Bantu Ideology of the Primordial
Batwa, this work has provided a new framework for interpreting references to
mythical first-comers found in the oral traditions of central and southern
African societies. Until now such references have been treated as anecdotal
and inconsequential, or in the case of the more southern regions, as memories
of actual autochthonous populations that existed in the past. When viewed as
local manifestations of deeply rooted cosmological beliefs, however, these
myths and traditions help us to understand the intellectual and incorporeal
elements of ancient Bantu peoples' lives.

The second period of interrelational transformations was engendered by
the social, political, and economic upheavals of the Atlantic Age (1500–1900
C.E.). In the regions of the southwest where centralized kingdoms had come to
exist, the rise of middlemen traders led to the eventual decline of traditional
authority. The accumulation of personal wealth became the principal source
of political power from the seventeenth century on, while slave raiding and
violence disrupted the political and economic systems that had formerly held
kingdoms together. As a result, local authorities once again became the focus
of political power, and primary producers began to suffer at the hands of more
powerful slave-trading chiefs. In this environment, the Batwa, like many agriculturalists of the region, were forced to enter into exploitative relations of
clientage or slavery simply to survive. Their loss of status was exacerbated by
the fact that in many regions, their role as procurers of forest products, especially ivory, began to be usurped by Bantu groups.

In the more northern regions of the rainforest Batwa communities were
able to retain a much greater degree of autonomy late into the Atlantic Age.
This was partly due to the political history of these regions, for centralized
polities had never come to exist, and agriculturalist societies were unable to
assert the same kind hegemony as those in the south. Also important was the
fact that the violence associated with the Atlantic era did not penetrate this
region until the late nineteenth century. Because this period also saw a dramatic increase in the European demand for ivory, Bantu societies depended
heavily on the skills of forest specialists for access to this valuable item of
trade. Thus, although exploitative systems of clientage and slavery eventually
came to prevail among the agriculturalists of the region, the economic contributions of Batwa communities afforded them a certain degree of bargaining
power throughout most of the Atlantic Age. This situation was altered however, as colonial systems were set in place. Europeans imposed harsh systems
of forced labor on agriculturalist societies, especially for the collection of forest products such as rubber and copal. In turn, agriculturalists became

increasingly hegemonic toward their Batwa neighbors, using tactics of violence and intimidation to force them to gather these products in their stead.

These examples illustrate that the reconstruction of Batwa histories must be approached on regional terms because the nature of agriculturalists' social, economic, and political systems play a large role in determining the opportunities available for Batwa societies as well. Although this phenomenon prevailed in earlier times, it was during the Atlantic Age that Batwa communities suffered their greatest socioeconomic decline.

In the earlier stages, this came about through their role as primary producers whom local chiefs and traders could dramatically exploit. By the nineteenth century however, their unique socioeconomic niche was beginning to be usurped. The high demand for ivory led numerous agriculturalists to take up elephant hunting as a specialized trade, thereby reducing the role that Batwa communities had played as procurers of ivory for two centuries or more. Then, as a result of the imposition of colonial rule, the demand for forest products (except rubber and copal) began to be limited to the much more local sphere. Patron-client relations that had been established during the Atlantic era continued to hold sway, and agriculturalists adopted Western notions of social evolution to justify policies of socioeconomic marginalization they imposed on their Batwa "clients." It is thus the dynamics of more recent history, intimately tied to the impact of the Atlantic trade, that explains how Batwa societies have come to occupy the lowest social, economic, and political strata of central African societies today.

An understanding of this history helps to explain an issue that has long perplexed scholars of central Africa: how myths that honor the ancestral Batwa could coexist alongside modern-day practices of such extreme social disdain. If we view the shift in attitude toward the Batwa as the result of recent historical events, one can posit that Bantu societies simply have not had enough time to readjust their myths so that they explain the socioeconomic realities of today. However, as was noted in chapter 6, this process has begun in some regions of the rainforest, where agriculturalists have begun to claim that it was their ancestors who civilized the Batwa by capturing them and introducing them to fire, food, iron, and clothes.

The historical hypotheses I have provided in this book will undoubtedly be challenged in a number of ways. Although I will be pleased if they withstand the test of time, my ultimate goal in putting them forth is to stimulate an interest in reconstructing the history of the Batwa. To that end, I hope that the methods and results I have developed here will encourage other historians to take up the task. As this work has shown, the reconstruction of Batwa history is not only possible, but it also turns out to be a history instrumental in the founding of social, political, and religious institutions of central Africa at large. Likewise, a more thorough understanding of central African history is essential to the reconstruction of Bantu histories across the continent, for, as the example of the Ideology of the Primordial Batwa has shown, the rain-forest served as a breeding ground for some of the most fundamental cultural, political, and religious beliefs that continue to define Bantu-speaking societies today.

NOTE

1. Jan Vansina, "New Linguistic Evidence and the 'Bantu Expansion,'" *Journal of African History*, (1995): 191.

BIBLIOGRAPHY

DICTIONARIES, LINGUISTIC ATLASES, AND LINGUISTIC SOFTWARE

Archevêché de Libreville. *Dictionnaire Ndumu-Mbede-Français et Français- Ndumu-Mbede*. Libreville, Gabon: Archevêché de Libreville, 1969.

Bouquiaux, L. *Dictionaire Sango-Français*. Paris: SELAF, 1978.

Calloc'h, J. *Vocabulaire Français-Ifumu (Batéké)*. Paris: Librairie Paul Geuthner, 1911.

————. *Vocabulaire Français-Gmbwaga-Gbanziri-Monjombo*. Paris: Librairie Paul Geuthner, 1911.

Coupez, A., Y. Bastin, and E. Mumba. *Bantu Lexicale Reconstructions 2* (database and software). Tervuren: Musée Royale de l'Afrique Centrale, 1998.

Dugast, I. *Lexique de la Langue Tunen*. Paris: Libairie C. Klincksieck, 1967.

Galley, S. *Dictionaire Fang-Français*. Neuchâtel: Messeiller, 1964.

Gusimana, B. *Dictionnaire Pende-Français*. Bandundu: Ceeba Publications, 1992.

Guthrie, M. *Lingala Grammar and Dictionary*. London: Baptist Mission, 1988.

Helmlinger, P. *Dictionnaire Duala-Français*. Paris: Editions Klincksieck, 1972.

Hulstaert, G. *Grammaire du Lomongo*. Tervuren: Musée Royale de l'Afrique Centrale, 1961.

Kadima, K., H.-M. Mutombo, M. Bokula, K. Kabuyaya, P. Mbula, and N. Tshimbombo. *Atlas Linguistique de L'Afrique Centrale: Le Zaire*. Paris: ACCT/CERDOTOLA, 1983.

Lekens, P.B. *Dictionaire Ngbandi*. Annales Du Musée du Congo Belge, series 8.1, Tervuren, 1952.

Lumwamu, François, and Josué Ndamba. *Atlas Linguistique de L'Afrique Centrale: Le Congo*. Paris: ACCT/CERDOTOLA, 1987.

Sammy-Mackfoy, P. *Atlas Linguistique de L'Afrique Centrale: La Republic Centrafricaine*. Paris: ACCT/CERDOTOLA, 1984.

Schadeberg, T. *Bantu Map Maker 3* (Linguistic Mapping Software). University of Leiden, 1996.

Swartenbroeckx, P. *Dictionnaire Kikongo et Kituba-Français*. Kinshasa: CEEBA, 1973.

Walker, A. "Dictionaire Getsogo-Français." Unpublished manuscript, n.d.

Whitehead, J. *Grammar and Dictionary of the Bobangi Language*. London, 1899. Reprint, Ridgewood, New Jersey: Gregg Press, 1964.

Willems, E. *Dictionnaire Français-Tshiluba*. Kananga: Editions de la Archdiocèse, 1986.

BOOKS, ARTICLES, AND DISSERTATIONS

Adams, W., M. A. S. Goudie, and R. Orme, eds. *The Physical Geography of Africa.* Oxford: Oxford University Press, 1996.

Anonymous. *Historia Do Reino de Congo.* Edited and translated by A. Felner. Angola: Coimbre, 1933.

Antilla, R. *Historical and Comparative Linguistics.* Amsterdam: John Benhamins, 1989.

Aristotle. *Histoire des animaux.* Edited by P. Louis. 3 vols. Paris: Les Belles Lettres, 1969.

Arom, S., and J. M. C. Thomas. *Les Mimbo: Génies du piégage et le monde surnaturel des Ngbaka-Ma'bo (Republique Centraficaine).* Paris: SELAF, 1974.

Bahuchet, S. "Notes pour l'histoire de la région de Bagandou." In *Pygmées de Centrafrique: Études ethnologiques, historiques, et linguistiques sur les Pygmées "Ba.Mbenga" (Aka/Baka) du Nord-Ouest du Bassin Congolais,* edited by S. Bahuchet, 57–76. Paris: SELAF, 1979.

———— "Utilisation de l'espace forestier par les Pygmées Aka, Chasseurs-cueilleurs d'Afrique Centrale." *Social Sciences Information* 16, no. 6 (1979): 999–1019.

———— "Linéaments d'une histoire humaine de la forêt du Bassin Congolais." *Memoires du Muséum Nationale d'histoire nationale,* series A, vol. 132 (1986): 297–315.

———— "Les Pygmées d'Afrique, maillon de l'histoire?" *Le Courier du CNRS* 69–70 (1987): 56–60.

———— "Les Pygmées Aka et Baka: Contribution de l'ethnolinguistique a l'histoire des populations forestiers d'Afrique Centrale." Thése de Doctorate d'Etat, Université René Descartes, Paris, 1989.

———— "Les Pygmées d'aujourd'hui en Afrique Centrale." *Journal des Africanistes* 61, no. 1 (1991): 5–35.

———— "L'Invention des Pygmées." *Cahiers d'Études Africaine* 129, no. 33 (1993): 153–181.

———— *La Recontre des agriculteurs: Les Pygmées parmi les peuples d'Afrique Centrale.* Paris: Peeters, 1993.

Bahuchet, S., ed. *Pygmées de Centrafrique: Études ethnologiques, historiques, et linguistiques sur les Pygmées "Ba.Mbenga" (Aka/Baka) du Nord-Ouest du bassin Congolais.* Paris: SELAF, 1979.

Bahuchet, S., and H. Guillaume, eds. "Relations entre chasseurs-collecteurs Pygmées et agriculteurs de la forêt du Nord-Ouest du Bassin Congolais." In *Pygmées de Centrafrique: Études ethnologiques, historiques, linguistiques, sur les Pygmées "Ba.Mbenga" (Aka/Baka) du Nord-Ouest du Bassin Congolais,* edited by S. Bahuchet, 189–211. Paris: SELAF, 1979.

Bahuchet, S., D. McKey, and I. de Garine. "Wild Yams Revisited: Is Independence from Agriculture Possible for Rainforest Hunter-Gatherers?" *Human Ecology* 19, no. 2 (1991): 213–243.

Bahuchet, S., and J. M. C. Thomas. "Linguistique et histoire des Pygmées de l'Ouest du Bassin Congolais de l'Ouest du Bassin Congolais." *Sprache und Geschichte in Afrika* 7, no. 2 (1986): 73–103.

Bailey, R. C., G. Head, M. Jenike, B. Owen, R. Rechtman, and E. Zechenter. "Hunting and Gathering in the Tropical Rainforest: Is it Possible? "*American Anthropologist* 91, no. 1 (1989): 59–82.

Balandier, G. *Afrique Ambiguë.* Paris: Plon, 1957.

————. *La vie quotidienne au Royaume du Kongo du XVI au XVIII siécle.* Paris: Hachette, 1965.

Bancel, P. "Étude comparée des noms de mammifères dans les langues du Groupe Bantou A.70." D.E.A. des Sciences du Langue Memoire, Université Lumière Lyon II, 1986–87.

Banier, M. l'abbé. *Explication historique des fables ou l'on decouvre leur origine et leur conformité avec l'histoire ancient et où l'on rapporte les époques des Héros et des principaux évenements dont il est fait mention.* Paris: Chez Francais Le Breton, 1711.

Barnes, J.. *The Ashmoelum Ostracon of Sinuhe.* Oxford: Oxford University Press, 1952.

Bastin, Y. "Reconstruction formelle et sémantique de la dénomination de quelques mamifères en Bantou." *AAP* (Köln) 38 (1994).

Bastin, Y., A. Coupez, and B. de Halleux. "Classification lexicostatistique des langues Bantoues (214 relevés)." *Bulletin des Séances: Academie Royale des Sciences d'Outre Mer* 27, no. 2 (1983): 173–199.

Bastin, Y., A. Coupez, and M. Mann. *Continuity and Divergence in the Bantu Languages: Perspectives from a Lexicostatistic Study.* Tervuren: MRAC, 1999.

Baumann, H. *Schopfung unde Urzeit des Menschen in Mythus der africanischen Volker.* Berlin: Deitrich Reimer/Andres & Steiner, 1936.

Bennett, P. R., and J. R. Sterk. "South Central Niger-Congo: A Reclassification." *Studies in African Linguistics* 3, no. 8 (1977): 240–273.

Bergsland K., and H. Vogt. "On the Validity of Glottochronology." *Current Anthropology* 3, no. 2 (1962): 115–153.

Biesbrouck, Karen, Stefan Elders, and Gerda Rossel, eds. *Challenging Elusiveness: Central African Hunter-Gatherers in a Multidisciplinary Perspective.* Leiden: CNWS, 1999.

Bird-David, N. "Beyond the Original Affluent Society: A Culturalist Reformation." *Current Anthropology* 33, no. 1 (1992): 25–47.

Birnbaum, Henrick. *Linguistic Reconstruction: Its Potential and Limitations in New Perspective.* Washington: Journal of Indo-European Studies, 1978.

Bittremieux, J. *Mayombische namen.* Leuven: Drukkerij der HH Harten, 1934.

Bleek, W. H. I. *A Comparative Grammar of South African Languages.* Part 1, *Phonology.* London: Trübner, 1862.

Blench, Roger. "The Niger-Congo Languages: A Proposed Internal Classification." Internet communication, 2000.

———— "Are the African Pygmies an Ethnographic Fiction?" In *Challenging Elusiveness: Central African Hunter-Gatherers in a Multidisciplinary Perspective,* edited by Karen Biesbrouck, Stefan Elders, and Gerda Rossel, 41–60. Leiden: CNWS, 1999.

Bouquet, A., and A. Jacquot. "Essai de géographie linguistique sur quelques plantes medicinales du Congo Brazzaville." *Cahiers Orstom* 5, no. 3–4 (1967).

Bouquiaux L., and J. M. C. Thomas. "Le peuplement oubanguien: Hypothèse de reconstruction des mouvements migratoires dans la région oubanguienne d'après les données linguistiques, ethnolinguistiques, et de tradition orale." In *L'Expansion Bantoue,* edited by L. Bouquiaux, 807–824. Paris: SELAF, 1980.

Bouquiaux, L., J. M. C. Thomas, and Simha Arom. *Enquête et description des langues a tradition orale.* Paris: SELAF, 1976.

————. *L'Expansion Bantoue: Actes du Colloque International du CNRS, Viviers (France) 4–16 Avril 1977.* Paris: SELAF, 1980.

Bowcock, A., et al. "High Resolution of Human Evolutionary Trees with Polymorphic Microsatellites." *Nature* 368, no. 6470 (1994): 455–458.

Boyd, W. C. *Genetics and the Races of Man: An Introduction to Modern Physical Anthropology*. Boston: Little, Brown, 1950.

————. "Four Achievements of the Genetical Method in Physical Anthropology." *American Anthropologist* 65 (1963): 243–252.

Boyer, P. "Pourquoi les Pygmées n'ont pas de culture?" *Gradhiva* 7 (1990): 3–17.

Boyi, J. "Problematique des langues Pygmées de la Republique Populaire du Congo: Communication a la table-ronde sur la problematique de l'integration des Pygmées au processus du development socio-economique du Congo." Brazzaville, 18–19 Avril, 1990.

Bradford, P. V., and H. Blume. *Ota Benga, The Pygmy in the Zoo*. New York: Delta, 1992.

Brandt, S., and D. J. Clark. *From Hunters to Farmers*. Berkeley: University Press of California, 1984.

Bruel, G. "Les populations de la Moyenne Sangha: Les Pomo et les Boumwali." *Revue d'Ethnographie et de Sociologie* 1 (1910): 3–32.

Budge, E. A. W. *A Guide to the Egyptian Collections in the British Museum*. London: The Trustees, 1909.

Buffon, G.L.L. *Histoire naturelle, générale, et particulière: Tome 11, Oiseaux*. Paris: Sanson, 1787.

Bynan, Theodora. *Historical Linguistics*. Cambridge: Cambridge University Press, 1977.

Cahen D., and G. Mortelmans. "Une site Tshitolien sur le Plateau de Bateke, Republique du Zaire." *Annales du Musée Royale de l'Afrique Centrale*. Series 8, vol. 81, 1973.

Calvocoressi, D., and N. David. "A New Survey of Radiocarbon and Thermoluminescence Dates for West Africa." *Journal of African History* 20, no. 1 (1979): 1–29.

Cartmill, M. *A View to a Death in the Morning: Hunting and Nature through History*. Cambridge: Harvard University Press, 1993.

Cavalli-Sforza, L. L., ed. *African Pygmies*. London: Academic Press, 1986.

Cavalli-Sforza, L. L., P. Menozzi, and A. Piazza, eds. *The History and Geography of Human Genes*. Princeton: Princeton University Press, 1994.

Cavazzi, G. *Istorica Descrizione dei tre Regni Congo, Matamba, et Angola*. Milan, 1690.

Celis, G. "Fondeurs et Forgerons Ekonda (Eqateur, Zaire)."*Anthropos* 82 (1987): 109–134.

Celis, G., and E. Nzikobanyanka. *La Métallurgie traditionnelle au Burundi. Techniques et croyances*. Tervuren: Musée Royale de l'Afrique Centrale, Archives d'anthropologie 25, 1976.

Chamberlain, C. "Competition and Conflict: The Development of the Bulk Export Trade in Central Gabon During the Nineteenth Century." Ph. D. diss., University of California, Los Angeles, 1977.

Chen, Yu Sheng, Antonio Torroni, Laurent Excoffer Santachiara-Benerecetti, and Douglas Wallace. "Analysis of mtDNA Variation in African Populations Reveal the Most Ancient of All Human Continent Specific Haplogroups."*American Journal of Human Genetics* 57 (1995): 67–73.

Childe, V. G. *Man Makes Himself*. London: Watts, 1956.

Clist, B. *Gabon: 100,000 ans d'histoire*. Libreville, Gabon: Centre Cultural Français Saint-Exupery/Sepia, 1995.

————. "Traces de trés anciennes occupations humaines de la forêt tropicale au Gabon." In *Challenging Elusiveness: Central African Hunter-Gatherers in a Multidisciplinary Perspective*, edited by Karen Biesbrouck, Stefan Elders, and Gerda Rossel, 75–87. Leiden: CNWS, 1999.

Coke, C. M., and D. T. Cole. *Contributions to the History of Bantu Linguistics*. Johannesburg: Witwatersrand University Press, 1961.

Collet, D. P. "Metaphors and Representations Associated with Pre-colonial Iron-Smelting in Eastern and Southern Africa." In *The Archaeology of Africa: Food, Metals, Towns,* edited by T. Shaw, P. Sinclair, B. Andah, and A. Okpoko, 499–511. London: Routledge, 1993.

Coon, C. *The Origin of Races.* New York: Alfred A. Knopf, 1962.

Coquery-Vidrovitch, C. *Le Congo au Temps de Grandes Compagnies Concessionaires, 1898–1930.* Paris and La Haye: Mouton and Co., 1972.

Courboin, A. "Les populations de l'Alima, Congo Français." *Bulletin de la Societe Royale de Geographie d'Anvers* 28 (1904): 273–275.

Crader, D. "Faunal Remains from Chencherer 2 Rock Shelter, Malawi." *South African Archaeological Bulletin* (1984): 37–52.

Cuvelier, J. "Traditions Congolaises." *Congo,* II, 2 (1931): 193–208.

Cuvelier, J., and O. de Bouveignes. *Jerome de Montesarchio, apôtre du Vieux Congo.* Namur: Grand Lacs, 1951.

Dapper, O. *Naukeuridge beschrijvinge der Afrika.* Amsterdam, 1668.

Dassen, V. "Dwarfism in Egypt and Classical Antiquity: Iconography and Medical History." *Medical History* 24, no. 2 (1988): 253–276.

Davison, S. "Namaso and the Iron Age Sequence of Southern Malawi." *Azania* 26 (1991).

Dawson, W. R. "Pygmies and Dwarfs in Ancient Egypt." *Journal of Egyptian Archaeology* 8, no. 2 (1938): 185–189.

de Bayle des Hermens, R. "Résultats d'ensemble des missions de recherches préhistoriques effectuées en 1966–1967 et 1968 en Républic Centrafricaine."*Bulletin de la Société Royale Belge d'Anthropologie et de Préhistoire* 80 (1969): 5–20.

———. *Recherches préhistorique en République Centrafricaine.* Paris: Labethno, 1975.

De Beir, L. *Les Bayaka de M'Nene N'Tombo Lenge-Lenge.* St. Augustine: Anthropos-Institut, 1975.

de Heusch, L. *Le Roi Ivre ou l'origine de l'etat.* Paris: Éditions Gallimard, 1972.

———. *Le roi de Kongo et les monstres sacrés.* Paris: Éditions Gallimard, 2000.

de Langhe, E., R. Swennen, and D. Vuylsteke. "Plantain in the Early Bantu World." In *The Growth of Farming Communities in Africa from the Equator Southwards,* edited by J.E.G. Sutton, 147–160. *Anzania* special vol. 29–30. London/Nairobi: British Institute of eastern Africa, 1994/95.

Delatte, A., and Ph. Derchain. *Les entailles magiques Gréco-Égyptiennes.* Paris: Bibliotheque Nationale, 1964.

Delobeau, J.-M. "Les Pygmées dans la Colonization," *Afrika Zamani-Revue d'Histoire Africaine (Yaoundé)* 14 and 15 (1984): 115–133.

de Maret, P. "Ceux qui jeux avec feu: La place du forgeron en Afrique Centrale." *Africa* 50, no. 3 (1980): 263–279.

———. "Preliminary Report on 1980 Fieldwork in the Grassfield and Yaounde, Cameroun." *Nyame Akuma*17 (1980): 10–12.

———. "New Survey of Archaeological Research and Dates for West-Central Africa and North-Central Africa." *Journal of African History* 23 (1982): 1–15.

———. "Recent Archaeological Research and Dates from Central Africa." *Journal of African History* 26 (1985): 129–148.

———. "The Smith's Myth and the Origins of Leadership in Central Africa." In *African Iron Working,* edited by Randi Halland and Peter Shinnie, 73–208. Oxford: Oxford University Press, 1985.

———. "Pits, Pots, and the Far-West Streams." In *The Growth of Farming Communities in Africa from the Equator Southwards,* edited by J. E. G. Sutton, 318–323. *Anza-*

nia special vol. 29–30. London/Nairobi: British Institute of eastern Africa, 1994/95.

de Maret, P., B. Clist, and C. Mbida. "Belgian Archeological Mission in Cameroon: 1983 Field Season." *Nyame Akuma* 23 (1983): 5–6.

de Maret, P., B. Clist, and W. Van Neer. "The Ngovo Group: An Industry with Polished Stone Tools and Pottery in Lower Zaire." *The African Archaeological Review* 4 (1986): 103–133.

———. "Résultats des premières fouilles dans les Abris-Sous-Roche de Shum Laka et Abeké au Nord-ouest du Cameroun." *L'Anthropologie* 91, no. 2 (1987): 559–584.

de Maret, P., and F. Nsuka. "History of Bantu Metallurgy: Some Linguistic Aspects. *History in Africa* 4 (1977): 43–65.

de Maret, P., and G. Thiry. "How Old Is the Iron Age in Central Africa?" In *The Culture and Technology of African Iron Production,* edited by P. Schmidt, 29–39. Gainesville: University Press of Florida, 1996.

Demesse, L. *Changements techno-économiques et sociaux chez les Pygmées Babinga, Nord-Congo et Sud-Centrafrique.* Paris: SELAF, 1978.

Denbow, J. "Congo to Kalahari: Data and Hypotheses about the Political Economy of the Western Stream of the Early Iron Age." *The African Archaeological Review* 8 (1990): 139–176.

de Quatrefages, A. "Les Pygmées d'Homère, d'Aristote, de Pline, d'après les découvertes modernes." *Journal des Savants* (June–August 1882): 345–363, 457–478, 694–712.

———. *Les Pygmées.* Paris: Baillère, 1887.

Deschamps, H. *Traditions orales et archives au Gabon: Contribution à l'ethnohistoire.* Paris: Éditions Berger-Levrault, 1962.

de Vitry, J. *Historian Orientalis.* Meisenheim am Glan, reprint, 1971.

Diamond, J. M. "Why Are Pygmies Small?" *Nature* 354 (1991): 111–112.

Digombe, L., M. Locko, J. B. Mombo, V. Moulengui, and P. Schmidt. "The Development of an Early Iron Age Prehistory in Gabon." *Current Anthropology* 29, no. 1 (1988): 179–184.

Doke, C. M. "The Growth of Comparative Bantu Philology." *Bantu Studies* 2, no. 1 (1943).

———. "The Growth of Comparative Bantu Philology." In *Contributions to the History of Bantu Linguistics,* edited by C. M. Doke and D. T. Cole. Johannesburg: Witwatersrand University Press, 1961.

Dolisie, A. "Notice sur les chefs Bateke avant 1898." *Bulletin de la Recherches Congolaises* 8 (1927): 44–49.

Doutreloux, A. *L'ombre des Fetiches: Société et Culture Yombe.* Louvain and Paris: Nauwelaerts, 1967.

Dubow, S. *Scientific Racism in Modern South Africa.* Cambridge: Cambridge University Press, 1995.

Du Chaillu, P. "Le pays d'Ashango." *Annales des Voyages* 2 (1867): 256–290.

———. *The Country of the Dwarves.* 1872. Reprint, New York: Negro Universities Press, 1969.

Dudley, E., and M. E. Novak. *The Wildman Within: An Image in Western Thought from the Renaissance to Romanticism.* Pittsburgh: University of Pittsburgh Press, 1972.

Dulloo, A. G., Y. Shahkalili, G. Atchou, N. Mensi, J. Jacquet, and L. Girardier. "Dissociation of Systemic GH-IGF-I Axis from a Genetic Basis for Short Stature in African Pygmies." *European Journal of Clinical Medicine* 50 (1996): 371–380.

Dupré, G. *Un order et sa destruction: Économie, politique, et histoire chez les Nzabi de la République Populaire du Congo.* Paris: ORSTOM, 1982.

Dupré, M. C. "Pour une histoire des productions: La métallurgie du fer chez les Teke: Ngungulu, Tio, Tsaayi (République Populaire du Congo)." *Cahiers Sciences Humaines* (ORSTOM) 28, no. 2 (1981–92): 195–223.

———. "Naissances et renaissances du masque Kidumu: Art, politique et histoire chez les Téké-tsaayi, Republique Populaire du Congo." Thèse d'État, Paris V, 1984.

Dupré, M. C., and B. Pinçon. *Métallurgie et politique en Afrique Centrale: Deux mille ans de vestiges sur les plateaux Batéké Gabon, Congo, Zaire.* Paris: Karthala Press, 1997.

Eggert, M.K.H. "Imbonga and Batalimo: Ceramic Evidence for Early Settlement of the Equatorial Rainforest." *The African Archaeological Review* 5 (1987): 129–145.

———. "Remarks on Exploring Archaeologically Unknown Rain Forest Territory: The Case of Central Africa." *Beiträge zur Allgemeinene und Vergleichendend Archäologie* 5 (1987): 283–322.

———. "Central Africa and the Archaeology of the Equatorial Rainforest; Reflections on Some Major Topics." In *The Archaeology of Africa: Food, Metals, Towns,* edited by Thurstan Shaw, Paul Sinclair, Bassey Andah, and Alex Okpoko, 289–329. New York: Routledge, 1993.

Ehret, C. "Linguistics as a Tool for Historians." *Hadith* 1 (1968): 119–133.

———. "Bantu Origins and History: Critique and Interpretation." *Transafrican Journal of History* 2 (1972): 1–9.

———. "Historical Inference from Transformations in Cultural Vocabularies." *Sprache und Geschichte in Afrika* 2 (1980): 189–218.

———. "Linguistic Inferences about Early Bantu History." In *The Archaeological and Linguistic Reconstruction of African History,* edited by C. Ehret and M. Posnansky, 57–65. Berkeley: University of California Press, 1982.

———. "Language Change and the Material Correlates of Language and Ethnic Shift." *Antiquity* 62, (1988): 564–574.

———. "The Establishment of Ironworking in Eastern, Central, and Southern Africa: Linguistic Inferences on Technological History." *Sprache und Geschichte in Afrika* 17 (1996): 125–175.

———. *An African Classical Age: Eastern and Southern Africa in World History, 1000 B.C. to A.D. 400.* Charlottesville: University Press of Virginia, 1998.

———. "Subclassifying Bantu: The Evidence of Stem Morpheme Innovation." In *Bantu Historical Linguistics: Theoretical and Empirical Perspectives,* edited by J.-Marie Hombert and L. Hyman. Stanford: Stanford University Press, 1998.

———. "Testing the Expectations of Glottochronology against the Correlations of Language and Archaeology in Africa. In *Time Depth in Historical Linguistics,* edited by Colin Renfrew, April McMahon, and Larry Trask, 373–399. Vol. 2. Cambridge: McDonald Institute for Archaeological Research, 2000.

———. "Bantu Expansion: Re-Envisioning a Central Problem of Early African History." *The International Journal of African Historical Studies* 34, no. 1 (2001): 5–41.

———. *The Civilizations of Africa: A History to 1800.* Charlottesville: University Press of Virginia, 2002.

Ehret, C., and M. Posnansky. *The Archaeological and Linguistic Reconstruction of African History.* Berkeley, Los Angeles: University of California Press, 1982.

El-Aguizy, O. "Dwarfs and Pygmies in Ancient Egypt." *Annales du Service des Antiquities de l'Egypte (Le Caire)* 71 (1987): 53–60.

Embleton, S. *Statistics in Historical Linguistics.* Bochum: Brockmeyer, 1986.

Fagg, A. "A Preliminary Report on an Occupation Site in the Nok Valley, Nigeria: Samun Dukiya." *West African Journal of Archaeology* 2 (1978): 75–79.

Fagg, B. "The Nok Culture: Excavations at Taruga." *West African Journal of Archaeology* 1 (1968): 27–30.

Fernandez, J. W. "Tabernathe Iboga: Narcotic Ecstasis and the Work of the Ancestors." In *Flesh of the Gods: The Ritual Use of Hallucinogens,* edited by P. Furst, 237–260. New York: Praeger, 1972.

———. *Bwiti: An Ethnography of the Religious Imagination in Africa.* Princeton: Princeton University Press, 1982.

Foley, R. "Hominids, Humans, and Hunter-Gatherers: An Evolutionary Perspective." In *Hunters and Gatherers.* Vol. 1, *History, Evolution, and Social Change,* edited by T. Ingold, D. Riches, and J. Woodburn. Oxford: Berg, 1988.

Fourneau, A. "Ouesso-Gabon (Dec. 1898–1899)." Afrique Equatoriale Française, carton 4YI (Mission Forneau). Archives d'Outre Mer, Aix-en-Provence, France.

Fourshey, C. "Agriculture, Ecology, Kinship, and Gender: A Socio-Economic History of Southwestern Tanzania, 500 B.C. to 1900 A.D." Ph. D. diss., University of California, Los Angeles, 2002.

Friedman, J. B. *The Monstrous Races in Medieval Art and Thought.* Cambridge: Harvard University Press, 1981.

Froment, A. "Le peuplement de L'Afrique Centrale: Contribution de l'anthrobiologie." In *Paléo-Anthropologie en Afrique Centrale: Un Bilan de l'archéologie au Cameroon,* edited by M. Delneuf, J-M. Essomba, and A. Froment, 13–90. Paris: Editions L'Harmattan, 1998.

Fu Kiau, A. *Le Mukongo et le monde que l'entourait.* Kinshasa: Office National de la Recherche et du Developpement, 1969.

Gardner, W. C. "Language Use in the Epena District of Northern Congo." Masters thesis, University of North Dakota, 1990.

Garn, S. *Human Races,* 2nd ed. Springfield, Illinois: Charles C. Thomas, 1965.

Gollnhofer, O., and R. Sillans. *La memoire d'un peuple: Ethnohistoire des Mitsogho, ethnie du Gabon Central.* Paris: Presence Africaine, 1997.

Gould, S. J. *The Mismeasure of Man.* 1981. Reprint, New York: W. W. Norton, 1996.

Grainger, A. "Forest Environments." In *The Physical Geography of Africa,* edited by W. M. Adams, A. S. Goudie, and R. Orme, 173–195. Oxford: Oxford University Press, 1996.

Griffith, F. Ll., and H. Thompson. *The Demotic Magical Papyrus of London and Leiden.* Vol. 2. Milan: Istituto editoriale Cisalpino, 1976.

Grinker, R. R. *Houses in the Rainforest: Ethnicity and Inequality among Farmers and Foragers in Central Africa.* Berkeley: University of California Press, 1994.

Guenther, M. G. "From Brutal Savage to Harmless People: Notes on the Changing Western Image of the Bushman." *Paideuma* 26 (1980): 123–140.

Guthrie, M. "Some Developments in the Pre-history of Bantu Languages." *Journal of African History* 3 (1962): 273–282.

———. *Comparative Bantu.* 4 vols. Farnham, England: Gregg Press, 1967–71.

Guyer, J. "Indigenous Currencies and the History of Marriage Payments: A Case Study from Cameroon." *Cahier des Études Africaines* 36 (1986): 577–610.

Guyer, J., and S. M. E. Belinga. "Wealth in People as Wealth in Knowledge: Accumulation and Composition in Equatorial Africa." *Journal of African History* 36 (1995): 91–120.

Hagenbucher-Sacripanti, F. *Les fondemenys spirituals du pouvour au royaume de Loango.* Paris: Orstom, 1973.

Hamy, E. T. "Essai de coordination des materiaux recemment recueillis sur l'ethnologie des Negrilles ou Pygmées de l'Afrique équatoriale." *Bulletin de la Société d'Anthropologie de Paris* 2 (1879): 79–101.

Harlan, J. R., Jan M. J. de Wet, and Ann B. L. Stemler, eds. *Origins of African Plant Domestication.* Paris: Mouton, 1976.

Harms, R. *River of Wealth, River of Sorrow; The Central Zaire Basin in the Era of the Slave and Ivory Trade, 1500–1891.* New Haven: Yale University Press, 1981.

———. *The Diligent: A Voyage through the Worlds of the Slave Trade.* New York: Basic Books, 2002.

Harraway, D. *Primate Visions: Gender, Race, and Nature in the World of Modern Science.* New York: Routledge, 1989.

Hauser, A. "Les Babinga." *Zaire* 7, no. 2 (1953): 147–179.

Headland, T. N. "The Wild Yam Question: How Well Could Independent Hunter-Gatherers Live in a Tropical Rain Forest Ecosystem?" *Human Ecology* 15, no. 4 (1987): 463–491.

Heine, B. "Zur genetische Gliederung der Bantu-Sprachen." *Afrika and Uberseei* 56 (1973): 164–184.

Heine, B., H. Hoff, and R. Vossen. "Neuere Ergebnisse zur Territorialgeschichte der Bantu." In *Zur sprachgeschichte und Ethnohistorie in Afrika.* edited by W.J.G. Möhlig, F. Rottlan, and B. Heine, 57–72. Berlin: Reimer, 1977.

Herbert, E. *Red Gold of Africa: Copper in Precolonial History and Culture.* Madison: University of Wisconsin Press, 1984.

———. *Iron, Gender, and Power: Rituals of Transformation in African Societies.* Bloomington: Indiana University Press, 1993.

Hewlett, B. "Cultural Diversity among African Pygmies." In *Cultural Diversity among Twentieth-Century Foragers: An African Perspective,* edited by Susan Kent, 215–244. Cambridge: Cambridge University Press, 1996.

Heywood, L. *Central Africans and Cultural Transformations in the American Diaspora.* Cambridge: Cambridge University Press, 2002.

Hladik, A. "Structure and Production of the Rain Forest." In *Food and Nutrition in the African Rain Forest,* edited by Hladik, C. M. S. Bahuchet and I. de Garine, 8–13. Paris: Unesco/MAB, 1990.

Hladik, C. M., S. Bahuchet, and I. de Garine. *Food and Nutrition in the African Rain Forest.* Paris: Unesco/MAB, 1990.

Holl, A. "Cameroun." In *Auxorigines de L'Afrique Centrale,* edited by R. Lanfranchi and B. Clist, 149–154, 193–196. Libreville, Gabon: Centre Culturels Français, 1991.

Homberger, L. *Étude sur la phonétique historique du Bantou.* Paris: Édouard Champion, 1914.

Hughes, M. R. "Wetlands." In *The Physical Geography of Africa,* edited by W. Adams, M. A. S. Goudie, and R. Orme, 265–286. Oxford: Oxford University Press, 1996.

Jacquot, Andre. *Les classes nominales dans les langues Bantoues des groupes B10, B20, B30 (Gabon-Congo).* Travaux et documents de L'O.R.S.T.O.M. Paris: O.R.S.T.O.M, 1983.

Jadin, L. "Apercu de la situation du Congo et rites d'election des rois en 1775, d'apres le P. Cherubino da Savona, missionaire au Congo de 1759 à 1774." *Bulletin de l'Institut Historique Belge de Rome* 36 (1963): 185–483.

Jenyns, S. "On the Chain of Universal Being." In *The Works of Soame Jenyns, Esq.*, edited by C. N. Cole. London: T. Cadell, 1790.

Johnston, H. A. *A Comparative Study of the Bantu and Semi-Bantu Languages.* Oxford: Oxford University Press, 1920.

Jordon, M. *Encyclopedia of the Gods.* London: Kyle Cathie Unlimited, 1992.

Keita, S.O.Y., and R. Kittles."The Persistence of Racial Thinking and the Myth of Racial Divergence." *American Anthropologist* 99, no. 3 (1997): 534–544.

Kent, S., ed. *Cultural Diversity among Twentieth Century Foragers: An African Perspective.* Cambridge: Cambridge University Press, 1996.

Kervegant, D. *Le bananier et son exploitation.* Paris: Societé d'Edition Geographiques, Maritimes et Coloniales, 1935.

Kittles, R., and S.O.Y. Keita. "Interpreting African Genetic Diversity." *African Archaeological Review* 16, no. 2 (1999): 87–91.

Klieman, K. "Hunters and Farmers of the Western Equatorial Rainforest: Economy and Society, 3000 B.C. to A.D. 1880." Ph.D. diss., University of California, Los Angeles, 1997.

———. "Hunter-Gatherer Participation in Rainforest Trade Systems: A Comparative History of Forest vs. Ecotone Societies in Gabon and Congo, c. 1000–1900 A.D." In *Challenging Elusiveness: Central Africa Hunter-Gatherers in a Multidisciplinary Perspective,* edited by Karen Biesbrouck, Stefan Elders, and Gerda Rossel, 89–104. Leiden: CNWS, 1999.

———. "Comments in Response to Christopher Ehret, 'The Bantu Expansions: Re-envisioning a Central Problem of Early African History.'" *The International Journal of African Historical Studies* 34, no. 1 (2001): 48–52.

———. "Towards a History of Pre-colonial Gabon: Farmers and Forest Specialists along the Ogooué, c. 500 B.C.–1000 A.D." In *Culture, Ecology, and Politics in Gabon's Rainforest,* edited by Michael C. Reed and James F. Barnes. Lewiston, NY: Edwin Mellen Press, 2003.

Koch, J. "Sind die Pygmaen Menschen." *Archiv fur Geschichte der Philosophie* 40 (1931).

Köhler, A. "Forest, Hearth and Home: Baka Village Life in Northwestern Congo." Ph.D. thesis, University of Manchester, 1998.

———. "The Forest as Home: Baka Environment, Housing, and Sedentarisation." In *Challenging Elusiveness: Central African Hunter-Gatherers in a Multidisciplinary Perspective,* edited by K. Biesbrouck, S. Elders, and G. Rossel, 207–220. Leiden: CNWS, 1999.

———. "Half-Man, Half-Elephant: Shape-Shifting among the Baka of Congo." In *Natural Enemies: People-Wildlife Conflicts in Anthropological Perspective,* 50–77. London and New York: Routledge, 2000.

Köhler, A., and Jerome Lewis. "Putting Hunter-Gatherer and Farmer Relations in Perspective: A Commentary from Central Africa. In *Ethnicity, Hunter-Gatherers, and the "Other": Association or Assimilation in Southern Africa?,* 276–305. Washington and London: Smithsonian Institution Press, 2002.

Kopytoff, I. "The Internal African Frontier: The Making of African Political Culture." In *The African Frontier: The Reproduction of Traditional African Societies,* edited by I. Kopytoff, 3–84. Bloomington: Indiana University Press, 1987.

Laburthe-Tolra, P. *Les seigneurs de la foret: Essai sur la passé historique, l'organisation social et les norms ethiques des Anciens Beti du Cameroun.* Paris: Publications de la Sorbonne, 1981.

Laman, K. *The Kongo.* Stockholm: Victor Pettersons Bokindustri Aktiebolag, 1953.

Laman, K. E. *The Kongo III, Studia Ethnographica Upsaliensis.* Uppsala: Almqvist and Wilsells, 1962.

Lanfranchi, R., and B. Clist, eds. *Aux origines de l'Afrique Centrale.* Libreville, Gabon: Centres Culturels Français/CICIBA, 1991.

Lanfranchi R., and D. Schwartz, eds. *Paysages quaternaires de l'Afrique Centrale Atlantique.* Paris: ORSTOM, 1990.

Lange, H. O.. *Der Magishe Papyrus Harris.* 8th ed. Copenhagen: Høst & Son, 1927.

Lavachery, P. "De la pierre au metal: Archéologie des depots Holocènes de l'abri de Shum Laka (Cameroon)." Ph. D. thesis, Université Libre de Bruxelles, 1997–1998.

Lewis, J. "Forest Hunter-Gatherers and Their World: A Study of the Mbenjele Yaka Pygmies of Congo-Brazzaville and Their Secular and Religious Activities and Representations." Ph.D. thesis, London School of Economics and Political Science, 2002.

Livingstone, D. A. "Interactions of Food Production and Changing Vegetation in Africa." In *From Hunters to Farmers: The Causes and Consequences of Food Production in Africa,* edited by J. Desmond Clark and Steven Brandt, 22–25. Berkeley: University of California Press, 1984.

Lovejoy, A. O. *The Great Chain of Being.* Cambridge: Harvard University Press, 1953.

MacEachern, S. "Genes, Tribes, and African History." *Current Anthropology* 41, no. 3 (2000): 357–385.

MacGaffey, W. "The Dwarf Soldiers of Simon Kimbangu: Explorations in Kongo Cosmology." Unpublished article, 1986.

———. *Religion and Society in Central Africa: The BaKongo of Lower Zaire.* Chicago: Chicago University Press, 1986.

———. *Kongo Political Culture: The Conceptual Challenge of the Particular.* Bloomington and Indianapolis: Indiana University Press, 2000.

Mankenda, A. *L'Initiation au Kimpasi et les rites Nkita chez les Kongo.* Mémoire de Licencié, Université Libre de Bruxelles, Belgium, 1971.

Marche, A. *Trois voyages dans l'Afrique Occidentale.* Paris: Hachette, 1882.

Marks, J. *Human Biodiversity: Genes, Race, and History.* New York: Aldine de Gruyter, 1995.

Marshal-Nasse, C. "Esquisse de la langue Tsogho: Phonologie-Morphologie." Mémoire de Licencié, Université Libre de Bruxelles, Belgium, 1979.

Martin, P. *The External Trade of the Loango Coast, 1576–1870. The Effects of Changing Commercial Relations on the Vili Kingdom of Loango.* Oxford: Oxford University Press. 1972.

Mayer, R. "Langues des groupes des Pygmées au Gabon: Un état de lieux." *Pholia* 2 (1987); 111–123.

Mbida, C. M. "L'Emergence de communautes villageoises au Cameroon Meridional; Étude archéologique des sites de Nkang et de Ndindan." Ph. D. thesis, Université Libre de Bruxelles, 1995.

Mbida, C. M., H., D'Outrelepont, C. M. Mbida, W. Van Neer, and L. Vrydaghs. "Evidence for Banana Cultivation and Animal Husbandry during the First Millenium B.C. in the Forest of Southern Cameroon."*Journal of Archaelogical Science* 27 (2000): 151–162.

Meadows, M. "Biogeography." In *The Physical Geography of Africa,* edited by W. Adams, M. A. S. Goudie, and R. Orme. Oxford: Oxford University Press, 1996.

Meeks, D. *Génies, anges et démons: Égypt, Babylone, Israel, Islam, peuples altaïques, Asie du Sud-Est, Tibet, Chine.* 1971. Reprint, Paris: Editions du Seuil, 1987. 8th ed. Source Orientales, 1971.

Merlet, A. *Vers les Plateaux de Masuku: 1866–1890: Histoire des peoples du basin de l'Ogooué, de Lambaréné au Congo, au temps de Brazza et des factoreries.* Libreville, Gabon: Centre Culturel Français Saint-Exupéry/Sepia, 1990.

Mesquita Lima, A. G. "Le Fer en Angola." *Cahiers d'Études Africaines* 66–67, no. 27 (1997): 345–351.

Mgomezulu, G. G. Y. "Food Production: The Beginnings in the Linthipe/Cangone Area of Dedza District, Malawi." Ph. D. diss., University of California, Berkeley, 1975.

Miller, J. *Way of Death: Merchant Capitalism and the Atlantic Slave Trade, 1730–1830.* Madison: University of Wisconsin Press, 1988.

————. "Central Africa during the Era of the Slave Trade, c. 1490s–1850s." In *Central Africans and Cultural Transformation in the American Diaspora,* edited by Linda M. Heywood, 21–69. Cambridge: Cambridge University Press, 2002.

Misago, K. "Zaire." In *Aux origines de L'Afrique Centrale,* edited by B. Clist and R. Lanfranchi, 175–178, 213–218. Libreville, Gabon: Centre Culturel Français/Saint-Exupery, 1991.

Monino, Y. *Lexique comparatif des langues oubangiennes.* Paris: LACITO, 1988.

Mukhopadhyay, C. C., and Y. T. Moses. "Reestablishing 'Race' in Anthropological Discourse." *American Anthropologist* 99, no. 3 (1997): 517–533.

Murdock, G. P. *Africa: Its Peoples and Their Culture History.* New York: McGraw-Hill, 1959.

Myers, N. "Biodiversity and Biodepletion." In *The Physical Geography of Africa,* edited by W. Adams, M. A. S. Goudie, and R. Orme, 356–366. Oxford: Oxford University Press, 1996.

Nurse, D. "The Contributions of Linguistics to the Study of History in Africa." *Journal of African History* 38, no. 3 (1997): 393–422.

Obenga, T. *La cuvette Congolaise—Les hommes et structures: Contribution a l'histoire de l'Afrique Centrale.* Paris: Presence Africaine, 1976.

Olmstead, D. L. "Three Tests of Glottochronological Theory." *American Anthropologist* 59 (1957): 839–842.

Oslisly, R. *Préhistoire de la moyenne Vallée de l'Ogooué (Gabon).* 2 vols. Paris: ORSTOM, 1992.

————. "The Middle Ogooué Valley: Cultural Changes and Palaeoclimactic Implications of the Last Four Millennia." In *The Growth of Farming Communities in Africa from the Equator Southwards,* edited by J. E. G. Sutton, 324–331. *Anzania* special vol. 29–30. London/Nairobi: British Institute of eastern Africa, 1994/95.

————. "Archéologie et paléoenvironnement dans la Réserve de la Lopé: Rapport final." Groupement AGRECO/C.T.F.T. Unpublished manuscript, 1996.

————. "Hommes et Milieux à l'Holocène dans la moyenne vallée de l'Ogooué (Gabon)." *Bulletin de la Société Préhistorique Française* 95, no. 1 (1998): 93–105.

Oslisly, R., and R. Deschamps. "Découverte d'une zone d'incendie dans la Forêt Ombrophile du Gabon ca. 1500 B.P.: Essay d'explication anthropique et implications paléoclimatiques." *Comptes-Rendus de l'Académie des Sciences de Paris* 318, no. 2 (1994): 555–560.

Oslisly, R., and B. Peyrot. *L'Art préhistorique Gabonais.* Libreville, Gabon: Rotary Club International Multipress, 1987.

———. "L'Arrivée des premières metallurgists sur l'Ogooué (Gabon)." *African Archaeological Review* 10 (1992): 129–138.

———. *Les gravures rupestres de la Vallée de l'Ogooué (Gabon).* Paris: Sepia, 1993.

Patterson, K. D. *The Northern Gabon Coast to 1875.* Oxford: Oxford University Press, 1975.

Pechuel-Loesche, E. *Die Loango Expedition.* Leipzig: Verlag Paul Frohlig, 1907.

Pepper, S. C. *World Hypothesis: A Study in Evidence.* Berkeley: University of California Press, 1942.

Peyrot, B., and R. Oslisly. "Sites archèologiques associant pierres taillées, ceramique, coquilles marines, et outils en pierre polie à Tchengué, Province de l'Ogooué-Maritime (Gabon)." *Nsi* 7 (1990): 13–19.

Phillipson, D. *African Archaeology.* Cambridge: Cambridge University Press, 1993.

Phillipson, G. "The First South African Pastoralists and the Early Iron Age." *Nsi* 6 (1989): 127–134.

Pincon, B. "L'Archéologie du Royaume Teke." In *Aux origines de L'Afrique Centrale,* edited by R. Lanfranchi and B. Clist, 243–249. Libreville, Gabon: Centres Culturels Français/CICIBA, 1991.

Posnansky, M. "Bantu Genesis." *Uganda Journal* 25, no. 1 (1968): 86–93.

Purseglove, J. W. "The Origins and Migration of Crops in Tropical Africa." In *Origins of African Plant Domestication,* edited by J. R. Harlan. Paris: Mouton, 1976.

RapondaWalker, A., and R. Sillans. *Les plantes utiles du Gabon.* Paris: P. Lechavalier, 1961.

Ravenstein, E. G. *The Strange Adventures of Andrew Battell of Leigh, in Angola and the Adjoining Regions.* Liechtenstein: Hakluyt Society, 1901.

Regnault, Dr. M. "Les Babenga: Negrilles de la Sangha." *L'Anthropologie* 22 (1911): 261–288.

Robineau, C. *L' Évolution économique et sociale en Afrique Central: L'Exemple de Souanké (République de Congo Brazzaville).* Paris: ORSTOM, 1966.

———. "Contribution à l'histoire du Congo: La domination Européene et l'exemple de Souanké (1900–1960)." *Cahiers d'Études Africaines* 7: 26(2) (1967): 300–344.

Rossel, G. "Musa and Ensete in Africa; Taxonomy, Nomenclature, and Uses." In *The Growth of Farming Communities in Africa from the Equator Southwards,* edited by J. E. G. Sutton, 130–146. *Anzania* special vol. 29–30. London/Nairobi: British Institute of eastern Africa, 1994/95.

———. *Taxonomic Linguistic Study of Plaintain in Africa.* Leiden: CNWS, 1998.

Sato, H. "The Potential of Edible Wild Yams and Yam-like Plants as Staple Food Resource in the African Tropical Rain Forest." *African Study Monographs* (Kyoto), no. 26 (2001): 123–134.

Sautter, G. *De L'Atlantique au fleuve Congo: Une géographie du sous-peuplement.* Paris: Mouton & Company, 1966.

Saxon, D. E. "Linguistic Evidence for the Eastward Spread of Ubangian Peoples." In *The Archeological and Linguistic Reconstruction of African History.* edited by C. Ehret and M. Posnansky. Berkeley: University of California Press, 1982.

Schadeberg, T. "Batwa: The Bantu Name for the Invisible People." In *Challenging Elusiveness: Central African Hunter-Gatherers in a Multidisciplinary Perspective,* edited by K. Biesbrouck, S. Elders, and G. Rossel, 21–39. Leiden: CNWS, 1999.

Schmidt, P. *The Culture and Technology of African Iron Production.* Gainesville: University Press of Florida, 1996.

Schoenbrun, David Lee. *A Green Place, A Good Place: Agrarian Change, Gender, and Social Identity in the Great Lakes Region to the Fifteenth Century.* Portsmouth, New Hampshire: Heinemann, 1998.

Schwartz, D. "Les paysages de L'Afrique Centrale pendant le quaternaire." In *Aux origines de l'Afrique Centrale,* edited by R. Lanfranchi and B. Clist, 41–45. Libreville, Gabon: Centre Culturel Français/CICIBA, 1991.

———. "Les sols de l'Afrique Centrale." In *Aux origines de l'Afrique Centrale,* edited by R. Lanfranchi and B. Clist, 26–27. Libreville, Gabon: Centre Culturel Francais/CICIBA, 1991.

Schweinfurth, G. *Au Cœur de l'Afrique.* Paris: Hachette, 1875.

Shanklin, E. "The Profession of the Color Blind: Sociocultural Anthropology and Racism in the Twenty-First Century." *American Anthropologist* 100, no. 3 (1999): 669–679.

Shaw, T. *Nigeria: Its Archaeology and Early History.* London: Thames and Hudson, 1978.

Shaw, T., P. Sinclair, B. Andah, and A. Okpoko. *The Archaeology of Africa Food, Metals, Towns.* London: Routledge, 1993.

Simmonds, N. W. *The Evolution of the Edible Banana.* London: Longmans, 1962.

———. *Bananas.* London: Longman, 1966.

Simmonds, N. W., and K. Shepherd. "Taxonomy and Origins of Cultivated Bananas." *The Journal of the Linnean Society of London* 55 (1955): 302–312.

Siroto, L. "Masks and Social Organization among the Bakwele People of Western Equatorial Africa." Ph. D. diss., Columbia University, 1969.

Slenes, R. "The Great Porpoise-Skull Strike: Central African Water Spirits and Slave Identity in Early-Nineteenth-Century Rio De Janeiro. In *Central Africans and Cultural Transformations in the American Diaspora,* edited by Linda M. Heywood, 183–208. Cambridge: Cambridge University Press, 2002.

Smith, B. "Rock Art in South Central Africa." Ph. D. thesis, Cambridge University, 1995.

Smith, W. S. *The Art and Architecture of Ancient Egypt.* Harmondsworth: Pelican History of Art, 1981.

Stadler, H. "Albertus Magnus de Animalibus." *Beitrag zur Geschichte der Philosophie des Mittelalters.* 16 vols. 1920.

Steindorff, G. *Catalogue of the Egyptian Sculpture in the Walters Art Gallery.* Baltimore: The Trustees, 1946.

Stepan, N. *The Idea of Race in Science: Great Britain 1800–1860.* London: MacMillan, 1982.

———. "Race and Gender: The Role of Analogy in Science." In *Anatomy of Racism,* edited by David Theo Goldberg, 38–57. Minneapolis: University of Minnesota Press, 1990.

Stoler, A. L. *Race and the Education of Desire: Foucault's History of Sexuality and the Colonial Order of Things.* Durham, North Carolina: Duke University Press, 1995.

Struyf, Y. "Langues et coutumes congolaises." *Missions Belges de la Compagnie de Jésus* (Brussels) 8 (1906).

Stuiver M., and G. Pearson. "High Calibration of the Radio-Carbon time Scale, A.D. 1950–500 B.C." *Radiocarbon* 28 (1986): 805–838.

Sulzmann, E. "Batwa und Baoto: Die Symbiose von Wildbeutern und Pflanzern bei den Ekonda und Bolia (Zaire)." *SUGIA* 7, no.1 (1987): 369–389. Translated into French, "Batwa et Baoto: Symbiose chasseurs-ceuillers et planteurs chez les Ekonda et les Bolia (Zaire, region de l'Equateur et de Bandundu). *Revue d'Ethnolinguistique (cahiers du LACITO)* 4 (1989): 39–57.

Sutton, J. E. G. *The Growth of Farming Communities in Africa from the Equator Southwards.* *Azania* special vol. 29–30. London/Nairobi: British Institute of Eastern Africa, 1994/95.

Swadesh, Morris. "Towards Greater Accuracy in Lexicostatistical Dating." *International Journal of American Linguistics* 21 (1955): 121–137.

Tamari, T. "The Development of Caste Systems in West Africa." *Journal of African History* 32, no. 2 (1991): 221–250.

Tastevin, C. "Les Pygmées." *Missi* 14, no. 3 (1949): 73–77.

Teeter, K. V. "Lexicostatistics and Genetic Relationships." *Language* 39, no. 4 (1962): 638–648.

Terashima, H., and M. Ichikawa. *Aflora Catalog of Useful Plants of Tropical Africa.* Kyoto: Center for African Area Studies, 1991.

Terashima, H., M. Ichikawa, and M. Sawada. *Wild Plant Utilization of the Balese and the Efe of the Ituri Forest, the Republic of Zaire.* Kyoto: Center for African Area Studies, 1988.

Thomas, J.M.C. "Emprunte on parenté? À propos des parlers des populations forestières de Centrafrique." In *Pygmées de Centrafrique: Études ethnologiques, historiques, et linguistiques sur les Pygmées "Ba.Mbenga" (Aka/Baka) du Nord-Ouest du Bassin Congolais,* edited by S. Bahuchet, 141–169. Paris: SELAF, 1979.

——— "Relations sociales et projections ideologiques: Exemple de Ngbaka-Ma'bo et des Pygmées Aka d'Afrique Centrale. *Cahiers du LACITO* 2 (1987): 15–30.

———. "Organisation sociale." In *Encyclopédie des Pygmées Aka: La société,* edited by J. M. C. Thomas and S. Bahuchet. Paris: SELAF, 1991.

Thomas, J.M.C., and S. Bahuchet, eds. *Encyclopédie des Pygmées Aka: La langue.* Paris: SELAF, 1991.

———. *Encyclopédie des Pygmées Aka: Le monde des Aka.* Paris: SELAF, 1991.

———. *Encyclopédie des Pygmées Aka: La société.* Paris: SELAF, 1991.

Thornton, J. *The Kingdom of Kongo: Civil War and Transition, 1641–1718.* Madison: University of Wisconsin, 1983.

———. *Africa and Africans in the Making of the Atlantic World, 1400–1680.* Cambridge: Cambridge University Press, 1992.

———. *The Kongolese Saint Anthony: Dona Beatriz Kimpa Vita and the Antonian Movement, 1684–1706.* Cambridge: Cambridge University Press, 1998.

Turbane, C. M. *The Myth of the Metaphor.* Columbia: University of South Carolina Press, 1970.

Turnbull, C. *The Forest People.* New York: Simon and Schuster, 1961.

Tylleskar, T. *Phonologie de la langue Sakata (BC 34).* Paris: Université de la Sorbonne Nouvelle, Paris III- U.E.R. Linguistique et Phonetique, 1987.

Tyson, E. *Orang-outang sive Homo Sylvestrus, or the Anatomy of a Pygmie compared with that of a Monkey, and Ape, and a Man.* London: Dawsons of Pall Mall, 1699.

Van der Veen, L. J. "Étude comparée des parlers du groupe Okani, (B-30 Gabon)." Ph.D. thesis, Université Libre de Bruxelles, 1991.

Van Grunderbeck, M.-C., E. Roche, and H. Doutrelepont. "L'age du Fer Ancien au Rwanda et au Burundi: Archéologie et environment." *Journal des Africanistes* 52, nos. 1–2 (1982): 5–58.

Van Roy, H. "Les Bambwíiti, peuplade préhistorique du Kwango." *Anthropos* 68 (1973): 815–880.

Vansina, Jan. "Long Distance Trade Routes in Central Africa." *Journal of African History* 3, no. 3 (1962): 375–390.

————. "The Bells of Kings." *Journal of African History* 10, no. 2 (1969): 187–197.

————. *The Tio Kingdom of the Middle Congo – 1880–1892.* London: Oxford University Press, 1973.

————. *The Children of Woot: A History of the Kuba Peoples.* Madison: University of Wisconsin Press, 1978.

————. "Western Bantu Expansion." *Journal of African History* 25 (1984): 129–145.

————. "Esquisse historique de l'agriculture en milieu forestier (Afrique Equatoriale)." *Muntu* 2 (1985): 5–21.

————. "Do Pygmies Have a History?" *Sprache und Geschichte in Afrika* 7, no. 1 (1986): 431–445.

————. *Paths in the Rainforest: Towards a History of Political Tradition in Equatorial Africa.* Madison: University of Wisconsin Press, 1990.

————. "A Slow Revolution: Farming in Subequatorial Africa." In *The Growth of Farming Communities in Africa from the Equator Southwards,* edited by J. E. G. Sutton, 15–26. *Anzania* special vol. 29–30. London/Nairobi: British Institute of eastern Africa, 1994/95.

————. "Historians, Are Archaeologists Your Siblings?" *History in Africa* 22 (1995): 369–408.

———— "New Linguistic Evidence and the 'Bantu Expansion.'" *Journal of African History* 36 (1995): 173–195.

Van Wing, J. *Études Bakongo: Sociologie, religion, et magie,* 2nd ed. Brussels: Desclée-DeBrouwer, 1959.

Walker, R. K. *Les tribus du Gabon.* Libreville, Gabon: Centre Culturel Français/Saint-Exupery, 1924.

————. "Initiation a L'Ebongwe, langue des Negrilles." *Recherches Congolaises* 23 (1937): 129–155.

Westminster Abbey Library. Image of a pygmy, three-faced giant, and sciopod. MS 22, fol. 1v, thirteenth century.

White, H. "The Forms of Wildness: Archaeology of an Idea," in *The Wildman Within: An Image in Western Thought from the Renaissance to Romanticism* edited by E. Dudley and M. E. Novak, 3–38. Pittsburgh: University of Pittsburgh Press, 1972.

Whitehouse, H. "In Praedis Iuliae Felicis." *Papers of the British School at Rome* 45 (1977): 52–68.

Whitmore, T. C. *An Introduction to Tropical Forests.* Oxford: Clarendon, 1990.

Wiber, M. *Erect Men, Undulating Women: The Visual Imagery of Gender, "Race," and Progress in Reconstructive Illustrations of Human Evolution.* Waterloo/Ontario: Wilfrid Laurier University Press, 1997.

Wijsman, E. J. "Estimation of Genetic Admixture in Pygmies." In *African Pygmies,* edited by L. L. Cavalli-Sforza, 347–358. London: Academic Press, 1986.

Willoughby, W. C. *Nature Worship and Taboo.* Hartford: Hartford Seminary Press, 1932.

Wilmsen, E. *Land Filled with Flies: A Political Economy of the Kalahari.* Chicago: University of Chicago Press, 1989.

Wilson, M. *Communal Rituals of the Nyakusa.* London: Oxford University Press, 1959.

Wrigley, C. "Review Article: The Long Durée in the Heart of Darkness." *Journal of African History* 33 (1992): 129–134.

INDEX

Wildcats, symbolism, 142
Wilmsen, E., 17
Wilson, Monica, 139
Wind, symbolism, 136
Woot, children of Mboom, 136
Wsir Mr-wr (bull), 5
Wumbu, 69, 70

Xhosa people, 151

Yaka peoples: cosmology, 145–47; notion
   of primordial water, 136; politics, 200;
   social structures, 145
Yams, 41, 117
Ya Mwei (mother *mwei*), 135, 137, 141, 142
Yaoundé site, 58

"Zambezi" language, 50
Zame ye Mebege, 141

About the Author

KAIRN A. KLIEMAN is Assistant Professor in the Department of History, University of Houston.